VOLPONE IN CONTEXT

Anthem Perspectives in Literature

Titles in the **Anthem Perspectives in Literature** series are designed to contextualize classic works of literature for readers today within their original social and cultural environments. The books present historical, biographical, political, artistic, moral, religious and philosophical material from the period that enable readers to understand a text's meaning as it would have struck the original audience. These approachable but informative books aim to uncover the period and the people for whom the texts were written, their values and views, their anxieties and demons, what made them laugh and cry, their loves and hates. The series is targeted at high-achieving A Level, International Baccalaureate and Advanced Placement pupils, undergraduates following Shakespeare and Renaissance drama modules and an intellectually curious audience.

VOLPONE IN CONTEXT

BITERS BITTEN AND FOOLS FOOLED

Keith Linley

ANTHEM PRESS

Anthem Press
An imprint of Wimbledon Publishing Company
www.anthempress.com

This edition first published in UK and USA 2016
by ANTHEM PRESS
75–76 Blackfriars Road, London SE1 8HA, UK
or PO Box 9779, London SW19 7ZG, UK
and
244 Madison Ave #116, New York, NY 10016, USA

British Library Cataloguing-in-Publication Data
A catalogue record for this book is available from the British Library.

Library of Congress Cataloging-in-Publication Data
Names: Linley, Keith, author.
Title: Volpone in context: biters bitten and fools fooled / Keith Linley.
Description: New York, NY: Anthem Press, 2016. |
Series: Anthem perspectives in literature |
Includes bibliographical references and index.
Identifiers: LCCN 2016032063 | ISBN 9781783085583 (paperback)
Subjects: LCSH: Jonson, Ben, 1573?–1637. Volpone. | Literature and society –
England – History – 17th century. | Theater and society – England –
History – 17th century. | BISAC: LITERARY CRITICISM / General.
Classification: LCC PR2622.L56 2016 | DDC 822/.3–dc23
LC record available at https://lccn.loc.gov/2016032063

ISBN-13: 978-1-78308-558-3 (Pbk)
ISBN-10: 1-78308-558-4 (Pbk)

This title is also available as an e-book.

CONTENTS

INTRODUCTION

About This Book

This book is not a scene-by-scene guide to *Volpone*. It concentrates on the contexts from which the play emerges, those characteristics of life and thought in early Jacobean England which are reflected in the values and views Ben Jonson brings to the text and affect how a contemporary audience might have responded to it.

The book is for students preparing assignments and examinations for Renaissance literature modules. The marking criteria at any level explicitly or implicitly require that students show a consistently well-developed and consistently detailed understanding of the significance and influence of contexts in which literary texts are written and understood. This means responding to the play in the ways Jonson's audience would have done. The following material will enable you to acquire a surer grasp of this cultural context – the social-political conditions from which the play emerged, the literary profile prevailing when it was written, and its religious-moral dimension. The setting is foreign, but this is merely a literary fashion of the time and is not meant to be taken seriously or literally. It is not a dramatized travel guide to Venice, but a warning to London. Furthermore, since the play was written in an age of faith, when the Bible's teachings and sermons heard in church formed part of every man and woman's mindset, it is vital to recreate those factors, for the actions of the characters will be assessed by Christian criteria. You may not agree with the values of the time or the views propounded in the play, but you do need to understand how belief mediated the possible responses of the audience that watched the play in 1606. A key concept in this book's approach is that *Volpone* is full of sins, transgressions, boundary crossing and rule breaking in the personal world and in the public and political arenas as well. Alerted to the transgressive behaviour of Mosca, Volpone and the predatory legacy hunters in the opening scenes, an audience member, who would not know the story (as it is largely a fabrication of the author), would expect they be punished. Though biblical values would be applied to the action, there is much more going on scene-by-scene than a series of echoes of or allusions to what the Bible says about virtue and vice. Interwoven are concerns about rule of self (a recurrent theme in all the comedies of the time), about the loss of an ethically driven value system, the dangers of appetite unrestrained, about patriarchy and marriage.

What Is a Context?

Cultural historians aim to recover 'the commonplaces, the unargued presuppositions', and 'the imperative need, in any comparative discussions of epochs, [is] first to decide what the norm of the epoch is'.[1] Once the typical and orthodox values are established, it is then essential to register significant divergences from them. Any document – literary or non-literary – comes from an environment and has that environment embedded in it, overtly and covertly. Its context is the conditions which produced it, the biographical, social, political, historical and cultural circumstances which formed it, the values operating within it and affecting the experience of it. A text in isolation is simply an accumulation of words carrying growing, developing meanings as the writing/performance progresses. It is two dimensional: a lexical, grammatical construct and the sum of its literal contents. It has meaning and we can understand what it is about, how the characters interact and the complications they create at a simple storyline level, but context provides a third dimension, making meaning comprehensible within the cultural values of the time. Context is the sum of all the influences the writer brings to the text and all the influences the viewer/reader deploys in experiencing it. This book concentrates on the archaeology of the play, recovering how it would be understood in 1606, recovering the special flavour and prevailing attitudes of the time, and displaying the factors that shaped its meaning for that time and that audience. *Volpone in Context* offers the views, prejudices, controversies and basic beliefs buried in the play – all the significations of society embedded in the text that added together make it what Jonson intended it to be or as closely as we can be reasonably sure. Recovering the mindset, nuances and values Jonson intentionally or unconsciously works into the play, and how his audience would have interpreted them, means recreating the Jacobean period. 'Jonson's art is intimately related to the popular tradition of individual and social morality'.[2] We need therefore to

1 E. M. W. Tillyard, *The English Renaissance: Fact or Fiction?* (27, 28).
2 L. C. Knights, *Drama and Society in the Age of Jonson*, 151.

recreate the terms of those two polar expressions of Jacobean morality, the personal and the civic. To achieve that a range of aspects is considered, but two key contextual areas dominate the approach of this book: the religious and the sociopolitical. The multiple transgressions represented in the play would be interpreted by the audience in terms of the scriptural upbringing most of them would have had and in the light of their ideas on how the gentry should behave. The social range of the cast spreads from a Magnifico (a wealthy man from the top layer of society), through a Venetian gentleman and two representatives of the English gentry, magistrates, a lawyer, a merchant and servants to the ordinary citizens of Venice. But it is largely concerned with the values of the middling and better sorts of people, even though in Mosca we have a servant who inverts social normality and rules his master. The play automatically activates some political considerations related to rule, mostly of self but partially rule of the state. We are invited to judge Volpone as a representative of the governing rank but mostly are aware of the presentation of his flawed personal life. The other characters too are all set up for us to judge according to the expectations of their ranks and also within the parameters of their shared ethical framework. Such subjects were constantly debated in pre-Civil War England and, though they are of limited scope in this piece as compared with the history plays and tragedies of the time, where they extend to the dimension of state politics, they have some small specific relevance to the hothouse court of James I because they relate to conduct, the conduct of supposedly better educated, better brought-up people from the rank that called itself 'the better sort'.

Sin, subversion, transgression and reversals abound in the play and part 1 looks broadly at the contemporary 'world view', the inherited past which shaped how Jacobeans thought about God, the world, sin, virtue, death, the Devil, the social structure, family, gender relationships, social change and political matters. These topics establish the orthodox understandings and expectations of the time so that the subversions of natural order and hierarchy displayed on stage can be seen in their ethical framework. Part 2 discusses contemporary contexts – politics, literature, authority, history and morality – that enhance and clarify specific issues the play addresses. It does this by looking, in separate chapters, at comedy as a genre, at aspects of the author's life and work, at the political context, at aspects of the central characters and at the literary influences and sources that triggered the thinking behind the play.

Connections are also made between *Volpone* and the wider literary world. Most importantly, the book considers the religious beliefs informing the likely judgements made of the actions viewed and suggests a number of sociopolitical allusions giving the drama a topical dimension.

Crucial to the religious context are moral frameworks against which conduct in the play would have been measured – the Ten Commandments, the Seven Deadly Sins, the Seven Cardinal Virtues, the Corporal and Spiritual Works of Mercy – the ethical framework in which the action is set and by which it is to be judged. (These are looked at in chapters 3 and 4.) These ethical contexts decode the hidden nuances and inflexions of meaning by which a contemporary audience would have mediated their responses to the distasteful conduct of the five central participants. There would have been many different responses to the characters, dependent on the viewer's rank and personal views, but in the area of the religious and moral values there would have been many shared reactions.

A gulf always exists between what people are supposed to do or believe, and what they actually do or believe. The play demonstrates what happens when idealized fantasies of expected conduct and rule are countered by the harsh realities of how people actually behave. Niccolò Machiavelli's version of 'the mirror for princes' claimed,

> I have thought it proper to represent things as they are in real truth, rather than as they are imagined. [...] The gulf between how one should live and how one does live is so wide that a man who neglects what is actually done for what should be done learns the way to self-destruction rather than self-preservation.[3]

Ignorance, indifference, rebelliousness, purposeful wickedness, laziness and weakness account for these discrepancies. No one in the audience would have missed the blasphemy in Volpone's opening adoring eulogy to his treasure. Some would have applauded the two hustlers duping such greedy fools. Most would have gradually turned against the central actors and longed for their humiliation. Duplicity and deception were essential ingredients in a comedy, and though they were not morally acceptable they reflect what happened in real life: the putting of personal obsession and private will before social and Christian responsibilities. But here, the excess of evil is there from the start and simply increases. There is little light-heartedness. It is all one sustained bitter snarl about humanity's corruption. The tension between what people should do and what they actually do creates dramatic conflicts not just for the characters but also for the audience who may be torn between enjoying the dextrous scamming of Mosca and Volpone yet feeling they ought to be condemned and must be punished in the end. And the questions

3 *The Prince*, 15, 90–1.

remain: should they be laughing at any of it and how can they not laugh at such a mad mixture of mistakes, such crass stupidity and such evil greed?

Further Reading

Useful Editions

Introduction, *Volpone* (ed. Philip Brockbank), New Mermaids (London: Ernest Benn), 1968.

Introduction, *Volpone* (ed. Brian Parker and David Bevington) Revels Student Editions (Manchester: Manchester University Press), 1999.

Introduction, *Volpone* (ed. Robert N. Watson), New Mermaids (London: Methuen Drama), 2003.

Critical Works

Ann Barton, *Ben Jonson, Dramatist* (Cambridge: Cambridge University Press), 1984.

Harold Bloom, *Ben Jonson's* Volpone, *or the* Fox: Modern Critical Interpretations (New York: Chelsea House), 1988.

Ian Donaldson, *Jonson's Magic Houses: Essays in Interpretation*. Oxford: Oxford University Press, 1997.

Richard Dutton, ed., *Ben Jonson*, Longman Critical Readers, 2000.

Jonathan Goldberg, *James I and the Politics of Literature: Jonson, Shakespeare, Donne, and Their Contemporaries* (Baltimore: Johns Hopkins University Press, 1983).

W. David Kay, *Ben Jonson: A Literary Life* (London: Macmillan, 1995).

L. C. Knights, *Drama and Society in the Age of Jonson* (London: Penguin Books), 1937.

Edward B. Partridge, *The Broken Compass* (Westport, CT: Greenwood Press), 1976.

Robert N. Watson, ed., *Critical Essays on Ben Jonson* (New York: G. K. Hall, 1997).

Articles

Jonas A. Barish, 'The Double Plot in *Volpone*', *Modern Philology* 51 (1953).

Mark Bland, 'Jonson, Scholarship, and Science', www.cts.dmu.ac.uk/occasional papers/ Bland.2013.pdf.

Stephen Greenblatt, 'The False Endings in *Volpone*', *Journal of English and Germanic Philology* 75 (1976).

Harriet Hawkins, 'Folly, Incurable Disease, and *Volpone*', *Studies in English Literature, 1500–1900* 8 (1968).

Harry Levin, 'Jonson's Metempsychosis', *Philological Quarterly* 22 (1943).

Howard Marchitello, 'Desire and Domination in *Volpone*', *Studies in English Literature, 1500–1900* 31, no. 2 (1991).

Susan Wells, 'Jacobean City Comedy and the Ideology of the City', *English Literary Renaissance* 48 (1981).

PART I

THE INHERITED PAST

PROLOGUE

'Ha! ha! the fox!' and after hym they ran,
And eek with staves many another man:
Ran Colle our dogge, and Talbot, and Gerland,
And Malkyn, with a dystaf in hir hand.[1]

The fox, standing on hind legs, wears a bishop's mitre. His left paw grasps his staff of office, the crozier, its headpiece shaped like a question mark in reverse. It looks like a ram's horn, so that the symbol of power also resembles a shepherd's crook, referencing the guardian aspect of a bishop's role. The right paw is raised. Is it in blessing or exhortation to the flock before him? His 'congregation' is a collection of birds – two chickens, a cockerel, three ducks, a swan and a heron. This scene, in the lower border of what is a manuscript possibly produced in France between 1300 and 1340, bears testimony to the longevity of the connection of the fox, in folklore and satire, specifically with anticlerical satire but always with cheating people.[2] The manuscript scene alludes to the old European-wide tale of Reynard the Fox masquerading in ecclesiastical robes in order to mislead the foolish. To the right of the scene is a housewife in a blue dress, white apron and white headcloth. She is swatting at a fox with what looks like a distaff with wool on it. The fox is running away with a large bird, its head trapped between his jaws. Both the fox-bishop and the fox-thief pictures rest on a painted long vine-like tendril so that both scenes are linked as if the before/after parts of the same story. The second scene seems to be the outcome of the first. It is therefore a sharp satirical comment on the rapacity and duplicity of the church, but works also as a scene from everyday rural life with a fox which has raided the hen coop. It carries with it resonances relating to the greediness and deceitfulness of man, the gullibility

1 Chaucer, *The Nonnes Preestes Tale*, 615–18.
2 Smithfield Decretals, British Library, Royal Ms. 10 E.IV, fol. 49v.

of the general populace and, more particularly, the oft-repeated connection of the church with avaricious predation. What the fox does to the fowls, appearing as guide, mentor and comforter, luring them into false security and then attacking them, is what many saw the church doing to its flock.

The fox is a creature of the night, a predator, a thief. He is a border raider, crossing from wild nature into man's domestic domain. Nightstalker, elusive, devious, he is embedded deep in the European psyche as a trickster and deceiver. This persona goes back to ancient Greek times when the various fox fables of Aesop mix with other beast tales. The linking of humans to animal characteristics is part of the language: snake in the grass, wolf in sheep's clothing, brave as a lion, timid as a mouse, busy as a bee, slimy toad, whoreson dog. At the most practical level, for a world almost entirely rural, he is the enemy of farmers and shepherds and individual poor households rearing just a few chickens, the feared killer which could annihilate a henhouse or ravage a warren. He was thus a food burglar, stealing food before it could be put on the table and as such a threat to the family's economy and perhaps even a threat to its survival. To a peasant labourer, nurturing a few chickens only, a fox in the henhouse could wreak appalling damage within seconds. Geoffrey Chaucer's 'Nun's Priest' tells of a poor widow who has three pigs, a sheep, three cows, a cockerel and seven hens. The fox that catches and abducts the cock is 'of sly iniquitee', a 'false mordrour [murderer], lurkynge in thy den!', a 'newe Scariot' (Judas), a 'false dissimulour' (dissembler, cheat).[3] To the warrener, breeding rabbits on a lord's estate, a fox's predations could be similarly devastating. He was everyone's enemy, with a price on his head. Understandably, every man's hand was against him and he was everywhere hunted. But he has an even more potent existence as a metaphor. In Western iconography, from ancient times, the fox (*vulpes vulpes*) was a symbol of deviousness, of the hypocrite who smiled and cajoled and wheedled and then, when your defences were down, would cheat you. He could be admired for his clever evasions, his lies and excuses, his wriggling out of apparently impossible situations – unless you were a victim. Niccolò Machiavelli, who stared unblinkingly into the corrupt hearts of men, warned, 'Princes who have achieved great things have been those who have given their word lightly, who have known how to trick men with their cunning, and who, in the end, have overcome those abiding by honest principles'.[4] He further asserts,

> as a prince is forced to know how to act like a beast, he should learn from the fox and the lion; because the lion is defenceless against traps

3 *The Nonne Preestes Tale*, 449–62.
4 *The Prince*, chap. 18, 99.

and a fox is defenceless against wolves. Therefore one must be a fox in order to recognize traps, and a lion to frighten off wolves. Those who simply act like lions are stupid. So it follows that a prudent ruler cannot, and should not, honour his word when it places him at a disadvantage [...] If all men were good, this precept would not be good; but because men are wretched creatures who would not keep their word to you, you need not keep your word to them. [...] those who have known best how to imitate the fox have come off best. But one must know how to colour one's actions and to be a great liar and deceiver. Men are so simple, and so much creatures of circumstance, that the deceiver will always find someone ready to be deceived.[5]

Many in the audience would not know that the play's title, *Volpone*, referenced the Latin name for the fox, but the subtitle, 'or the Fox' would activate a host of responses from those not privileged to learn Latin. Some responses would be traditional and rural, others more topically related to the tricky twists and turns of scurvy politicians. Deceit, self-interest, self-deception, greed, stupidity, gullibility, flattery – these are the characteristics of those who fox and those who are foxed in Ben Jonson's play. They are the key ingredients too of any comedy.

The Setting

[...] with my wife to the King's house, there to see *Vulpone*, a most excellent play – the best I think I ever saw, and well acted.

(Samuel Pepys, *Diary*, 14 January 1665)[6]

The trumpet has blared to announce a performance is about to begin. The Globe is its usual heaving, noisy mass of humanity. Later, those standing in the pit will make a good extension of the Piazza crowd watching Volpone in his second disguise as Scoto of Mantua. They are a cynical and very vocal lot, munching nuts, chewing fruit, pushing, joking, calling out to friends, making bawdy comments to the prostitutes squeezing through the crowd (a different sort of hunter to those who will stalk the stage). But there are predators among them. There are the whores, and there are pickpockets too looking for victims.

5 *The Prince*, chap. 18, 99–100. Jonson had some knowledge of Machiavelli as evidenced in *Sejanus*. See Daniel C. Bourghner, 'Sejanus and Machiavelli' *Studies in English Literature, 1500–1900* 1, no. 2 (1961).
6 The 'King's house' is Samuel Pepys' name for the Theatre Royal, Drury Lane, built by Thomas Killigrew in 1663. Much frequented by Charles II, it was also where Nell Gwyn acted.

Everyone there is, in some senses, a scavenger on the lookout to snaffle up whatever they can steal, lift, scrounge.

Humanity preys on itself. The gallery seats around them too are full of those on the make or already made. They are more restrained, more refined perhaps. Certainly they are better dressed, as befits their rank and purses. This London crowd knows all about the greedy cannibalism of life, man's inhumanity to man, how rampant consumerism destroys families and greed destroys the soul. They have all struggled, elbowed and scratched a living, some of them very evidently more successfully than others. All humankind is here – except perhaps the very bottom of society, the beggars, incapables, insane and unemployed. Some of the finely decked spectators in furred robes are deep in credit (or discredit), owing thousands perhaps, though you would not know it from their silken appearance. Their finery may not have yet been paid for (and may never be), but it lends them a little brief authority. Orazio Busino, generalizing about London playgoers, describes them thus,

> People devoted to pleasure, who, for the most part, dress grandly and colourfully, so that they appear, if possible, more than princes, or rather they appear actors. Similarly in the King's court after Christmas day begins a series of sumptuous banquets, well performed plays, and very graceful masques of knights and ladies.[7]

The audience might even contain the usurers who loaned them the gold to acquire their gorgeous attire. Look at those young men leaning on the balustrade chatting to a pretty girl and her nurse – another sort of rapacious hunting in train. In the top box left of stage a ruffed, bejewelled nobleman is accompanied by several ladies in gold and silver and pearl bespangled dresses, some no better than the whores in the pit or the famous courtesans of Venice. And the gentleman with them? Their father? A respectable, successful merchant out with his family? Some grandee of great estate? Perhaps a courtier who has the ear of the king? Or a libertine with money to spend and 'loving' ladies to help him spend it? The whole food chain is here, all feeding off each other, off anyone who has anything they want.

From its first performance in spring 1606 Jonson's acid attack on greed and lust had pleased audiences. Nearly 60 years later it retained the same bite, for its satire on society, its mockery of pretension, gullibility and the lust for wealth was as relevant to Samuel Pepys and Restoration England as it

---

7 Orgel and Strong, *Inigo Jones*, 1, 282. The prices are six pence, one shilling, half a crown, respectively. Sixpence was a twelfth of a workman's average weekly pay. Busino was chaplain to the Venetian Embassy.

had been to the increasingly greedy money- and sex-mad world of Jacobean London. With thriving commerce, expanding trade, with the rich pickings of developing colonization, the London of the real world was becoming like the fictional Venice they are about to see. The play has continued to please, for its subject is eternal.

Jonson's comedies were more to the popular taste than his tragedies. *Sejanus, His Fall*, performed 1603, not only failed at the box office, booed by the groundlings, but it also got its author into trouble with the authorities. Its political content was deemed too openly critical of the contemporary governing system despite its setting in ancient Rome. *Catiline, His Conspiracy* (1611) fared no better. He had earlier been in trouble with *The Isle of Dogs* (coauthored with Thomas Nashe, 1597) and *Eastward Ho!* (a collaboration between Jonson, John Marston and George Chapman, 1605) had landed all three authors in jail on a charge of disrespect to the Scots nation, for an actor had mockingly used a Scots accent. The charge was brought by a touchy Scots lord and was backed by the king, eager to assert his new authority. It was a time when the usurpation of political power at Westminster and in the royal palace of Whitehall by James's fellow countrymen, friends and favourites, had begun to niggle the English public in general and the eclipsed English politicians in particular. By the time of *Volpone*, Jonson had established a reputation for acerbic commentary on the topical contemporary social scene and as critic of the universal human follies.

The Globe production was staged by the King's Men of which William Shakespeare was a member and who may have been in the cast. The play has much of the black cynicism found in *Troilus and Cressida* (1601–2), *All's Well That Ends Well* (1602–4) and *Measure for Measure* (1604). The Venice of *Volpone* is a cruel world of predators preying on each other. That Christmas of 1606 Shakespeare was to preach to the court, through his tragedy *King Lear*, that

> [i]f that the heavens do not their visible spirits
> Send quickly down to tame these vilde offences,
> It will come,
> Humanity must perforce prey on itself,
> Like monsters of the deep. (4.2.46–50)

For all its being a comedy, Volpone's world is just such a Hobbesian nightmare.

It is impossible to identify or quantify the degree to which the so-called Mermaid Tavern group influenced each other, but there is a uniformity of bilious criticism of the world in the work of Jonson, Shakespeare, Thomas

Middleton and Marston at this time and *Volpone* certainly has a similarly jaundiced view of the parasitism and predatory greed of humankind. So confident was the company in the quality and attraction of the play that when in the summer of 1606 plague closed the theatres in London they removed to Oxford and Cambridge to perform.

When the piece was printed by Thomas Thorppe in 1607 the author added an epistle, dated 11 February 1607 'From my house in the Black-Friars'. It was dedicated to the two universities, the 'most equal Sisters' and used the opportunity to outline some of his lofty aims as a poet:

> He that is said to be able to inform young men to all good disciplines, inflame grown men to all great virtues, keep old men in their best and supreme state, or [...] recover them to their first strength; that comes forth the interpreter and arbiter of nature, a teacher of things divine, no less than human, a master in manners; can alone (or with a few) effect the business of mankind.[8]

The combative and difficult Jonson did not always in his own life conform to the behaviour of a 'master in manners', but his art, often overly intent on displaying his learning, is always morally exemplary. He admits that not only writers' manners but also their natures have been 'inverted' and the 'dignity of Poet' become an 'abused name' due to the 'ribaldry, profanation, blasphemy, [and] all licence of offence to God, and man' that had become the pattern of '*stage poetry*' (italics in original). This is Jonson again announcing his crusade to reform the drama aesthetically and morally. His idea of structure and adherence to the unities – which is strenuously the case in *Volpone* – gives the play an intensity and pace that is sometimes temporarily hindered by his cumbrous verse, but the drive of his condemnation helps keep the play moving. He acknowledges that his opposition to folly is such that some have levelled 'the imputation of sharpness'. He denies any particular 'public person' or particular 'nation, society, or general order, or state' has been specifically targeted. Only 'creatures' deserving 'for their insolencies' are 'taxed' (censured). He identifies the types as mimics (those who copy or imitate – that is, hypocrites, who ostensibly personify a virtue but are just acting the part); cheaters (a very broad class of sinners); bawds (pimps and procuresses)' and buffoons (gullible fools). The main characters in *Volpone* all fall into at least one of these categories and almost all are subject to Jonson's *saeva indignatio* (savage indignation) against human folly and corruption. In this play exposing avaricious criminal corruption outweighs the mockery of gullible fools or the

---

8 'The Epistle' to *Volpone*, 23–30 (Brockbank edition).

virtuous. Like his favourite Roman satirist, Juvenal, he portrays and punishes an age and the types that swarm in his city. His aim overall is to

> [r]aise the despised head of *Poetry* again, and stripping her out of those rotten and base rags, wherewith the Times have adulterated her form, restore her to her primitive habit, feature and majesty, and render her worthy to be embraced, and kissed, of all the great and master-spirits of our world.[9]

As for 'the vile and slothful', he will, as a servant of Poetry, 'out of just rage [...] spout ink in their faces'. 'Just rage' is his gloss on *saeva indignatio* and *Volpone*, on stage and on the page, is Jonson spitting venom at the corrupt. Rarely has any piece of satire presented such a sustained vilification of human rottenness.

As such the play seemed to retain an attraction throughout the seventeenth and eighteenth centuries. It was performed for Charles, Prince of Wales (1624) and again for him as king in 1637 at the Cockpit-in-Court, a private theatre within the grounds of Whitehall Palace.[10] John Evelyn's diary records him seeing a production at Charles II's court on 16 October 1662. It was onstage again the following year in the public theatre at Drury Lane, acted by the King's Men under Thomas Killigrew and then at the same venue two years later when Pepys was impressed by it. Richard Steele refers to a performance of it in 1709 in *The Tatler* and John Genest's history of the drama cites more than 50 performances up to 1770.[11] Thereafter it fell into disfavour due partly to the elaborate Latinism of its verse and critical condemnation of act 5 as unbelievable. By then the more elegant satire of Richard Sheridan's *The Rivals* and *The School for Scandal* and the more up-to-date comedy of Oliver Goldsmith's *She Stoops to Conquer* and George Colman's *Clandestine Marriage* were more to the current taste. The targets were much the same and the need to expose folly just as great, but the style of doing so had changed.

Thereafter, Shakespeare's reputation rose and Jonson's was eclipsed.

9 'The Epistle', 127–32.
10 Inigo Jones was not only the royal architect but also chief designer of stage sets and machinery for court masques. In this role he collaborated closely with Jonson, who wrote a large proportion of such court entertainments. Refitted in 1662 the theatre survived the fire of 1698, but by then had ceased to house performances, becoming government offices and accommodation for the growing band of civil servants.
11 *Some Account of the English Stage from the Restoration in 1660 to 1830*, Bath, 10 vols., 1832.

Chapter 1

THE HISTORICAL CONTEXT

1.1 The Jacobean Context: An Overview

Elizabeth I died in 1603 and James VI of Scotland became James I of England. The play was written in 1605, so falls into the Jacobean period (after *Jacobus*, Latin for James). In the wider European literary and political contexts, the period is the waning of the High Renaissance. Historians today call it Early Modern because many features of it are recognizably modern while being early in the evolutions that shaped our world.

The new king, ruling until 1625, was of the Scottish family the Stuarts. They were a dynastic disaster. None was an effective king. James I, a learned man but a flawed ruler, shirked the routines of work government involved; disliked contact with his people; was extravagant, constantly in debt and in perpetual conflict with Parliament; was a hard-line right-winger in religion who backed the repression of Catholics and Puritans; drank heavily and was impulsive and tactless. Sir Anthony Weldon, courtier and politician, banished from court for a book criticizing the Scots, dubbed him 'the wisest fool in Christendom'.[1] The epithet captures something of the discrepancy between his writings on political theory and his practice as a lazy man only intermittently engaged with his role. London celebrated with bonfires when he succeeded peacefully. His apparent engagement with his regal duties generated hope, reflected in the mass of appalling, sycophantic eulogistic verse published.[2] During the 15 March 1603 royal procession through the City two St Paul's choristers sang of London as Troynovant (New Troy),[3]

---

1 Weldon, *The Court and Character of King James I*.
2 See Nichols, *The Progresses, Processions, and Magnificent Festivities of James the First*.
3 Troynovant was the ancient name for London, supposedly founded by Brutus leading a band of Trojan exiles. This pseudohistory in Geoffrey of Monmouth, filtered through Holinshed into a play, *Locrine*, performed c. 1595.

no longer a city but a bridal chamber, suggesting a mystical union and new hope.[4]

This sense of promise soon evaporated when his failings and inconsistencies quickly emerged. *Volpone* is underpinned by concerns about rule (or misrule) of self and others. The central character is a *magnifico* from the governing ranks of Venice, thus his misrule of self, his failure to live up to the expectations of his degree, is a significant theme running throughout the play. The moral failings of the other characters too relate to their social positions and become a part of the general criticism.

The previous monarch, Elizabeth, a Tudor, much loved and respected, had been a strong ruler, indeed strong enough to suppress the addressing of many problems which by James I's time had become irresolvable. The Tudors – Henry VII, Henry VIII, Edward VI, Mary I, Elizabeth – ruled 1485–1603 and brought relative stability after the turmoil of the Wars of the Roses (though there were various short-lived rebellions against them). Questions of succession, the nature of rulers, the use and limits of monarchical power, the influence of court and the qualities of courtiers were matters that concerned people throughout the period and are part of the broader contexts of *Volpone*. Religion too was a major conflict area.[5] Catholic opposition to the new Church of England and Puritan desires for freedom from tight central control created a constant battleground. The effects on society and individual morality of the wealth that the new capitalism and the expansion of trade were creating also worried Jacobean writers. The new individualism, another context, emerges in the self-centred ruthlessness of all five central characters. Each is driven by his own will to acquire wealth and power and seems to exist outside the ethical framework of the time. The increasing influence of such a disconnect between the old values of public duty and private morality was a source of much anxiety to moralists and writers. Deceit and selfishness seemed to be banishing openness and altruism.

Henry VIII's great achievement (and cause of trouble) was breaking with the Catholic Church of Rome and establishing an independent English Church. This inaugurated a period of seismic change called the English Reformation. In 1536 the first Act of Supremacy made Henry Supreme Head of the Church of England. Its rituals and doctrines remained essentially Catholic until the reforms of his son Edward aligned it with the Protestant movements on the

---

4 James's inaugural speech to Parliament declared, 'I am the husband, and the whole island is my lawful wife; I am the head and it is my body' (McIlwain, 272). Revisionist historians have tried to rehabilitate James but the overwhelming evidence of the time is highly critical of him.

5 Davies, 7.

Continent. There was some limited alliance with the Protestant Reformation led by Martin Luther, but in many ways the English went their own way. Monasteries and convents were dissolved, the infrastructural features of Catholicism banished, altars stripped of ornament (leaving only the cross and flanking candles), churches emptied of statues and relics and some murals whitewashed over or scratched out. New services and prayers were in English rather than Latin, new English translations of the Bible began to appear and there was a Book of Common Prayer to be used in all parish churches. Holy shrines, saints' statues and saints' days were done away with as idolatrous superstitions. The vicar was to be the only intermediary between a person and God. After a brief, fiery, bloody return to Catholicism under Mary I (1553–8), Elizabeth succeeded and bedding in the new church continued. The freedom of a reformed English religion, supposedly stripped back to its simple original faith, encouraged the rise of more extreme reforming Protestant sects (not always to the liking of the infant Established Church). These groups, called Non-Conformists, Independents or Dissenters, included Puritans, Calvinists and Presbyterians – all Protestant, but with doctrinal differences. Some eccentric sects emerged too – like the Anabaptists, the Brownists and the Family of Love.[6] Religious differences, tensions between different faiths and disagreements within the same faith are persistently present at this time, but despite all the official changes to religion, the essential beliefs in sin, virtue, salvation, the centrality of Christ and the ubiquity of the Devil (the idea that he was everywhere, looking to tempt man) were the same as they always had been, as were the beliefs that sin was followed by punishment and possible damnation and that the world, in decline, would shortly come to an end.

Also persistent is the political discourse on kingship. Elizabeth (adoringly nicknamed 'Gloriana' after her identification with a character in Edmund Spenser's *The Faerie Queene*) ruled 1558–1603, a time long enough to establish her as an icon, particularly as she headed up strong opposition (and victory) against the Spanish. External threats repulsed, the regime was consolidated (though relentlessly under covert attack by Catholicism), but the Elizabethan-Jacobean period was one of unstoppable internal changes, gradually altering the profile and mood of society.[7] Religion, commerce, growing industrialization, increase of manufacture, social relationships, kingship and rule were all in flux. One unchanging feature of the period was the unceasing rise in prices,

6 After John Calvin the radical French Protestant reformer. His *Institutions of the Christian Religion* (1536) was very influential.
7 Niccolò Machiavelli had referred to 'the great changes and variations, beyond human imagining, which we have experienced and experience every day' (130). In 1606 the European world was still morphing from its medieval past. *The Prince*, written 1513, was not published until 1532.

particularly of food, bringing an unceasing decline in the living standards of the poor, for wages did not rise. The rich and the rising middle class could cope with inflation, but the state of the poor deteriorated. Enclosure of arable land (labour intensive) and its conversion to sheep farming (requiring less labour) raised unemployment among the 'lower orders' or the 'baser sort' who constituted the largest proportion of the 4–5 million population (between 80 and 85 per cent). Rising numbers of poor put greater burdens on poor relief in small, struggling rural communities and added to the elite's fear of some monumental uprising of the disenchanted. Most of the population worked on the land, though increasing numbers were moving to the few existing cities. Later ages, regarding the Elizabethan era as a 'Golden Age', talked of 'Merry England'. It was not, except for a small section of rich, privileged aristocrats. Also enjoying greater luxury and comfort were canny merchants (making fortunes from trading in exotic goods from the 'New Worlds' of Asia and the Americas) and the increasingly wealthy, acquisitive 'middling sort' manufacturing luxury goods for the aristocracy. Awareness of the state of the poor and the governing class's emotional detachment from that deteriorating condition is not a feature of *Volpone* but it does concentrate on the self-centred concerns of the rich. An audience in 1606 would see the play as an indictment of the greed, shiftiness and corruption of its capital city and its leading ranks. On Sunday 13 March 1603, the Puritan divine Richard Stock, delivered a Lent sermon at the Pulpit Cross in St Paul's churchyard, commenting,

> I have lived here some few years, and every year I have heard an exceeding outcry of the poor that they are much oppressed of the rich of this city [...] All or most charges are raised [...] wherein the burden is more heavy upon a mechanical or handicraft poor man than upon an alderman.[8]

The Jacobean period was quickly perceived as declining from the high points of Elizabeth's time, with worsening of problems she had been unable or unwilling to rectify. Economic difficulties, poverty, social conflict, religious dissent and political tensions relating to the role and nature of monarchy and the role and authority of Parliament, all remained unresolved. Charismatic, strong rulers (like Elizabeth) inspire loyalty though often through fear.

Emerging problems are ignored or masked, because the ruler disallows discussion of them and councillors fear to raise them. Elizabeth, for example, passed several laws making it treason to even discuss who might succeed her.

---

8 Historical Manuscripts Commission, *Calendar of the Manuscripts of ... the Marquess of Salisbury*, vol. 12, 272.

Such a ruler's death exposes the true state of things. Volpone's detachment from any form of civic-political duty highlights the growing perception that James I's court and government were more concerned with pursuing their own pleasures and milking the system than with addressing the problems growing in the nation at large.[9]

Under James I strong, purposeful central rule dwindled into rule by whim and capricious diktat. His court became more decadent and detached from the rest of the population than his predecessor's. Commerce and manufacture expanded rapidly, triggering a rise in the middle class that provided and serviced the new trades and crafts. Attitudes to religion and freedom from church authority began to develop into resistance, and science began to displace old superstitions and belief in magic. Like all times of transition the Jacobean period, and the seventeenth century in general, were exciting for some but unsettling for most, profitable for a few but a struggle for the majority. As always the rich found ways to get richer, and the poor got poorer. Gradually the disadvantaged found men to speak up for them in the corridors of power, in the villages of England and the overcrowded streets of the cities. *Volpone* is about the fall of a man who could have had power but who lives entirely for himself. The fall of Volpone is not a tragic story, not a Renaissance *de casibus* tragedy.[10] Unique as it is, it is also a typical Jacobean play – dark, cynical, deeply satirical, violent, psychological – but it explores character and motive only in broad terms. While much concerned with sin and punishment, there is little of repentance, redemption, reconciliation. Its first audience was probably the broad social mix of The Globe. Many of the clientele would appreciate the exposure of their so-called betters. Others would find it an embarrassing experience.

9 Linda Peck's work uncovers how privy councillors gathered advisers from court, scholarly and merchant communities, thus slightly broadening the social range from which parasites were drawn. Many advisers used their entry into the corridors of power as a means of self-interested profit making, bribery and jobbery. The king ignored what would not increase his revenue or simply went his own way, exercising absolute, personal power. No social improvement policy was in place or even conceived of.

10 After Giovanni Boccaccio's collection of stories of the tragic falls of illustrious men, *De Casibus Virorum Illustrium*.

.

Chapter 2

THE ELIZABETHAN WORLD ORDER: FROM DIVINITY TO DUST

Strict hierarchy (everything having its place according to its importance in God's order) and organic harmony (everything being part of a whole and having a function to perform) were the overriding principles of the broad orthodox background to how the audience thought their universe was structured (cosmology), how they saw God and religion (theology) and how their place in the order of things was organized (sociology). The disorders and disharmonies upsetting roles and expectations stem from Volpone's and Mosca's massive deception (already three years old). Both contravene Christian and humanist teaching about conduct. Mosca has usurped control over his master, and Volpone fails to live according the rank to which he belongs. Their transgressions, while theatrical, impressive and fascinating, are entirely immoral. An audience might be amused by their trickery and admire their skills, but would expect (even demand) ultimate punishment. *Volpone* is like other Ben Jonson pieces in that the action becomes increasingly complex in the last act. The outcome remains unsure as unexpected new twists make the audience wait. Suspending retributive justice prolongs the excitement as the plot winds up into a whirlwind of complications, as the sins reach excessive proportions and as the audience wonders how and whether it will all be resolved. Christian beliefs and values demanded punishment, but it looks as if Mosca will get away with his final scam – betraying his partner in crime. Both characters, at the beginning of the play, are already deeply implicated in the breaking of the Commandment not to bear false witness. Both commit the sins of avarice and covetousness.

Volpone's household and clients form a small court, but it is a place of corruption and predation, not a centre of amity, harmony, elegance or moral example. The source of that subversion is the very man who should be an exemplar. His little world is a reflection of the greater society with its cheats and scavenging parasites, a place of dishonesty, theft and a form of cannibalism where men prey on their own kind. This linking of the microcosm with the macrocosm, the idea that the world of Volpone's palazzo reflects the world of the Venetian state, that the spiritual dimension is connected to and has an influence over the fleshly world, that the inner world is a model of the outer, is central to Renaissance thought about order, hierarchy, nature and God. The distortions of right conduct witnessed in Volpone's court act as enveloping emblematic metaphors of a world turned upside down. A series of other reversals are presented before the play reaches a degree of harmony when the literal, judicial court pronounces sentences on the perpetrators of the evil witnessed through the narrative.

Such reversals of normal order, such monstrous greed, such deforming of nature were unsettling to an audience that followed a strict etiquette of precedence, where social power depended on a person's place in the hierarchy being seen (in clothing and other signs of wealth, title, rank and office) and accepted as superior by those below them in society. Disturbingly, underpinning the action seen is the knowledge that this is no fiction, that this is how humans behave.

2.1 Hierarchy

Everyone was fairly clear where they were in the universal order, the Great Chain of Being. God ruled all, was omnipotent (all powerful) and omniscient (all knowing). Man was inferior to God, Christ, the Holy Ghost, all the angels, apostles, saints, the Virgin Mary and all the blessed, but superior to all animals, birds, fish, plants and minerals. God ruled Heaven, kings (and princes, dukes, counts) ruled on earth and fathers ruled families like God at home.

The chain stretched from God through all the hierarchies of existence to the very bottom in descending order of importance – from divinity to dust – all interconnected as contributory parts of God's creation. The chain links were each a separate group of beings, creatures or objects, each connected to the one before and the one after, semiseparate, dependent but partly independent, both separate and part of something greater. Within each link there was a hierarchy. The human link contained three different ranks – 'the better sort' (kings, nobles, gentry), the 'middling sort' (merchants, shopkeepers, farmers) and the 'baser sort', or 'lower orders' (artisans, peasants, beggars). Within each of these orders there were further rankings of superiority and inferiority. The word 'class' was not used then, but these ranks, degrees or estates represent our upper, middle and lower classes as we know them today.

2.2 Cosmology

In astronomical terms, medieval and Renaissance man thought of creation, the cosmos, as an all-enveloping godliness that incorporated Heaven, the human universe and Hell.[1] The universe was thought of as a set of revolving, concentric, transparent crystal spheres, one inside the other, and each containing a planet. It was a geocentric model, with the earth in the middle encased in its sphere, enveloped by the moon's sphere, and then by Mercury, Venus, the sun, Mars, Jupiter and Saturn, like the rings of an onion.[2] Each of these bodies in its sphere circled the earth at different orbital angles and different speeds.

After Saturn came the firmament or fixed stars (divided into 12 seasonal zodiac sectors). Volpone mentions how he is more glad to see his gold than the earth is to see the spring sun 'peep through the horns of the celestial Ram' (1.1.5), referencing Aries, the sign that relates to late March–late April. Next were the 'waters [...] above the firmament' (Genesis 1:7) encased by sphere ten, the Primum Mobile (the first mover), which drove the spheres. Finally, everything was held within the all-surrounding empyrean, the domain that was all God's and all God – Heaven. Here the Deity was accompanied by his Son, the Holy Ghost, the Virgin Mary, the angels, the saints and the blessed. The set of concentric crystal balls was imagined by some to hang from the lip of Heaven by a gold chain. This cosmological organization, called the Ptolemaic system, was formulated by the second-century AD Egyptian astronomer-geographer Ptolemy (Figure 2.1). In Tudor times his *Cosmographia* (Geography of the universe) was still recommended by Sir Thomas Elyot for boys to learn about the spheres.[3]

A man could see the stars and some of the planets, but not beyond, his vision being blocked by the 'waters'. As the empyrean, the destination for the virtuous saved, was thus made invisible, people needed a visualizable image. It was easier to imagine the blessed 'living' in a celestial city rather than existing vaguely and spiritually in the heavenly ether, so the idea grew of a fortified city with towers and gates made of different substances. At the gate of pearl

---

1 The Catholic Church had imagined another level – Purgatory – a sort of halfway house between earth and Heaven. It was for venial sinners who, after death, could purge their souls of sin and make themselves suitable for Heaven. Masses, paid for by money left in wills, were believed to assist in cleansing the soul of the departed. Protestantism saw this as a corrupt money-making scheme and doctrinally suspect. It banished the idea from its own teachings.

2 Uranus was only discovered in 1781.

3 In *The Boke Named the Governour* (1531).

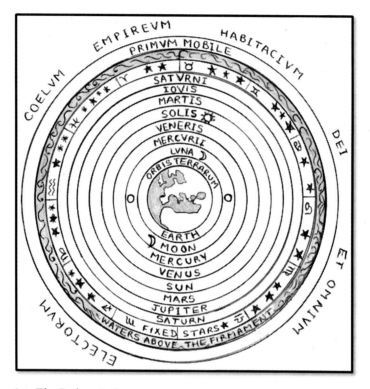

Figure 2.1 The Ptolemaic System
Source: Adapted from the engraving for Peter Apian's *Cosmographicus liber* (Book of the universe, 1524). Enclosing the spheres is the *Coelum Empireum Habitacium Dei et Omnium Electorum* (Empyrean sky, home of God and all the elect, that is, those judged worthy of heaven).

St Peter was supposed to receive each approaching soul and consult his 'Book of Life', recording all the good and evil a person had done, to see if the soul was worthy of entry. Medieval paintings show the *civitatis Dei* (city of God) resembling the walled cities of Italy, France or Germany. Painters often simply depicted the city they knew.

This system was beginning to be undermined. The great Copernican revolution, supported by Galileo Galilei, Johannes Kepler and others, put the sun at the heart of the universe. Entering the public domain with Nicolaus Copernicus's study *De revolutionibus orbium coelestium* (On the revolutions of the celestial spheres, 1542), the idea was only slowly accepted by scientists and took even longer to filter down to the mass of ordinary people. Dissemination was impeded by church authorities and the slowness of information spread in those times. In 1603 Sir Christopher Heydon, displaying his knowledge of the new advances, declared, 'Whether (as Copernicus saith) the sun be the centre of the world, the astrologer careth not'.[4] This references the triple belief system in which most people lived: (1) Christian doctrine existing uneasily alongside (2) the new astronomy and sciences and (3) old semimagical belief in the authenticity of astrology. The new heliocentrism (with the sun as the centre of the universe), opposed by the scepticism of some astronomers (like John Dee), was frighteningly repressed by very conservative, dogmatic churches. The Catholic Church's Inquisition enforced conformity persuasively with thumbscrews, the rack and many other grizzly tortures. The English Church had its own courts to question and punish deviations from customary practice and belief.

Visitations within their diocese enabled bishops to keep vicars and congregations in line. Serious infractions could be brought before the Star Chamber, but torture (with or without legal sanction) was endemic in Protestant Britain too.[5]

Ferdinand Magellan's circumnavigation of the world in 1522 without falling off the edge showed the flat earth theory was inaccurate. Sir Francis Drake's 1580 voyage brought this home more directly to British people when the queen permitted an exhibition to publicize his discoveries. A map displayed at Whitehall Palace made the spherical world graphically clear. But how many people saw it? William Shakespeare knew of the new development in thinking about the world's shape as evidenced by Puck's referring to putting 'a girdle round about the earth' (A Midsummer Night's Dream, 1595–6) and Lear's demand that the gods 'strike flat the thick rotundity of the earth' (King Lear, 1606). He clearly also knew much about the travel writing describing the discovery and conquest of the Americas. Presumably Jonson, an informal member of and writer for the King's Men and a member of the Mermaid Tavern coterie of friends and writers, was also up to date. To most people, unenlightened by new discoveries, the earth's roundness and the centrality of the sun were unimportant and perhaps still unknown. In an age when the nearest town was often as alien as the moon, 'New Worlds' were places of fantasy and nightmare, inhabited by unnatural beings like the cannibal anthropophagi 'whose heads/Do grow beneath their shoulders' (Othello,

4 Heydon, A Defence of Iudiciall Astrologie, 371, quoted in Keith Thomas, Religion and the Decline of Magic, 414.
5 A court comprising privy councillors and judges, instituted to try cases of suspected treason by powerful lords whom the ordinary courts were unable to bring to book. Under the Stuarts it became a means of curbing the Crown's political opponents, most of whom belonged to the dissenting religions.

1.3.144–5) and a whole bestiary of strange animals.[6] As long as the sun rose
to grow corn, ripen fruit and assist in telling the time and the season, most
people were indifferent to and ignorant of new discoveries. The centre of
their universe was their village. The old world of the ancient fields and the
more ancient woods around them was a world of mystery and magic not quite
banished by the new religion. The ordinary farmer or villager knew the stars
and some of the planets, but thought of them as belonging to the mystical
world of superstition, astrology, weather lore and magic rather than to the
measurable world of science and astronomy. Their everyday world contained
frightening shadows and unsettling possibilities; spirits could be conjured
up, demons lurked in the dark and fairies were not necessarily benign little
fluttery things.

2.3 The Great Chain of Being

Earthly creation was thought to be arranged in a set of hierarchical links
that made the world order. Man was at the top, followed by animals, birds,
fish, plants and minerals. Each stratum of existence was internally organized
in order of importance. Man was the pinnacle of God's animal creation,
though not entirely perfect. Flawed by original sin, with animal weaknesses
and negative passions, he was nevertheless part angel, endowed with soul,
reason, language, intelligence and sensitivity. A human being acting morally
was an imitation of Christ. Choosing the left-hand way, the path of sin, he
resembled the Devil. The conflict between these two aspects made man an
angel with horns, but the tensions between virtue and passion, the perpetual
psychomachia of life, sparked the interest of literature.[7]

   The Great Chain of Being was a construct of human imagination helping
people from the early medieval period to the Renaissance picture how the
universe was put together socially and how it worked physically. It was a
general view still held by the majority of people in Jacobean times, though its
physical structure was increasingly challenged by new astronomical research
and by socio-economic changes. Most people still thought the universe was

6 A tribe with eyes in their shoulders and a mouth in their chest was reported by Raleigh
   after his 1595 trip to Guiana and recorded in Richard Hakluyt's *Voyages*, viii. Richard
   Hakluyt, personal chaplain to Sir Robert Cecil, was a leading petitioner to James I for
   granting the Virginia Company charter.
7 *Psychomachia* is the struggle between good and evil for the mind/soul of man. Often
   portrayed on stage as a good angel and a bad angel, advising or tempting the protagonist
   (as in *Dr. Faustus*), by the 1600s they lost their allegorical state and were integrated
   into secularized characters, like a good friend and a false friend or a wise, disinterested
   adviser and a flattering self-seeker.

geocentric. The Renaissance is regarded as a time of change, new learning and new knowledge. Men were discovering new lands and new ways of thinking about God and society, but this only slowly affected everyday life. The iconoclastic, rationalist, free-thinking Renaissance Man, daringly breaking through barriers, questioning old orthodoxies, was a rarity, an oddity often in conflict with the authorities. Such men were confined to small minority groups of progressive artists/scientists/intellectuals. The seventeenth-century Everyman was conservative, backward looking in his beliefs and daily lifestyle. If literate, he would have few books apart from a Bible.[8] He still went to the wise woman for semimagical medical help, believed in divination, went to an astrologer to predict a suitable day for travelling or a suitable mate, and still believed the Chain of Being was constructed by God.

Hierarchically arranged, reflecting descending importance, usefulness and diminishing perfection, the chain was sometimes imagined instead as a ladder, the *scala naturae* (ladder of nature). The ladder image was agreeable to Christian thinkers because it suggested rising toward the divine (or descending toward perdition), as each person was supposed to do through a life of virtue which cleansed away their earthly faults, purifying them as they metaphorically climbed rung by rung to a holiness that prepared their soul for Heaven. The title of Walter Hilton's book *The Ladder of Perfection* (written between 1386 and 1396) reflects the image of rising step by step from sin to virtue, presented as a spiritual journey toward the peace given by Christ and the peace which is Christ. He is the perfection achieved by climbing the ladder, reached by denying the primacy of the 'anti-Trinity' of mind, reason and will, and trusting faith alone.[9] In the busy, corrupt world of the 1600s, the same belief persisted among the godly sort.[10] These were not just fervent Puritan zealots but also those ordinary folk who believed their Christian duty was to live the good life. The good life meant not the carnal life of fleshly pleasures but rather the hard-working, devoted life of the family man or woman, who struggled through their days with the example of Christ as their perpetual model. It is important not to underplay the general piety of most people at this time. They listened frequently to preachers of different sorts and attended church regularly.[11] The

---

8 Literacy was accelerating and cheap books and pamphlets, increasingly numerous, were sold at the door by itinerant, cheap, general goods dealers called chapmen.

9 Its reliance on mind, reason, will, is one marker of the Renaissance's divergence from medievalism.

10 The word 'godly' is used throughout to mean those with faith and not just Puritans.

11 Apart from their own parish priest there were various official open-air preachers (like those in the pulpit in St Paul's churchyard) and, increasingly, informal speakers from the ranks of the Puritans, Calvinists and other sects.

literate bought, borrowed, read or had read to them the religious pamphlets pouring off the presses.

The production of printed pamphlets accelerated from a trickle to a flood by the Civil War.[12] Though people lived physically 'by the rule of the flesh', as St Augustine put it, they were dominated by 'the rule of the spirit'.[13] While most lived dedicated Christian lives, others lived at various intermediate stages ranging from occasionally lapsing piety to a more sinful existence, less concerned with virtue, more interested in bodily pleasures and shading down toward outright irreligion and criminality. This vast spectrum was much represented in the city comedies of the 1600s and in the revenge tragedies (1580s–1630s). Shakespeare's problem plays and the late romances are all concerned with the ethical complexities and ambiguities focused on the tensions between flesh and spirit. So too is Jonson, but from his earliest stage work he had always exhibited a cynical and satirical attitude. The spirit of his plays is persistently critical and contemptuous of most of mankind – its greed, selfishness, shallow materialism, pretension and endless deviousness. He is consistently more directly topical than Shakespeare. Both writers, nevertheless, addressed questions of conduct in areas that were of contemporary interest, and the audience (often the same type of people for both writers and in the same venues – The Globe, Blackfriars, the court) would have responded largely within the same Christian, Bible-based context.[14]

Between the Creator and dust are all the many phases of existence. The chain image was equally apt in suggesting unbroken interconnection. This idea of hierarchies originated in the pre-Christian philosophy of Plato and Aristotle. In medieval times Christian theology assimilated the heavenly hierarchy to fit above the feudal system of human society and the descending levels of the rest of creation. Below earthly life (physically and morally) came the hierarchy of hell traditionally thought to be in the bowels of the earth. In his *Inferno* (1321) Dante placed it below Gehenna, the rubbish dump outside Jerusalem.[15] The orderliness of God's creation was so embedded in people's minds that any disassembling of it was like an

12 The church tried to keep track of unlicensed presses producing heretical or treasonable matter, but smuggled imports from Holland and the mobility of printers made it very difficult to police thought.

13 St Augustine, *City of God*, 548.

14 The Globe was most socially diverse, Blackfriars (being more expensive) was less inclusive and the court was positively exclusive.

15 See *L'Inferno*. In *Paradise Lost* (1667) John Milton has Hell specially created by God from the materials of Chaos to receive the falling angels after their defeat and expulsion from Heaven.

attack on the foundations of life and faith. Order was part of everything and the maintenance of order was a form of worship, an acceptance of God as the author of that order. Within each dominion – Heaven, earth, Hell – there was a series of graduated structures. In Christian thought the domains of Heaven and Hell, equivalents of the classical world's Olympus (home of the gods) and Hades (the underworld, the place of the dead), had their inhabitants ranked according to priority and power like the various types of earthly creation. All three realms had rulers and below them were ranks of diminishing power and diminishing virtue. This was 'a society obsessed with hierarchy'.[16]

Hierarchy of Heaven – God > Christ > the Holy Ghost > seraphim > cherubim > thrones > dominations > principalities > powers > virtues > archangels > angels > the Virgin Mary > the disciples > the saints > the blessed (saved, elect, good souls admitted to Heaven after a virtuous life)[17]

Praying to saints as intercessors for some particular concern was intermittently still practised in Protestant England. Though the church disapproved, having banished such idolatry, it took generations to change a mindset integral to thought and belief for centuries.

Hierarchy of Earth – man > animals > birds > fish > plants > rocks/minerals

Hierarchy of Hell – Devil > First Hierarchy (nobility of hell): named devils like Beelzebub, Mephistopheles, Mammon, Belial and so forth > Second Hierarchy: demons > goblins > imps > incubi/succubi[18] > familiars

Familiars are spirits acting as assistants to witches/wizards, either in the imp/demon form or disguised as an animal. Volpone calls Mosca 'my fine devil' (5.3.46) and Voltore mistakes Volpone as 'doubtless some familiar' (5.10.8) of Mosca, suggesting devilish chicanery is afoot. On the surface this means 'a fellow of the household, that is, someone you are familiar with'. But it has a double meaning, suggesting Mosca is a devilish assistant, as indeed he is. Volpone had already just previously called him a basilisk (5.8.27). This creature of fable was thought to be snakelike in form, venomous and able to kill with its look. Here Volpone wants Mosca to verbally attack Voltore by disproving his accusations. The snake reference alone is sufficient to suggest Mosca is linked to evil, as indeed he is. Often familiars were in animal form. Black cats were thought to be the standard witch's demon familiar, but records

---

16 Beier, *Masterless Men*, 125.
17 Formalized by St Thomas Aquinas, one of the seminal Christian thinkers of the medieval period. Hell's hierarchy is variously organized by different writers.
18 Incubi were male demons thought to have sex with sleeping women. Succubi were female demons coupling with men in their sleep. Both helped explain why people had lustful dreams; it was the work of the Devil.

include frogs, dogs and toads, and demonic forms.[19] They could take human shape too. Seventeenth-century witch confessions regularly describe a witch being aided by a good-looking blonde-haired young man, but with giveaway cloven hoofs. A familiar attached to a necromancer/witch was thought to be a malevolent servant/assistant imp/demon, a limb of Satan, sometimes even Satan himself. In *The Devil Is an Ass* (1616), Pug, a 'less devil', visits London to do mischief, but finds humans so corrupted he is appalled and outdone by them. If a familiar was benevolent and assisted a white wizard/cunning woman it was sometimes called a fairy. The latter could have mischievous tendencies as Puck and Ariel do (*A Midsummer Night's Dream, The Tempest*). They were capable of appearing as three-dimensional forms or remaining invisible. Magic occupied an ambiguous role in the thinking of the time, opposed by the church and law, but resorted to regularly by all sectors of society. The majority of the population saw black magic as malevolent and diabolic and white magic as benign and helpful. The law and the church saw both forms as illicit, dangerous and punishable.

2.4 Human Hierarchy

Society was arranged in three main ranks, degrees or orders – the 'better sort', the 'middling sort' and the 'baser sort' ('lower orders', 'commoners'). It was thought those of the highest rank were there by the grace of God and were therefore automatically considered to be more virtuous and more intelligent. They certainly thought themselves superior. The lower orders were thought to be naturally sinful, the middle ranks dour money-grubbers. The three-tier medieval feudal system (those who fight, those who pray, those who work) was refined during the Renaissance. The remaining clergy personnel, diminished by the Dissolution of the Monasteries, were assimilated into the upper ranks. 'Those who work' were split into 'the middling sort' and 'commoners'. They had to work in order to live, as opposed to the idle rich living off inherited fortunes and the income from their landholdings. The aristo-gentry had immense power, locally and nationally. They had psychological power over people's thinking because they could severely punish disrespect, had money and connections to impose other forms of subordination and had a status they claimed was derived from God, like the Divine Right of the King. Those of middle station included the important expanding new masses of bourgeois entrepreneurs (bankers, projectors (speculators), merchants, wealthy clothiers, industrial manufacturers) that hardly existed before, but which were driving

---

19 James I, in *Demonology* (1597), describes the Devil himself appearing 'either in likeness of a dog, a Catte, an Ape, or such-like other beast; or else to answere by a voice onlie', 19.

the astonishing explosion of culture and commerce that was the Renaissance. As money and investment spread through the arteries of European trading, so the bourgeoisie expanded.

This rising class was to be a vital feature in Elizabethan-Jacobean social change, hugely increasing the numbers of the 'middling sort', creating confusion about whether money-powerful 'merchant princes' and 'captains of industry' belonged within the middling rank or among the better sort. In *Volpone* the top tier is represented by Volpone himself, Corbaccio and the briefly appearing magistrates. Voltore, as an advocate is partially associated with the governing elite. Judges were clearly part of the governing echelon, but a lawyer occupied a slightly ambiguous position. He worked to earn a living (a signifier of the middling and lower sort), but education, profession and contacts allied him to the establishment. Volpone, a magnifico, is nominally a part of the wealthy patricians from among whom the ruling oligarchs of Venice were chosen, but he has no political role. The middle rank is represented by the merchant Corvino, while the baser sort are present in Mosca, Nano, Androgyno and Castrone (servants, entertainers), and the crowd gathered to hear Scoto of Mantua.

In general terms, the old, simple world of the Middle Ages, unified in religion by Catholicism, and unified socially by the simplicity of the feudal system, was morphing into dynamic new forms. Rising wealth created new social classifications. Developing industries created new roles and services. The broad social stratifications were still the same, but within them the three levels were diversifying into complex new divisions while social/political/ commercial interactions were changing in destabilizing, disturbing ways with which many could not easily cope. The framework in which *Volpone* is set is this consumer/acquisitive society where people consume each other and seek to acquire each other's property. It is a world where people are treated as commodities to possess as Volpone seeks to acquire control of Celia (to 'buy' her with a luxurious lifestyle) and seeks to acquire 'presents' from his dupes. It is a world where quack doctors sell their commodities to gullible customers, advertising the miraculous qualities of worthless wares. Volpone (an actor playing the part of a character pretending to be an old man close to death), plays another part as Scoto of Mantua pretending to sell an all-purpose elixir while really seeking contact with the object of his lust. He later masquerades as a would-be lover and as a commendatore. It is pretence within pretence, scam within scam, and becomes an emblem of the destabilization of a rapidly changing world of expanding commercialism. Every pretence is a lie and therefore a sin. Each pretence aims to gain material goods, so is the sin of greed. Volpone's failure to engage with his civic duty is a form of sloth and thus also a sin.

Hierarchy applied in everything. The hint of tensions between the ranks, focused on Mosca's persistent plotting to fool men who were ranked above him, and eventually in his attempt to outwit his master, was a major theme in the plays of the 1600s as the governing elite detached itself more and more from the rest of the population, a process already advanced by the end of Elizabeth's reign. The state of official corruption was part of that disconnect and was highlighted in the oration delivered to James I on his arrival in the City. It demanded that 'no more shall bribes blind the eyes of the wise, nor gold be reputed the common measure of a man's worth'. (This sets Volpone's gold obsession in a critical light.) The burden of monopolies, generating taxes that went into the pockets of the monopoly owner rather than into the national purse, was described as 'most odious and unjust' and sucking the marrow out of the life of the people. Elizabeth promised to deal with this corrupt and burdensome matter, but the Commission set up to do so had made little progress by the time of her death. James I promised to deal with monopolies, but extended them. The oration indicts the legal profession too: 'Unconscionable lawyers and greedy officers shall no longer spin out the poor man's cause in length to his undoing and the delay of justice'. (The law and lawyers are unfavourably presented in all Jonson's plays.) The speaker demanded benefices no longer be sold, the nobility be encouraged to shoulder their responsibilities to the poor, and placemen rebuked for their 'abuse [of] the authority of his Majesty to their private gain and greatness'.[20] The court, a place of extensive financial and personal corruption, became an emblem of the weakness, greed and selfishness that was thought to be sweeping through all levels of society. Specific anti-court satire is minimal in *Volpone*, but there is a general sense that the leaders of the Venetian state are as untrustworthy and dishonest as the Whitehall and City worlds of Jacobean London.

2.5 The Social Pyramid of Power

Each man was placed within different hierarchies relating to (1) society in general, (2) work and (3) family (Figure 2.2). It is usual nowadays to see human hierarchies as layered pyramids. This simple sociological model classifies according to priority, power and function. First you had a place in the social pyramid (better, middling, lower sorts), and within every rank there was a hierarchy with expectations, duties and roles to play. At work you were in another pyramid where position depended on age, experience, seniority,

20 John Nichols, *The Progresses, Processions, and Magnificent Festivities of James the First*, 128–32. 'Placemen' were those who held court or government posts, often through family influence, and regardless of their ability to fill the post.

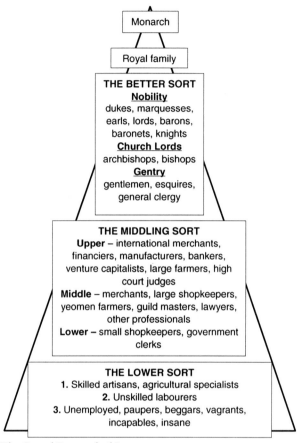

Figure 2.2 The Social Pyramid of Power

qualification and success. Within the family pyramid an unmarried man was subordinate to his father and other male elders. Once married, he was still subordinate within his extended patrilineal family but ruled his own nuclear family – wife, children, servants. For each of these social structures obedience to those above was paramount, resistance to change was the default attitude and threats to order were seen as blasphemy defying God's arrangement. Those with the most to lose were the most in favour of things staying the same, and so in history and literature noblemen and kings promote order and hierarchy as God ordained and not to be overthrown; maintaining the status quo, guaranteeing the perpetuation of their power and privilege. The Bible, as so often, authorises this view: 'Remember them that have the rule over you' (Hebrews 13:7) and the Commandment 'Honour thy father and thy mother'.

For all the comradeship in crime shared by Mosca and Volpone, their witty collusion is a subversion of proper order, of deference and respect.

At the pyramid's pinnacle the ruler reflected God's dominance. The idea of Divine Right rests on the belief that kings are chosen by God as his earthly representatives. This endows monarchs with immense psychological (or superstitious) influence and protection. As God's vice-regents kings could no more be questioned, tried, imprisoned or executed than you might think of questioning or dethroning God. In 1528 William Tyndale, a radical thorn in the church's side, affirmed in *Obedience of a Christian Man*,

> He that judgeth the King, judgeth God and damneth God's law and ordinance [...] the King is, in this world, without law; and may at his lust [will] do right or wrong, and shall give accounts to God alone.[21]

James I believed monarchs were not to be judged by their subjects. It was to become a contentious topic as his authoritarianism and unswervable intention to rule as he wished created more and more serious differences with his Parliaments. Elizabeth had been similarly resistant to advice, similarly determined to do as she chose. Her stalwart opposition to Spain had created a reason for loyal adherence and she had become an icon of English independence of spirit. In some senses, as married to her state and refusing to marry any of the foreign princes brought to court her, she had unsexed herself. She could become aggressively angry when opposed, but that was the way of monarchs, reflecting the wrath of God. The queen's will was sufficient for anything to be done unquestioningly by willing courtiers. It was the magic password for absolute power. Elizabeth's will could be implacable and she frequently acted outside the law. James I was much the same, but was never able to activate love and loyalty so much as fear and contempt. Here we encounter the uneasy tension between the divine aura attributed to monarchs and the daily experience of their human failings. Given the ritualistic, emotional reverence accorded to monarchs and the customary obedience to hierarchical superiors, Volpone, though his theatrical ability may amuse and amaze, his immoral life and conduct would not ultimately be endorsed by the audience.

2.6 The Better Sort

Below the king come the royal family, the nobility and gentry. The descending ranks of the nobility, titled aristocrats – dukes, marquesses, earls, viscounts, barons, baronets, knights – were highly stratified, jealously preserving

---

21 www.godrules.net/library/tyndale/19tyndale7.htm.

distinctions of precedence. This upper section included archbishops and bishops, men of immense power and wealth. Part of the upper sort, but untitled, was the gentry – men eligible to be called esquire and gentleman – ranked upper, middle and lower according to size of fortune, size of landholding, civic profile and ancientness of family title. Because many of the older generation of gentry families lived in the country they effectively ruled vast areas of the nation. As Sir Walter Raleigh put it, 'The gentry are the garrisons of good order throughout the realm'.[22] They traditionally tended to live on their country estates, but were by the 1600s beginning to spend more of their time in London. This was a growing trend particularly among the younger generation of gentry families whose sons were entered at one of the several Inns of Court (though not necessarily studying seriously). Many more hung about the court, hoping to get a government place or catch an heiress.

'The better sort', the quality, was the governing elite. What did they actually do? Some were ministers, Privy Councillors, government officers (place men), Members of Parliament, army or navy officers (when there was a war) or local magistrates. Those with estates might manage them (though probably through a steward who, acting as a deputy, did most of the actual administration).

They were essentially idle, a leisured class pursuing their own pleasures (hunting, gambling, drinking, whoring, lounging about court), a do-nothing aristocracy doing nothing. Yet they had clear social duties as outlined in the Works of Corporal Mercy (chapter 4). Increasingly there were men who never had an estate (or had lost it through debt) but who called themselves gentlemen on the grounds of having (or having had) some sort of independent means, university education, officer rank, skill with weapons, no need (or intention) to work for a living, gentry parents and a coat of arms. The city comedies are filled with impoverished gentlemen, living on the edge of high society, scrounging meals, hustling for an heiress or favour at court.

The better sort in *Volpone* are not laudable. They are as shabby as the atmosphere and subject of the play they are accomplices in. Though individual aristo-gentry characters in Jonson's work have virtuous qualities and conduct themselves suitably, like Bonario and Celia, they are rare. Most of his characters, whatever rank, are less than exemplary. His view of life is jaded. Most of his characters expose the age's increasing sense that the governing elite was essentially no better morally than others of lesser station and in practical terms often behaved badly and were undeserving the respect they demanded or the access to money and power they had traditionally

22 Quoted in Mortimer, *The Time Traveller's Guide to Elizabethan England*, 49.

monopolized. Volpone himself is a magnifico (a great one, a fine one, that is, of the ruling elite) but has no role in governing the city. There is no mention in any part of the play of his having any official position. He is a drone, a voluptuary who lives entirely for his own pleasures. That in itself is sinful, but made worse by the quickly emerging fact that his pleasures are dishonest. The second *avocatore* calls him 'a true voluptuary' (4.5.10) and Volpone admits to being a sensualist (1.5.88). Corbaccio is an old gentleman, but is another parasite, living off his wealth and trying to scavenge Volpone's, even prepared to risk disinheriting his son in Volpone's favour in order to appear even more devoted to Volpone and increase his chances of going to the top of the list of legatees. This dishonourable behaviour is not that expected of his degree, but while it echoes the predatory cannibalism rife in the play, it also reflects the debasement of gentry status in James I's time. Much of that was due to James I's ludicrous knighting of hundreds of unworthy men, his sale of peerages and his gentrification of hundreds.

The distinguishing material feature of the aristocracy and gentry was land ownership. Estates meant tenants (farmers and land workers) paying rents. Rent rolls provided the basic unearned family income. Many titled men held sinecure government posts (requiring little actual work) enabling them to sell other places to family members, friends and political contacts who formed an obligated clientage. This nepotism (giving jobs to relatives), once a sin, now accepted, added to growing grievances about court and government corruption.

Wealth could be materially improved if the monarch gave or sold you a monopoly giving you control of the taxes and other charges on a commodity or service, like imports of wine, tobacco, sugar, spices and starch. This provided further opportunities for selling posts within the infrastructure. The upper sort thought themselves superior in virtue, born with innate leadership abilities, with better moral qualities than other ranks. *Probitas* (physical and moral courage) was believed to pass through the male bloodline (a reason for ensuring your heir's legitimacy), giving each generation the qualities of prowess, honour, magnanimity. Noble in rank, supposedly noble, courageous, generous in nature, they thought themselves deserving of respect from all below them. They were the evolution of the medieval warrior class, now demilitarized and without apparent function. Many were fine and decent people, living on their estate and doing their social-moral duties. Many others were simply weak personalities, extravagant, in debt, idle, sexually decadent, syphilitics, drunks, fools, inveterate gamblers, incompetent estate managers and indifferent to their role as social exemplars and leaders.

Venetian nobles were similar, owning fine palaces in the city, but also villas and estates on the mainland to which they retired in the hot summer months (as English aristocrats returned to their country mansions in the summer), relying on vineyards and farmland to provide produce and rents. They were also, again like the English aristo-gentry, increasingly involved in commercial and industrial enterprises.

The discrepancies between the expected conduct of the ranks and their actual behaviour were regular targets for satire. Knowing how to behave and actually conducting themselves decorously, respectfully, modestly, were two different matters. Running after the latest fashion or innovation was becoming a feature of court life, fed by leisure and the expanding availability of luxury goods as commerce and capitalism took hold in England. It was encouraged too by the increasingly closed nature of the court as a separate world in a protected bubble. Being involved in fraudulent activity of the sort Volpone thrives on is a step-stage down in immoral conduct even for an already corrupt better sort. His play-acting as the terminally old man, his charade as a mountebank, his attempted rape would also have been regarded as degrading his rank.

Contemporary plays are full of men claiming gentlemanly status, but behaving badly. Drunken, roistering, lecherous misconduct highlights serious discrepancies between the expected behaviour of aristo-gentry men and their actual comportment. Inconsistently, bad behaviour often coexisted with oversensitive alertness to offences to their honour. Reacting to the slightest perceived insult to their conceived status and the respect they believed it deserved, that response was usually angry and violent. In an age when gentlemen habitually wore swords the ready resort to arms was all too easy, especially when alcohol played its part in the constant outbreaks of street and tavern brawls. This gives a very topical context to the swaggering braggadocio of the Montagu-Capulet bravo boys in *Romeo and Juliet*. Such intemperate violence was a slur on the honour of any gentleman, but never seemed to be seen as such by the hotheads involved. Elizabethans and Jacobeans were obsessed with genealogy and proving the ancientness of their noble or gentry origins. Many family trees, however, were fabricated, claiming descent from Norman knights, Saxon thegns, the pre- Roman Trojan roots claimed for the British nobility by pseudohistorians like Geoffrey of Monmouth, even from Old Testament kings. Suitable payment to the College of Heralds bought you an 'authenticated' coat of arms and genealogy. The public audience knew full well that young men of titled or gentry background often behaved like rowdy boors and that some of them were currently watching the play – or probably ogling the female spectators. In the 1600 city comedy *Eastward Ho!* Francis Quicksilver claims gentlemanly status because his mother was a gentlewoman and his father a senior Justice of the Peace. He feels it is beneath him being apprenticed to a goldsmith, and spends his time drinking, whoring and scamming money out of other gallants.[23] To him idleness, drunkenness, violence and carelessness over money are gentlemanly markers:

> do nothing [...] be idle [...] Wipe thy bum with testons [sixpences; approximately 5p], and make ducks and drakes with shillings [10p]. [...] As I am a gentleman born, I'll be drunk, grow valiant, and beat thee.[24]

Golding, the industrious apprentice, scorns Quicksilver as 'a drunken whore-hunting rake-hell' (1.1.125). Sexual licence was common in the elite. A 'rake-hell' was a troublemaker and alludes to the gang mentality and hooliganism of the many unsupervised, upper-rank young men floating around London. The only people in *Volpone* who behave with the honour expected of their status are Celia and Bonario. Everyone else behaves dishonourably.

Noticeably, no one speaks of their family history, though among the patrician Venetians the family tree and the contribution of ancestors to the success of the state were as important for status and eligibility for office as in England. Even the officers of the court are somewhat flexible in their morality. They are more influenced by Voltore's adversarial condemnation of Bonario than by any desire to establish the truth and administer justice fairly. One even sees the opportunity of arranging an advantageous marriage between his daughter and Mosca when he thinks the parasite is a rich man. He is fooled by the fine clothes the parasite has adopted. The *Scrutineo* is fooled by show and words rather than motivated to rigorously question to find the truth. The *Scrutineo* was a court housed in the Senate building which was part of the Doge's palace. Such cynicism is typical of Jonson and of the mood of the early 1600s.

Despite the intense stratification of society, dividing lines between social groups were becoming blurred by individual cases of social mobility, the proliferation of new knights under James I, growing bourgeois wealth and the increasing complexity of society in general. People became obsessively fussy about precedence, about being treated according to their rank, preserving fine differences that made them feel superior and calling on their genealogy to prove their family pedigree. Ambition is a subset of pride or vanity, so overambition is seen as pushy, selfish and sinful. A little ambition was proper use of your God-given talents. However, to avoid the hubris of becoming overproud of advancement, you should humbly thank God for the good fortune of your rise, downplaying the extent and effect of your own efforts.

---

23 Many aristo-gentry families put younger sons to professions and trades so they should have an income, since property, land and fortune were bequeathed to the eldest male.
24 1.1.114–16, 138 (New Mermaid edition, 1994).

Political theorists and moral polemicists formulated programmes emphasizing the upper rank's duty to serve the state and the people. Elyot's *The Boke Named the Governour* (1531) proposed careful education combining a reverence for virtue and a readiness to assume social responsibilities. This meant residing on your estate, leading the community, helping the poor and establishing schools and almshouses, as enshrined in the Corporal and Spiritual Works of Mercy. These justified living comfortably off income derived from the labours of tenant farmers and tenant labourers. Rank and privilege were counterbalanced by a requirement to put something back into the community, but one of the features of the growing new individualism was that civic spirit and charitable work were discarded by elite-group young men. This was assisted by the growing tendency of the governing class to gravitate to London and become detached from their locality. A responsible role for the ruling classes, built on a virtue-based humanist education, was promulgated by many writers throughout the decades leading to the Civil War, but the actual behaviour of many gentlemen conformed more to Viscount Conway's definition: 'We eat and drink and rise up to play and this is to live like a gentleman; for what is a gentleman but his pleasure?'[25] Courtiers were docile yes-men and yes-women, obsequiously bowing and scraping at the monarch's whim. They were intent on pleasure and advancement. Advancement depended on others so aspirants to place and promotion tended to be morally indifferent. To stand by principles could lose you favour and the pursuit of personal pleasures dulled the ability or willingness to make moral distinctions if they threatened enjoyment.

2.7 The Middling Sort

The next layer down is the newly enlarged bourgeoisie or 'middling sort'. In the Middle Ages, the feudal system included them with 'those who work' (anyone earning a living – 90 per cent). This group comprised everyone from day labourers to the wealthiest merchant. The country arrangement was village centred, with the lord of the manor (living in or near the village) governing and guarding his 'flock' of farmers and labourers like a shepherd protects and guides his sheep. The workers lived in or near the village, where the priest represented 'those who pray'. The professional 'middling sort' (lawyers, doctors, produce factors, clothiers) hardly existed in country areas, tending to cluster in market towns, and were numerically an insignificant demographic nationally. By the Renaissance the pattern had changed. With the growth of commerce and the growth of towns, the 'service' industries expanded and

25 Cited in Stone, *The Crisis of the Aristocracy*, 27.

with them the numbers of the bourgeoisie. Eighty per cent of the population was still rural – farmers and labourers – but 15 per cent were now largely town-dwelling middle class. The growing bourgeoisie of Elizabeth's time expanded much more in the trade boom of the seventeenth century. The remaining 5 per cent was the aristo-gentry. The upper ranks thought the middling sort were greedy, obsessed with making money and virtuous enough, but lacking taste, elegance, culture. They were mocked as 'cits' (citizens, city dwellers, that is, not landowners), derided as social climbers whose wives and daughters were snobbish, fashion mad, empty headed and easy prey for lascivious, gold-digging courtiers (as with Volpone's pursuit of a merchant's wife). Some were like that, but many were educated, cultivated people, looking after their families (especially their children) better than many of the nobility. Most were hard working, eager to put some comfort buffer between themselves and poverty, but showed civic spirit, were modest in lifestyle and personal behaviour, pious and were drivers of conservative church reform.

The rise of the middling sort was *the* big social change in Elizabethan-Jacobean England. Division into upper, middle and lower classifications distinguishes between, say, a very rich international merchant, the farmer of a largish thriving farm and a small shopkeeper. The upper echelons were protocapitalists – merchant bankers, venture financiers, large-scale traders, major clothiers, wealthy manufacturers, leading lawyers and judges, and large-scale farmers; men of wealth and local (and increasingly national) power. The middle group would be comfortably wealthy merchants and masters of guild trades, professionals like doctors and lawyers, living in cathedral cities and market towns and substantial farmers. The lower 'middling sort' were small shopkeepers, small farmers owning only a little land and growing numbers of lowly paid metropolitan-based government clerks. What differentiated between the upper, middle and lower 'middling sort' was money. More money meant access to mayorships, masterships of guilds, alderman or councillor status. Money brought the capacity to invest in speculative enterprises and loan cash, thus becoming a sort of local banker or simply a moneylender. Usury (lending money at interest), a sin in medieval times, was acceptable though not loved by the seventeenth century, a natural development of the growing cash richness of the expanding commercial world. As the economy grew fortunes were made and wasted. Satire against moneylenders, money-amassing citizens and the debt-fuelled lifestyles of parasite gentlemen, became regular features in contemporary plays.

In Venice all were citizens, but the very rich did have mainland estates, so were not forced to live all the year round on the central islands that formed the city. The richest families, from whom the Doge and Senators, the ruling oligarchy, were elected, were often merchants too. But their trading ventures were an add-on to their patrician status. They were rich magnificos by birth and entrepreneurs by choice, while the Corvino-type merchant hoped to make a fortune big enough to enable him to gain noble rank at some later point in his life. Just what commodities Corvino trades in we are not told, but he is as avaricious as the lawyer and the old gentleman. His vulnerability through his wife is a character feature that could easily be understood to reflect the uneasy tension between the City and Westminster/Whitehall. It was a commonplace (in real life and in literature) that men of the better sort preyed sexually on merchants' wives and daughters. Volpone's readiness to predate Voltore's wife recurs in literature from Giovanni Boccaccio in the fourteenth century to novels and plays in the eighteenth. Corvino is a recognizable English type in fiction and real life; the cuckold, the dull money-mad monomaniac.

The middle ranks looked up to the aristo-gentry and showed public respect. Privately they thought themselves morally better than the upper sort. Pious, hardworking, earning their living, living moderately, paying their debts, establishing schools and hospitals, doing civic duties and giving their children disciplined home lives, education and love, they saw the better sort as vain, idle, showy wastrels, parading in silks they did not pay for, gambling, drinking, promiscuous and demanding deference not always deserved. Yet, many merchants longed to rise and put on the outer show of gentleman status – a title, fine country house, coach and horses, fashionable clothes, social power. 'The old English gentry were powerfully reinforced

> by an influx from the professional and mercantile classes. Lawyers, government officials, and successful merchants bought land not only to better their social standing but also to increase their incomes.[26]

As England became a more active trading nation the middle ranks expanded, became wealthier and more upwardly mobile. Those at the very top could be awarded or buy titles. They tended also, with this status rise, to move into the country, selling their business, cutting themselves off from the taint of trade or distancing themselves from it by hiring a manager. Legislation restricting bourgeois land ownership was increasingly ignored, circumvented or simply not applied. The bourgeoisie was unstoppable, buying estates, thinking of themselves as equal to the nobility. Some became nobility. Money power enabled such men to push out the cash-strapped yeoman farmer. Agricultural depression led to many of these freemen, owning their own farm, selling up to opportunist incoming merchants turned landowners looking to

26 Ashley, 18.

add to their holdings. Small, independent farmers were also under pressure from gentry seeking to augment their estate.[27] A gentleman wanting to annex land adjoining his estate had the advantage over the small farmer facing hard times.

Another expanding bourgeois group was top civil servants administering the proliferating departments of government. The three most prestigious power posts were those of lord treasurer, lord chancellor and the king's secretary. These were political as well as royal household appointments. Below them was another internal pyramid of court power – the bureaucrats – reaching down to the lowliest 'base pen clerks'.[28] The most junior dreamed of catching the eye of a superior or a titled courtier and being promoted. Once you were in a higher place your future was made. Place was gained by patrimony, patronage or purchase. A poor clerk without family connections or money to help him advance had to find a patron. It was difficult to penetrate 'the grand efflorescence of nepotism' if you could not buy promotion or inherit a post from your father.[29] The court was awash with idle young men seeking opportunities for advancement. In *Eastward Ho!* the idle apprentice, Quicksilver, cast off by his irate master, declares, 'I'll to the Court, another manner of place for maintenance […] than the silly City!' (2.2.54–5).

If your courtier patron had some measure of power you were made. In the plots, counterplots and intrigues of the Elizabethan-Jacobean courts there are innumerable examples of servants ready to bear false witness, cheat, slander to get on. It was another sort of 'food chain' fight for survival of the fittest or, rather, the most ruthless and devious.

2.8 The Lower Orders

The mass of the population formed the broad base of the pyramid. Skilled artisans were at the top along with farm workers who had a specialism (shepherd, horse man, cattle man).

Apprentices, learning a trade or craft, would count themselves as being in the middle of the lower orders, but with diligence and industry aspired to become masters of their craft and move into guild membership and shop ownership, thus becoming bourgeois. Below was the mass of unskilled day labourers, then the unemployed, paupers, beggars, vagrants, the insane and

---

27 Ashley, 18.

28 From Thomas Wilson, *State of England* (quoted in *Camden Miscellany*, vol. 16, 43).

29 Mark Kishlansky, *A Monarchy Transformed: Britain 1603–1714*, 44, describing the huge network of family members given posts under the influence of the Duke of Buckingham, James I's favourite.

incapable at the very bottom. Farm labourers were severely squeezed at this time. Many were day labourers, hired as and when needed, and subject to the seasonal fluctuations of employment needs. The irregularity of work made household budgeting difficult. Prices of essentials rose steeply throughout Elizabeth's reign and continued to do so in James I's.

Common land, where game could be caught, firewood gathered, vegetables cultivated and animals grazed, was being enclosed by greedy landowners. Thus, the options for augmenting food and comfort were diminishing. This sector of society too was growing alarmingly, not because of a high birth rate but because the changing economy caused 'casualties' falling out of working society into unemployment. The growing unemployed poor put pressure on local poor relief resources (organized on a parish basis) and represented a dangerous underclass with the potential for social unrest and riot. A 1597 law aimed at reducing poverty by banishing vagabonds to Newfoundland and the East and West Indies, but remiss or reluctant justices of the peace meant the law failed to reduce or repress the problem.

The lower orders were thought by those above them to be lazy, delinquent, ignorant, feckless and vicious (in the physically brutal and morally unsound senses). There was much truth in that, particularly among the growing numbers of urban poor, many of whom were 'masterless men', unemployed and detached from their original rural communities. The commoners thought much the same of their so-called betters. And there was truth in that too. There were hard-working men and women living godly lives and bringing up families despite hardships. Those living in the countryside were particularly susceptible to rent rises, fluctuations in labour needs, prices of produce and winter feed for livestock and changes in land usage brought about by local enclosure. A series of disastrous harvests in the 1590s exacerbated matters, bringing famine to many doors. Piety, thrift, frugality, hard work and decent living could not feed hungry children nor protect you from market shifts caused by the greed of others in higher ranks. The self-satisfied courtly members of the audience knew well that outside the comfort of Whitehall and Westminster beggars thronged the streets. There were about 12,000 in London in 1600. Some were indolent fraudsters preferring begging or thieving to work, but many were genuine victims of hard times. They were all the responsibility of those with wealth, rank and privilege. They were all morally and metaphorically (some literally) sons and daughters of the nobility. The king and their local lord was a 'father', they his children. It was the job of the monarch and court to look after them. Most did not. Shakespeare's *Measure for Measure* (1603) and *King Lear* (1605–6) criticized the detachment of the rich from the poor. Social tensions underlie and overlay Jonson's comedies. The social range in *Volpone* is narrow, but in *The Alchemist* (1610) a broad spectrum of the ranks is portrayed and in *Bartholomew Fair* (1614) the cast forms a microcosm of society. In the opening to Shakespeare's *Coriolanus* (1607–9), the privileged senator Menenius and the arrogant Martius clash with the starving citizens of Rome. A Citizen sums up the class tensions that similarly underlay Jacobean England:

> 1 *Citizen*: We are accounted poor citizens, the patricians good. What authority surfeits on would relieve us. If they would yield us but the superfluity while it were wholesome, we might guess they relieved us humanely. But they think we are too dear. The leanness that afflicts us, the object of our misery, is as an inventory to particularize their abundance. (1.1.13–19)

If the governing orders have responsibility to aid the poor, the poor have a duty of grateful, controlled conduct and respect for those above them. Social difference and tensions between the ranks is not a major theme in *Volpone*, but underlying it is the sense that Volpone fails to engage at all with his duty of governorship, his Christian duty of charity, the concept that brothers (in Christ) and neighbours should take care of one another and that he is a 'father' to his family, his household. What is presented is a world where humans all prey on each other. Commerce and imperialism are founded on predation and the spirit of that has permeated the circle of characters centred on Volpone. Those who are meant to lead society and be an example are shown as scavenging and greedy. Even in the Scoto scene, where the mountebank is followed in by a crowd, the gentry characters alone, Sir Politic and Peregrine, speak and the common sort are voiceless apart from the cry 'Follow, follow, follow, follow, follow' (2.2.28).

2.9 The Theory of the Humours

There was a hierarchy of the inner man too. The head, like a monarch, ruled (theoretically) as a symbol of the primacy of reason. The major organs, the nobility and gentry, came next as key to the functioning of the body. The limbs, the commoners, were the mere labourers. This loose, imprecise image was less important than the connection of the body to the outer world, the macrocosm. The alignment of stars, planets and the ascendant zodiac sign at the precise hour of your birth fixed your fate and personality, enabling predictions to be made concerning your future fortune. There was a correspondence too between your inner self and the outer world. From classical times until the end of the eighteenth century people believed that the body contained four fluids (humours) influencing personality, attitude and behaviour.

This had been particularly developed by the Roman physician Galen and persisted into Renaissance times, though it was beginning to be modified by new scientific/medical discoveries. While your astrological sign provided your broad personality characteristic, the proportions of the four humours determined more precisely your temperament. Whatever these proportions were at birth defined your personal normal state and psychological type. The humours were phlegm, yellow bile (choler), blood and black bile. Four temperaments were associated with the humours. The phlegmatic person was easy going and stoical, remaining calm in crises and seeking rational solutions. The choleric man was inclined to temper, was bossy, aggressive, ambitious and liked to take charge. The sanguine man (in whom blood predominated) tended to be positive, active, impulsive, pleasure seeking, self-confident, sociable, open, friendly and warm hearted. Those in whom black bile was dominant tended to be melancholic, negative, overly introverted and considerate of others but inclined toward pessimism about the imperfections of the world. The greediness of the central five characters in *Volpone* betokens a form of aggressiveness linked to the choleric temperament. Each too has a monomaniac fixation on gain. Between these four cardinal types there were many permutations, many mixed proportions of humours explaining the huge variety of human personalities and the range of emotional phases to which an individual might be subject.[30] Illness was thought due to increase or decrease in one fluid and led to (and explained) mood changes. The medical practices of bloodletting and purges were thought to rebalance the body, getting rid of an excess of one humour, while certain foods or drinks redressed deficiencies. Some natural philosophers (scientists and rationalists) were beginning to question this theory, believing parental attitudes, early life experiences and education formed personality. Some physicians were beginning to ascribe other causes to illnesses, though today's knowledge of chemical imbalances causing maladies and mental aberrations shows the humours theory was not entirely wrong. Belief in these characteristics led to 'humour' stereotypes in literature that were sources of comedy (grumpy fathers, shrewish wives, romantic lovers, bloodthirsty soldiers, gold-mad misers, sex-mad widows, scheming villains). The character flaws of tragic heroes and villains fall easily into these broad categories as well.[31] There were those who rejected astrological origins of personality and claimed they created their own destiny. *King Lear's* Machiavellian individualist, Edmund, rejects the idea of the stars

---

30 Robert Burton's *The Anatomy of Melancholy* (1621) explores this multiplicity of psychoemotional types.
31 Lily B. Campbell's *Shakespeare's Tragic Heroes* interprets heroic flaws from physiological/psychological diagnoses.

forming personality. Conceived 'under the dragon's tail' and born 'under Ursa Major' he was expected to be 'rough and lecherous' (1.2. His belief in himself as maker of his own destiny ('I should have been that I am had the maidenliest star in the firmament twinkled at my bastardizing') was a minority view. In *Volpone* the dominant humour displayed is the choleric tendency to aggression sublimated into the fury for gain. The miser was a traditional humour type in literature and the expectation was that his greed would be punished by a thief stealing his darling gold. Jonson doubles his miserly characters (with Volpone and Mosca) and then adds three more greedy villains whose lust for gain gulls them into a situation where they are being conned of their wealth little by little, present by present. The dominant pair are also punished by each other as Mosca betrays his master and aims to be the superpredator. His apparently successful greed is finally brought down by institutional retribution. It is a close-run thing and the supercarrion ultimate scavenger, Mosca the fly, nearly gets away with it. The characterization is simple and shallow. Each character is initially presented, their humour displayed, and there is no attempt to show them changing, becoming repentant and cleansed. Redemption/reformation does not take place. Exploration of deep psychological patterns is not part of this play. The characters are deeply sinful but not deeply complex. It is what people do that signifies. and the consequences of their actions drive the plot and create comedy. There are some other serious issues related to patriarchy, arranged marriage, the workings of lust, the inadequacy of the judicial system, but, while entertainment and laughter dominate, the main focus is on the characteristics and effects of greed in a dog eat dog world.

Renaissance people believed in a network of complex correspondences flowing through the outer world and the inner world, linking all things. The planets affected and reflected moods (the moon was particularly influential), herbs and weather and foodstuffs affected health.

Fogs were thought to carry poisons and disease and certain organs were affected by particular types of food or drink and were also linked to moods and psychological states. The stomach was supposedly the seat of courage, the liver supposedly the organ involved with love. Overcome with lust for Celia, which he mistakes for love, Volpone tells Mosca, 'My liver melts' (2.4.9). He refers to Cupid and the fires of love/lust.

2.10 The Rest of Creation

Below humankind come the other animals – mammals, birds, fishes, insects – able to move, reproduce, experience appetites (hunger, thirst, heat, cold, sexual urges), with limited sensory responses, limited problem-solving intelligence, lacking the capacity for a spiritual life and without the ability to reason or make moral decisions. Animals were thought not to have souls, logic or language.

Animals were also ranged hierarchically though less precisely than humankind and often according to conflicting ideas about their nature. The lion topped the mammal world because of imagined links to courage, nobility and kingship (reflected in the use of lions as royal heraldic emblems). Yet it was also associated with lofty pride. To Machiavelli the lion lacked the worldly wisdom of the wily fox and was rather a brave but intellectually limited creature.[32] Wolves, jackals, hyenas and foxes were ranked low for their scavenging, savage, predatory, untrustworthy and devious nature. Lady Would-be is called a 'she-wolf' (5.2.66). The leopard represented sexual promiscuity. The hyena was a symbol of treachery for imitating a human cry to lure its victims. (Lady Would-be refers to this when accusing Celia in court, 4.6.3.) Tigers were noted for ferocity. A mother tiger's protectiveness of her young is admired but tigers could also display an unreliable, savage aspect – a quality ascribed to ruthless humans. The fox was traditionally linked (particularly in fables) to ingenious plotting, hence the use of its Latin name (*vulpes vulpes*) for the title character. This animal figures in a number of Aesop's *Fables* as a predator using trickery and a sharp understanding of weaknesses in others. Apes and goats were thought particularly lustful. An angry Corvino accuses Celia of displaying herself at the window and allowing the crowd to gaze upon her 'with goatish eyes' (2.5.34). Goats were also associated with the Devil for their horns and cloven feet and often linked with black magic rituals. Other creatures were attributed with lustfulness. Corvino in court accuses his wife of being a 'a whore,/Of most hot exercise, more than a partridge' (4.5.16–17) and neighing 'like a jennet'. He means that in orgasm she makes a noise like a horse in heat neighing to call a stallion. Reptiles were low in the hierarchy, snakes particularly being associated with evil, linked to temptation and original sin in the Bible. Mosca is likened to the venomous, mythological basilisk, and Corbaccio asserts Voltore, the lawyer, has a 'forked tongue' (5.10.46), suggesting he is a liar, a bearer of false witness, unreliable, evil. Frogs, toads and bats had witchcraft associations.[33]

Lowest of all were rats, mice and other vermin. Domesticated animals were ranked by usefulness. Dogs (guards and hunters), listed with the working creatures, could be highly prized. Elizabethan-Jacobean gentlemen endlessly discussed the qualities of their hunting dogs. Canine loyalty was

---

32 'The lion is defenceless against traps and a fox is defenceless against wolves. Therefore one must be a fox in order to recognize traps, and a lion to frighten off wolves. Those who simply act like lions are stupid' (*The Prince*, chap. 18, 99).

33 'No animal fawns so much as a dog, and none is so faithful' (Erasmus, *Praise of Folly*, 134).

highly regarded, but there were negatives – a fawning, flattering nature, greediness, readiness to follow anyone who fed them. Mosca talks of parasites at court:

> With their court-dog-tricks, that can fawn, and fleer,
> Make their revenue out of legs and faces [bows and obsequious smiles],
> Echo my lord, and lick away a moth: [remove vermin]. (3.1.20–2)

'Whoreson dog' and 'cur' are common abusive epithets in plays. Apart from the beast fable names given to the central characters there is wide use of animal imagery throughout the play. This helps emphasize the savage nature of the human activities represented. The range is drawn from all areas of living creatures, but there is a preponderance of negative images (frightening, savage, predatory or evil) over positive or neutral images. Images of trapping, snaring, baiting hooks link the similarity of man in his brute form to the trickery that is rife in the play. Disease imagery, even if Volpone's illness is fabricated, establishes the sense of a decaying society that is morally sick. Images of assertions claimed to be true but which are lies link too with the action's deceptions and illusions. These clusters of overlapping imagery create an atmosphere in which it is impossible to tell what is true.

Birds were highly thought of because of flight's association with air, thought to be a divine element along with fire. Hierarchy applied again within the group of birds used for hunting; the eagle as *the* hunting bird for an emperor, the gerfalcon for kings and other birds of prey, used for the chase, ranked according to their suitable social level; peregrine (nobility), goshawks (yeomen – landowning small-scale farmers), sparrow-hawks (priests) and the smallest hawk, the kestrel, for servants or knaves. After the birds of prey (including the owl, synonymous with wisdom), the hierarchy breaks down. The carrion eaters, as scavengers, were ranked low, like hyenas in the mammal hierarchy. Kites (combing rubbish tips in London) are always represented negatively, linked with the parasitical behaviour of those feeders and sycophants hanging around the households of men of power, but Jonson adds a vulture to his crow and raven:

> Now, now, my clients
> Begin their visitation! vulture, kite,
> Raven, and gor-crow [carrion crow], all my birds of prey,
> That think me turning carcass. (1.2.88–91)

Such opportunists, watching a dying animal, waiting to pick over the flesh, become metaphors for human predation of its own species.[34] Erasmus had a similar jaded view of mankind. In *Praise of Folly* he refers to 'all the evil man does to man, [...] the infliction of poverty, imprisonment, slander, dishonour, torture, treachery, betrayal, insult, litigation and fraud' and 'the countless hordes of mortals [...] a swarm of flies or gnats quarrelling [...] fighting, plotting, stealing, playing, making love'.[35] Many of these evils are perpetrated in the play.

The humans are shown as worse for preying on those still living while knowing they should behave better. In *Timber* Jonson offers a context for his human predators: 'The net was never spread for the hawk or buzzard that hurt us, but the harmless birds'[36] for they are good meat. This statement, based on a remark in Terence's play *Phormio*, focuses the injustice of nature, how the innocent and weak are victimized. It also implies how one species devours another. These images are both central to the play. Jonson adds a quote from Juvenal Satire II to clinch the point: 'Dat veniam corvis, vexat censura columbas' ('You pardon the ravens, but censure the doves').[37] This has a resonance for the justice system of his time, which allowed many guilty men to escape sentence because they were rich and powerful, while the poor were harshly punished.

Writers began to register anxiety that, as more people moved into towns, the businesses that grew there, particularly those that appealed to the acquisition of status symbols and luxury goods, encouraged men to lure others into buying what they did not need. The whole expanding commercial world was based on entrepreneurs luring money out of customers' purses into their own coffers. The parasite (the yes-man toady, like Mosca and Oswald in *Lear*) was a familiar figure of scornful fun on stage, originating in Roman comedy and satirical poetry. A parasite was anyone attaching himself to a rich, powerful man in order to curry favour, be rewarded for running errands (including pimping), and for flattering his master's self-esteem. At the very least he hoped to be invited to dinner, at most retained as a household member and personal assistant-cum-fixer. Mosca, the paragon of parasites, is so called after the Latin for fly (*Musca domestica*) since flies are the lowest carrion eaters.

Jonson names his fortune hunters after allegorical animal figures in line with the medieval-Renaissance iconography of didactic fables – Voltore (a

---

34 'Those who have deliberately preferred a life of irresponsible lawlessness and violence become wolves and hawks and kites' (Plato, *Phaedo*, 134). See also Leviticus 11:14, where kites are listed with many other birds that are 'an abomination'.
35 *Praise of Folly*, 108, 143.
36 *Timber*, 43.
37 *The Sixteen Satires* (trans. Peter Green).

vulture-like advocate), Corbaccio (the raven, an old gentleman) and Corvino (the crow, a merchant).[38] Below the scavengers came the worm- and insect-eating birds and then the seed eaters. Abusive name-calling occurs plentifully in Jacobean drama, often involving animal/avian epithets that use negative characteristics associated with these creatures. Some animal epithets are positive, but linking human behaviour with animals is mostly negative, a reminder that the animal side of man was sinful – lustful, brutal, devious, greedy, slothful. The worst type of connection involves monsters – unnatural, mythical, animal hybrids. They are the stuff of myth and nightmare, like the dark Anglo-Saxon dreamings of weird beasts found in illuminated gospels, the multiplicity of strange hybrid creatures painted in the margins of medieval manuscripts and the ugly monster mutants in paintings of hell. These are the imaginings of mankind's worst fears, suggesting the darker side of life, fears that emerge in dreams, the monsters men can be made into by love or hate or greed, and of course the forms the Devil takes. The word 'monster', applied to humans, connotes anyone behaving outside the acceptable parameters of civilized conduct and signifies an extreme shift from decent, normal human form and behaviour to brutal and uncivilized in manners and deformed in appearance, like that travesty of nature an ass-headed/ass-eared man. Medieval and Renaissance people believed outward ugliness expressed inner deformity and sinfulness. Beauty was thought a guarantee of inner grace and purity. In *The Tempest* Shakespeare has a savage, Caliban, described as being as deformed in mind as he is body and regularly called 'monster'. He represents the primitive savagery in man and the ungovernable sex drive of the brute, man reduced to his lowest, what King Lear calls 'unaccommodated man'. Jonson's birds represent human nastiness. Each should be an example of humankind at its best. Voltore is an educated man of law, supposedly bringing the orderliness that reason and justice impose on the wild brutality of society. He actually represents the king of scavenging birds, tracking wounded creatures and waiting for their death before moving in to strip them to the bone. Lawyers were regarded as unscrupulous, money-grabbing, self-serving vultures who preyed on the living. Vulture in Italian is *avvoltoio*, but Voltore sounds Italian and is recognizable as vulture to the English ear.

There is some confusion over the naming of the other two *captators*. In Italian a raven is *corvo* and crow is *cornacchia*. Yet Corvino is supposedly a crow and Corbaccio a raven. Corbaccio, an old gentleman (perhaps dressed in sober, dignified black, suited to his age), is called a raven (Volpone calls

---

38 An allegory is a story with a secondary meaning, usually moral and with characters representing abstract qualities (Courage, Justice, Cunning, Lust, Virtue and so forth). *Volpone* has a surface storyline about legacy hunters and so on, but the characters stand for various sins and the overall story has moral lessons embedded in it.

him 'the old raven', 1.4.81). He should represent all those good qualities supposedly associated with his rank and the dignity of age, but, like the raven (traditionally thought to be a harbinger of death), he is a bird of ill omen, contemplates the legal death of his son by disinheritance and is a scavenger. The largest of the crow family, the raven, eats carrion but also kills for itself and forages for eggs, reptiles, insects and seeds. As previously said, the Italian for raven is *corvo* (Latin, *corvus corax*), but that sounds too like Corvino, so Jonson had to fabricate another name for him. There was a prose work by Boccaccio, written circa 1355. It was called *Il Corbaccio*, usually translated as *The Crow*.

Jonson knew something of Boccaccio's work (probably through Florio), so he takes the name, though changes the character into a raven rather than a crow.[39] Coincidentally, a simple switch of the letters of the first syllable of Boccaccio gives Ccobaccio (almost Corbaccio), so perhaps this spoonerism suited him as a further private joke when choosing the name for this character. Corbaccio has linguistic resonances too (again perhaps provided by Florio). In central Italian dialect the word *corvaccio* means something/someone nasty and little – a dirty nasty crow. The 'v' is pronounced in dialect as a 'b', so becomes *corbaccio*. The third fortune-hunting bird-man is Corvino the crow. In Italian a crow is *cornacchia*. This is perhaps too close to Corbaccio and would cause confusion to an audience in the sometimes speedy succession of characters entering and exiting. *Cornacchia* is partially suggestive of *corno* (horn) – signifying a cuckold (which is what Corvino was prepared to make himself in the name of gain). Jonson avoided that pun and went to the Italian *corvo* (raven) – perhaps as an echo of the Latin *corvus corone corone*, the carrion crow. Hated by farmers for its predation of grain, root crops, eggs and chicks, it also feeds on carcases. Jonson's Latin was better than his Italian and a more ready source. These linguistic confusions matter little, for just as ravens and crows are easily confused and look similar, so too, though in their own way, Corbaccio and Corvino are similarly corrupt and disgusting. Both subvert two foundational aspects of society.

As explorers and exploiters opened up the world and contact was made with other cultures, questions began to be asked about just how truly civilized European society was with its institutionalized torture, witch burnings, rampant urban sex trade and epidemic sexually transmitted diseases, its wars,

---

39 In *The Devil is an Ass* he has a character use a trick found in Giovanni's Boccaccio's *Decameron*, 3.6. Though different attitudes to love are a unifying theme, the 100 stories pivot on many types of trickery. Quick-witted resourcefulness is valued, but so too are loyalty and piety. Churchmen are regularly mocked for their hypocrisy, lustfulness and general corruption. Money and the greediness of merchant figure as themes too. The work thus shares common ground with that of Jonson.

assassinations, politically motivated executions and religion-based massacres. Its selfish, ruthlessly individualistic conduct, beginning to disregard the ancient traditions of respect for the old and vulnerable, is another collision of old and new philosophies that casts doubt on European cultures and how much progress had been made in the achievement of virtue. Courtiers wore silks, adorned themselves in jewels, acted out elaborate rituals of etiquette, listened to intricate and beautiful music, read philosophy and poetry and watched charming and elegantly written plays. Manners had improved greatly. The surface gloss was supershiny, but people starved, syphilis raged, the plague killed thousands, torture and brutal punishments were institutional, and courts were hotbeds of promiscuity, intrigue, power struggles and murders. Jonson peels back the cultured surface to reveal the animal beneath, each preying on the other in a struggle but not one for survival. What is done by man to man in the play is not of necessity but choice, self-elected, fabricated – for gain. Volpone and the legacy hunters are all comfortably off, as far as is possible to tell. They are examples of what Burton saw as one of the symptoms of covetousness: 'the more he hath, the more he wants'.[40] This is animal behaviour of a sort. If food is available an animal will eat more than it needs on the grounds that it does not know when food will be available again. But a man who is not in want can choose to be moderate, a virtue most of the characters in Jonson do not display.

The final groupings of animals were the fish, reptiles, amphibians, insects, sessiles (unmoving shellfish). Fish were ranked low as water was thought to be a dull heavy element like earth. Reptiles, amphibians and insects were thought of as even lower, fleas and lice being seen as verminous like rats. Bees and ants were positively regarded for their industry and apparent social organization, which suggested something approaching intelligence.[41] This period valued any form of corporate, civic or community cooperation as a mark of moral engagement with civilized behaviour.

One hundred and three animal references in the play indicate the density and dominance of this particular type of image and reinforce the central idea that men have become like animals. The play is a carnival of beasts, many, but not all, grotesque. There are multiple references to vultures, crows, ravens snuffing (smelling) a carcase and pecking for carrion. Inevitably there are many mentions of the fox. Viper, basilisk, snake and 'fork-tongued' allusions emblematize the evil loosed in the piece, focusing Mosca (along with some mention of flies). Metaphors of man as an ass and mankind as 'herds of fools', indicate a generally accepted view of the species. Significantly there are verbs

---

40 *The Anatomy of Melancholy*, 247.
41 Socrates calls bees, wasps and ants 'social and disciplined creatures' (Plato, *Phaedo*, 134).

denoting baiting, trapping, catching and consuming. Phrases like 'drown kitlings', 'wolvish nature', 'flayed ape' and 'roasted bitch's marrow' create distasteful pictures. The sheer number suggests a clear imaginative purpose and many of the type of animals emphasizes the brutality of nature having seeped into human society. Most of the mammals, birds, reptiles or insects have negative connotations and many are related to the secondary imagery of devouring, swallowing and eating. This imagery relates not to hospitality, bonding, companionship, family and sharing, but expresses eating as a greedy act similar to the lust for riches, material gain and sensual pleasures. It is not an activity of civilized, cultured man, but the insatiable wolfing down of consumables displayed when scavengers fight over a carcase. Much of Volpone's world is expressed in terms of eating to metaphorically reflect the psychology of acquisition which is the monomania that drives Voltore, Corbaccio and Corvino. It is the addiction that drove Venice, the obsession that was turning London into the temple of money worship.

Lower still the plant world had only the ability to grow and reproduce. It too had a loose hierarchy. Trees were at the top with the oak as the prime form – useful, because of its hardness, for building ships and houses – associated with stability, rootedness, imperturbable fortitude, Englishness. A king was seen as a great oak, sheltering his people as the tree did birds and insects. Shrubs and bushes came next, along with flowers as symbols of the beauty of God's creation. The rose was thought to be the most beautiful, associated with love and with the Virgin Mary (the rose without a thorn). The lily signified purity, chastity and death. There was a wide range of floral/herbal significations – pansies for thought, rosemary for remembrance, rue for repentance, violets for faithfulness, daisies for unhappy love and so on. Next came the useful plants – corn crops and herbs with their medicinal and edible uses.

Ferns, weeds, moss and fungus were such basic forms they often furnish pejorative metaphors for useless, troublesome, threatening humans. Their tendency to spread and choke other vegetation expressed the fear that mob violence, vulgar attitudes threatened always to engulf virtue and cultured living. The rising middle class were sometimes described as 'so many early mushrooms, whose best growth sprang from a dunghill'.[42]

At the bottom of creation were rocks and minerals. Even they were ranked by their values as gemstones, precious metals or their usefulness for building or yielding minerals. Pearls were much prized in the Renaissance – by Queen Elizabeth particularly – and long associated with purity. Among the metals gold was king, succeeded by silver, iron (and steel), bronze, copper and lead. Gold had particular power over the Renaissance imagination. It was the regal

42 Flamineo in John Webster's *The White Devil* (1612), 3.3.49–50.

metal, used for crowns and sceptres, prized above silver and lowly lead, but also had its negative side as a symbol of man's greed. It is the means to suborn, seduce and corrupt. Its corrupting power is most forcibly, comically and sadly expressed in this classic play where, blasphemously, gold has become Volpone's god. (For more on gold, see chapter 14.)

Among rocks marble was most prized as a princely adornment for palaces, followed by granite, sandstone, limestone. Even lowly chalk and clay had their uses (for lime and bricks), though clay was connected metaphorically with man's mortality. Last of all are the particle forms – sand, gravel, soil, dust. Sand and gravel represented the precariousness of man's attempts to build a solid life as in the parable of the house built on sand. Earth, while the growth bed for all edible vegetation and fruits, was thought a dull, heavy element (the other main elements were fire, air and water), appropriately typifying man's last state: 'earth to earth, ashes to ashes, dust to dust'.[43]

2.11 Order

Not only were humans ranked in an order reflecting how they were valued but also the preservation of that order was seen as a guarantee of social harmony. Orderliness reflected, therefore affirmed, God's ordering of the universe. Hierarchy is not under great threat in *Volpone*, but it is distorted. Though the organizing dominance of Mosca appears to be a reversal of normality and the servant often appears to be the master, it is a subversive arrangement in which Volpone is complicit. In this, Volpone ('By blood, and rank a gentleman' 5.12.117) subverts his own rank. In his behaviour he transgresses even further. Order, however, is subverted by the conduct of the five central male characters. Each behaves contrary to the theoretical demands of their rank. Corvino subverts marriage, Voltore subverts the law, and Corbaccio subverts the father/son bond and the custom of inheritance by the son. To promote his standing with Volpone, he is ready to name the magnifico as his heir in the hope he will in turn be sole inheritor of Volpone's fortune. He claims disinheriting Bonario is only temporary and will make greater gains for he will have more to bequeath his son. As a result of Mosca's lies he is ready to disinherit Bonario for real. The would-be legatees not only display immense greed but also bad taste and bad manners in the way they talk of what they believe is a sick, deaf and nearly blind old man. The ruling elite's misconduct was regularly criticized. Both Elizabeth and James I themselves sometimes subverted hierarchy and decorum in their own personal conduct in public. Both exhibited character flaws in publicly humiliating servants, courtiers and

---

43 *Book of Common Prayer*, prayer 'For the Burial of the Dead'.

great men. That could be a process of just punishment, part of the role of a ruler, but it was often rather the reaction and retaliation of personal anger, spite, petty-mindedness and was therefore unacceptable behaviour.

The increasingly elaborate ritualization of all aspects of the monarch's life meant nobles and titled men doing menial tasks not in accord with their rank. Some enjoyed the honour, some found it degrading but necessary to maintain their influence. Sir Philip Gawdy describes the king's dinner served not by ordinary household servants but by titled courtiers:

> [The king] was serued wth great State. My Lo: of Southa [Southampton]: was caruer [carving the meat], my L. of Effingham Sewer, and my Lo: of Shrewsberry cup bearer, my poore selfe carried vp ij [2] dishes to his Maties [Majesty's] table.[44]

Courtiers struggled indecorously for these places, flattering, bribing and defaming rivals. Loss of favour unsettled the order of things by rearranging the tenancy of these posts. The tense uneasiness and jealous ever watchfulness of the court was something the audience well understood. A precarious world; power and place struggles were everyday happenings. Loss of post meant shame, dishonour, loss of influence with the monarch and loss of valuable patronage saleable to those wanting your help accessing the queen or king. It was a vicious world, a jungle, animal against animal. *Volpone* is no more than a mirror of the times.

In the latter part of her life Elizabeth was increasingly volatile and unreliable. Fears about the end of her long reign, uncertainty about who would succeed, created a general mood of uneasiness in a society believing the world in inevitable decline. This worsened as hysterical anxieties clustered round the approaching end of the century. The precariousness of the balances of power at the top, evident enough in the rise and fall of favourites, would soon be displayed more prominently when James I came to the throne. James I was worse in his erratic moods. New monarchs usually brought in favourites, but James I gave unprecedented power to men regarded as foreigners. This Scottish usurpation generated grievances to add to others accumulating around the wholesale Scots incursion into London and Whitehall. Giovanni Scaramelli, Venetian ambassador, recounted how English courtiers complained,

> no Englishman, whatever his rank, can enter the Presence Chamber without being summoned, whereas the Scottish Lords have free entrée of the Privy Chamber, and more especially at the toilette; at which

44 Gawdy, 132. A sewer seated you at table and might also serve you.

time they discuss proposals which, after dinner are submitted to the Council, in so high and mighty a fashion that no one has the courage to oppose them.[45]

James I's blatant favouritism had the effect of uniting rival English courtiers and politicians. Scaramelli observed, 'The English, who were at first divided amongst themselves, begin now to make common cause against the Scots'.[46] This weakness of the king worsened when favourites began to emerge; the Carr and Villiers factions gained huge influence and huge amounts of money. The same had been experienced during the 'reigns' of Elizabeth's many favourites – Leicester, Essex, Raleigh and others. She regularly dismissed councillors who gave advice she disliked. And this was the court of the so-called Gloriana. The audience for Jonson's play would not be shocked by the misconduct of his high status characters. They were already used to seeing it on the stage and hearing of it in real life.

Though Volpone's actions are those of an unconscionable criminal, he is punishing men who deserve to be humiliated. It is controlled and directed anger at their temerity in trying to dupe him, but they are being entrapped by him for his own gain, which is just as reprehensible. He seems unaware how far his own behaviour deviates from proper conduct, but this is a world without a moral compass. His barely suppressed anger stems from his greed, for underlying greed is an anger against the world that you do not have enough to satisfy your soul. Michel de Montaigne's comment 'No passion disturbs the soundness of our judgement as anger does' echoes a theme schoolboys knew from studying Seneca's essay *De Ira* ('On Anger').[47] James I was well established as an intemperate, irascible monarch liable to burst into incandescent anger if opposed. Hasty actions, un-thought-through, rash judgements are unwise. When the actor is a monarch the consequences are national. In his essay 'On Anger', Bacon quotes Seneca: 'Anger is like ruin, which breaks itself upon that it falls'.[48] Volpone's anger, combined with his belief that he will inevitably succeed and his blindness to wrong, will prove self-defeating. His fiery drive to gain, to acquire, to amass will break on him and break him. His and Mosca's hubris, offending morality, offending God, will spiral out of their control as the chief brute turns on his partner. All are sold and the perpetrators of it all

---

45 Quoted in Leanda De Lisle, *After Elizabeth*, 205. Scaramelli revealed to the Signory that English politicians, aristocrats and courtiers blamed the government for 'having sold England to the Scots'.

46 Quoted in De Lisle, 210, from *The Calendar of State Papers Relating to English Affairs, existing in the archives and collections of Venice* (London, 1900), vol. 10. 1603–7.

47 Michel Montaigne, 'On Anger', *The Complete Essays* (ed. M. A. Screech), 810.

48 'Of Anger', *The Essays*, 226. The translation is Bacon's.

will be sold too. Wrath is one of the Seven Deadly Sins and Ephesians 4:26 warns, 'Be angry, but sin not'. Luke 21:19 exhorts, 'In your patience possess ye your souls'. Greed too is a deadly sin and the Bible is full of exhortations against it. Jeremiah 6:13 has a warning that applies to the world Jonson has created: 'For from the least of them even unto to the greatest of them every one is given to covetousness; and from the prophet even unto the priest every one dealeth falsely'. St Luke 12:15 too has an apposite comment about identity not residing in material goods: 'And he said unto them, Take heed, and beware of covetousness; for a man's life consisteth not in the abundance of the things which he possessth'. I Corinthians 6:10 puts the matter in terms of the afterlife and its consequences: 'Nor thieves, nor covetous, nor drunkards, nor revilers, nor extortioners, shall inherit the kingdom of God'. From line 1 Volpone's state of soul is clear and from 1.1.75 we know he is not alone in his sinful greediness. Keeping order, preserving the distinctions of rank, was essential; they are eventually restored by the judgement of the human agents of the High Court of the *Scrutineo*.

Orderliness is given its most famous and detailed definition in Shakespeare's *Troilus and Cressida* (1602). Ulysses upbraids the bickering Greek leaders for neglecting 'The specialty of rule'. If the clarity of 'degree' is blurred the unworthy will appear no different from the meritorious. 'The specialty of rule' is founded on the traditional belief that some were born to rule, the rest to obey. Ulysses points out that the whole universe follows ordained rules:

> The heavens themselves, the planets, and this centre,
> Observe degree, priority, and place,
> Insisture, course, proportion, season, form,
> Office, and custom, in all line of order. (1.3.85–8)

If orderliness is disturbed,

> what plagues and what portents, what mutiny,
> What raging of the sea, shaking of the earth,
> Commotion in the winds. (1.3.96–8)

Disorder affects human society when rank is disrespected:

> O, when degree is shaked,
> Which is the ladder of all high designs,
> The enterprise is sick! How could communities,
> Degrees in schools, and brotherhoods in cities,
> Peaceful commerce from dividable shores,

> The primogenitive and due of birth,
> Prerogative of age, crowns, sceptres, laurels,
> But by degree, stand in authentic place? (1.3.101–8)

Order is the cement bonding human society and Ulysses warns of the consequences of disassembling order:

> Take but degree away, untune that string,
> And hark what discord follows! each thing meets
> In mere oppugnancy: the bounded waters
> Should lift their bosoms higher than the shores,
> And make a sop of all this solid globe;
> Strength should be lord of imbecility,
> And the rude son should strike the father dead. (1.3.109–15)

Shakespeare was always concerned with order – nationally, socially, personally and spiritually. Rebellion, usurpation and collapse are political themes found in all his history plays (including the Roman ones). They are found in Jonson too. *Sejanus, His Fall* (1603) and *Catiline, His Conspiracy* (1611) – two historical Roman tragedies – are concerned with the personal and political consequences of excess and the subversion of order. Disorder, excess and misrule figure too in his comedies. Loss of 'degree' means force would dominate society, justice would be lost, illegitimate power, will, appetite ('an universal wolf') would rule. In 1598, James I warned his son, 'beware yee wrest not the World to your owne appetite, as over many doe, making it like A Bell to sound as yee please to interpret'.[49] Restraint of appetite is not a personal quality Volpone possesses. Neither is it evident in those around him. Ulysses uses images of natural order reversed, unnatural human behaviour and the dominance of sin. The irony is that while theoretically God's Nature should be our model, history shows repeatedly that what is natural for man is that the strongest oppress the weak, the brutal take control and the ruthless rule. The need and desire to cooperate creates society and unites community, but such bonding is often weak when faced by strong men backed by pitiless, armed henchmen ready to shed blood to gain power or by clever criminals prepared to lie. History plays and tragedies show time after time how devious men gain power and how decency and virtue are slow to react. In the comedies, virtue, right thinking and right action win through and tragedy is averted, but there are always latent dangers in the plot situations that develop, dangers that could lead to misery if not death. In a

---

49 *Basilikon Doron*, 4. All quotes from EEBO Editions' reprint of the 1682 edition.

Christian context evil was thought ever present, the Devil constantly trying to tempt people into sin. Constant vigilance was crucial. The personalities in *Volpone* exhibit what happens when the old value of moderation gives way to the new impulse toward immoderate individual will, while immoderate greedy acquisitiveness and negative humours are allowed to dominate men's actions.

The sixteenth century was much concerned with political theory. Playwrights, especially Shakespeare, picked up on the interest in how society was best to be administered. Elyot's *The Boke Named the Governour* (1531) and the various editions of *A Mirrour for Magistrates* (between 1559 and 1603) were influential. Before becoming king of England, James I contributed two theoretical conduct books on kingship – *The True Law of Free Monarchies* (1598) and *Basilikon Doron* (1598). Sadly, there was a discrepancy between his ideas and his actions and both works exposed the shortcomings of Elizabeth too. The theory of order, the desire for peace and harmony were belied by the actualities of life. Order seemed continually under attack and the fear of disorder added to the growing Elizabethan end-of-era angst. The queen and the century were close to death. The end of a century always raised fears of disasters to come, especially in an age that believed the world was in decline and the end of the world imminent. Rising crime figures contributed to the general gloomy sense of decay. These factors feed into those dramas which reflected the feeling of increased dishonesty, licentiousness, greed and brutality. This is precisely the Venice of *Volpone*. Though he is not a political leader, the magnifico is yet another example of the top echelon of society behaving badly. The city comedies are peopled by petty criminals, shysters, cozeners, cony-catchers, usurers, legacy chasers, greedy merchants and braggart penniless heiress-hunting gentlemen and immoral noblemen. London emerges as the subject and often the setting of critical dramas in the 1590s. Though foreign cities (especially Italian) also figure, the virulent satire, the abuses and 'ragged follies' are transparently English and associated with London. Venice is London. The increase in the crowded metropolitan population (200,000 in 1600; 575,000 in 1700)[50] provided a huge variety of human types. Writers revelled in portraying the seedier characters, enjoying their vitality while deprecating their immorality and trickiness. Jonson's comedies are far more topically specific than *Measure for Measure* or *King Lear*, and in its overall mood *Volpone* reflects current neurotic fears of a society in free fall. It is a feature of comedy that the sins and transgressions that destroy peace, harmony and lives in other dramas are successfully neutralized. It has to be said, however, that the Elizabethan period, stable insofar as the

50 M. J. Daunton, *Progress and Poverty*, 137.

queen reigned for 45 years, was constantly afraid of destabilization by Spanish invasion, wholesale Catholic insurrection or individual Catholic attempts to assassinate of the queen. The year 1605 had seen the shocking exposure of the Gunpowder Plot. For the Jacobeans it was a very edgy time and such neurotic paranoia seeps into the atmosphere of many plays and is reflected in the frenetic action of comedies. In 1572, after the Massacre of St Bartholomew in Paris, when up to some six thousand Protestants were slaughtered, the queen's printer published a book of penitential prayers conveying something of the persistent anxiety of the Elizabethans:

> Oh Lord, the counsel of the wicked conspireth against us: and our enemies are daily in hand to swallow us up. They gape upon us with their mouths as it were ramping and roaring lions.[51]

Much of the fear was well founded and never quite went away, though the Tudor polity became more settled and secure as Elizabeth's reign went on. The Church of England became more solidly entrenched and recruited increasing numbers of the population, though it too faced constant attack from Catholics without and reformers within. The times were both settled and unsettled. Constant vigilance was needed. There was the constant fight with the Devil and the constant fear of Spain and the Catholics. James I had been king only just over two years when the Gunpowder Plot panicked him and unsettled politicians in general. The young Francis Walsingham, even before he became Elizabeth's spymaster with a network of agents all over Europe and England, summed up the situation: 'there is less danger in fearing too much than too little'.[52] Less danger perhaps, but it did nothing to calm the frightened psyche of the nation. The feeling of being at siege, the fear of being destabilized by the Antichrist in Rome, were there all the time. Any form of threat to hierarchy was very unsettling and in Jonson's play the top end of society seems rotten through and through.

The geographical arrangements of the nation reflected the authoritarian orderly social structure. Divided into a network of counties, each with a sheriff or lord lieutenant, hierarchy imposed order on what might otherwise be, and sometimes was, a restless population. Below the sheriff, a patchwork of estates owned by rich, titled, powerful men, imposed local authority. Estates varied in size, but within reach (sometimes within the actual perimeter) of even the smallest would be villages, parishes, individual dwellings rented by families dependent on the landowner's good will. Grandees often owned huge estates in different parts of the country, each providing income from rents and

---

51 The prayer combines elements of Psalm 22.
52 Quoted in Alford, 54.

farm produce. The local 'great house' was an ever-present, looming influence on localities, a brooding presence that reminded the commoners who had the power. Increasingly, though land gave status its value was diminishing. Landowners were becoming entrepreneur-employers exploiting mineral deposits on their domains and other natural advantages like water, timber, rush for thatching, clay for bricks. Men of lesser title and less money, with smaller estates, still had dependent tenants and a home farm to provision the family. The gentry might only own one house, maybe a fortified manor, and land no more than a small acreage surrounding it, but as part of the ruling class – magistrates and Justices of the Peace – they further imposed the values of their privileged elite. Hierarchy penetrated parish churches where the better sort might have boxed-in family pews near the pulpit, the middling sort might sit on benches and the poor might stand at the back. The gentry monopolized parish councils through the so-called 'select vestry' that barred lower ranks from attending. Local politics was controlled by landed families and Parliament was 88 per cent upper orders and 12 per cent merchants and civic authorities. The top 5 per cent had the whole country under their nominal control. The few large cities – London, Bristol, Norwich, York – also had their networks of power, with aldermen, beadles, mayors and wealthy liveried companies. Richard Stock's 1603 Lent sermon in St Paul's churchyard, directly addressed the mayor of London, the aldermen, nobility and privy councillors:

> You are magistrates for the good of them that are under you, not to oppress them for your own ease. I would speak to him who is chief of the city for this year. What is past cannot be remedied, but for the future, as far as lies in your power, prevent these things.[53]

'The wealthier sort feared sudden uproars and tumults, and the needy and loose persons desired them'.[54] The gentry largely resided in the country while titled men spent much of their time at court and Parliament, but the gentry too was beginning to be drawn to the capital. In a period of high produce prices and little profit to be made from agriculture by any except the great farmers, landowners raised rents, reducing the profit margins of husbandmen holding leases from them and forcing many labourers into homeless unemployment. Increasingly gentry heirs and younger sons, drifted to the capital, forming a large, shifting population of troublesome young men, some hanging about the court seeking posts or heiresses. They saw London as a pleasure ground,

53 Historical Manuscripts Commission, *Calendar of the Manuscripts of … the Marquess of Salisbury*, vols. 12, 14, 15.
54 Clapham, *Elizabeth of England*, 98.

removed from immediate parental disapproval. Drinking, whoring, gambling, fighting, theatre-going and chasing rich merchants' daughters, they were generally a nuisance.

Many titled families were founded by men who, coming to power under Henry VIII, bought, or were given by the king, church lands that came onto the market at the Reformation. These once new families were now the old upper-rank families. A few titled dynasties could trace their ancestry to the Conquest. Most were of relatively recent authority, some paying the College of Heralds to manufacture fake genealogies that gave them more respectable and ancient descent. This network of power and privilege was intended to keep the king's peace. It largely did so, despite outbursts of local unrest, but at the expense of the physical and political repression of the 'baser sort'. Generations of psychological pressure established a fear of the upper ranks, a belief that, like the king, they were part of God's order and that opposing them was a grave blasphemy, pitting your puny, sinful self against the divinely ordained state of creation.

The civil power was not the only repressive network controlling England. Hand in hand with government, often synonymous with it, the church attempted to guide conformity and forcibly dissuade dissent. In 1549 Thomas Cranmer, Archbishop of Canterbury, had reinforced this in upbraiding rebels: 'Though the magistrates be evil and very tyrants against the commonwealth and enemies to Christ's religion, yet the subjects must obey in all worldly things'.[55] This encouragement to submit even to injustice was repeated in the 1571 *Book of Homilies* in the sermon 'against disobedience and wilful rebellion'. The tyranny of a monarch was a divine punishment against a sinful people who should not 'shake off that curse at their owne hand'.[56] The attempt to identify hierarchical deference with submission to God is part of seeing the social order as God ordained. By making it an aspect of church doctrine the Anglican hierarchy aimed to curb rebellion, maintain power and enforce doctrinal uniformity. Social and religious submission to the established power structure, however unjust its actions, would work for the mass of fearful superstitious people. But opposition was slowly rising.

Each English diocese had a bishop responsible for ensuring priests and congregations followed the Anglican form of worship. These dioceses comprised in total some nine and half to ten thousand parishes each (theoretically) with a priest. The average number of souls in country parishes was 300. In the less controllable, expanding cities it was 450. Pluralism (holding more than one

---

55 Strype, *Memorials of Thomas Cranmer* (1690), rec. 114.
56 *Homily against Disobedience*, from Wootten, *Divine Right and Democracy: An Anthology of Political Writings in Stuart England*, 94–98

living) was a growing practice whereby a poorly paid vicar could augment his stipend and an already rich one could add to his fortune.[57] Nonresident priests employed curate substitutes so there was religious presence to oversee the social and spiritual state of the congregants. The priest, representing the church's might, was a figure to be respected, part of the ruling Establishment, part of the control troika of magistrate, lord of the manor, priest. Often the lord of the manor was also a magistrate, thus narrowing the power base to two. Part of the priestly power aura was education. The ability to read and write (though not all priests were highly literate) gave special, magical status. As mediator between this world and the next, he had immense psychological influence. Education made him able to advise about moral and practical matters, and his spiritual role made him a privileged mentor in matters related to living the virtuous life. Not everyone in a village would necessarily defer to the priest. Some vicars were ineffective – drunks, ignorant, more interested in hunting. Closet Catholics and Dissenters would only pay lip service. Puritan dissidents were slowly increasing in number and were increasingly vocally critical of the church. More worrying for the episcopal elite was the spread of vicars of Puritan sympathy. In the 1590s large numbers of progressive, radical-thinking young ordinands graduated from Cambridge University, adding yet another destabilizing factor to an age already undergoing disturbing changes. Principles absorbed from the lectures and writings of Cambridge don William Perkins inclined them to be less obsequious to their gentry parishioners and more mindful of the hardships of the poor, though some gentry families, sympathetic to reform, protected Puritan-minded vicars from church persecution.

Another source of anti-Establishment attacks was playwrights coming from the universities where they had contact with radical views. Vitriolic in criticizing purse-proud citizens, their ostentatious wives, the explosion of greed, the obsession with luxury, vanity, lust, the idle and incompetent aristocracy and particularly those many ungentlemanly gentlemen buzzing like flies round the court, they also deplored the state of the lower orders. City comedies, set in the contemporary city, were essentially morality based, harking back to medieval values. Shakespeare tended to skirt round overt attacks on his own times by setting his plays in other countries or in other periods. *Volpone's* Italian setting should not fool us into thinking the play is not about current issues or situated within contemporary values. The original

---

57 Entering the priesthood was a common career path for younger sons of gentry families. Faith and devotion were not always their chief motives. Barred from inheriting by the custom of primogeniture, such men could access wealth and power by carefully targeted promotions within the ecclesiastical hierarchy.

audience would not be gulled either and the conduct of the characters would be judged by the religious and humanist ethics of the time.

James I expressed the principle that concern for 'the well-fare and peace of his people' identifies a king 'as their naturall father and kindly maister'. In 'subjecting his owne private affections and appetites to the weale and standing of his subjects' he shows himself better than the tyrannical king who 'thinketh his people ordained for him, a pray to his passions and inordinate appetites'.[58] Volpone shows none of this paternalistic concern for the Venetian citizenry. He only minimally interacts with his substitute 'family' of Androgyno, Castrone and Nano and then only to command they entertain him or accompany him in his charade as Scoto of Mantua. His isolation from normative social and personal relationships parallels his abnormal status. His only active bond, with Mosca, is antisocial and criminal and is another of the many illusions the play represents – for it is not a true bond. Other fundamental bonds – marriage and the father-son relationship – are similarly shown to be faulty.

Detachment from people encourages desensitization which leads to brutal attitudes to them. Rank divisions were becoming a growing tension in English society. They would worsen under James I and then worsen still more under his son Charles I. Living just for his own pleasures and ends Volpone represents the idle and privileged who neglect their duty to help the poor and neglect showing God gratitude for being wealthy by not wasting their excess fortune on pointless extravagances but put it to the good of the whole polity. The Bible authorized this: 'For unto whomsoever much is given, of him shall be much required' (Luke 12:48). The middling and lower orders had obvious work to do to live, while those with wealth and rank did not need to work. However, the standard view was that 'None are less exempted from a calling than great men'.[59] The bible story of Dives and Lazarus (Luke 16:19), a popular text for sermons, told how the rich Dives refused to pass the crumbs off his table to the poor Lazarus. When Dives dies, he goes to hell and in his sufferings sees Lazarus among the elect in Heaven. The rich and powerful had a duty to be fathers to their neighbours, shepherds to the flock around them. Jonson declared 'a prince is the pastor of the people. He ought to shear, not to flay his sheep'.[60] He worked for a king that made 'his exchequer a receipt for the spoils of those he governs', and mixed with a nobility that saw the people as a purse which they were entitled to empty. Brathwait put it starkly: 'The higher place the heavier the charge'.[61] Many privileged lords and ladies sent unwanted food

58 *Basilikon Doron*, 18, 19.
59 Brathwait, *The English Gentleman* (1631), 115.
60 *Timber*, 41.
61 Brathwait, 115.

to the poor, endowed almshouses and schools and did other acts of charity. Many did not. Each new generation inheriting wealth needed reminding that

> charity [...] should flow
> From every generous and noble spirit,
> To orphans and to widows.[62]

It is ironically just that Volpone's fortune will, as part of his punishment, be put to the good he never bothered to do and donated to the hospital of the *Incurabili*. The concept of *caritas* (love expressed through charitable acts), integral to medieval church teaching, derived from canon law's delineation of the basic duty of the rich to assist the needy.[63] It was taken up in Protestant thinking too. Compassion, a necessary virtue in a Christian, was essential in those who had never experienced adversity or affliction. The governing classes had detached themselves from the rest of society, living their own self-interested, selfish, narcissistic lives at court or isolated in their mansions on their estates. The self-indulgent, libertine life of Volpone should be a prick to the consciences of the pampered, self-obsessed courtiers in the audience. Probably some of them would endorse his behaviour. Mankind never readily acknowledges its failings when displayed. Corrupt, ineffective and arrogant kingship was another feature of the time and the period is full of admonitions to prince figures and nobility.[64] In 1609 the Earl of Northumberland wrote,

> There are certain works fit for every vocation; some for kings; some for noblemen; some for gentlemen; some for artificers; some for clowns [country people]; and some for beggars; [...] If everyone play his part well, that is allotted him, the commonwealth will be happy; if not then it will be deformed.[65]

God's judgement against Adam and Eve at the Fall condemned men to live by the sweat of their brow. Adam had a second chance. Saved from destruction by the mercy of God, he left Eden and sought salvation elsewhere. Volpone and Mosca are given another chance when they are exonerated after the first court appearance and Celia and Bonario are sentenced thanks to the specious

---

62 John Webster, *The White Devil*, 3.2.64–6.
63 The ancient and medieval world conceived of three types of love: *eros* (erotic love), *agape* (non-sexual love) and *caritas* (social, charitable love).
64 At the time the word 'prince' was generically applied to anyone who ruled of a state, be that person count, duke, governor, prince, king or queen.
65 Percy, *Advice to His Son*, 119.

pleading of Voltore and the witness statements made by Corvino and Lady Would-be. Though aware they have had a lucky escape, they cannot resist further deceptions. Addicted to gain, addicted to the game of imposture, they do not take the opportunity to repent and reform. They are like 'the thief that had a longing at the gallows to commit one robbery more before he was hanged'.[66] Some people are incorrigible. The Bible is full of figures given a second chance and Ezekiel, Proverbs, Ecclesiastes, the Epistles to the Thessalonians and Timothy all strongly criticize idleness and recommend employment. That included kings, courtiers … and magnificos.

66 Jonson, *Timber*, 9.

Chapter 3

SIN, DEATH AND THE PRINCE OF DARKNESS

People's sinfulness was the greatest threat to order. The Jacobeans were neurotically alert to the temptations surrounding life. Conflicting Christian sects shared basic beliefs when it came to right and wrong. Man was perpetually open to sin, temptation was all around him and evil existed. The Devil was to be defied, and Christ was man's redeemer and the way to salvation. The moral bases of life were agreed.

The Ten Commandments (abridged from Exodus 20:19)

1. Thou shalt have no other gods before me.
2. Thou shalt not make unto thee any graven image.
3. Thou shalt not take the name of the Lord thy God in vain.
4. Remember the Sabbath day, to keep it holy.
5. Honour thy father and thy mother.
6. Thou shalt not kill.
7. Thou shalt not commit adultery.
8. Thou shalt not steal.
9. Thou shalt not bear false witness.
10. Thou shalt not covet […] any thing that is thy neighbour's.

It is this last Commandment that is the key failing exposed in *Volpone*.

The Seven Deadly Sins

1. **Pride** (arrogance, vanity, vainglory, hubris)
2. **Wrath** (anger, violence)
3. **Lust** (lechery, wantonness, lasciviousness)
4. **Envy** (covetousness)

5. **Greed** (avarice)
6. **Gluttony** (including drunkenness)
7. **Sloth** (laziness, despair)

Commandments 1, 6, 7, 8, 9 and 10 are transgressed or contemplated throughout the play and all the sins too are present, even Sloth (in Volpone's idle dereliction of his duties).

Sin and Satan were as much a part of religious consciousness as the desire to emulate Jesus and live virtuously. The church's cultural monopoly meant even those indifferent to religion would acknowledge that faith was the common, underlying feature of life at all levels. The passing year was marked by religious events, each day was punctuated by aspects of faith, the parish church bell indicated the times of services, pious families gathered for morning and evening prayers and individuals might visit the church during the day. Schoolboys had communal classroom prayers with their teacher. A master craftsman, his journeymen and apprentices might start the working day with prayers. The formal ceremonies of their guild involved prayers, readings and sermon-like addresses. Children were taught the Bible, learned texts, creeds, catechisms and prayers and would kneel by their bedside to ask for protection during the dangerous hours of darkness. Those of weak faith attended Sunday service rather than be fined in a church court. Those not particularly pious in their everyday life had scriptural grounding as children and like everyone else would know how they were expected to behave as Christians and would be aware of biblical allusions, echoes and ethics in what their neighbours said and did. They would observe too how plays displayed, reinforced and debated the basic Christian values of society. The church was omnipresent. When you were born, married, committed adultery, defamed a neighbour, were rowdy, sharp-tongued and shrewish, or opened your shop on Sunday, the church was there approving or wagging its finger. You lived in public, your discovered sins were made public and your punishment was public.

Mosca and Corvino are both sentenced to public punishment. Your misdemeanours were spied out by constables, beadles, the watch, servants and neighbours and dealt with in the local church court. These wrongdoings dealt not just with religious matters like blasphemy, heresy, contempt for the vicar's authority, or absence from service. Secular misdemeanours too came within within the jurisdiction of the church courts: perjury, slander, incontinence (excessive sexuality, excessive gluttony, excessive anything), sorcery, adultery, domestic disputes, marital quarrels, probate of wills. Anglicans were rarely left to solve a problem alone. Individual conscience was too weak to deal with matters of sin and morality without help. In times of national or personal stress many people turned to the consolations offered by being part of communally held belief. When you were afraid of imminent disaster, the support of others was a coping mechanism; the church was a mental, spiritual and physical refuge.

All Jacobean plays either verbally echo or allude to well-known biblical texts and are situated explicitly or implicitly within a value matrix of sins and virtues. Unspoken, indirect, implicit biblical contexts evoking Christian values, reactions and assessments are inescapable in the literature of the time. Every action in *Volpone* is starkly silhouetted against a backdrop of Christian ethics. The second agent in mediating a text – the responder (reader or viewer) – provided a religious assessment. The text may lack a direct allusion to Christian dogma, but Ben Jonson, like William Shakespeare, knew his audience would make the connections. The play is nominally set in Venice, but this is a shallow fiction that provides the opportunity to give his characters the exotic effect of Italian names. This would appeal to a cultivated audience and lend an air of authority and courtliness. It was an established feature of comedies that the upper-rank characters bore Italianate or classical names. There are the usual references to classical deities and figures from myth (Jove, Mars, Venus, Europa, Cupid and so forth). The setting and names are merely a blind. The literature, philosophy, history and mythology of the classical world was the lingua franca of learned discussion. It was the common depository for allusion as a result of the education of most of the male and some of the female audience. Increasingly too, writers and works from Renaissance Italy were introduced to lend an air of modish elegance. But that did not preclude that other parallel moral system – the Bible. In discussing the early humanist reformers of the 1520s, A. G. Dickens put it thus,

> It became a natural tendency in a classically-educated age to co-ordinate the teaching of the great pagan moralists with that of the New Testament, to see in Christianity a mode of this life rather than a way of salvation for the next, even to envisage a cool, reasonable religion, a Christianity without tears.[1]

The two systems overlapped considerably, but the value system by which the audience would be expected to judge actions, attitudes and outcomes was almost entirely Christian – and Protestant. Every scene provokes a Christianity-focused judgement of what is said and done. Whatever the level of engagement with faith, Christian upbringing triggered a vigorous conscious or subconscious religious reaction to everything seen. Debauched libertines or audience members who had lost their religion still had vestigial

---

1 A. G. Dickens, *The English Reformation*, 101.

memories of the values they had learned as children. The Bible was the standard of all conduct. To Protestants canon law and episcopal rules and regulations meant little: 'Christian doctrine and conduct have only one sure basis – the New Testament'.[2] Responses might vary according to education, upbringing, class, political and/or religious allegiance, and experience of and attitude to the world, but there would be broad agreement, since all the viewers – from the pit to the top gallery – shared this common Bible-based background. The ways in which time after time the characters offend the commandments or commit sins would be glaringly obvious to the audience. It is an absolutely fundamental aspect of the play, informing every motif in it.

Life was a journey, a pilgrim's progress toward holiness and union with God.[3] Volpone has several moments of confrontation with self, with loss of self, with temptation, a coming face-to-face with fear, frenzy and disorientation. He has chances to reassess his behaviour and re-establish orthodox values, but he is too in love with his sin, enjoys deception too much and is too addicted to the games he plays. Surviving the first court appearance should lead to a new vision of the world, a new understanding of self and others, and a sense of gratitude for a second chance to reform. It should be the beginning of a healing process that would regenerate him morally and re-establish more firmly the basis of his life and his relationship with Mosca. It is an opportunity not missed but purposely ignored.

From birth people were to pursue virtue, shun sin, imitate Christ, keep the soul pure and progress toward death, ready to pass through to the life everlasting. Earthly life was a transient state preparatory to the afterlife. In John Ford's late revenge tragedy *'Tis Pity She's a Whore* (c. 1629–31; hereafter *'Tis Pity*), when sexual sins and violent plots begin to gather and drive the drama, the character Richardetto states the basic situation of Christian existence: 'No life is blessèd but the way to heaven' (4.2.21) and encourages his niece to flee a vile world by entering a convent: 'Who dies a virgin lives a saint on earth' (4.2.28). The virtuous life gained Christ's favour and a state of grace. No advantage in the fleshly world was of any value if you lacked grace. Ford presents even the standard view of good looks in a religious context:

> Beauty that clothes the outside of the face
> Is cursèd if it be not clothed with grace. (5.1.12–13)

2 Dickens, 124.
3 Volpone, as Scoto, mentions 'so short is this pilgrimage of man (which some call life)' (2.3.231–2).

Volpone and Mosca represent those people who are unregenerate, unrepentant, who refuse to atone. They reject grace; they are irredeemable. Back home after the court ordeal, Volpone expresses a sense of lucky escape:

Well, I am here; and all this brunt is past:
I ne'er was in dislike with my disguise,
Till this fled moment. (5.1.1–3)

The hustle was fine whilst it was kept within the private sphere, but the danger of public exposure has given him some symptoms of a panic attack. His left leg began cramping and he felt a paralysis come on him. But a couple of hearty swigs of 'lusty wine' set him up and made him ready for 'any device [...] of rare, ingenious knavery'. He calls Mosca, who asks if 'the day look clear again?' and 'Is our trade free, once more?' In calling his servant Volpone has summoned the Devil who leads him into temptation again. Volpone is as morally blind as the men he dupes. When Mosca starts planning how his master can seduce Celia, Volpone calls him 'my better Angel' (2.4.21). He makes the basic mistake of thinking that his servant, though he lies to everyone else with his 'quick fiction', will act honestly with him. With no moral compass, he trusts an accomplished liar to direct him and encourage what he knows are the sins of adultery, fornication and lust.

Uncontrolled appetite (a spiritual or physical imbalance) was something the church feared and punished. Lust was the most common sin, but any of the Seven Deadly (or Mortal) Sins could damn you eternally if unrepented.[4] Dramatists relied on their audience seeing the danger of unfettered sexuality and the guiding restraint Christian morality offered. They relied too on their seeing how the court did not fit the moral framework of the time. The characters in *Volpone* are from the upper two ranks. The servants and the crowd gathered to watch Scoto are a passive presence. The social mix at the public theatre would comprise many of the common sort and the other ranks as well. They might have been more mockingly vocal about the mountebank's miraculous claims than the Venetian mob, but would all have had enough biblical knowledge (even if their faith was weak) to put the actions and words before them into a moral context that reflected poorly on their own attitudes to money, love, marriage, greed and honesty. They might have been less vocal about that.

The permeating religious atmosphere made identifying sin instinctive. Sin was the Devil's portal, giving access to your soul to damn you. The Devil was

4 For the growing prosecution of prenuptial sex, adultery and bastard birth, see Faramerz Dabhoiwala, *The Origins of Sex: A History of the First Sexual Revolution*, 41.

a very real entity to people, not a metaphor of evil, but a very real, horned, hoofed, forked tail and whiff of burning sulphur presence. Progressive thinkers tried to internalize the Devil as the evil in man, but most people believed he was a real creature. His earthly work, assisted by legions of demons, imps, goblins, incubi and succubi, was devoted to corrupting man and thwarting God's will. The Book of Revelation describes 'the great dragon' who 'was cast out, that old serpent, called the Devil and Satan, which deceiveth the whole world' (22:9). In John's Gospel he is called 'the prince of this world' (22:31) and in II Corinthians 'god of this world' (4:4), suggesting that the fleshly world of greed, brutality, cheating and lust (ever present in the plays of the 1590s and 1600s) is the Devil's domain. Paul's Epistle to the Ephesians (2:2–3) goes further, placing the Devil firmly in this world, embodied in the waywardness and violence of men. Volpone's world is one where evil has been released – by transgressing decorous conduct and by rampant greed, lust, immodesty, disobedience, betrayal and recklessness.

Good resides in Celia and Bonario and in a tainted form in the judges at the *Scrutineo*, but how weakly it speaks. The Devil is loosed when Christian values and cultivated, civilized, sensitive and sympathetic behaviours are ignored. Volpone is no ordinary miser and no ordinary voluptuary. Addicted to his greed and to the thrill of cheating people, he cannot, even after the danger of being nearly exposed in court, leave it alone. He courts danger, enjoys the challenge. He is aware of this, asserting, 'What a rare punishment/ Is avarice, to itself!' (1.4.142–3). Knowing this he persists in his sin. It is hubris inviting retribution. After he leaves the first court hearing he voices a similar sense of how close he had been to being caught:

> To make a snare, for mine own neck! and run
> My head into it, wilfully! With laughter!
>
> When I had newly scaped, was free, and clear!
> Out of mere wantonness! (5.11.1–4)

Ultimately he makes a greater fool of himself than he makes of any of his dupes and does so by overmuch greediness (in going into a more public arena in seeking Celia to satisfy his lust). It is lust that lures him, not love. It is a lust not just for her body but also a lust to possess her as if she were an object, like the many other objects he has been given by the legacy hunters. A similar warning is delivered by the deceiver Follywit in Thomas Middleton's *A Mad World My Masters*:

> Let the usurer look for't; for craft recoils in the end like an over-
> charged musket and maims the very hand that puts fire to't. There

needs no more but a usurer's own blow to strike him from hence to
hell. (3.3.9–12)

The view of orthodox morality is left to the chief judge in the closing lines:

Mischiefs feed
Like beasts, till they be fat, and then they bleed. (5.12.150–1)

Volpone's mischiefs certainly thrived and his hoard grew, until his lust led
him to overreach and he fell due to a combination of the hand of his own
parasite feeder (how foolish to trust a deceiver), the charge of attempted rape
and overconfidence in his own ability to read and control circumstances. The
feeding image works in a double sense and is associated with the prevalent
animal imagery. The greed of beasts merely fattens them for the abattoir, the
butcher's stall and the table. Literally, feeding is a life-maintaining activity (if
moderate) and a life-enhancing one when shared amicably between men, but
when avarice has taken hold on the psyche it becomes an insatiable need.
Greed for wealth is a psychological gluttony, blurring the moral vision of
even the cleverest. A similar conclusion closes Thomas Middleton's play *A
Trick to Catch the Old One* (1605): 'Who seem most crafty prove oft times
most fools'. Dante defined nobility in terms of virtuous conduct not rank or
title.[5] Baldassare Castiglione highlights this too when, during a discussion on
what makes the best sort of courtier, he has Pallavicino remark that while
some 'of the most noble blood, have been wicked in the extreme' there were
'many of humble birth, who, through their virtues, have won glory for their
descendants'.[6] Conduct is the determinant of true nobility. Nobility of spirit,
expressed in courteous, gentlemanly, noble behaviour, counts for more than
all the titles, estates and cultured accomplishments a lady or gentleman
may have. Daily experience showed how badly young men of noble blood
could behave. There was ample proof too showing that older men of rank
could demonstrate how eternal and universal were the violence, greed and
corruption of man. Volpone and his three victims are examples of that.

Educated viewers would see the piece not simply as a traditional Roman
comedy tale of miserly greed and legacy-hunting predators. It is permeated
by sin and is at the same time a morality play for the times, displaying sin
punished and Venice redeemed. Though not written in the style of the earlier
morality plays, the subject and ethics have similarities.

---

5 See Chaucer, *The Wife of Bath's Tale*, 1109–30.
6 Castiglione, *The Book of the Courtier*, 55.

Vicars loved loosing their imaginations in sermons describing the workings of the Evil One and the torments of Hell awaiting unrepentant sinners. Creative writers too enjoyed the opportunities for fantasy descriptions offered by ideas of Hell, sin, death and the Devil. The awareness that sin is ever present, that life is a persistent battle between good and evil and that the lure of vice has to be constantly rejected, was reinforced by witch trials. Witchcraft was another subject on which King James I delivered his opinions. His *Demonologie* (1597) captures the contemporary mood of fear and suspicion. Many artists painted representations of demons, and the Devil gave visual concreteness to the fears haunting people. Hell and the sufferings of the damned were popular subjects. Hieronymous Bosch (1450–1516) graphically depicts the horrors of perdition in *The Last Judgement*. Many medieval churches had depictions of 'Christ in Majesty', but in the late medieval period (in response perhaps to the holocaust of the Black Death) artists took to painting scenes of 'The Last Judgement'. Many (but not all) were scratched out or whitewashed over during the Reformation, but there were other means by which the idea of suffering was established in the minds of people. It was an age when hanged bodies were routinely displayed strung up in chains, 'heretics' were burnt at the stake and traitors had their entrails cut out and burned in front of them. The rack, thumbscrew and strappado were regularly used to extract information.

Noses slit and ears cropped for criticizing royalty or the church, thieves branded and blasphemers having their tongue pulled out or a hole bored through it, and birching, blinding and being broken on the wheel were all part of institutionalized cruelty. The gruesome acts portrayed in plays reflect a violent culture. Sin against the state or sin against God, and you could suffer similar pain. These brutal punishments reflect the age and how people imagined the damned were tortured in Hell.

The threat of damnation and eternal torture for extreme sinners was a useful moral control device to frighten naughty children and was a moral corrective for adults, but there were those who did not care about hellfire and damnation, and those who did not believe in Hell.

Christopher Marlowe's Faustus declares 'hell's a fable' (scene 5, line 128). Despite Mephistopheles asserting, 'this is hell, nor am I out of it' and 'where we are is hell', Faustus arrogantly laughs off the possibility:

Faustus: Think'st thou that Faustus is so fond to imagine
That, after this life, there is any pain?
Tush, these are trifles and mere old wives' tales.

Mephistophelis: But, Faustus, I am an instance to prove the contrary,
For I am damn'd, and am now in hell.
[…]

Faustus: How! now in hell!
Nay, an this be hell, I'll willingly be damn'd here. (scene 5, lines
134–44)

People were beginning to question Hell's existence, claiming this life was
our Hell. In *'Tis Pity*, the reckless Giovanni, a scholar like Faustus, thinks
reasoned argument can demolish the idea of Hell, and confidently announces
to his confessor,

The hell you oft have prompted is nought else
But slavish and fond superstitious fear,
And I could prove it too. (5.3.19–21)

The friar replies, 'Thy blindness slays thee'. Giovanni's trust in rational
arguments led him to believe sex with his sister was permissible. This is a
moral blindness. His actions result in spiritual death and physical slaughter.
Most of the audience, if they thought about it, probably believed in both
Heaven and Hell as real places of reward and punishment in the afterlife.

Most, except extreme libertines, believed sin was everywhere and virtue
needed to be cultivated. This would not have prevented most people from
committing sins or encouraged living a particularly good life. Like most people
they would probably experience guilt and fear, resolve to improve, then lapse
into the normal not-very-bad-but-not-very-good everyday life. An affecting
play might well prick their consciences – temporarily at least.

In *King Lear* the mad king makes a brief mention of Hell in a comment
on female lust that shifts from describing how from the waist down 'is all
the fiend's' domain to a recognizable description of the Christian idea of the
Devil's kingdom:

There's hell, there's darkness,
There is the sulphurous pit – burning, scalding,
Stench, consumption. (4.6.)

In *'Tis Pity* the friar, trying to frighten Annabella into repentance for
fornication and incest, describes hell:

There is a place [...] in a black and hollow vault,
Where day is never seen. There shines no sun,
But flaming horror of consuming fires,

A lightless sulphur, choked with smoky fogs
Of an infected darkness. In this place

Dwell many thousand thousand sundry sorts
Of never-dying deaths: there damned souls
Roar without pity. (3.6.8–16)

He continues with specific punishments meted out for specific sins:

There are gluttons fed
With toads and adders; there is burning oil
Poured down the drunkard's throat, the usurer

Is forced to sup whole draughts of molten gold;
There is the murderer forever stabbed,

Yet can he never die; there lies the wanton
On racks of burning steel, whiles in his soul
He feels the torment of his raging lust. (3.6.16–23)

Neither Volpone nor Mosca voice any fear of Hell. They seem to operate in a moral and religious vacuum.

3.1 Sin and Death

The Prince of Darkness was inexorably linked with temptation, reminders of what awaited after death and the very fact of death itself.[7] In medieval and Renaissance art reminders of death are ubiquitous. Skulls, skeletons and the Grim Reaper appear regularly in paintings in churches and in the funerary furniture surrounding the congregation. Sin and death are linked as a hellish duo in opposition to Christ and the Holy Spirit. The everyday world was a minefield for the morally unwary, full of devils waiting for any hint of ungodly, impure thought. Momentary lapses – a nasty comment, bitchy gossip, a bad-tempered snappish reply, blasphemous expletives, temptations to gluttony, theft, the prickings of lust – were opportunities for 'the Enemy of Mankind'. Wary Christians prayed regularly for protection. Prayers at bedtime were especially important, calling guardian angels as night security. A habit grew of eventide self-examination of your day, casting up your account of good and bad acts, making resolutions to improve, repenting and praying for salvation.

---

7 Lucifer was a prince of light before he fell. The Testaments call the Devil a prince and as darkness denotes sin joining the two terms is natural. Edgar's phrase 'The Prince of Darkness is a gentleman; Modo he's called, and Mahu' (*King Lear*, 3.4.) takes names from Samuel Harsnett's anti-Catholic pamphlet, *A Declaration of egregious popish impostures* (1603), and links evil with the sham politeness of gentlemen that masks devious intent.

It was end-of-the-day quiet time for assessing how well you had passed the day and resolving to be better if need be. James I recommended,

> remember ever once in the foure and twentie houres, either in the night, or when yee are at greatest quiet, to call yourself to account of all your last dayes actions, either wherein yee have committed things ye should not, or omitted the things yee should doe, either in your Christian or Kingly duty.[8]

He adds a marginal note referencing I Corinthians 11:31: 'For if ye judge your selfe, ye shall not be judged'. Temptation was everywhere and everyone knew 'the wages of sin is death' (Romans 6:23). You had to fight constantly to win the gift of eternal life through Jesus Christ. What made it more difficult was that you were born a sinner with the susceptibility to sin already in you. This original sin was the curse Adam and Eve's Fall brought to mankind. Their disobedience meant all successive generations were weakened by being open to temptation – a weakness played on by omnipresent devils. This idea provoked a rich language of condemnation among moralists – pamphleteers or preachers – and a delight in describing the pains of Hell.

In the turbulent times when *Volpone* was written there was no shortage of targets named as the source of sin. Sin bred like disease (medical and spiritual) in the growing capital. Disease itself was God's punishment for sin – not just the usual bodily sins of lust, gluttony and sloth but also pride in rank, the vanity of fashion, the greed of moneymaking, the abuse of power. Society seemed to be falling apart. Crime was rising and sexual debauchery and alcoholism too. Heresy and religious dissent were rife. Anglicans blamed Puritans, Puritans blamed Anglicans and everyone blamed the Catholics, the Pope (the Antichrist), the French, the Spanish, the court and increasingly the king.

Life was a battle to preserve your virtue and live like Christ, cleansing sin by prayer. Prayer would involve repentance and begging forgiveness ('Forgive us this day our daily trespasses'.). Accumulated, unrepented sins, particularly grave ones, could damn you when you died, though repentance (even at the last minute) could save you. The terrified Faustus, about to be dragged down to Hell as payment of his side of the bargain with Satan, cries out,

> See, see where Christ's blood streams in the firmament!
> One drop would save my soul, half a drop. Ah, my Christ!
> Ah, rend not my heart for naming of my Christ!
> Yet will I call on him. (scene 19, lines 146–9)

8 *Basilikon Doron*, 12–13.

Death was never far away in those days of plague and illnesses easily brought on by poor diet, unhealthy living conditions and ignorance of basic hygiene. Infections were a leveller making no distinction between rich or poor, though the better off might be better protected by superior food. The world was an insecure place, made more uncertain by persistent Puritan claims that epidemic diseases were punishment for tolerating Catholicism or changes to church ritual, the performance of plays, not keeping the Sabbath holy, the sinfulness of the court and the sinfulness of everyone in general.[9] There was no escape. Poverty, illness and sudden disaster were constant anxieties people lived with. As Michel de Montaigne put it, 'We do not know where death awaits us: so let us wait for it everywhere'.[10] Starting and ending the day with family prayers was part of that protection/salvation process and behaving piously during the day was another. James I advised his son, 'Pray [...] God would give you grace so to live, as yee may everie houre of your life be readie for death'.[11] This life, though the gift of a bountiful God, was short, miserable and merely preparatory to the life eternal, spent in the torments of Hell or among the blessings of Heaven.

Increasingly in the seventeenth century small coteries of scientists and intellectuals questioned the authority and authenticity of the concepts of sin, damnation and salvation. Part of a growing rationalist movement, they encouraged cynicism, secularism and individualism.

The idea that the individual was responsible for his own soul and for his personal relationship with God was refreshing and liberating, facilitating independence from an Anglican Church already as mired in corruption and entangled in the Establishment power structure as the Church of Rome had been. But individualism, emerging simultaneously with the capitalist practices of a profit-driven, go-getting, selfish commercial world, threatened old ideas of humble self-effacement and dedication to the community's good. This individualism discounted others, prioritized your needs, disconnected you from moral restraints and promoted a world where personal will and private appetite were the measure of actions, where villainy and ambition thrived. Traditional morality demanded the bad be punished in fiction. In real life villains often got away with skulduggery and dishonesty. Niccolò Machiavelli was demonized because his works 'openly and unfeignedly [...] describe what

---

9 The anonymous *Memorial* (addressed to James I on his accession) demanded the reintroduction of the Edwardian reforms, more practising preaching ministers, strict observance of the Sabbath, the banishment of the ring exchange in marriage and other 'superstitious' remnants of popery.

10 Montaigne, 'To philosophize is to learn how to die', 96.

11 *Basilikon Doron*, 13.

men do, and not what they ought to do', yet plays do exactly the same.[12] The discrepancy between moral expectation and actual behaviour shows that rule breakers succeed. Man's unique features – the virtues of charity, mercy, sympathy, intellectual ability, reason and the emotional faculties (imagination, love, sympathy) – raised him above animals and closer to godlike status. But the pinnacle of God's earthly creation, part-divine, part-animal hybrid, was too easily tempted by fleshly failings. Mankind was God's second attempt after some of his first angelic creations rebelled with Satan. Because humans had animal traits life was a constant battle between the animal promptings of appetites and passions and the angelic demands of reason and virtue. The exploration of that struggle between our baser and our better nature is the domain of literature. The Ten Commandments, the Seven Deadly Sins and the Seven Virtues, are conduct guidelines implicit in all Elizabethan-Jacobean drama against which characters can be measured. They specifically address the need to repress impulses toward lust, bloody acts, all violence, theft, gluttony and sloth. The presence of these appetites, in such density, gives *Volpone* its dark and grim aspect. A light-hearted comedy it is not, but rather a bleak and depressing picture of human failing.

The list of sins, revised by Pope Gregory I in 590 AD, was used by Dante in his influential poem *The Divine Comedy* (1321). Originating in Catholicism, these mortal, capital or cardinal sins were still much referred to by the very sin-conscious Anglican Protestants of Jonson's time and obsessively so by dissenting sectarians. They are cardinal because they were thought grave enough to require God to renew his grace to the sinner and for the sinner to show repentance before forgiveness could be shown. They are mortal or capital because they were serious enough to warrant death ('For the wages of sin is death'.). God was thought able to strike down great sinners by sudden death or to use human agents. The Book of Proverbs lists looking proud of yourself, lying, shedding innocent blood, having a heart ready to devise wickedness, a readiness to do mischief and stirring trouble. St Paul offers a longer list, any of which will lose you the kingdom of God: adultery, fornication, uncleanness, lasciviousness, idolatry, witchcraft, hatred, variance, emulations, wrath, strife, seditions, heresies, envyings, murders, drunkenness, revellings 'and such like' (Epistle to the Galatians 5:19–21). Fornication was sex between a couple not married to each other. The principle was that sex should not take place at all unless within matrimony. Elizabeth's court, for all her surveillance of her gentlewomen, was a hotbed of promiscuity, ambition, petty rivalry, plotting for promotion and blatant vanity and display. These failings and more would increase during the reign of James I. Ranked below the Deadly Sins are many

12 Francis Bacon, *The Advancement of Learning* (1605), 157.

other negative behaviours and vices regarded as sinful, though less serious. These are called Venial sins. Committing them would not lead to you losing the grace of God, and thus you could still be cleansed and saved – with effort on your part.

The idea of Hell as below the earth, imagined as a fiery pit structured like a funnel with terraces circling inside, is formalized by Dante in *L'Inferno* [Hell], the first part of *The Divine Comedy*. Each sin was tabulated and allocated its sector. The lower Dante goes in his visit to the nine circles of Hell, the worse the sins committed by the damned he meets. In 'Upper Hell' are those who committed sins of incontinence, failings effected by those constant enemies of mankind, the appetites. These mainly personal failings, tied closely to the Seven Deadly Sins, are in descending order – the lustful, the gluttonous, hoarders and spendthrifts, the wrathful, suicides. In 'Nether Hell' – getting closer to Satan at the bottom of the pit – are sinners who, like Mosca and Volpone, committed planned transgressions – fraud or acts of malice. In descending order they are panders and seducers (pimps and fornicators), flatterers, simoniacs (those who sold church offices), sorcerers, barrators (who abused the legal system to profit by groundless cases or false claims), hypocrites, thieves, those encouraging fraud, sowers of discord, falsifiers and traitors (to kindred, country, guests, their lord).[13] These broad definitions comprise a number of sins against the community and against probity in public office. Some occur in the play and the audience would easily identify them.

Pride was the first sin, committed by the Devil in thinking so well of himself he rebelled against God to replace him. As Lucifer ('the bright one'), he was God's favourite angel, but becoming ambitious, thinking that though God favoured him above the other angels he deserved even better and higher status, he rebelled, was defeated and cast out of Heaven. He and his co-conspirators fell through Chaos into Hell, a fiery pit full of sulphur and smoke, specially created by God. Vanity is a form of pride. At a venial level it is conceit about your physical looks, clothes or status. Stephen Bateman's *The Christall Glasse of Christian Reformation* (1584) has two engravings depicting 'Pride'. The first shows a well-dressed woman looking in a mirror. Her foot rests on a skull. Behind her is a winged, horned devil, with clawed feet like a bird of prey, a man's torso, a balding skull-shaped head and a long curved beak of a nose. The accompanying description reads, 'The woman signifieth pride: the glasse in her hand flattery or deceate – the deuil behind her temptation: the death head which she setteth her foote upon, signifieth forgetfulness of the life to come, wherby commeth destruction'. Volpone and Mosca exhibit overly

---

13 Sorcerers used occult, diabolic powers, as opposed to conjurors or white magicians (not intending evil), using natural magic and harnessing Nature's forces.

high self-esteem, an overblown perception of their skill and a sense that they are untouchable. While they are not concerned about their appearance (a vanity much evident among the rich, power-broking, fashionable elite), their obsession with material gain and cheating has encouraged them to forget 'the life to come'.

Their vanity, amusing in its effects in predating the would-be predators, is also setting itself up for a fall. In a lesser way Sir Politic's pose as international man-of-the-world also cries out for humiliation. The arrogance of thinking yourself better than others is a small vanity until it becomes active disregard and bad treatment of others, behaving as if you were above common courtesy, decency and the law. The fool is perhaps the last to become aware of his folly. Volpone is. Bateman's view of 'Pride' has a verse heading (an epigraph) that reads, 'When daintie dames hath whole delight: with proude attyre themselves to [ar]ray/Pirasmos shineth in the sight: of glittering glass such fooles to fray [frighten]'. This simply means that when a woman delights solely in ostentatious appearance, the Devil will appear reflected in her mirror to frighten her into remembrance of what is truly important in life. *Peirasmos* is the Greek word used in the New Testament to mean temptation or testing. Bateman's second example of 'Pride' shows a rich man, fashionably dressed, striding past a beggar and ignoring the supplication for alms. He is 'such a one as careth for no poore man [...] the poore man signifieth the pouertie general [general poverty], whose petitions of such are not heard, nor once relieued'. The situation behind this social complaint, made in 1584, had worsened by 1606.

Vanity related to appearance and fashion, and any reference to clothing as a shallow, fleshly distraction, is relevant to an audience with many peacock young men and young women in it, whose wasteful extravagance on clothes was becoming increasingly disturbing to moralists and playwrights. Personal display was a common target in drama and moralistic pamphlets. The most extensive and hysterically extreme attack is to be found in the Puritan Phillip Stubbes's *Anatomie of Abuses* (1583). Apart from Lady Would-be's brief vanity about her appearance as she arrives at Volpone's palazzo, ostentation is not in Jonson's sights, though it was in some of his other plays and was a recurrent theme in works by other dramatists. Pride is the besetting sin of those with power, privilege, rank and wealth (like some of the audience). The Bible required such people to disregard their advantages and be humbly ready to serve those whom it was their duty to help. A king is most likely to be proud, but overweening self-regard was rife among courtiers too. Pride in personal power underlies Corvino's heavy insistence on his patriarchal dominance. It is wrong because it is so extreme, so bullyingly autocratic. Its wrongness is pointed up when it is perverted by his threats when Celia is reluctant to prostitute herself just because he commands her to do so. The anti-patriarchal element is minor in a play so full of wrongdoing, but it is there and contributes to the decayed moral state portrayed. The pride of Mosca and Volpone in their ability to maliciously defraud everyone is a major form of the sin.

Wrath ranged from any moment of anger that flares and soon dies away, through escalating losses of temper to the irrational rage that becomes violent against someone else. This is relevant to those men in the audience ready to fall out and fight. Men (not just gentlemen) wore swords, carried concealed daggers and were prepared to use them. Too much wine, and tempers frayed easily – over cards, dice, women, a word taken the wrong way. The Day of Judgement, known as the *Dies Irae* (The Day of Wrath – the term used in the Anglican Communion), was when God's ultimate anger would be shown. In Him it was thought of as divine judgement and justice. Irascibility (a tendency to hot temper) is a sin liable to occur in any rank of society, but particularly among hot-headed young men. Those of rank and wealth were most susceptible to it, believing themselves superior to others and ready to defend any perceived slur against their honour. Bateman's engraving *Wrath* shows a helmeted, armed man carrying a sword and a flag. He sits astride a boar. He represents a standard view of anger as the soldier's key quality, but his flag bears a figure in ecclesiastical dress. In front of the boar a man stabs himself with a dagger and a stream of blood cascades to the ground.

Behind the boar a woman raises her arms to the sky. The explanation reads, 'The boar signifieth Wrath, and the man on his backe mischief: the Pope in the Flag destruction, & the Flag vncertain religion, turning and changing with euery blast of winde: the man killing him selfe desperation: the woman madness'. Ira (anger) is commonly depicted at this time as a sword-bearing man often armoured and helmeted as well. Cesare Ripa's engraving has his figure dressed thus but also holding a flaming torch to signify the burning blaze of temper.[14] Anger renders a man beastlike. In *'Tis Pity* calm reason is recommended to a jealous, vengeful husband: 'Sir you must be ruled by your reason and not by your fury: that were unhuman and beastly' (4.3.83–5).

Anger is not the inciting emotion of the play, though it occurs briefly at different times in the discussions between Mosca and the various predators. They feel some slight anger that Volpone's life is lingering longer than they

---

14 Ripa's *Iconologia* was the most famous and influential of iconographical handbooks. Published in 1593, with a second edition in 1603, it had 684 separate emblem/allegory descriptions and 151 woodcuts. Apart from the Seven Deadly Sins there are depictions of Dignity, Liberality, Harmony, Justice, Ambition, Sin, Arrogance, Authority and Power, Reason, Counsel, Idolatry and other personifications.

would like. There is wrath too in Peregrine's desire to trick and humiliate Sir Politic for his persistent snooty assumption of superior knowledge about Continental affairs. Mixed with this is the instinctive impulse of the hawk (a peregrine falcon) to swoop down on its prey. In Robert Burton's view, anger underlies covetousness and most of the miseries of our life.[15] Anger against the world may lurk beneath Volpone's desire to deceive. His compulsion to cheat bespeaks a contempt for other humans. It is not motivated by a sense of the justice of deceiving greedy men. It is perhaps his revenge on a society that is to him dull and unstimulating.

Lust was a universal sin, felt by both sexes, all ranks and most ages. The 'disease of lust' was to St Augustine persistently intrusive and the most destructive of the appetites.[16] Necessary for the continuation of the species, it was difficult to control. The human sex drive considerably concerned all churches. The sin of fornication was defined as any prohibited sex, that is, outside marriage. Consensual sex between two unmarried adults was forbidden. Sex with someone other than your husband or wife was both fornication and adultery. Conception of a child alone justified intercourse within marriage. Sex for pleasure alone was lust and fornication. Lust comprised all unclean thoughts and unclean acts, including unnatural ones like bestiality, incest and homosexuality (condemned in Romans 1:26). Masturbation, rape and sexual thoughts were all lust. A perceived growing libidinousness in society, with an increase in unwanted pregnancies in all ranks, worried preachers and playwrights alike. 'In political libels, lampoons, satires, and other forms of writing and action, upper-class immorality is almost inevitably the object of sharp disapproval, reflecting the growing grip of Protestant attitudes to sin, social order, and divine vengeance'.[17] Church attitudes to sexuality focus on two problem areas: the medieval church's view of women as the source of sin (particularly the belief that women were more lascivious by nature than men) and the church's central principle that appetites (passions) made men more like animals than angels and needed to be controlled or suppressed. The Christian ascetic tradition required avoiding all excess: simple food, simple clothes, a focus on the spiritual rather than the carnal. Every deadly sin is an appetite developed to excess. Unruly appetites (of different sorts) were the subject of play after play. Very slowly, over centuries, marriage was established within Christian Europe as a means of controlling and channelling lust. While theoretically chastity was regarded as preferable in order for full spiritual perfection to be achieved, it was gradually conceded that marriage was the

---

15 See Robert Burton, *The Anatomy of Melancholy*, 244.
16 Augustine, *Confessions*, book 7, sect. 7, p. 169.
17 Dabhoiwala, 42.

second-best course if you could not effectively control your sexual impulses.[18] Marrying was preferable to engaging in promiscuity, but even within wedlock lust had to be restrained.

Lust was a major topic for admonition in sermons and religious writing. Men and women sat separately in some churches. The Puritans, though in favour of marriage, had considerable difficulty with the whole area of sexuality. Criticism of rampant lust is recurrent in plays of the 1600s. Sexuality has a part to play in *Volpone*. It begins as an apparently insignificant side issue, but develops as the trigger for catastrophe and the fall of the villains. Leaving aside the lust for gain, sexual lust proves to be Volpone's downfall when he tries to woo, seduce and then rape Celia. Lust is the means by which the first part of the drama is drawn out of the closed, claustrophobic atmosphere of Volpone's bedroom. His predatory natures transmutes in this second phase from vulgar greed for acquisition to the cliché of upper-rank male habits and values, leading him to think his wealth and position will lure a mere merchant's wife into becoming his mistress. He displays the recognizable, traditional ploys of amatory literature – offering her a more affectionate and more comfortable life, serenading her with a translation of a famous poem by Catullus. In yet another shape shift he presents himself as far from bedridden and geriatric, promising a more active and exciting sex life. He denigrates Corvino's 'earth-fed' mind and offers 'the true heaven of love' (3.7.140), assuming that, married to a merchant (probably an arranged union), she will not have experienced genuine love and physical passion. Once again he seems to enjoy the trickery involved for he anticipates 'secrecy, and pleasure', seeking to clinch his argument by the display of his treasure and promises of pearl necklaces and diamonds. Ironically, the satire here presupposes that many women would have been convinced and that there would almost certainly have been bourgeois housewives among the audience who had already given in to such temptation. The offer of 'sensual baits' in the decadent and exotic food he promises ('The heads of parrots, tongues of nightingales [...] brains of peacocks, and of ostriches', 3.7.202–3) is rejected, so he offers pampering baths, expensive drinks and a range of Ovidian sexual antics and fantasies. All in all he offers a more affluent lifestyle and a taste of patrician pleasures. Her calm, reasoned rejection, her assertion of virtue and readiness to pray for him and report his virtuousness, rouses his anger and makes him show his true self when he declares, 'Yield, or I'll force thee' (3.7.266). It is the expected nobleman's reaction. Here is bourgeois virtue rejecting the traditional aristo-gentry male tendency to have its way by force. When Bonario (a gentleman's

---

18 'if they cannot contain, let them marry: for it is better to marry than to burn' (St Paul, I Corinthians 7:9).

son) rescues the damsel in distress, such misconduct is 'unmasked, unspirited, undone' by goodness in one of his own station. Lust is thwarted, but punishment is delayed.

Envy or covetousness is jealous desire for what others have, a form of mental theft and discontent with the lot God gave you. It is the overriding sin of the play and closely allied to avarice. The two are similar enough to overlap. It is the greediness of a child coveting what another has. The greed of these older men is for things, for objects of material wealth. The *captators* covet Volpone's property and portable wealth by becoming a legatee. (A *captator* is a legal term for one who fraudulently attempts to gain from another's will.) They even strive to outdo each other and become the principal heir named in his will. Volpone uses their greed by encouraging them to make him gifts on the pretence it will enhance their chances of being made a valuable bequest. In tempting them into covetousness, he expresses his own greed, his longing to accumulate. He claims it is the thrill of tricking them that is most important, but he still accepts the bribes they bring. The play is not interested in exploring deep psychological states, but there are hints that Volpone's state (and to lesser extents the states of soul and mind of the legacy hunters) are deep-seated, ingrained weaknesses that lead them into other serious sins (lies, callousness, hypocrisy, rank betrayal). Volpone makes no attempt to hide the naked desire to acquire rich gifts from the greedy predators. They make little attempt to hide their desire for Volpone's wealth. Both reactions were aspects of contemporary life in Jacobean England among the upper ranks. The aristo–gentry, neither trained for nor desiring to work, had to scavenge to maintain their standard of living or to regain it if depleted by thriftlessness, gambling, whoring, buying clothes or keeping up expensive households. Their struggle to survive is a recurrent feature in life and literature through to the nineteenth century. Yet survival is not Volpone's problem. He faces no difficulties of that material sort. The better and the middling sort are exposed as shameless parasites in the play. The constant suspicion that your neighbour was doing better than you, that he made a better showing in society, was a persistent impulse motivating the envious tensions of society.

Venice is a small city and, like the restricted circle of the English court, generated the hothouse jealousies of any limited group. Jonson reworks envy as an unsettling, potentially destructive yet integral aspect of the human make-up, releasing deceit, cheating, lies, plots and ploys in the attempt to outdo the hated rivals for social standing. Family relationships are absent for Volpone and disregarded by Corbaccio. Love and marital harmony are strangers to Corvino. Envy is a frequent theme in revenge plays. The Mary Tudor/Elizabeth relationship had had its uneasy jealousies and the Mary Queen of Scots/Elizabeth cousin rivalry bedevilled English politics until the former was executed for yet another plot against the queen. James I's court was riven by envious struggles for dominance among courtiers vying for favour, for royal favour meant money, status and power.

Bateman has two engravings for 'Enuie' and two for 'Couetousnes'. One illustration for envy has a clearly religious, anti-Catholic focus. It shows a cardinal astride a dragon that is trampling two sheep. There is a tonsured clerical figure too cutting the throat of a third sheep. The animals represent the ordinary faithful Christian flock. 'The Dragon signifieth the enemie to all that professe the worde of God: the Cardinall persecution [...] of the same – the Fryer murther'. The epigraph reads, 'To Serpent like I may compare: those greedie wolues that lambes deuoure:/Awayting still to catch in snare: all such as gette they may by power'. The second 'Enuie' picture has a recognizable rural scene that reminds the viewer that loving thy neighbour as thyself did not always happen in small, closed communities. It shows an open field where 'the true labourer' sows seed. He is 'dilgence of mind [...] sowing the seedes of veritie' (truth). A sack of seed lies open at the side of the field. In the foreground another man is pouring seeds from a bag into the stream flowing by. He is 'a deceatful person, seeking by all meanes to waste and spoyle the seedes of veritie'. It is unclear whether the second man has stolen seed from the first, but the message, though using the common farming image (with allusions perhaps to the parable of the sower), transforms into a comment on how some people (Catholics, heretics or Non-Conformists) tried to pervert the truth of the true faith (Anglicanism). The epigraph says, 'Enuie seeketh where to finde: to hurt hys neighbour if he can:/And neuer ceaseth but to purloyne [steal]: which hath been the vndoing of many man'. One picture for covetousness shows a man on a throne with a supplicant on either side. The enthroned man has power and has four hands and four arms: 'two to deliuer & two to receaue'. The giving hands have papers – the official notice of appointment to a place ('preferment for small gaine'). The receiving hands are outstretched for the money the placemen are donating to his private fortune, the bribe that is the price of their advancement. The transaction is a 'deceit' and is done 'priuily' (privily = secretly). This picture relates to the growing problem of bribery and corruption in government, a persistent subject for cartoonists and polemicists through to the end of the nineteenth century. The more powerful engraving of 'Couetousnes' shows a man dressed in fool's motley wearing the traditional three-horned cap with bells at the tips and garters with bells on them. The Devil offers him three swords, a money bag and an armillary sphere (three forms of earthly power). Bateman's gloss asserts, 'The deuil is Enuy, the swords in his hand betokeneth mischief, the purse couetousness, the globe the world, the man in fooles weede signifieth carelesse couetousness, a man ouercome with Enuy and couetousness, may be likened to a fool that is not able to rule himselfe, and so the ende is death'. The epigraph reads, 'To delight in treasure, is a daungerous pleasure'. *Volpone* is a dramatized demonstration of this *sententia* or moral maxim.

Greed and gluttony are sins of physical excess. Avarice (greed), or excessive desire for material goods or wealth, is the miser's sin, hoarding for its own sake. It overlaps with Envy or Covetousness and stems from envy of what others have and you do not. It extends into the obsession to acquire more. It is the sin of the moneymaker – the financier, speculator, entrepreneur – accumulating more than he needs. It is the sin of the skinflint who has money but will not spend readily, the sin of conquistador explorers like Sir Walter Raleigh and the Virginia Company, like the founders of the East India Company, looking to loot luxury materials from the Americas and Asia and make huge profits. From the religious standpoint it is the sin of the man who does not 'shake the superflux' (his unwanted excess food or money) to the needy, a theme much discussed in the increasingly hard times of the 1590s and 1600s. The rise of capitalism saw an increase in obsession with physical shows of wealth. The affluence of some people precipitated countless writings deploring luxury, extravagance, waste and display (all forms of conspicuous consumption). Between the miser and the prodigal is the charitable man who gives to the poor, the man of largesse who feasts his neighbours at times of celebration and in times of hardship. Ripa's illustration to 'Avaritia' shows a young woman dressed in classical Greek robes holding a large money bag. Behind her stalks a wolf, the traditional symbol for avarice, based on its reputation for having a voracious appetite and always being hungry.[19] The hunger was not only for material gain but also included political ambition. *Volpone* and the city comedies present many wastrels, some mean men, but few who are generous of spirit and open-handed.

Gluttony is bodily excess, largely applied to overindulgence in food and drink. It reminds that 'enough is as good as a feast'. As long as you had eaten and drunk in moderation, sufficient for the body's needs, anything more was unnecessary indulgence. The leftovers could be given to the old and the poor. It is the Dives and Lazarus story again, a story reminding the rich and comfortably off to do their duty to the community. It was part of the harmony of society, payment for deference, putting back into the community. But gluttony also related to the loss of moderation and balance. Bateman interprets 'Gluttonie' as incontinence of feeling such as leads to the tavern brawl he depicts, with a man lying dead after a quarrel has broken out. The setting in a tavern implies that overeating and certainly overdrinking can

---

19 At the beginning of *L'Inferno* Dante meets a she-wolf who 'seemed, in her thinness,/To have nothing but excessive appetites' (canto 1, verses 49–50).

cause heated and excited passions that may lead to violence. Volpone exhibits a degree of gluttony in the extravagant meals he promises Celia if she becomes his mistress. But it is avarice (greed for material things) that is the overriding sin in the play.

Jonson knew of Dante for Lady Pol refers to him. There is evidence he was familiar with *The Divine Comedy* and that in *L'Inferno* Dante has the avaricious and the prodigal (the misers and spendthrifts) condemned to the Fourth Circle, where they eternally push in front of them heavy weights (substituting for their amassed wealth). He comments,

> all the gold there is [...]
> And all there ever was, could never give
> A moment's rest to one of these tired souls.[20]

This image captures something of the endlessly driven greed of Volpone and the legacy hunters. In *Il Purgatorio*, the second book of Dante's epic, repentant misers are bound face to the ground to remind them how earthly and materialistic they had been, neglecting their spiritual side.

Excess was a moral hot point. Any excess was disapproved. The early church was built on moderation, on asceticism, fast days, lack of material possessions and the simple life. It failed to live up to that ideal, becoming a monolithic edifice of accumulated wealth, land, power, corruption and self-indulgence. Its decadent worldliness triggered various reforming heresies violently suppressed in the name of preserving the faith, but actually defending Catholicism's monopoly hold over the people of Europe. The theoretical basis was moderation and simplicity. The Apollonian religion of ancient Greece prioritized controlled moderation. 'Nothing in excess' was inscribed on Apollo's temple in Delphi. The concept persisted. A late-fourteenth-century proverb said, 'There is measure in all things'. St Augustine wisely remarked that 'to some, total abstinence is easier than perfect moderation'.[21] The Puritans revitalized the traditions of asceticism, leading to them being seen as killjoys, but excess was a moral danger marker. In tragedy (classical and Elizabethan–Jacobean), once a character behaves excessively in one aspect of their life, disaster becomes possible. In comedy too we find excesses – Sir Toby's persistent drunkenness, Malvolio's social aspirations, Orsino's obsession with Olivia (just to take examples from *Twelfth Night*). In *Volpone* it is excess that drives the plot. Any form of obsessive/excessive behaviour is open to mockery. There is something spiritually mean in the excitement Volpone and Mosca

---

20 *L'Inferno*, canto 7, verse 64.
21 *On the Good of Marriage*, chap. 21.

experience through their deceptions. It is all focused on gain, then getting more. They experience a selfish pleasure too in cheating others, proving their superiority. It is a form of power. And they revel in it. A Jacobean audience would assume both will somehow get their comeuppance, while enjoying their assumed mistaken confidence that they will succeed. There is irony and hubris in their complacency that tempt Providence to reverse their fortunes. For a long time it is unclear who is to be the agent of their humiliation and how (even whether) it is to be achieved. Where will justice come from? The denouement is long suspended and not always certain of a just outcome, though once Mosca reveals his plan to cheat his master we may suspect they will expose their crimes in the attempt to outdo each other. The audience may imagine the first trial will expose the wrongdoers, but it is a trick, postponing justice, showing how easily fooled the *avocatori* are by the 'faith, and credit' (4.5.19) claimed by Voltore and his fine oratory when backed by the lies of the *captators* (legacy hunters) and the disabled, derelict appearance of the alleged rapist. Jonson plays with the audience further when he lets Volpone and Mosca revel in their escape and push their deceits a final stage further. Mosca, dressed as a *clarissimo* (Venetian grandee), and Volpone as a *commendatore* (law officer) invert their social status. They show no mercy in victory (indeed, they exult in it) and thereby bring down retribution for hubris. By going over the top and initiating new tricks after escaping from due punishment for their previous scams they exhibit further excess and invite God's punishment.

Excess is the standard in *Volpone*. Even Celia's stance is excessive in her virtue, unnaturally upright, even self-righteous. Neither she nor Bonario are characters we warm to yet they represent what the Christian was expected to be like. Neither is developed enough as a personality for the audience to identify or sympathize with. We may dislike the greed of the five central characters and condemn them, but where will the toppling impulse come from? Mosca and Volpone seem invincible; they are vigorous, they incite action and they evoke reactions from the audience. In attempting to clear themselves from soliciting fornication and rape, Volpone and Mosca are drawn into a legal confrontation. It is this institution which will eventually, and not entirely satisfactorily, constitute the restoration of justice and order. But that is actually activated by those who deserve punishment eventually defeating each other and bringing each other down, rather than by exposure by the court officers. Venetian society is shown to be a jungle where each is out to devour the other, so it is entirely right that those deserving punishment should do so by trying to do each other down in court, exculpate themselves and incriminate their rivals. Comedy is usually cruel for the victim of the joke. As spectators, outside the action, not too emotionally involved and knowing it is only a fiction, we can laugh, though occasionally the suffering a mistake or trick can cause may be too much to be acceptable. We enjoy seeing the biters bit. Amused initially, we support how Mosca and Volpone punish the greedy predators, but turn against them with the attempted rape. True morality should, however, condemn them from the outset. They are liars, cheats, frauds and too full of themselves. Portraying a cruel and selfish world, they are so vile we gradually long to see them shamed, humiliated, exposed for the vermin they are. It is a near-run thing and trickery nearly wins. Emotional identification probably does not take place in watching *Volpone* for the characters are not likeable enough for us to feel empathy. The piece aims to entertain, to amuse and to instruct. But we are watching a disturbingly ugly play.

Virtuous, rational living was thought to be its own reward. Moderation, abstinence, chastity and renouncing and avoiding temptation were all ways to concentrate devotion to God and virtue, though not much practised at court and certainly not on display on the stage. The principle of moderation was integral to Christian belief from its beginnings. The simple life of John the Baptist, Jesus, the hermits of the Thebaid Desert and many saints prioritized spiritual cleansing over the demands of the body. Regular fasting and leading a frugal life, were practices that continued in Protestant England. Periods of contemplation and prayer were encouraged as was the rejection of luxury. Excessive, ostentatious displays of your spirituality were sinful too, the overpiety of the Puritans being commonly mocked in drama. The aim was to put the corrupting influence of this world into perspective. Diminishing its power over you gave you time to focus on the next world. But balance had to be kept. It was acceptable to work hard, enjoy your family, be an active, useful member of your community and take pleasure moderately in the good things of this world. Courtiers were an ostentatious, drunken, promiscuous, gambling-obsessed, garrulous and debt-ridden lot, mostly living away from home and thus neglecting their families and their local social duty, and needing more instruction than most. Given the noisy, inattentive, food-munching, giggling, gossiping nature of audiences, we can only hope that the spectators were suitably receptive to the lessons taught in *Volpone*.

Sloth, another sort of excess – an overdeveloped laziness – was not just a disinclination to work but also a psychological/spiritual state of not bothering. Your duty to God was to work hard at your trade and at being virtuous. Many didactic stories and plays illustrate the spiritual and material rewards of industry. A popular one compared two apprentices – one, hard-working, gets on well in his trade and gains his master's daughter, while the other, idle, falls into bad habits and ends up in prison for debt, as demonstrated in *Eastward Ho!* (1605). But industry not only meant working at your livelihood but also at being a committed, active Christian, helping the community and actively working at guarding and improving your own spiritual state. The Latin word for sloth, *acedia* (or *accidia*), also applies to spiritual slothfulness or despair, the state in which you lost the belief that God cared for and watched over you. It was a state akin to melancholy or depression.

The parade of sins is unrelieved in this play and would be easily spotted. An audience of the time would be of the mindset to interpret the drama before them in the light of these moral waymarkers. It would take the point, made multiple times, that mankind is a foolish species.

Man had two basic characteristics not shared by the rest of creation: sensibilities and reason. Altruistic feelings of kindness, empathy and caring led to charity. Such sensibilities showed in family love and community care which rationally accepted that some loss of self-will was needed if the benefits of group cooperation were to be accrued. Despite the positive aspects of some feelings there were many others that lured men into folly. Folly was the first step toward sin. It was, however, his ability to reason that raised him far above the animal world and drew him closer to the angels. It was the capacity to postulate action, speculate on causes, effects and consequences and then decide what course to take. Hamlet sums this up most aptly:

> What a piece of work is a man! How noble in reason! how infinite in faculty! in form, in moving, how express and admirable! in action how like an angel! in apprehension how like a god! the beauty of the world! the paragon of animals! (2.2.303–7)

This ideal Renaissance man, rational and civilized, had cultured accomplishments, could play and write music, write poems, dance well, converse easily and fluently, had impeccable manners, was cultivated and learned and could talk equally with paupers or kings. All of this was very possible if you had position and money – but rare. Moderate in behaviour, he was charitable, judging the sinner mercifully and helping unquestioningly those in need, but strip away the fine clothes and airs of the man of rank, remove the protection money and power give and he was a 'bare, forked animal' (*King Lear*) and as susceptible to sin as the lowliest dependent on his estate.

The year *Hamlet* described man's perfectibility, another picture of what man could be (and generally was) is voiced by the jester Feste (*Twelfth Night*, 1601) telling Viola/Cesario, 'Foolery Sir, does walk about the Orb like the Sun, it shines everywhere' (3.1.39–40). In theory rational, in practice foolish is Shakespeare's presentation of mankind. Jonson is harsher. Human kind for him is greedy and corrupt. Everyone acknowledged man at his best – planning ahead, being practical and reasonable, using common sense, adjusting to changed circumstances, doing what was just and kind, constructing social agencies to fit the needs of a community, sympathetically desiring to redress imbalances of food, wealth and power caused by individual greed, laziness and intemperance and formulating this into a judicial system, and developing a power-hierarchy that (theoretically) enabled society to work effectively. It was the other aspect, however, the failure to achieve perfect social harmony and perfect personal government, that most exercised the pens and tongues of satirists, moralists and playwrights. Acts of folly, the first steps on the road to sin, provided an endless, rich ground for description of failure and prescriptions for improvement. Man's infinite capacity for spoiling things was a much more exciting, titillating, sensational and fruitful subject for dramatists and religious polemicists, than theorizing about ideal sociopolitical-personal structures. Silly judgements, making a fool of oneself, deceiving others, self-deception, trickery for gain, greed, the minefields of sex and love, power, money and outright wrongdoing provided a complex network of failed right conduct and a wonderful parade of fools. In *Volpone*, man's essential evil dominates. The main characters act with apparent rationality, but their aims are foolish – they risk their immortal souls for the sake of brief temporal pleasure and glittering trinkets. Their actions are excessive, their appetites excessive.

Rational, balanced judgements (that is, virtuous, moderate judgements) are taken out of the hands of most of the characters as their humours dominate, making them puppet playthings of their own character, addicted to greed, incapable of acting considerately and moderately. As Bacon said, 'Prosperity doth best discover vice, but adversity doth best discover virtue'.[22] Jonson echoed this view: 'He knows not his own strength that hath not met adversity'.[23] Neither Volpone nor his victims are materially poor. Mosca alone actually needs to build a safety buffer of money. That explains but does not excuse his criminal deceptions, his lies, his betrayals. His master and the birds of prey have less excuse for their behaviour, being greedy without needing to acquire more. The play is uniformly dark. The laughter it provokes is grim, derisory, sneering contempt. It is not light-hearted, tolerant amusement at man's folly, but the contented snort of seeing sin caught out.

There is a range of different types of humour, including commedia dell'arte slapstick farce, but always with serious underlying issues. Whatever the topical targets, the constant target is the universal condemnation of man's sinfulness. The play displays will devoid of consideration for others, appetite unfettered by morality. Its logical outcome, unless some punishment is imposed from above

22 'Of Adversity', *Essays*, 75.
23 *Timber*, 3.

(from Heaven or from the legal authorities), is the unfettered ruthless struggle of animals squabbling for food. The judgement of the court almost misfires, chillingly reminding the audience that corruption goes to the very top of society and that more often than not justice is not done and the ruthless win. Not being part of the action, the audience's superior knowledge of just what is going on enables us to be amused at the characters' confusions, but generates a sense of helplessness. We watch evil's cleverness and the naive vulnerability of innocence but are unable to step into the scene and help justice prevail. This is part of the magic of theatre, but also part of its frustratingly closed nature. It is its own world and we are only spectators.

Chapter 4

THE SEVEN CARDINAL VIRTUES

If the Seven Deadly Sins were the warning signs for avoiding damnation, the Virtues were waymarkers to salvation.

The Seven Cardinal Virtues

1. **Temperance** (abstinence, moderation)
2. **Prudence** (providence, foresight, circumspection, consideration, wise conduct)
3. **Justice** (justice, equity, fair judgement)
4. **Fortitude** (strength under pressure)
5. **Faith** (piety, duty to and belief in God)
6. **Hope** (hope of salvation)
7. **Charity** (love of, benevolence to, others)

A godly life won a heavenly crown. If life was a journey and each person a pilgrim on the highway, conduct determined destination. Virtue's path was hard – steep, thorny, stony, winding, tiring. The way for the carnal man of weak character, Mr Worldly Wiseman, was easy, a 'primrose path', as Macbeth puts it, but leading to an 'everlasting bonfire' and 'sulphurous pit'. Virtue requires steadfastness of belief. Stephen Bateman's engraving *Of Faith* depicts a knight, fully armoured in the Elizabethan style. He is a warrior for Christ, bears a shield with the cross of St George on it and has a lance and a sword. He stands on the body of the Devil sprawled on his back and looks out across a bay where a ship is sailing and over which the clouds have opened to reveal, in Hebrew, the words of God. The accompanying signification reads, 'The man in armour signifieth all stedfast beleuers [believers] of the veritie being armed with constant zeale of Christianitie, and weaponed with the shielde of liuely faith, the spere of continuance and the sworde of the word of God: the Deuil vnder him is temptation being ouercome by faith in Christ Iesus'. In *Of Justice*, Justice carries the scales of equity, a sword to 'cut off all rebellious persons and offenders' and has one eye in the middle of her forehead representing 'vpright iudgement'.

Volpone follows a course much like a tragedy. The 'hero', that is, the central character, has a fatal flaw, is presented at the height of his power and skill as a deceiver, makes a misjudgement that almost leads to disaster, is given a chance to recognize his fault, fails to reform, eventually falls, is judged and punished. As the play is not designed as a tragedy, the trajectory of the plot does not lead to his death and the destruction of those about him, but to public exposure and punishment. Volpone, Mosca and the greedy would-be legatees are all punished and the innocent survive and are ultimately exonerated. Sin pervades the narrative and its potential to take hold of and take over its victims is persistently displayed. Its potential to destroy the innocent is also represented but eventually turned aside. The sins and sinners hold our attention because they are intriguing and are potentially dangerous. Virtue is evident and opposes sin. Celia clearly argues her position in rejecting Volpone, and Bonario's physical championing of virtue is decisive in itself though nearly perverted by the survival tactics of clever and well-practised deceivers supported by a naive court. The sins provoke questions that hold our attention for they create tension and drama between the characters and a tension between the play and the audience. It is unusual for the central and inciting characters to be so clearly evil and yet hold the majority of our attention for the majority of the drama. The characters we are most interested in are ones we wish to be caught out, stopped and punished.

That is a way of displaying how widespread Ben Jonson saw sinful conduct, how dominantly he felt it represented human beings. The Old Adam far outweighed the new humanist. Sin takes over the play. It is the play. Further tension is evoked by the growing suspicion that good will not succeed in ending the free range of corruption. Contemporary morality demanded evil be seen to be punished, but there is always the feeling that when it does so it has been achieved by artificial manipulation of the story and that in real life sinners are winners.

The centrality of virtue to living the good life was not only recognized in Christian thought. Classical writings, particularly Plato's Socratic dialogue *Protagoras*, Aristotle's *Ethics*, Cicero's *De Officiis* (On Duty or Obligation) and Seneca's *De Ira* (On Anger) and *De Clementia* (On Mercy), extolled virtue. Each listed those qualities required to live the good (that is, virtuous and wise) life. Plato names wisdom, courage, justice, kindness, circumspection and holiness as essential components of excellence. Aristotle identifies courage, temperance, liberality, magnanimity, proper ambition, patience, truthfulness, friendliness, modesty and righteous indignation. Schoolboys studied Cicero's works particularly as models of good Latin style, elegant but direct. In an age when one's first public duty was to others and not to selfish individual desires, *De Officiis* became the key exemplum of good citizenship. Studied at university as an essential guide to the moral life and public conduct for young men who might be active in national arenas, it advised how to discern false flattery from wise counsel and how to divert unreasonable, angry demands. Seneca too was studied and his essays were of particular relevance in the formation of a wise ruler. The qualities identified evolved into the four virtues of Christian thinking, then extended to seven with faith, hope and charity, originating in Paul's letter (I Corinthians 13:13), with charity elevated as the greatest.

Charity means not only donating alms to beggars or assistance to the poor, but the extension of love and sympathy to all fellow living beings. In Epistle to the Galatians 5:22–3, Paul also said, 'The fruit of the Spirit is love, joy, peace, longsuffering, gentleness, goodness, faith, meekness, temperance'. Such characteristics are part of the moral excellence that constitutes a person's virtue. The Christian fathers, St Ambrose, St Augustine and St Thomas Aquinas (*Summa Theologica*, first part of part 2, sect. 61), reacting to and refining St Paul, discussed and detailed what became the seven key characteristics of the pious Christian and incorporated them into the main body of church teaching. By the Renaissance their meanings had proliferated into an extensive didactic and mentoring literature aimed not just at individual Christians but also at any sort of leader or governor. Temperance was a crucial characteristic for a prince. For James I temperance meant not only the opposite to gluttony but moderation in all things, particularly in the exercise of justice, power and anger. However, temperance was not something he actually followed himself, being an intemperate drinker and given, like Queen Elizabeth, to immoderate rage when thwarted. To Thomas Elyot self-control and emotional balance were crucial qualities in someone with the immense potential for arbitrary, extra-legal punishment available to a king.

Prudence is the patience of the circumspect or wise ruler who does not react impulsively but weighs up options, considers possible outcomes and makes decisions calmly and with the advice of trustworthy counsellors. Wise patience (prudence), perseverance, courage (the bravery to do the right thing and combat evil), fairness (justice for all who deserve it), tolerance, truthfulness and honesty, respect for others, kindness, generosity and forgiveness were key to right conduct.

Justice (along with appropriate mercy) was a key quality in a king for in those days a monarch had absolute power and could act outside the law. That might be a good thing if it meant showing fairness and merciful pardon for all who deserve it, but absolutism, authoritarianism and arbitrary whim in the hands of bad monarchs litters the pages of the chronicles. Willam Shakespeare's history plays alone demonstrate the all-too-human spitefulness, pettiness and brutality of kings, queens and overmighty noblemen.

Fortitude is strength in the face of hardships. It is inner strength that helps a person persevere through negative situations and strive to deal with them.

Faith, **Hope** and **Charity** are all religious characteristics thought to be absolutely vital for a Christian prince. No ruler could govern justly and properly unless he was a committed follower of Christ and could reasonably hope for salvation at the end of life. Charity was largely interpreted as the sort of generous largesse traditionally expected of any prince figure. But it had a more than material dimension relating to a general love of a ruler for his people. Caritas was expressed in the protection a shepherd gave his flock and the care a father took to look after his family. 'Shepherd' and 'father' were terms used to describe a governor's concern for his people. Bateman's gloss to his engraving 'Of Charitie' is virtually a verbatim repetition of the Corporal Works. Charity is 'to fede the hungry, to clothe the naked, to harbour the harbourless, & lodge the stranger, to visite the sicke, and to relieve the prisoners and poor afflicted members of Christe, this is the dueties of all faithfull people'.

Cesare Ripa's allegorical personification of 'Carita' is less socially oriented. It portrays family love, a woman, a mother, leading two children and suckling a third.[1] His personification of 'Liberalita' (Largess or Generosity), the readiness of the rich man to 'shake the superflux', that is, give liberally from his excess to the poor shows a woman bearing two large cornucopias. The horn of plenty in her left hand is full of fruits, while that in her left is inverted in order to spill out its gifts. Tucked into the right hand is a pair of dividers symbolising the idea of apportioning her liberality so that each needy person receives a due and equitable share.

Along with prudence or circumspection, moderation was fundamental to kingly rule. Not jumping to conclusions but considering options and outcomes carefully is a vital skill for any civic leader whose actions and judgements have widespread consequences. James I contributed to the discussion of princely duty in *Basilikon Doron* (1598). Only seven copies were printed and privately circulated. All doubt about authorship was removed when, on succeeding to the English throne, James I had thousands of copies reprinted and circulated in London. Both *Basilikon* and *The Trew Lawe of Free Monarchies* (1598) promulgated absolutism and shared many of the basic concepts of princely conduct already currently accepted. There was broad agreement by most writers on the subject. Of course Volpone is not

---

1 Ripa, *Iconologia.*

a prince. He is not the Doge of Venice nor even a member of the *Signory*, the oligarchic senatorial rulers of the state from whom the official head, the Doge, was elected. But he is a patrician, an upper-rank grandee. This immediately brings into play a host of responsibilities to the community and presupposes he has certain personal and public qualities entitling him to the respect of his inferiors. Volpone very publicly does not have those qualities. He is immersed in the greedy pursuit of his own private ends. To an audience of the time this puts him incontestably into the category of sinner and irresponsible member of the polity. One wonders how many at The Globe squirmed in their seats at recognizing as their own failings the standard virtues transgressed in the selfish avarice, selfish trickery and sexual rapaciousness on stage. Patience, perseverance, courage (the bravery to do the right thing and combat evil), fairness (justice for all who deserve it), tolerance, truthfulness and honesty, respect for others, kindness, generosity and forgiveness were key to right conduct, but not displayed by Volpone. He has perseverance, but it is perseverance in sin. Apart from the greed he releases in them, Corvino is persuaded to prostitute his wife, Corbaccio to disinherit his son and Voltore to debase his profession by knowingly presenting a false case in court. The opposites of the princely virtues are presented in *Volpone* – pride, intemperance (in the form of bad temper), greed, sexual licence, envy, indulgence, irreverence, dishonour, violence, deceit – and are enacted at excessive levels.

Three other moral schemas had become part of the automatic thinking about how men should behave toward each other.

The Seven Corporal Works of Mercy

1. To tend the sick
2. To feed the hungry
3. To give drink to the thirsty
4. To clothe the naked
5. To harbour the stranger
6. To minister to prisoners
7. To bury the dead

Bateman's gloss to the engraving *Of Charitie* is virtually a verbatim repetition of the Corporal Works. Charity is

> to fede the hungry, to clothe the naked, to harbour the harbourless, & lodge the stranger, to visite the sicke, and to relieve the prisoners and poor afflicted members of Christe, this is the dueties of all faithfull people.

Ripa's allegory for Prodigality similarly has a woman bearing the classical symbol of the Horn of Cornucopia, but this time the woman spills out its contents carelessly and is blindfold too. This is thoughtless waste not sensible magnanimity.

The Seven Spiritual Works of Mercy

1. To convert the sinner
2. To instruct the ignorant
3. To counsel those in doubt
4. To comfort those in sorrow
5. To bear wrongs patiently
6. To forgive injuries
7. To pray for the living and the dead

The Seven Gifts of the Holy Ghost

1. Counsel
2. Fear of the Lord
3. Fortitude
4. Piety
5. Understanding
6. Wisdom
7. Knowledge

Bateman's depiction *Of Wisdome* alludes to a parable. It shows two houses, one solidly built on rock, the other a rickety hovel about to collapse. The former represents 'the stedfaste belief of the faythfull'. The house built on sand is 'the church of Antichrist and all popishe preaching'.

These schemas all officially disappeared at the Reformation, but were still in people's heads and hearts, becoming absorbed into Protestant thinking, particularly in relation to social responsibilities. These are the positives by which the sinful onstage action would be judged by the contemporary audience. Volpone endorses Mosca's laudatory assertion:

> You loathe the widow's, or the orphan's tears
> Should wash your pavements; or their piteous cries
> Ring in your roofs. (1.1.49–51)

Widows and orphans are regularly used as icons of those who need the help of the rich. Volpone's detachment from social responsibility is focused sharply here.

Though the fun of clever deceptions, pleasure at seeing the ills of the time identified and criticized and the desire to see how the intriguing complications of the plot would work out are probably the dominant feelings the audience had in watching the play, the moral values of the time would persistently be operative as the audience watched and judged.

Chapter 5

KINGSHIP

Now what shall I say about the courtiers? For the most part they are the most obsequious, servile, stupid and worthless creatures, and yet they're bent on appearing foremost in everything.

(Erasmus, 176)

... the aim of the courtier is to make his prince virtuous.

(Castiglione, 320)

They do abuse the king that flatter him:
For flattery is the bellows blows up sin.

(*Pericles*, 1.2.39–40)

Volpone, of course, is not a king. Nor is he a governor. He has no public role to play in Venice, is not a senator or magistrate. But he is a magnifico (a member of the better sort), a member of the leading rank, the governing class and therefore, though he only has responsibility for the governance of his household, should act and be seen to act as an example to other citizens of the Republic. He has no trading links or other 'common way' of making money:

.... I use no trade, no venture;
I wound no earth with ploughshare; fat no beasts
.... Have no mills ......
....
I blow no subtle glass; expose no ships
....
I turn no moneys, in the public bank;
Nor usure private – (1.1.33–40)

He is then simply a man of inherited wealth who is not involved in any of the usual commercial ventures for which Venice was famous and which enriched her fabulously. The leading families of the city often had landed estates on the mainland of the Veneto and made money by selling farm produce in the city's markets. They did not, of course, get their own hands calloused by such work. They had stewards and tenant farmers to do that. They owned olive oil mills and glass factories, and were presidents of banking concerns, much as English aristocrats were beginning to do as land values dropped throughout the seventeenth century. Volpone does none of this. He is a decadent, idle libertine who indulges in a series of confidence tricks to enrich himself. He shows no inclination to do public work of any sort. He festers in his *palazzo* letting his servant do the work of luring in his prey. In this he reflects the idleness and corruption of many of the better sort in Renaissance Europe.

A persistent theme in the work of all dramatists at this time was the exposing of the conduct of the top layer of society, the political nation (or rather the only rank with access to political place). The concern of playwrights like John Marston, Thomas Middleton, Thomas Dekker and Ben Jonson is a reflection of the growing anxieties people of all levels felt about the disconnection of the monarch and growing numbers of the aristocracy and gentry from the lifestyles and difficulties of the other two degrees, particularly the commons. Political, social and religious theory was clear about the duties of the better sort in regard to their role as guardians or shepherds of the poor. Glaringly evident is Volpone's selfish, narcissistic detachment from the outer community. He is solely focused on the pursuit of his own pleasures and goals. As often in the city comedies and in Shakespeare's and Jonson's work, self-rule is the central question. In Volpone's case it is his misrule of himself that is foregrounded. His greed, his covetousness and his self-centredness (a form of pride) immediately place him in a state of sin. Corbaccio, Voltore, Corvino and Mosca too fail to match the expectations of proper conduct. Each fails to behave as demanded of their role and all fail to match the Christian model with which all Elizabethans and Jacobeans were fully conversant. The reformed church, the Church of England, had since 1547, promulgated a series of homilies that laid down clearly the moral guidelines for all Anglicans. There were 33 by 1563. These homilies were to be read or preached in all churches throughout England. They were intended to address some theological issues but also to offer moral instruction. Essentially they were laying down the ground rules of the new church. The 1563 homily 'Against Idleness' declares,

> Forasmuch as man, being not born to ease and rest, but to labour and travail, is by corruption of nature through sin so far degenerated and grown out of kind, that he taketh idleness to be no evil at all, but rather a commendable thing, seemly for those that be wealthy [...] is greedily imbraced of most part of men, as agreeable to their sensual

affection, and all labour and travail is diligently avoided, as a thing painful and repugnant to the pleasure of the flesh; it is necessary to be declared unto you, that, by the ordinance of God [...] every one ought, in his lawful vocation and calling, to give himself to labour; and that idleness, being an intolerable evil; to the intent that [...] ye may diligently flee from it, and [...] earnestly apply yourselves, every man in his vocation, to honest labour and business.[1]

The sermon makes it clear that work involves not simply 'handy labour', that is, physical, bodily employment, but also

governing the common weal publicly, or by bearing public office or ministry, or by doing any common necessary affairs of his country, or by giving counsel, or by teaching and instructing others, or by what other means soever he be occupied, so that a profit and benefit redound unto others, the same person is not to be accounted idle.[2]

Idleness is the deadly sin of Sloth and 'idleness is never alone, but hath always a long tail of other vices hanging on, which corrupt and infect the whole man [...] that he is made at length nothing else but a lump of sin'.[3] The conclusion is direct: 'idleness, the mother of all mischief'.[4] Contemporary proof of this idleness among the better sort is Viscount Conway's definition of a gentleman: 'We eat and drink and rise up to play and this is to live like a gentleman; for what is a gentleman but his pleasure?'[5]

As a consequence of this perennial concern about the disengagement of the better sort from their social duty an extensive literature developed focusing on the proper upbringing of all who were destined to govern. Renaissance humanist writers were particularly exercised by this matter, but its history stemmed from long ago.[6] Erasmus's *The Education of a Christian Prince* (published 1516) had great influence throughout Europe. In England concern over training men for public office and social leadership had a

---

1 *The Two Books of Homilies* (ed. J. Griffiths), 516.
2 *The Two Books of Homilies*, 517.
3 *The Two Books of Homilies*, 519.
4 *The Two Books of Homilies*, 524.
5 Cited in Lawrence Stone, *The Crisis of the Aristocracy*, 27.
6 Plato's *Republic* is the starting point (much referenced in James I's *Basilikon Doron*), but others took up the theme – Xenophon (*Cyropaedia*), Isocrates (*Oration To Nicocles*), Cicero (*De Officiis*), Seneca (*De Clementia*), John of Salisbury (*Policraticus*, 1159), St Thomas Aquinas (*De regimine principum*, c. 1265), Erasmus (*Education of a Christian Prince*, 1516), Niccolò Machiavelli (*Il Principe*, 1532).

history going back at least to King Alfred's translation of Pope Gregory the Great's *Pastoral Care* which comments on the duties and responsibilities of those in governing roles. More contemporary with Jonson are Sir Thomas Elyot's *The Boke Named the Governour*, the successive editions of *The Mirrour for Magistrates* (1574, 1578, 1587, 1610) and James I's *The True Law of Free Monarchies* and *Basilikon Doron* (both 1598). James I's works reflect the common thinking on ruler and rulers. Relevant too as a handbook for the development of refined accomplishments and manners in courtiers is Baldassare Castiglione's *Il Cortegiano* (*Book of the Courtier*, 1528, translated by Thomas Hoby, 1561). These, and many sermons and pamphlets on the subject, indicate contemporary anxiety about what was suitable educational material, what was a workable stepped programme and above all how to properly train the minds and conduct of young men of rank. The education debate was not just about assimilating facts or developing skills. It was set within a basic belief that upbringing should be moral and the aim should be the production of a virtuous Christian prince. The term 'prince' applied to any ruler of a state (be they a duke, count, bishop and so forth) and all the way down the governing hierarchy to minor gentry acting as the 'prince' or leader of their community (comprising their household, estate and surrounding villages). It applied as well to fathers and heads of commercial enterprises. The alternative word used was 'governor' and comprised anyone in a governing, controlling role. Essential to the argument about what children should learn and how they learn, is the belief that nurture will not work if a person's nature is against it and that some types of personality resisted learning how to behave according to the Renaissance idea of the cultured civilized gentleman.

Magnifico he may be, but a gentleman Volpone is not. James I's handbook for a prince, *Basilikon Doron*, opens with an orthodox declaration that immediately places Volpone in the wrong:

> he cannot bee thought worthie to rule and commaund others, that cannot rule [...] his owne proper affections and unreasonable appetites, [...] Neither can [...] his Government succeed well with him [...] as coming from a filthie spring, if his person be unsanctified. (1)

Volpone has polluted his own household, and his greed (through the deception he plays, pretending to be old and dying) has tempted others into tainting their own lives and those close to them. Corvino's corruption affects his wife's life (though not her essential virtue), Corbaccio disregards his expected paternal affection, and Voltore betrays the expected probity of his profession. In reality, all of them reflect Jonson's cynical view of the fallen state of contemporary society. The matter of government – of people, of self – is common to all

Shakespeare's work. Kingship is inevitably an explicit theme in the history plays. Popular audiences seemed insatiable for dramas revisiting the English past, displaying the fortunes of heroes and villains, plotters arrested and executed, monarchs succeeding or failing. The stories of Henry V, King John, Richard III and Richard II were popular subjects that Shakespeare was to rework in his own way. The fall of kings was endlessly fascinating and the history genre continued popular at the Swan and Rose theatres even into the 1600s when other venues and other writers, doubtful and discontented about the running of public affairs and the direction in which society seemed to be going, turned to topical satire to voice their anxieties. Reading or watching the many chronicle plays infesting the stage, leads inevitably to the conclusion that though kings are theoretically honoured as God's vice-regents on earth, in practice history shows them as persistently opposed, plotted against, harried from battle to battle, disrespected, often removed from the throne and violently disposed of. Jonson was less drawn to history drama, though his two tragedies (*Sejanus* and *Catiline*) do focus on failed rulers. His social comedies, however, highlight in different ways the personal failings of others who have a duty to rule at a lower level and his work in general, like Shakespeare's, is concerned with the consequences of people not ruling themselves. Volpone is steeped in sin – greed, pride, false witness, lust, sloth. At the basic personal level each man was responsible for his own soul and responsible for maintaining his own virtue. As Phillip Stubbes put it, 'Is it not written, *unusquisque portabit suum onus*? Every one shall beare his owne burden'.[7] The vicissitudes inciting the drama in *Volpone* are not of a public nature but are made public, firstly to the audience and then to the judges in court – the sins paraded are all personal, but public virtue and probity originated at the private individual level. The consequence of unrepented sin was dire: 'the soule that sinneth shall dy'.[8] Jonson was no zealous Puritan, but would have probably agreed with Stubbes's analysis of society in England:

> notwithstanding that the Lorde hath blessed that lande with the knowledge of his truth above all other lands in the worlde, yet is there not a people more abrupte, wicked, or perverse, living upon the face of the earth.[9]

The ruler who organized his or her private life according to the prescriptions of the Bible and classical models and applied those values in public life had a

7 *The Anatomie of Abuses* (1583), 23.
8 *The Anatomie of Abuses*, 23.
9 *The Anatomie of Abuses*, 22.

good chance of ruling well. From his opening lines Volpone is seen to subvert the requirements of a Christian life, putting his own selfish ends before his duty, perverting worship of God into worship of gold. Good kings can be undermined by evil men, but evil rulers undermine themselves. Weak kings, however virtuous, can be misled by devious lords just as Mosca encourages his master into deeper and deeper sin. Bad kings have nasty ends, being shown as unworthy of their role, either on personal or political grounds. *Volpone* differs from many orthodox comedies in that we are hardly aware of the fortuitous outcomes for Bonario and Celia, because we are so relieved at the well-deserved punishment of the protagonists and their equally greedy victims.

Charismatic rulers generated powerful displays of patriotic loyalty and provoked a similar response in audiences when their stories were dramatized, but by the end of Elizabeth's life a general cynicism seemed to attach to real-life leaders (nobles and monarch). A strong leader's decline provokes consideration of failings that would be diplomatically ignored while the ruler's strength was feared. Elizabeth's death precipitated many long-repressed fears. The chronicle plays crowding the early public stage reflected not just an interest in rethinking the nation's past. They also sublimated contemporary anxieties about stability, masked and made palatable by dead personae and long-gone events. The approaching end of the century released many superstitious fears of apocalypse and gloomy anticipation of the new era inexorably coming. At Elizabeth's death there was considerable anxiety about the new monarch. Initial relief that James promised to be a good king was encouraged by his apparent readiness to engage with the concerns voiced in numerous petitions handed to him as he progressed south to London, his setting up of the Hampton Court Conference to address divisive religious issues and the reissuing of his principles of monarchy embodied in *Basilikon Doron*. The relief did not last long as James revealed his true nature as opposed to his declared views. His short-tempered authoritarianism, combined with his laziness, seemed in many respects not dissimilar to Elizabeth's shortcomings. People from all ranks of society began to fear that disengagement from pressing social problems had spread into the highest level of the pyramid of power. These fears transferred into negative representations of magistrate figures. Jonson's *Sejanus* and the numerous revenge tragedies do not portray leaders as divine or their courts and advisers as anything other than basely human, grasping and unscrupulous. Roman history and recent Italian city-state politics afforded a useful means of dealing with current English concerns under the mask of foreign settings. The question of government is not confined to the history plays. It is present too in Shakespeare's four great tragedies with a focus on the qualities that may enable proper or improper governorship of self or polis.[10] Be that polis a household, a city or a nation, the control of emotions, appetites and vices (and the consequences of not doing so) is at the heart of Jonson's drama too. Such serious concerns and outcomes are only minimally relevant here – since Volpone has no public responsibility his fall affects only himself – but as the comic complexities proliferate and the grim laughter mounts there are niggling questions that keep looming in the shadows. Jonson's plays focus on the personal politics and morality of small 'courts' and individual relationships. With restrictions on what aspects of contemporary life could be presented and with portrayal of the monarch prohibited, indirection was the only means. *Volpone*, while not a history play, is a study of faulty governorship (Volpone), faulty self-governorship (Volpone, Voltore, Corvino, Corbaccio, Mosca), faulty parenthood (Corbaccio), an inept judiciary and an exposure of a flawed society obsessed with acquiring material goods.

5.1 Preparation for Rule

In order to understand how people in the 1600s thought about princely conduct, the work of two writers on the subject is worth considering. They implicitly precipitate comparisons with the personal misrule of the characters in the play. Tudor conceptions of preparation for rule were dominated by Sir Thomas Elyot's *The Boke Named the Governour* (1531). The next generation would also have James I's *The True Law* and *Basilikon Doron*. Their thinking is in line with orthodox political philosophy and indeed echo Elyot in many ways. Elyot asserts the need of 'one souerayne gouernour [...] in a publike weale', but acknowledges the need for councillors and a nationwide group of 'inferior governours called magistratis'.[11] Volpone does not have such a role. Indeed, he seems to have no specific role in society. Like so many of the better sort in Jacobean England he has nothing to do – not even an estate to run. He lives only for himself. Was he thought unfit for public life? From what we see of his character he possibly was considered unfit. The basis for rule at any level is the proper upbringing of 'the chylde of a gentilman which is to have auctorite in the publike weale'. Elyot discusses lengthily the curriculum for this education because 'gentyllmen in this present time be not equall in doctrine to th'ancient noble men', due to 'the pride, avarice, and negligence of parentes', snobbery and a lack of teachers. Elyot complains that gentlemen

10 City-state (Greek). In theology, morality and political theory a person was seen as a state, governed well or ill.
11 All quotes from Elyot come from the 1970 Scolar Press unpaginated facsimile reprint.

believe 'it is a notable reproche to be well lerned'. The better sort of families pay high wages for skilled cooks or falconers, but not for a tutor to educate their child and inculcate virtue. Just what sort of education Volpone received we are not told, but his language is full of classical allusions and rhetorical embellishments. He displays the standard classical knowledge of gods and goddesses, so it is not his education that is at fault but the application of it in daily conduct. How true this was of young elite men in England. Girls were, by and large, chaperoned. Sons, away at university or roaming free in London, were an altogether more difficult problem. Clearly Volpone has been allowed as a youth to do the same, whether in Venice or elsewhere. He would have learned vice at home as easily as in another city. Venice had a well-established and deserved reputation for sexual laxness and for providing opportunities for other vices.

The general qualities needed by any man who was to govern at any level were prudence, industry, circumspection and modesty. Monarchs required comeliness in language and gesture, dignity in deportment and behaviour, honourable and sober demeanour, affability, mercifulness, placability, humanity, benevolence and liberality, well-selected friends, sharp discernment of the 'diversity of flatterers', a sense of justice, personal fortitude and 'the faire vertu pacience'. Volpone displays none of these; he has become a swollen monster of greed. From Greek and Roman comedy the monomaniac was a stock figure of comedy. Elyot recommends a set of passion-controlling virtues – abstinence, continence, temperance, moderation, sobriety, sapience (wisdom) and understanding. These requirements, echoing the Seven Virtues and the Works of Mercy, are very demanding, but Volpone fails to measure up to any of them. If Mosca is to be believed, his master has spawned a number of illegitimate children. This sexual predation, passed off as sowing their wild oats, was a frequent accusation laid at the feet of profligate young elite men (and not only young men), summed up in the contemporary adage 'untill everyone hath two or three bastards a peece, they esteeme him no man'.[12] Privilege, power and the money that comes with them, brought responsibilities and responsibilities mean sacrifice – of time and money. Has Volpone endowed any schools, made donations to a hospital? Does he have a list of dependent charity cases he regularly visits and helps? This was what was expected of a man in his position.

For Elyot, it is the governor's role to keep just harmony between the 'comunaltie' ('the base and vulgare') and those with honour and dignities (titles and responsibilities). Maintaining order is vital. The 'discrepance of degrees' (differences of ranks) is part of 'the incomprehensible maiestie

---

12 Quoted in Giles Milton, 201.

of God'. 'Take away ordre [...] what shulde then remayne? [...] Chaos. [...] perpeyuall [perpetual] conflicte [...] vniuersall dissolution'. This has an ideological affinity with Ulysses's degree speech in *Troilus and Cressida*. Elyot asserts that the hierarchies of Heaven are reflected on earth – the elements have their 'spheris' and men do not all have the same gifts from God. Potters cannot administer justice, and ploughmen and carters 'shall make but an feble answere to an ambassadour'.

Central to the situation as viewed by most orthodox Englishmen is that a ruler who subverted normative hierarchy, God's order, brings disruption to the whole chain of being. Though the scope of Volpone's actions are restricted to his own household (distorted and abnormal as that is), they spread (through the captators) into the world outside and affect the families of Corvino and Corbaccio. This disorder is metaphorically reflected in the human distortions with which the play is filled. Volpone, instead of being an exemplar of contagious benevolence is the source of sinfulness in others.

Key to the infant education of men destined to authority is that their early years be lived in a milieu of virtue, that the language and behaviour of mothers, nurses and maids be irreproachable.

At seven boys should be removed from 'the company of women' and tutored by 'an auncient & worshipfull man' with grave demeanour, gentle manners and impeccable morality. Then began a classics course that would develop rhetorical skills and perfect their Latin and the fluency and accuracy of their English. Elyot does not exclude physical exercise from his regimen, recommending hunting, hawking, dancing, wrestling, running, swimming and weapons training – in moderation. This is standard Renaissance elite male education. Elyot deplores the tendency of noble families to halt their children's education at 14 and 'sufre them to live in idelnes'. He believes education is a lifelong process and is essential for the production of governors if they are to resemble Plato's philosopher-king. James deprecated the tyrannical distortion of the state to suit the monarch, though both he and Elizabeth regularly did just that. Gentlemen should be 'trayned in the way of vertue' as Elyot recommended, and avoid the usual high-end lures of gluttony, avarice, lechery, swearing and dicing. Elyot exhorts young men to 'lerne wisdom & fal nat' [do not fall into sin] and abide by Christian precepts of behaviour, for 'from god only procedeth all honour' and God 'shal examine your dedes & serch your thoughtes'.

Since no one man can know all that is happening in a realm, kings need reliable deputies to act as his eyes, ears, hands and legs. The body image was often invoked. The nation was 'the body politic': the head was the monarch; the major organs were the nobility; and the hands, legs and muscles were the labouring part of society. All had a job to do and if one part did not work properly the whole became less effective. Such subsidiary governors (courtiers, councillors/counsellors, magistrates) should be men 'superiour in condition or haviour [...] [and] vertue'. Elyot demands they have 'their owne reuenues certeine, wherby they have competent substance to lyve without taking rewardes: it is likely that they wyll not be so desirous of lucre' [lucre = money]. This defence against bribery had disappeared by the time Jonson wrote *Volpone*, but the jobbery, corruption and greed that were standard at court are not explored. The play's focus is not a court (other than the grotesque one that comes to pretend homage to the fake invalid), though the trial scenes suggest that judicial procedure is as much prone to self-interest and stupidity as is shown in the streets with Sir Pol's multiple misunderstandings and the gullibility of the crowd gathered to hear Scoto's pseudomedical patter. Outside the play's fiction, in real life, two generations of luxurious living and extravagance had left many high-status English families financially embarrassed. The unseemly scrabble for lucrative posts, the lobbying for monopolies, cringing subservience to the queen and then the new king (or anyone who could advance your fortunes) and a readiness to offer and accept bribes were ways to help recoup family fortunes. This predatoriness is echoed in the universal scavenging displayed in *Volpone*.

5.2 A King's View of His Office

Volpone's personal misrule (of himself and his network of human contacts) is contextualized by a real king's contribution to conduct literature on the role and nature of kingship. *Basilikon Doron* was structured as an advice book to his son, Henry, Prince of Wales. It is in three books: 'Of a King's Christian Duty towards God', 'Of a King's Duty in his Office' and 'Of a King's Behaviour in Indifferent Things'. ('Indifferent' means matters relating to private time.) The first section, about a king's duty to follow the tenets of Christianity, establishes strongly the idea of kings as God's representatives. This becomes a running motif throughout. Many ideas parallel Elyot and there are verbal echoes of the earlier work. Marginal notes indicate how much the book owes to Plato's *Republic* and Cicero's seminal work, *De Officiis*, the common source for books on the perpetual need to remind the governing ranks what their function in society was.

Basilikon begins with an abstract of the 'Argument' in sonnet form:

> GOD giues not Kings the stile of Gods in vaine,
> For on his throne his sceptre doe they swey:
> And as their subjects ought them to obey,
> So Kings should feare and serve their God againe.

If then ye would enjoy a happy raigne,
Obserue the statutes of your heauenly King,
And from his Law, make all your Lawes to spring:
Since his Lieutenant here ye should remaine,
Reward the iust, be steadfast, true, and plaine,
Represse the proud, maintaining aye the right,
Walk always so, as euer in his sight,
Who guards the godly, plaguing the prophane:
And so ye shall in Princely vertue shine,
Resembling right your mightie King Diuine.

Overlapping the belief that kingship was divinely sanctioned with the image of God's 'Lieutenant here', the king almost becomes divine. Few Elizabethans or Jacobeans questioned that rule should be monarchical or doubted the continuing English system should have one-person government, but more and more they questioned kingship's divinity, the relationship between ruler and ruled and what should be the limits to princely authority.

Increasingly as Elizabeth's reign reached its end such questions were asked more urgently. It is usually assumed divine right was universally accepted. It was and was not. The unthinking mass accepted that the king – a distant figure of power and awe to them – was like a god on earth. Largely they were voiceless, but others spoke for traditional beliefs. Robert Filmer formalized these in *Patriarcha*. Written in the 1620s (published posthumously in 1680), it summarizes the accumulated ideology of divine right. Filmer believes the model monarchical state is founded on the idea of familial patriarchy and asserts Adamic dominion established by God (in Genesis) as the origin of patriarchy and kingship. As fathers rule the domestic polis, so do kings rule the nation state. Elizabeth's death was shortly to foreground discussions focused on the complex concept of divine right and how kings should govern. The justificatory line of argument went as follows: God made Adam lord of all creation, with dominion over his wife, family and the fruits of the earth. Male rule, therefore, was divinely sanctioned. Kings had similar incontrovertible, unopposable rule, reigning like the King of Heaven – autocratic and unquestionable. Disagreement was a sin against God, against nature.

Thus bulwarked against opposition, monarchy and patriarchy became firmly embedded in society and their power developed. Kings had absolute power over life and property, could have people imprisoned, executed or pardoned, declare war, make peace, levy taxes, regulate trade, charter markets, issue licenses for manufacture, legitimize bastards and send people to the Tower. Their will was law and the law bent to their will. Regal proclamations were made with the mantra 'The king wills it'. Laws were only passed if similarly authenticated. The monarch nominated government officers, bishops, judges and peers. His or her power was absolute, his or her favour vital. James I said, 'Kings are called Gods by the prophetical King Dauid, because they sit vpon GOD his Throne in the earth'.[13]

As already quoted, *Basilikon's* Book the First opens with an orthodox declaration that immediately places Volpone in the wrong:

> he cannot bee thought worthie to rule and commaund others, that cannot rule [...] his owne proper affections and unreasonable appetites, so can he not be thought worthie to governe a Christian People [...] that [...] feareth not and loveth not the Divine Majestie. Neither can [...] his Government succeed well with him [...] as coming from a filthie spring, if his person be unsanctified. (1)

This was an age much concerned with sin/virtue and right/wrong conduct. Comedy as a genre was particularly open to criticism as presenting immoral behaviour without sufficiently disapproving of that behaviour. However, a tendency to judge would have been more insistent in the minds of a Jacobean audience than today. To make moral judgements of the actions of the play is not to diminish the humour of it. To consider those serious issues that shadow its action is rather to enhance it and increase its underlying and unavoidable seriousness.

Book the First stresses the need for kingly piety and a life lived (as an example to his court and people) according to the demands of Christianity: virtue, self-control, respect for and obedience to scripture, conscience and faith ('the Golden Chaine that linketh the Faithfull Soule to Christ' 9). The series of guiding precepts are the following: 'wrest not the World to your owne appetite' (4); 'The summe of the Law is the Tenne Commandements' (6); 'wisely [...] discerne [...] betwixt the expres Commaundment and Will of God in his Word and the invention and ordinance of Man' (15); and 'kythe [show] more by your deedes then by your wordes the love of Vertue and hatred of Vice' (16). Volpone rather shows his vices through his deeds, has no virtues and seems to hate virtue anyway.

Book the Second, 'A King's Duty in his Office', links the lesson of being a good Christian to the prince's second calling – being a good king. This office is discharged through 'justice and equitie' (fairness), achieved by 'establishing and executing good lawes' and 'by your behaviour in your own person, and

---

13 *The Trew Law of Free Monarchies*, 64, in *King James VI and I: Political Writings*. The allusion is to Psalm 82:6.

with your servants, to teach your people by your example: for people are naturally inclined to counterfaite (like Apes) their Princes manners' (17–18). Mosca certainly seems energized by Volpone's conduct and outdoes him in duplicity and criminal inventiveness.

James defines the difference between a true king ('ordained for his people') and a tyrant (who 'thinketh his people ordained for him, a pray to his passions and inordinate appetites', 18). A good king 'employeth all his studie and paines, to procure and maintaine […] the well-fare and peace of his people […] as their naturall father and kindly maister […] subjecting his owne private affections and appetites to the weale and standing of his subjects' (18–19). Volpone is a model for his 'people', but a bad one, an evil and immoral one. James warns that good new laws are always being needed to deal with 'new rising corruptions' (20) and that 'a Parliament is the honourablest and highest judgement […] as being the Kings heade Courte' (21). He constantly called Parliament when he needed it to vote him money and regularly left the country in the charge of his Privy Council while he gallivanted off hunting for days on end. James did not deal with the old or new corruptions that surrounded him, did not settle the country 'by the severitie of justice' (22), but left in place the institutional corruption of many judges and lawyers. He did not 'embrace the quarrel of the poore and distressed' (26). Neither did he live up to the precept that you should 'governe your subjects, by knowing what vices they are naturally most inclined to, as a good Physician' (27). Elizabeth often went on long, meandering progresses, neglecting her political duties and avoiding addressing difficult problems. She had a similar contempt for Parliament as a threat to her absolutism. She did little to alleviate the hardships of the poor, but did make herself visible to her people. Her readiness to meet them, while she never relinquished her view that she was a lofty, divinely ordained being, nevertheless encouraged great love and loyalty. Superficially Volpone has a loyal household, but Mosca always has his own interests at heart.

When he came to power James simply found the English situation too complex and deeply ingrained, gave up trying to reform either court or country on the lines of Basilikon (if he had ever intended to) and, hypnotized by the immensely increased disposable income the English crown gave him, stopped bothering to be a good king and enjoyed the ritual, the status and the luxury. The failure to see that privilege, power and luxury come with responsibilities would lead James's other son, Charles, into civil war. Instead, James's court became a byword for the sort of greed that so completely permeates Volpone.

James never got to grips with any of the underlying social problems he inherited from Elizabeth, seeming to let the nobility act as they pleased, despite his admonitions in Basilikon about repressing aristocratic pride and supporting the poor. Elizabeth, in contrast, kept her nobility well in hand.

Echoing Elyot, James advises, 'Acquaint your selfe [...] with all the honest men of your Barrones and Gentlemen' (34) for 'vertue followeth oftest noble blood'(35) and such men 'must be your armes and executers of your lawes' (35). These words express the common belief that the nobility are born innately virtuous. This view, promulgated by the nobility, ignores both original sin (the belief that all men are born sinful) and the daily evidence of aristo-gentry misconduct. James's recommendation 'bee well acquainted with the nature and humours of all your subjects [...] once in the yeare to visit the principall parts of the country' (40) was not something he did. After reading Polydore Vergil's *Anglica historia* James agrees that a king's actions determined his country's fate.[14] The image of a 'filthie spring' polluting the stream (a ruler's corruption corrupting the country) occurs frequently in contemporary drama. Volpone is the 'filthie spring' which precipitates the latent sin in others.

The gap between precept and practice is made wider and more ironic when James discusses a prince and his court as exemplars:

> It is not enough to a good King, by the sceptre of good lawes well excute to governe, and by force of armes to protect his people; if he joyne not therewith his virtuous life in his owne person, and in the person of his Court and companie: by good example alluring his subjects to the love of vertue, and hatred of vice. [...] all people are naturally inclined to followe their Princes example [...] let your owne life be a law-book and a mirrour to your people. (45)

This was achieved 'in the governement of your Court and followers' and 'in having your minde decked and enriched so with all virtuous qualities, that there-with yr [sic] may worthilie rule your people. For it is not enough that yr [sic] have and retaine [...] within your selfe never so many good qualities and virtues, except ye imploy them, and set them on worke, for the weale of them that are committed to your charge' (45). Care was crucial when appointing public officers who had responsibility for 'the weale of your people' (50). They should be men 'of knowne wisdome, honestie, and good conference [...] free of all factions and partialities: but specially free of that filthy vice of Flattery, the pest of all Princes' (51).

As regards personal kingly virtues, James echoes many of Elyot's recommendations. A prince should follow the four cardinal virtues with 'Temperance, Queene of all the rest' (62). The synonym for temperance used by both Elyot and James is 'moderation'. A king needs the quality of 'wise moderation [...] first commanding your selfe [...] in all your affections

14 *A History of England*, cited in *Basilikon*, 62.

and passions, [...] even in your most virtuous actions, [so you] make ever moderation to bee the chief ruler' (63). If civility, education and cultured behaviour are to be part of social-civic interaction, moderation is vital in assisting the repression of those aspects of man's nature that are disruptive to the moral profile of a state. After temperance comes justice: 'the greatest vertue, that properly belongeth to a Kings office' (63). 'Use Justice [...] with such moderation as it turne not in Tyrannie' (63). James specifies 'Clemencie, Magnanimitie, Liberalitie, Constancie, Humilitie, and all other Princely vertues' (64) as essential.

The important second book of *Basilikon Doron* finishes with a series of pertinent precepts: 'Embrace true Magnanimitie [...] thinking your offender not worthie your wrath, empyring over your owne passion, and triumphing in the commanding your selfe to forgive' (71): 'Foster true Humility [...] banishing pride' (71). He warns, 'Beginne not, like the young Lords and Lairds, your first warres upon your Mother [...] O invert not the order of nature, by judging your superiours' (72). Volpone has inverted the relationship which puts humility before pride. He puts acquisitiveness before simple living. He prioritizes his sexual desires over respect for a woman's refusal and her chastity. He seems clearly unfit for any public role in Venice. The benevolence humans can show is absent in *Volpone*. Nature is perverted/ inverted, the world turned upside down and the strength of greed and malice overwhelms any good the characters may have in them. Philip Stubbes declared, 'All wickedness, mischief, and sinne [...] springeth of our auncient enemie the devil, the inveterate corruption of our nature, and the intestine malice of our owne hearts'.[15] The characters at the heart of the plot are all representatives of the ruling degrees in Venice and England (a magnifico, a gentleman, a lawyer, a merchant). Each of them is poisoned through and through with intended malice, persistent greed, a blatant disregard for others and the agreed decencies of life. James concludes with the admonition 'exercise true Wisedome; in discerning wisely betwixt true and false reports' (74), reminiscent of Michel de Montaigne's comments on the misuse of words. Montaigne deplored the art of fine speaking as 'deceiving not our eyes but our judgement, bastardizing and corrupting things in their very essence' so that feelings are 'inflated with rich and magnificent words' by passing off lies as truth, by appearing honest while being deceiving.[16] Mosca and the legacy hunters all abuse language by using it so duplicitously.

Volpone's blandishments to Celia, trying to bribe her into a sexual liaison by offering a range of glamorous rewards, and all the lies the legacy hunters

---

15 *The Anatomie of Abuses*, 22.
16 'On the vanity of words', 343.

speak, display the intricacy and unreality of words, ideas and emotions that inflate feeling and distort reality by creating a new pseudoreality of rhetoric. To a Jacobean audience, knowing the Devil was the Father of Lies, the trick and counter-tricks at the heart of the play represent the way to Hell.

James I's final dictum ironically resonates with failings of the central characters: 'Consider that God is the author of all vertue, having imprinted in men's mindes by the very light of nature, the love of all morall virtues [...] preasse then to shine as farre before your people, in all vertue and honestie; as in greatnesse of ranke [...] as by their hearing of your lawes, both their eyes and their eares, may leade [...] them to the love of vertue, and hatred of vice' (75).

All plays were licensed by the Revels Office and registered at the Stationers' Office only once the government officials were sure the work contained nothing treasonable or heretical. The meaning of treasonable was elastically expanded to mean any criticism of the monarch. Direct representation of or critical reference to a reigning monarch was prohibited and removed from the script. The author could face imprisonment as Jonson well knew from experience.

As a leading writer of masques for the court, Jonson could ill afford to upset his employer. His peripheral acquaintanceship with some members of the Gunpowder Plot and his interrogation and the subsequent surveillance of his movements would have made Jonson doubly aware of the need to be careful in expressing his satire. Flawed leadership and satire of the ruling classes become very evident in all his post-1600 plays as in those of friends and colleagues.

Shakespeare often removed his plays from immediate identification with contemporary England, its court or its monarch, by time and setting. *Measure* is set in Vienna, *Lear* in pagan times, *Macbeth* in the medieval past (but showing the restoration of a legitimate line from which James I was descended), *Antony and Cleopatra* in the Roman era, *Timon of Athens* in Athens, *Coriolanus* in Rome, *Cymbeline* in pre-Christian Britain, *The Winter's Tale* in Sicily and Bohemia and *The Tempest* on a Mediterranean island. Jonson was much more ready to expose England's sins. His early comedies are set in Italy (though later brought up to date and set in England). His two historical-political pieces deal with Roman events. His later plays, *The Alchemist, Epicoene, Bartholomew Fair, The Devil Is an Ass*, address English failings head-on. The exception is *Volpone*. Whatever the locational or time-frame indirection, the themes were resonantly of contemporary relevance. Ultimately, *Volpone* is a devastating indictment of a contemporary society that was becoming obsessed with getting and spending, becoming detached at the higher levels from any sense of responsibility to the wider community and disregarding the expectations of religion and humanism. The critique of personal misrule aims at provoking thought and at a possible adjustment of values. It may have entertained its audience, but the play failed to reform the society it tried to scourge. History shows that human greed persisted and increased.

Chapter 6

PATRIARCHY, FAMILY AUTHORITY AND GENDER RELATIONSHIPS

6.1 Patriarchy and a Woman's Place

Yet will not I forget what I should be
And what I am, a husband: in that name
Is hid divinity.

('Tis Pity 4.3.135–7)

Gender relationships occupy a small part of the play, but when the matter does emerge it provides the turning point. Corvino's insistence that his wife obey his command to make herself sexually available to Volpone is not only the nadir of the merchant's ethical corruption but also incites the moment when Volpone attempts to rape Celia. This leads to the court case which eventually brings down the overreaching libertine. Mosca hoodwinks Corvino with the fiction that Volpone can only be preserved if a young woman 'lusty, and full of juice [lively, sexually alluring] sleep by him' (2.6.35). He clinches the matter by inventing a doctor, Signior Lupo (Mr Wolf), who has offered his daughter. The thought of being outdone in preparedness to assist persuades the merchant to offer Celia. Thus a father/daughter (Signior and Signorina Lupo) and husband/wife bond are subverted through the display of male dominance and disregard. Volpone regards Celia as sexual goods he can acquire, assuming that because of his wealth and rank she, as a mere merchant's wife, will agree readily to become his property. This belief by men of high degree that women of lesser status are willing sexual partners or if unwilling can be forced, was reinforced by long custom. Title, money and social power encouraged such thinking.

The matter of gender relationships is full of ambiguities, contradictions and inconsistencies. Two features are definite: theoretically men ruled, and in practice women often subverted male domination. Corvino, about to command his wife to let herself be used by Volpone, asserts,

Do not I know, if women have a will,
They'll do 'gainst all the watches o' the world? (2.7.8–9)

Just as some men readily enforced their will physically, so some women got what they wanted if they wanted it badly enough. Custom, doctrine and law made husbands and fathers heads of families. God ruled creation, kings ruled nations and fathers ruled the home. God punished sin, kings punished earthly crime and a man could beat his wife, his children and his servants. Custom recommended moderation in corporal punishment, advocating its avoidance if possible, but its support in law meant it could happen. Beating causing bodily harm was not allowed. There were abusive and violent men who caused serious injury, but they could be protected by an all-male legal system. Husbands were authoritarian figures whose word was law and the law supported men. St Paul authorized male dominance in the New Testament, *the* primary conduct book.

> Wives, submit yourselves unto your own husbands, as unto the Lord.
> For the husband is the head of the wife, even as Christ is the head of
> the church.[1]

Theoretically then, husbands were dominant and wives supposedly subordinate in all things – in legal status, physical strength, intelligence, virtue. Celia is an articulate, intelligent woman, but very much under her husband's thumb.

Patriarchy originates in Genesis when God makes man first, gives Adam dominion over all animals, then makes Eve out of Adam's rib and gives him rule over her. She is designed as 'an help meet' (Genesis 2:18) – a companion and assistant. When Adam is tempted by Eve to eat the apple God upbraids him for listening to his wife and acting according to her encouragement rather than His command against eating the forbidden fruit. This story, written by men and endorsing male superiority and rule, reflects the hierarchy of the chain of creation and shows how society was organized and reinforced by a misogynistic Catholic Church deeply suspicious of women. To the fallen Eve God says,

> I will greatly multiply thy sorrow […] in sorrow thou shalt bring forth
> children: and thy desire shall be to thy husband, and he shall rule
> over thee.[2]

1 Ephesians 5:22–3. See also I Corinthians: 11:3.
2 Genesis 3:16.

The seventeenth century saw female inferiority as predating the Fall. Made after Adam, Eve was always secondary. So were all women. The poet-satirist George Wither summed this up: 'The woman for the man was made/And not the man for her'.[3] Advising his son about marriage, James I quoted Genesis 2:23 (where Adam claims Eve is 'bone of my bone, and flesh of my flesh'), commenting on the institution as 'the greatest earthly felicite or miserie, that can come to a man, according as it pleaseth God to blesse or cursse the same'.[4] His advice is largely orthodox. Henry should marry within his own religion and rank. There is awareness of the partnership aspect of marriage but it is patriarchal:

> Treate her as your owne flesh, commaund her as her Lord, cherish her as your helper, rule her as your pupil, and please her in all things reasonable [...] Ye are the head, as she is your body: [...] your office to commaund, [...] hers to obey; but yet with such a sweete harmonie, as shee should be as readie to obey, as yee to commaunde [...] suffer her never to medle with the politick government of the common-weale, but hold her at the Oeconomick rule of the house; [...] yet all to be subject to your direction: keepe carefullie good and chaste companie about her; for women are the frailest sexe.[5]

Publicly, it was a man's world. Whatever the theory, whatever the biblical and legal support, the reality varied greatly. In defining gender roles and attitudes it is always important to remember, whatever the stereotypes, in practice matters could be different and women subverted patriarchy in many ways and in a variety of arenas. There had been some liberalizing of opinion under the new Anglican Church and as a result of humanism. There was a lively discourse about the nature and role of women, but the bulk of thinking conformed to the old-established view of male superiority and dominance.

The traditional medieval position on women still persisted into the Renaissance, despite some changes. Orthodoxy saw women as the origin of sin, the source of temptation. This 'man's world' derived authority from the Bible. Paul told wives to submit to their husbands and keep silent in church (Colossians 3:18). In I Timothy (2:8–12) he wrote,

> I will therefore that the men pray [...] Let the women learn in silence with all subjection. I permit not a woman to teach, neither to usurp authority over the man, but to be in silence.

3 *Hallelujah* (1641).
4 *Basilikon Doron*, 54.
5 *Basilikon*, 60–1.

The Bible's good women, the Virgin Mary and the church's array of female saints, were outweighed by evil women from scripture and history and the diatribes of the Church Fathers. The biased selection of biased texts built up formidable prejudice against the sex. Tertullian (c. 160–c. 225 AD), saw women as 'the devil's gateway'.[6] St John Chrysostom (c. 347–407 AD) claimed, 'from beholding a woman [we] suffer a thousand evils […] The beauty of woman is the greatest snare'. Clement of Alexandria (c.150–c. 215), went further: 'Every woman should be ashamed that she is a woman' for they are 'the confusion of men, an insatiable animal […] an eternal ruin'.[7] Male mistrust of female sexuality underlies much of the patriarchal system. It was a factor in the intermittent waves of witch trials and executions. The *Malleus Maleficarum* (The hammer of witches, 1496) declared, 'All witchcraft comes from carnal lust, which in women is insatiable'.[8] Women's main role was keeping the house and largely keeping to the house. Corvino is incandescent with wounded honour when he thinks Celia has shown herself in public by looking out of her window. Accused of flirting with Scoto and letting the crowd gaze at her, she has little to say other than to deny it. Her husband's attitude attitude reflects how the English thought Italian husbands guarded their women, keeping them mostly at home, restricting their public appearances. English wives were, as commented on by many foreign visitors, rather freer in their daily lives. Corvino's overreaction betokens his insecurity as regards their relationship. Though many merchant's wives were godly, chaste women, there is a stereotype in drama of the bored bourgeoise seeking thrills outside the house and outside the marriage.

In rural areas women helped in the fields, but many of their tasks were home based – cooking, feeding poultry, tending vegetable gardens, cleaning, making clothes. A shopkeeper's wife or daughter might occasionally help behind the counter, but saleable products (pastry, clothes, crafted items) were made by men (apprentices, journeymen, masters) and shop assistants were largely men. Women were barred from the professions, public life and higher education. The standard view was that women were intellectually feeble, unreliable, irrational, shrewish gossips unable to keep a secret, bad tempered, sexually voracious, endlessly demanding, never satisfied and would interrupt and take over any public/social meeting. A common image in medieval comic writing was that while the man worked and the servants kept the house, the wife gossiped with friends, gallivanted wasting money shopping or entertained her lover. This view persisted. It was generally believed women were overemotional

6 From *De Cultu Feminarum*.
7 Clement also advocated equality of the sexes and women being admitted to leading roles in the church.
8 *Malleus Maleficarum*, sec. 1.

and easily overheated sexually. Belief in the insatiability of the female sex drive reflects male insecurity and uncertainty over whether the child he is bringing up is indeed his own, fears related to questions of inheritance and keeping the family bloodline pure. It explains the obsession with the chastity of daughters and wives. A tainted daughter shamed the family, had little value in the marriage market and remained a drain on family finances. A wife who was 'loose i'the hilts' degraded the husband's public reputation and honour, wounded his personal esteem, cast doubt on his children's legitimacy and made him the butt of jokes about cuckolds and horns.[9] Proverbs 12:4 put it thus, 'A virtuous woman is a crown to her husband: but she that maketh ashamed is as rottenness in his bones'. Patriarchy's dominance explains why so many men had low opinions of women, treated them unsympathetically and as sex objects. Such views are voiced frequently among the rakish male characters crowding Elizabethan-Jacobean comedies, though Hamlet and Iago are misogynistic too. This loose-living, loose-tongued, bawdy brotherhood stretches from Lucio (*Measure for Measure*, 1604) through Willmore (Aphra Behn's *The Rover*, 1677) to innumerable libertines in later dramas and novels. Symbolizing the upper-rank male on the prowl to seduce anything in a petticoat, they parallel the corrupt and rapacious control the governing class had over most of the workings of society. The law, land ownership and politics had for centuries all been organized in favour of the male elite.

A counterbalancing philosophy offers the *gentils domna* (gentle and genteel lady) of courtly love, the beautiful but virtuous woman whose example civilizes brutish men. She has the self-effacing quiet of the confident but restrained woman, not the silence of a downtrodden creature. Celia speaks for this type of woman. She is not aggressively independent, not rhetorically polished, but is clear in her standpoint and articulate in voicing it. While Volpone spouts the ritualized, artificial cliché images of praise for her beauty and the opulent paradise he offers – the orthodox poetry of male devices to lure a woman into bed – she speaks out for virtue, for female choice of when and to whom she gives herself. Left onstage with the supposedly near-moribund Volpone, she bewails her fate and the state of male honour:

O God, and his good angels! whither, wither
Is shame fled human breasts? that with such ease,
Men dare put off your honours, and their own?
Is that, which ever was the cause of life [love],
Now placed beneath the basest circumstance?
And modesty an exile made, for money? (3.7.133–8)

9 The incestuously obsessed Duke Ferdinand in *The Duchess of Malfi*, 2.5.6.

Rejecting the exotic lifestyle Volpone offers, she asserts innocence as her only wealth and the only quality 'worth th'enjoying'. For her there is 'nought to lose beyond it' (3.7.209) and untouched by 'these sensual baits' she appeals to his conscience. He rejects the concept as relevant only to beggars and itemizes the luxury life to be lived with him. She makes a final appeal to his heart, to his respect for the 'holy saints, or heaven' (3.7.243) and as a last resort to his generosity in killing her rather than subject her to a life of shame. She would rather have her beauty disfigured than live without her honour; she is a woman then who puts virtue above fleshly pleasures and the glitter of high living, valuing honour above good looks. This appeal is no more effectual than that made to Corvino in denying she displayed herself at the window in order to excite the viewers or that she made in arguing against his order to give herself to Volpone.[10] Her principles are disregarded in a world where males rule and material gain supersedes spiritual qualities. She is caught between obedience to her husband and the higher duty of God's requirements. The husband who should protect her virtue is the very one using his authority to debase her. With no male parent or relative to guide her, she is at risk.

Some in the audience would expect and endorse her relenting and obeying her husband, on the grounds that a wife should obey under any circumstances. The libertines would support her giving herself on the grounds that sexual pleasure was worth more than morality. These would be men who thought drinking, gambling and whoring were the marks of a gentleman. They would regard her as foolish for making such a fuss about her honour. Unusually, but perhaps because she is only a merchant's wife, she has no females around her to encourage her in her decision. Nurses, maids, friends and female relatives are often on hand in plays to contribute their views in any dilemma. Celia has no one other than the husband who has already betrayed her.[11] The underlying message seems to be that however self-reliant, resilient, confident or virtuous you are you can still make mistakes, particularly if judgement is distorted by passion (like Corvino's passion for gain) and your action inhibited by hierarchy. Celia's faith is strong, the Bible her guide. Opposition to Volpone seems physically impossible. Bonario's rescue may be seen as pure luck, the intervention of Providence or the invention of the playwright.

---

10 Venetian courtesans customarily displayed themselves at a window like goods in a shop.

11 Corvino mentions her mother, sister and aunt as potential go-betweens to her 'lovers'. She remarks how little she actually goes out (2.6.40–8).

The 1571 *Book of Homilies* sermon on matrimony declared woman was 'a weak creature, prone to all weak affections and dispositions of the mind', indicating that the Anglican Church was essentially little different from Rome. Celia's heroic stand gives the lie to the church's blanket judgement of women. Greater respect for women, though still wary, emerged among the Puritans, who demanded moderation by both sexes. Puritanism was, however, still a minority sect. Theatre commonly reverted to stock types of females for their humour or dramatic value. The garrulous nurse in *Romeo and Juliet*, the witty but overwhelming Beatrice in *Much Ado* and the scheming unscrupulous Lady Macbeth follow other stereotypical lines. Another stock character from drama, the widow – either rampantly free or easily victimized – reflects the standard views of predatory female sexuality or foolish vulnerability and echoes anxieties about overhasty second marriage for women. Dynastic and financial concerns are involved. Family fortunes could quickly be lost to a predatory second husband and the children of the first union disposed of in marriage or simply sent to a faraway estate and neglected. The 'merry widow' was not just a comic figure. *Hamlet* and *The Duchess of Malfi* present tragic examples of the difficulties a second marriage could bring. In practice second marriages were common among both sexes and all classes. Moralists admitted that humankind was inordinately lustful, but since most moralists were male they tended to be more tolerant of male libidinousness and more critical of female failings.

Nevertheless, there are female figures in plays who display strength of character and readiness to suffer for their principles. They are, however, rare. The common stage stereotyping is of the calculating flirt/widow/bored wife on the lookout for material advancement through becoming the mistress of a rich man, or the gossipy girl of easy virtue with more sexual need than sense. Neither the wildfire spread of syphilis nor the widespread ecclesiastical condemnation of intercourse outside marriage as a deadly sin for both sexes curbed the natural lustfulness of either. With the blatant hypocrisy, chauvinism and prejudice that each sex brings to stereotyping the other, there was, on the male side, a double standard accepting young men fornicating indiscriminately and regarding possession of a mistress as a sign of manhood, while demanding chaste behaviour among their women. In *Volpone* the men are at fault, while Celia honours the sacrament of marriage and adheres to Christian morality. Young Jacobean women were not allowed much freedom of access to young men. They were kept at home much of the time and chaperoned in public. Fiction and real life showed how predatory men of any age could be and the church was abundantly clear about the ubiquity of the temptations of lust.

The orthodox husband-wife relationship is defined in William Shakespeare's early sex-war comedy *The Taming of the Shrew* (1593–4).[12] Petruchio, marrying in order to refill his coffers (as many did), announces to the assembled wedding guests,

> I will be master of what is mine own.
> She is my goods, my chattels: she is my house,
> My household stuff, my field, my barn,
> My horse, my ox, my ass, my anything. (3.2.229–32)

At the end of the play Kate supposedly defines the theoretically submissive role of the wife:

> Thy husband is thy lord, thy life, thy keeper,
> Thy head, thy sovereign – one that cares for thee,
> And for thy maintenance commits his body
> To painful labour both by sea and land,
> To watch the night in storms, the day in cold,
> Whilst thou li'st warm at home, secure and safe. (5.2.146–51)

She sees 'love, fair looks, and true obedience' as a duty a wife owes like that 'the subject owes the prince' and deprecates the rebellious wife seeking 'rule, supremacy, and sway'. Is this sincere or has she, like women before and since, discovered she can get all she wants by appearing submissive while secretly gaining control of the household and of him? This is the comic discrepancy inherent in the gender relationship. Man plays the master and to all intents and purposes is so publicly, while the woman pulls his strings behind the scenes. No background to the Celia–Corvino marriage is given. We do not know whether he is older than she or whether the marriage was arranged. The little shown suggests she is strongly repressed by him. In reprimanding her for showing herself at the window as Scoto addressed her, he is verbally abusive and threatens to

>   strike
> This steel into thee, with as many stabs,
> As thou wast gazed upon with goatish eyes (2.5.32–4)

He calls her 'whore' and 'Lady Vanity' and accuses her of encouraging the crowd and of killing his honour. The irony of this is shortly revealed when

---

12 A similarly orthodox view is voiced by the unmarried Luciana in *The Comedy of Errors* (1588–93) 2.1.

his own commands destroy his honour. With further ironic prolepsis he suggests she is a 'dealer' (that is, in the flesh trade) and wants to mount the mountebank.[13] In the very next scene it is he who is the dealer, loosing his wife to Volpone in the ludicrous belief it will revivify him and that in gratitude he will name Corvino as his heir. Irrational jealousy and suspicion go beyond sensible bounds when he declares he will block up the window and in the meantime put a chalk line on the floor

> o'er which, if thou but chance
> To set they desp'rate foot; more hell, more horror,
> More wild remorseless rage shall seize on thee,
> Than on a conjuror that had heedless left
> His circle's safety. (2.5.52–6)

Manipulation, deviousness, sheer bloody-mindedness and simple evil (their weapons in the sex war) were attributed to women in the social comedies of the 1590s/1600s. Celia displays none of those all-too-common failings. Unfortunately her character profile is broadly drawn rather than deeply detailed. Given little to say, she is simply projected as a virtuous woman much put on by an authoritarian but hypocritical husband claiming concern for his honour yet ready to besmirch his wife for money. Responding with quiet denial of his lurid accusations, she says nothing in reply to his threat to lock her into a chastity belt and confine her to the back of the house. Thomas Coryat described how Venetian 'gentlemen do even coope up their wives alwaies within the walles of their houses for feare of these inconveniences [...] So that you shall very seldome see a Venetian Gentleman's wife'.[14] The 'inconveniences' are the general air of sex in a city so full of courtesans, and the numbers of men who visited Venice and who might tempt or be tempted by sight of a lady they mistook for one of the 'licentious wantons'.[15] The English believed that Italian women were more easily aroused sexually because of the hot climate and that their men were therefore more readily suspicious of them and kept them locked or shut away.

While female tenderness and sensitivity are acknowledged by dramatists, misogyny is accurate in its definitions too. In Thomas Middleton's *A Mad*

13 Prolepsis is a verbal or situational device by which a development or outcome later in the narrative is anticipated, foreshadowed or hinted at in an earlier part of the story.

14 From Coryat's *Crudities* (1608), quoted in *Volpone* (ed. Philip Brockbank), 163.

15 'For they thinke that the chastity if their wives would be the sooner assaulted, and so consequently they should be capricornified' (Coryat, 162). 'Capricornified' means given horns like the zodiac sign, Capricorn the Ram. Given horns or cuckolded means made the victim of his wife's adultery.

World My Masters the superior cleverness of the courtesan Frank (Frances) Gullman is openly admitted by a country gentleman surreally named Penitent Brothel:

> The wit of man wanes and decreases soon,
> But women's wit is ever at full moon. (3.2.159–60)

and

> When plots are e'en past hope and hang their head,
> Set with a woman's hand, they thrive and spread. (3.2.246–7)

He is right. The aptly named Gullman (man fooler) lures into marriage Follywit, the heir of Sir Bounteous Progress.[16] Shakespeare's comic heroines – Beatrice, Rosalind, Viola, Portia – are similarly clever, inventive, resourceful women, but their virtue prevents them intending or doing evil. Lady Macbeth, Goneril and Regan (*King Lear*) are prime examples of devious women whose ambitions are ruthless and destructive. In the real world theory and practice diverge once again, diversifying into a variety of relationships. Every marriage was unique – some paralleled the orthodox model, in some the woman ruled unopposed, in most a compromise was negotiated or appropriated. There were happy marriages, arranged or not. Many men and women married only for fiscal or dynastic reasons. Slowly a shift was taking place that saw marriage as a partnership of companions, physically and spiritually. Lord Montagu advised his son, 'In your marriage looke after goodness rather than goodes'.[17] Traditionally men sought love and sexual relief outside marriage. This was the negative aspect of arranged marriages where there was no initial attraction and none developed afterwards. The Earl of Northumberland advised his son: 'As you must love, love a mistress for her flesh and a wife for her virtues'.[18] Some women took lovers and others sublimated their emotional needs through running estates and raising children, while their husbands attended court or parliament, joined the army or spent their time in usual male activities – hunting, gambling, drinking, theatregoing, whoring. Many marriages were based on separate lives, but many thrived on the love and respect that formed the new companionate marriage. Puritan pamphlet/sermon input to the marriage debate promoted the development of the helpmeet/companion element.

16 A gull was a fool, someone gullible.
17 Cited in Stone, *The Crisis of Aristocracy*, 615.
18 Stone, 614.

A play marking the emergence of the strong, independent woman is John Fletcher's *The Woman's Prize, or The Tamer Tamed* (1610). Appropriating Shakespeare's Petruchio, the shrew tamer, Fletcher has him tamed (or humanized) by his second wife, Maria. She outwits the standard chauvinistic male. She, no longer 'gentle' or 'tame', has 'a new soul':

> Made of a north wind, nothing but tempest,
> And like a tempest shall it make all ruins
> Till I have run my will out. (1.2.77–9)

Her sister advises abandoning her plan and accepting her expected sexual destiny. Maria is implacable:

> To bed? No, Livia, there be comets yet hang
> Prodigious over that yet. There is a fellow (Petruchio)
> Must yet before I know that heat – ne'er start wench –
> Be made a man, for yet he is a monster;
> Here must his head be. (1.2.101–5)

Where does she point? To herself as his head, her breast where his head must rest lovingly, or under her foot? She is being transgressive, though expressing something of the rebalancing of the gender roles of the time. Her cousin, Bianca, contextualizes Maria's stand:

> All the several wrongs
> Done by imperious husbands to their wives
> These thousand years and upwards strengthen thee!
> Thou hast a brave cause. (1.2.122–5)

To her this is an opportunity for extreme gender revenge. Maria's apparent goal is less extreme though radical enough – equality in marriage. She declares

> that childish woman
> That lives a prisoner to her husband's pleasure
> Has lost her making and becomes a beast
> Created for his use, not fellowship. (1.2.137–40)

This play contributes to the lively late sixteenth-/early seventeenth-century debate about just what women were like and what their place in society should be. *Volpone* largely refers to women in terms of the traditional whore image with the unique exception of Celia's steadfast goodness. Mosca claims that his master has sired 'some dozen or more' (1.5.44) bastards on marginalized females – beggars, gypsies, Jews, blackamoors – suggesting Venice had an underclass of vulnerable females just as in London. Though this is probably a fabrication it reflects the truth, the 'common fable' (the common story) that men of the so-called better sort did regularly sexually abuse young women of all types, especially the vulnerable. Their inconsiderate, indiscriminate conduct echoes the general attitude of men toward women, adding to the contemporary perception that sexual decadence was widespread, that figures for illegitimacy were rising alarmingly and that London was fast becoming as immoral as Venice. The church's crusade against fornication, its active prosecution of offenders – mostly women – did little to stem the rising tide of the sex trade. It was a feature that went in parallel with the rise of commerce in London and the rise of luxury and would persist throughout the subsequent centuries. It was part of the dark side of London life that Ben Jonson and others attacked yet did little to affect.

Opinion was mounting against arranged marriages forced for dynastic and material reasons (characteristic of royal and aristocratic unions) where there was no attraction or love. Arranged royal marriages were traditionally a facade only, sometimes fruitful, sometimes not, often becoming a union of separateness. There were exceptions, but the recent example of Henry VIII shows how personal choice too could be mistaken, especially when driven by an absolute will. Thomas Becon, in his *Golden Boke of Christen Matrimonie* (1542), describes couples trapped unhappily in arranged/forced marriages cursing 'their parents even unto the pit of hell for coupling them together', though there were also many who coped or even found happiness. Celia and Corvino do not fall into that last category. Despite her strength of belief she seems daunted and cowed by him, saying little in her defence. Anger distorts his thinking and he does not believe in his wife's virtue (perhaps judging the world by his own conduct). A weakness of her character (and a cause of her suffering) is that she only stands up for herself verbally, but retreats quickly. The self-effacing modesty of virtue and its minority status in decadent Venice is one reason why it takes so long for goodness to fight back in the play.

The sex drive is one of the primal impulses. As the usually coy Ophelia sings in her unrepressed madness,

> By Gis and by Saint Charity,
> Alack and fie for shame,
> Young men will do't if they come to't –
> By Cock they are to blame. (*Hamlet*, 4.5.58–61)

She might have added that young women will do it too, if they get the chance. Jacobean dramatists, particularly in the city comedies, present such women, but they also acknowledge and present women like Celia. In *A Midsummer Night's Dream*, Lysander has 'bewitch'd the bosom' of Hermia and 'stol'n the impression of her fantasy' with all the paraphernalia of young love ('bracelets of thy hair, rings, gauds, conceits,/Knacks, trifles, nosegays' 1.1.33–4). Volpone's 'love' tokens are much more sophisticated and decadent as befits a denizen of the most opulent, 'glorious [...] potent [...] renowned a city' in Europe.[19] Volpone asserts that he is smitten with Celia at first sight, is 'wounded', on fire, his liver 'melts', he has 'longing'. These are the traditional words of love poetry, but they are no more true than most of the claims in this play. What he feels is lust and greed – lust to possess her physically and greed to possess her as another material commodity. Love at first sight is a recurrent device in romances and comedies. Volpone feels lust at first sight, the gluttony of a jaded palate to possess young flesh. It was an old story the audience would identify as a 'common fable' in London. Courtesans might not be as common there as reputedly in Venice, but there was plenty of such commerce.

The confrontation between Volpone's lust and Celia's virtue is a gender conflict between a nobleman (behaving ignobly) and a woman of the middling sort (behaving nobly). Jonson is suggesting that decency is to be found among the merchant ranks, that wives of such men are not always the stereotype of 'clap-fallen daughters/Night-walking wives [...] libidinous widows'.[20] It is a gender conflict between different age groups and between married female virtue and predatory unmarried male libertinism. This very contemporary situation occurs regularly in seventeenth- and eighteenth-century literature. Celia bears some resemblance to the heroines of Shakespeare's romances (Imogen, Hermione, Miranda), though her part as an agent of God's justice is minimal and almost accidental.

The increasing vocal presence of women in society and at court combined with their increased presence in print, ratcheted up the gender discourse. Though women were beginning to record their lives in private journals and letters, few are represented in print, but that was changing rapidly. Gender issues are addressed mainly through male dramatists. The public dimension of theatre and the growth in the practice of printing play texts for commercial sale foregrounded this persistent concern. But in privately circulated manuscripts and in occasional printed texts, women were emerging as authors

19 Coryat (Brockbank, 162).
20 As defined by Sir Gilbert Lambston in Middleton's play *No Wit, No Help Like a Woman's* (c. 1611–12), 4.3.52–3.

and raising gender issues.[21] *The Memorandum of Martha Moulsworth, Widow* (1632) offers a touching verse account of her life and three happy marriages. A loving father brought her up 'in godlie pietie [...] In modest chearfullnes & sad sobrietie'. Unusually, for her sex and rank (rural gentry), she was taught Latin, but lamented 'two universities we have of men/O that we had but one of women then!' (lines 33–4).[22] Martha married at 21 (quite late), was widowed at 26, mourned a year, remarried and was widowed again 37. At 40 she married a third time. Of this last relationship she writes,

> The third I tooke a lovely man, & kind
> such comlines in age we seldom find
> [...]
> was never man so Buxome to his wife
> with him I led an easie darlings life
> I had my will in house, in purse in Store
> what would a women old or yong have more?

She loved all her partners, was very happy with them and enjoyed domestic responsibility. She completes her autobiography with a neat and witty couplet in keeping with her satisfaction in marriage:

> the Virgins life is gold, as Clarks us tell
> the Widowes silvar, I love silvar well.

Martha is a positive example of a woman living in the provinces. There is insufficient evidence to form a distinct pattern or profile showing how widespread such education for girls was or how common such happiness in marriage.[23] Clearly there is little affection between Corvino and Celia. This is similarly true in the Would-Be's union. Lady Pol has some breadth of education if her claim to have read a representative list of Italian poets is to be believed (3.4.). She alludes to Baldassare Castiglione's *Book of the Courtier*, Giovanni Guarini's tragicomic pastoral, *Pastor Fido*, and has some knowledge of medicine, but her 'torrent of words' is merely the spilling out of bits and pieces of information she has picked up. It does not represent a

---

21 See Louise Schleiner, *Tudor and Stuart Women Writers*, for discussion of the small coteries of women authors.

22 *Norton Anthology of English Literature*, vol. 1. (1962), 1553–5.

23 The letters between the gentry couple Sir John and Margaret Winthrop, from the second decade of the seventeenth century, testify to both a loving marriage and a highly articulate woman.

solid programme of learning. Martha's education makes her an exception, but not unique. The bulk of women (and men) had little learning. How much love they found within arranged unions is impossible to tell. The Would-Be marriage seems to be formal, without true affection or warmth.

If working, running the estate or living for pleasure and leisure was a man's life in aristo-gentry circles, family tended to be the major part of the female sphere, along with overseeing the household economy (though responsible to her husband for expenditure in both areas).

Traditionally women were thought more naturally inclined to be loving and nurturing though many plays present women who are cruel, ruthless, selfish, vain and shallow. Many fathers were distant, even when at home. James I warned his son that when he had 'succession' (children) he should 'bee carefull for their virtuous education: love them as yee ought', but 'contayning them ever in a reverent love and feare of you'.[24] Some mothers too were distant (especially court ladies), so that noble offspring were often reared by nurses and maids. Fathers tended to be strict, concerned to discipline children to conform to society's expectations of their gender role and attitudes. Formality and ritual deference were more common among the elite. In their parents' presence children stood in silence, speaking only when spoken to. In very strict aristocratic families they knelt. Even a citizen's children asked father's permission and blessing before beginning any undertaking – making a journey, going to university, leaving home to marry, leaving the table, going to bed. The addressing of a father or mother could be very formal – using their title or calling them 'Sir' and 'Madam'. Similar formality could apply between husband and wife. We see this coolness between the Would-Bes, she even calling him Master Would-Be when she is angry with him. The Corvino marriage is similarly formal. He calls her Celia, like an angry father, and abuses her with the epithets 'Lady Vanity' and 'whore'. She addresses him as 'sir' or 'dear sir', but the 'dear' is not affectionate so much as extra formal. The only semblance of affection ('Where are you, wife? my Celia? wife!') is still wrapped in the formality of 'wife' and occurs when he wants to command her to lie with Volpone. He orders her, 'Come, kiss me', and 'Go, and make thee ready straight,/In all thy best attire, thy choicest jewels' (2.7.13–14), claiming to be free of 'jealousy, or fear', but only to soften her up for the appalling and immoral demand he will make of her. That said, in many families there was affectionate informality.

While Lady Would-Be is outspoken, wilful and endlessly chattering, Celia is reserved, respectful and cowed. Both the talking woman and the mouse were stock types in comedy. Humility (valued in men too) was not merely a

24 *Basilikon Doron*, 62.

device for keeping women quietly deferential. Overwhelming, garrulous adults were unacceptable whatever their sex. Knowing when to give your opinion and how to give it least offensively and most courteously was a social skill prized among courtly people. The idea that a young woman or man had the right to speak up independently and freely was centuries away. Deference, humility and self-effacing silence were expected, but human nature being what it is, were not always displayed.

As legally, biblically authorized head of the woman and the family, a man's wife's money and property became his, his claim to custody of the children took precedence over hers and theoretically he had the final say in all things. In practice many different arrangements were negotiated by individual couples. Some women were independent, bossy termagants. Some efficiently ran households with the power of decision over menus, furnishings, the hiring and firing of servants and the education of the younger children. Some were docile shadows. As Hugh Bicheno asserts, in discussing the constant manoeuvrings and blood-lettings of Renaissance Italian politics, 'No one should doubt that women were [...] as able, ambitious and even more devious than men, and that although sexual dimorphism ruled them out of actual combat in the era of muscle power they were probably braver as a sex and certainly no more gentle and peace-loving than men'.[25] There was an immense range of different male familial profiles too, from the ultrachauvinistic father/husband, through the liberal, kindly, affectionate and caring father/husband, to the weak henpecked nonentity.

Much debated was how fathers should behave toward their children and how best children could be brought up. Mostly it focused on boys. Michel de Montaigne and Francis Bacon have much to say on the subject. Largely, fathers were stern, distant and formal, partly because high infant/teenage mortality discouraged too close and affectionate a relationship developing, partly because strict fathers were thought better teachers of respect and discipline. Mothers were thought too lax, too inclined to be easily forgiving. Fathers reflected the loving sternness of God.

Children were thought to be like wild creatures needing taming and training if they were to be self-disciplined in later life and cope with the customs and practices of a highly stratified, ritual conscious, traditionalist society. The traditional suspicions men had of female irrationality, unreliability and emotional instability transferred to their attitude toward a mother's relationships with her children. In elite families boys were removed from female control at seven, were breeched and were put under a tutor until ready to be sent away to complete their education.

25 Bicheno, *Vendetta*, 6.

Affective family relations did exist as did companionate marriages. Not all was male chauvinism or female submission and not all marriages were perpetual conflict. Many widows were accepted as managers of estates and businesses and were very effective. It was an accepted thing and quite common. There were many more such women than one might think since men tended to marry later than women and die earlier. It was not unusual or unexpected for a woman to remarry. In business a widow commonly married one of the journeymen or a senior apprentice. A journeyman had completed his seven-year apprenticeship. Not yet master of his craft, he was sufficiently skilled and experienced for it to be a practical union keeping the business going and money coming in. Among high-status women there were many examples of very dominant, bullying characters who plotted for power at court. Among elite families marriage and family relationships were often thought of not as loving supports developing a child's personality within a sheltered environment with people who cared about him or her, but as units of child production that would enable the family title, status, money and property to be kept together and handed on. It is a chilling fact that one-third of marriages did not last longer than 15 years, many women dying in childbirth and old husbands dying first. Remarriage was common, and often swiftly followed the funeral. These dynastic concerns may seem inhumanly disagreeable to modern minds, but in an age when death was a constantly imminent possibility such severe considerations were crucial at every level of society where property (however minor) was held. At stake might be the tenure of thousands of acres and a place at court, a commercial enterprise or simply the hedging tools of a farm labourer and the lease on his cottage. Apart from biblical authority for patriarchy there were practical reasons for it. Among the aristo-gentry, who remembered the violent precariousness of the Wars of the Roses, men bred large families hoping at least one male would survive. This required a wife who was fertile and would be home based in order to rear the offspring. Lawrence Stone puts it thus,

> Among the landed classes in pre-Reformation England [...] (the) objectives of family planning were the continuity of the male line, the preservation intact of the inherited property, and the acquisition of further property or useful political alliances.[26]

Such objectives persisted into the seventeenth century.

Feminist historians and literary critics have drawn attention to the marginalized role and restricted potential of women throughout the ages.

26 Lawrence Stone, *The Family, Sex and Marriage in England, 1500–1800*, 37.

This perspective usefully counterbalances the male-dominated view of history and sociology but simultaneously overemphasizes the negative aspects of male domination and underemphasizes the forms of overt and covert female power. Strong women sought power and gained it, often ruthlessly.[27] The assumption has been that because male dominance was legally institutionalized it was the overwhelming norm. Archival evidence shows women more politically engaged than hitherto claimed. The most material sign of male dominance was the husband's appropriation of his wife's property and money to do with as he wished. Where husbands were cash-strapped, in debt, thriftless wastrels (whether the eldest son or a younger son) this led to dowries being swallowed up, provoking resentment and tension. Liberal, less chauvinistic men often left their wife's money in her hands. Less well advertised was the jointure arranged by parents and lawyers. This was an agreed annuity payable by the husband's family if he predeceased his wife. It could represent a considerable sum if paid over a long period of time. Also, all debts accumulated by a wife were legally payable by the husband. Female extravagance becomes a recurrent theme in literature as in life. Materially and emotionally every arranged union had two potential victims. Men too could be trapped unhappily inside an arranged marriage. The patriarch kept family property intact through primogeniture, but may himself have been forced into marriage with a wealthy but old, ugly, ill-tempered or extravagant woman. Younger offspring had to be found appropriate marriages. Sons were a problem, tending to drift into similarly cash-short homosocial groups in London, unsupervised, uncivilized and antisocial. They were increasingly pushed into high-status professions – the church, law, government service, the army – but often dropped out or pretended to study while pursuing a libertine lifestyle. Many young high-status women remained unmarried, without a vocation, without the chance to work other than at relatively trivial domestic and social accomplishments (sewing, embroidery, music).

While parental wishes, much influenced by financial, hierarchical or political interests, were dominant in choosing a partner, increasingly the child's consent was sought. This approach was particularly evident in the wealthy upper-middle ranks. If a child did not like and was not attracted to a possible partner, that could put an end to negotiations. In *'Tis Pity* Florio tells a fellow citizen who is seeking Florio's daughter as wife for his booby fop of a nephew,

> My care is how to match her to her liking:
> I would not have her marry wealth, but love;
> And if she like your nephew, let him have her. (1.3.10–12)

---

27 See Chris Laoutaris, *Shakespeare and the Countess* and Mary Lovell, *Bess of Hardwick*.

Ironically, this liberal approach is voiced while Annabella is in bed with her chosen lover – her brother.[28] There was fear attached, by parents and the church, to the exercise of sexual freedom by both sons and daughters. Daughters were kept under close guard because there were so many predatory young men looking for sex, so many heiress hunters seeking a meal ticket. Drama presents a mass of different conflicts over courtship and marriage because it offers excitement and more plot possibilities than demure agreement. However, in real life, parents commonly chose a suitor or bride when they saw there was already attraction. In the case of a candidate picked by the parents but unknown to the prospective bride/groom, proposed by the suitor/bride's family or self-presented by a free bachelor, again the son/daughter's response was taken into account. But, if a candidate was strongly preferred by the parents on material grounds and rejected by the son or daughter, then parental pressure and patriarchal weight (threats of disinheritance, imprisonment and other punishments) would be applied. Marriage without parental consent was illegal, putting the archetypal romantic lovers, Romeo and Juliet, outside the law. Lear, in his anger, disposes of Cordelia to the lowest bidder without her say. Prospero (*The Tempest*) is more caring. Egeus (*A Midsummer Night's Dream*) is not. Corvino is an autocratic husband with inconsistent principles. Volpone is a typical aristocratic predator.

Though the odds might appear against it, there is evidence of loving marriages and happy families 'long before the eighteenth century'.[29] Studies show that

> [p]atriarchal authority applied in theory to this period, but could be modified in practice, by illustrating the range of experiences of married couples in which much depended upon factors such as the personality and relative status of the husband and wife.[30]

More importantly, counterbalancing the idea of women being universally dominated,

> [f]ar from being passive subordinates, some women developed strategies to modify or resist patriarchal authority, including marshalling support through friends, neighbours and kin to circumvent their putative subordination to their husbands.[31]

---

28 The early 1600s saw accelerating punitive action by various authorities against fornication, adultery, incest, homosexuality and prostitution. See Dabhoiwala, chap. 1.
29 Helen Berry and Elizabeth Foyster, *The Family in Early Modern England*, 3.
30 Berry and Foyster, 3.
31 Berry and Foyster, 3.

Deep-seated institutional misogyny persisted through the 1600s. Though the Catholic Church held no sway in England, its ideas had bitten deep into the male psyche, and suspicion of women was endemic in masculine thinking. The Church of Rome, systemically anti-female in its doctrines, saw women's secondary role as part of God's plan. The Church of England was more of the mind that men and women should respect one another, that husbands and wives should work in harmony, but was clear that ultimately the man was in charge. Women, as Eve's descendants, were thought more inclined to sin. Men too were sinners but a neat argument mitigated that:

> though an husband in regard of evil qualities may carry the image of the devil, yet in regard to his place and office, he beareth the image of God.[32]

No one statement or view can be universally true of the complexities of male-female relationships, but in general a woman's place was subordinate to that of the males within her family and social sphere. There were, of course, numbers of strong-minded women who would not be dominated within their family or in any situation. Women did have status. Being married gave a woman greater status within her community. A mother had authority over her children (in the father's absence). A housewife had authority over her servants (in the master's absence). The wife of a guild master, a titled lady or a shop owner's wife was superior to anyone of an inferior station (male or female), but within her own rank was secondary to any adult male, even to a son of age if he had inherited from a dead father and was head of the family, though respect for her as a woman, as mother, as dowager (widow of a titled/propertied man) would partially mitigate his authority. However, irrepressible women dominated all these situations. It is clear that Lear regards his daughters as very much his property. As father and king he disposes of them as he sees fit. But once free of him, with his power diminished to a level where only affection might work in his favour, the two older daughters display a barbaric cruelty transgressing custom and civilized behaviour. Egeus too thinks of his daughter as a commodity, his property, and decides whom she will marry. Corvino similarly thinks he can decide for his wife.

The subordination of women was part of an unfair hierarchical system and accepted within a social structure that designated a place for everyone and in which most people (men included) were subordinate. It was unjust but most of the social and legal structure was unfairly organized in favour of the rich over the poor and men over women.

---

32 William Gouge, *Of Domesticall Duties*, 1622.

In 1558, the most strident statement of female inferiority was made by the Scottish radical Protestant John Knox, from his exile in Geneva:

> To promote a woman to bear rule, superiority, dominion or empire above any realm, nation or city is repugnant to nature, contumely to God, a thing most contrarious to his revealed will and approved ordinance, and finally it is the subversion of good order, of all equity and justice.[33]

Knox's views resonate with fear that transgressing the social, familial or gender order would herald anarchy and collapse. Montaigne, usually liberal and fair, declares that

> women should have no mastery over men save only the natural one of motherhood [...] It is dangerous to leave the superintendence of our succession to the judgement of our wives and to their choice between our sons, which over and over again is iniquitous and fantastic. For those unruly tastes and physical cravings which they experience during pregnancy are ever-present in their souls.[34]

This takes no account of the general tendency of women (1) to oppose by a variety of means all attempts by males to repress them, and (2) to achieve some independence for themselves by negotiation, by clandestine action or by default. Some women failed to win any area of domination. Some ruled every area of family life or a limited area. Some said, 'Yes, dear, no, dear' and then secretly did as they wished. Some men could not be bothered about household matters or child-rearing, so the wife/mother ruled by default. Some women gained rule of estates or businesses through their husband's decease, but largely Heaven's hierarchy persisted on earth and religion backed it. Thus, 'by marriage, the husband and wife became one person in law – and that person was the husband'.[35]

Just where women were placed in the day-to-day reality is problematic. The bulk of ordinary people were voiceless. Women provide even less evidence of their existence than men. Printed documents enabling the profiling of actual relationships are scarce and differ between court and country and between the aristo-gentry and other ranks. The lower down the social scale the less material is available. Archives hold a few personal diaries and letters

---

33 John Knox, *The First Blast of the Trumpet against the Monstrous Regiment of Women*, 1558.
34 Screech, 448.
35 Stone, *The Family, Sex and Marriage*, 136.

by women and probably more await discovery. It was a period in which few people committed personal feelings to paper, but that was changing. Cost of materials was one factor but the culture was only slowly coming to accept that an individual's thoughts and feelings were of value. The various intersecting sixteenth-/seventeenth-century conflicts did push more people to express their views. The expanding print culture enabled many individuals to publish pamphlets that contributed to a war of words on religion, politics, gender and a multitude of topics. Urban trading families needed literate heirs and from the mid-seventeenth century dissenting groups began establishing academies that provided excellent broad education, more liberal, practical and extensive than the limited classical studies of high-end families. In Elizabeth's time, education was much more narrowly focused. It was available to aristo-gentry boys and was rigidly classical in its curriculum. There were many grammar schools and these often had endowments, bursaries and scholarships that enabled boys from poor families to gain formal education. Little formal schooling was given to girls, even from high-status families (apart from the royal family and a few cultured aristocratic households). Literacy and numeracy, taught at home, was about the scope of it for girls. There were some formal institutions for girls set up by Puritans, but these are the exception not the rule. Sir Anthony Cooke was an exception in that all his daughters were educated to a very high level of competence, forming what was known as a little 'university'. The Cooke sisters were translators and commentators, Puritan in thinking, involved in contemporary polemic and annexed to the power hubs of the court.

It was common for Christians (Dissenters particularly) to make personal daily examination of their lives. In time this was written down in a spiritual journal and from then on more material is available. The decade prior to the Civil War saw many pamphlets (many by women) offering opinions on everything from politics to horoscopes (and religion particularly). By the Restoration (1660) there was a slightly higher proportion of female-to-male professional writers, reflecting some easing of male repressiveness, but as a demographic percentage figures for female writing are small. There are more questions than evidence to answer them. Did women write but not publish? Often. Did women just not write much? No. Were they unable to access reading material that triggered their own writing? Not in elite circles. Was female literacy just too low to make a showing? Not in elite circles.

Much female-authored fictional work circulated in manuscript among social networks like the court, London-based writers and literate and literary families and their friends. Prohibited from acting women seem not to have written for the public stage until Aphra Behn.[36] Any assessment of women from 1600 to 1620 can largely only be constructed from male perspectives.

The general picture seems to be that private individuals (male and female) were increasingly writing about their lives, opinions and personal struggles. This accelerated in the Civil War and afterwards. Most of this manuscript material is locked away in scattered archives, public and private. The later Stuart period provides many spiritual autobiographies, but an interesting early example of personal writing, giving insight into provincial life, comes from Lady Margaret Hoby's 1599–1605 diary. A Yorkshire heiress, educated in a Puritan school for gentlewomen, she married three times, making alliances with high-profile court dynasties (the Devereux, Sydneys and Hobys). Her life was spent near Scarborough, with a few visits to London. Her diary, the earliest known to have been written by an English woman, records local charity work and the running of the household and estate, details domestic activities – managing servants, paying them – describes mundane activities like gardening, arranging the washing and ironing and preparing medicines, and discusses her contacts with neighbours and estate tenants. It recounts her outer spiritual life – organizing household prayers and her personal devotions and reading – but does not delve into her inner feelings.

At every stage of life a woman was expected to be deferential, submissive and constantly aware of her different and separate expectations. Her infant education (if any) would be at home and limited to letters and figures, while her brothers attended school (or were home tutored), and once literate and numerate, moved on to Greek, Latin, mathematics, history and geography, followed by university. In a lower rank a schooled boy might be apprenticed or simply join his father in the family business. A girl stayed at home and learned housecraft and needlework skills. Farmers' daughters joined the women in planting, tending animals, spinning, cooking and nursing younger siblings, but brothers ploughed, reaped, herded animals, made and used tools, went to market and met the world. Once of marriageable age, whatever her rank, she might be contracted to a man of her father's choosing if it was profitable to the family; she might choose for herself and have parental approval; or she might remain at home unmarried as general help, that is, an unpaid servant. If lucky she might be sent away into service.

While exposing her to innumerable risks, this event opened better prospects. She might climb the ladder of service from housemaid to housekeeper. A prime fantasy was attracting her master's eldest son and marrying him. In practice parents reacted in horror at their son wishing to unite himself to a maid. Girls

---

36 Her first play was *The Forced Marriage* (1670). Some privately performed masques and dramas for private reading were female authored before this.

from the governing ranks and upper bourgeoisie had better opportunities for being educated but fewer for going into society or working, and largely waited to be courted. Numbers from all ranks simply never got married. The tediousness of such limited horizons is well detailed in the eighteenth and nineteenth centuries, but the bored girls of Renaissance England are relatively silent. Like their brothers, they had virtues to cultivate – piety, chastity, discretion, modesty, gentleness, decorum, prudence, diligence, industry. If from a comfortably off family, a girl was expected to join her mother in charity visits to the poor and other almsgiving. Lower down the social ladder things were better as regards active occupation, for you were expected to work and earn money to contribute to the family income. Middle- and upper-rank girls had to do much sewing and embroidery, cutting out and stitching clothes for younger siblings or for charity children. Often their only projection of identity was in the samplers they embroidered with their name on it. These acted as samples of patterns that might be later stitched onto cushion covers or quilts. They also acted as a measure of a girl's needlework skill to be shown off to a would-be courter who might never come calling. Thousands on thousands must have let their father marry them off to the first man who offered, simply to escape to another life and a home of their own to run. That seems to be the limit of Celia's life for she is virtually a prisoner at home, rarely let out except to the church 'and that, so seldom –' (2.6.46). Even that is further restricted by Corvino's jealous suspicions.

There were differences between how the court treated women and how they were expected to behave elsewhere. Court women were perceived (often correctly) to be promiscuous, fawning gold-diggers (therefore manipulative and devious hypocrites), overly interested in clothes and show, given to rumour-mongering and generally flirtatious and frivolous. There were differences in how men regarded and treated women and what was expected of them according to their rank. Common girls were regarded as skivvies and sexual prey, and middling ones as sexual prey and sources of fortune. A girl from a titled family could not easily be predated sexually if she had kinsmen to take revenge, but she could be courted for her money, married and left to nurture the offspring. Many girls in the two upper tiers did get a good education, depending as always on parental attitudes (the father particularly) and there was a swing toward humanist ideals that saw female education as essential for the next generation of wives and mothers.

6.2 Renaissance Improvements

Richard Mulcaster, first headmaster of Merchant Taylors' School, then High Master of St Paul's School, strongly favoured female education. His book,

Positions (1581), declares that as 'our' closest 'companions', women should be 'well furnished in mind' and 'well strengthened in body'. Fathers have a 'duty' to educate their daughters. God 'require[s] an account for natural talents of both the parties, us for directing them; them for performance of our direction'. Mulcaster believed women's education should be selectively targeted toward strengthening virtue, emphasizing four essential skills – 'reading well, writing faire, singing sweet, playing fine', plus languages and drawing. Maths, science and divinity were less useful, but not excluded. Women, he felt, were weak by nature, but education could strengthen intellect and soul. Men should be educated 'without restraint for either matter or manner'. Countering the stereotypical view that women's education was neglected he asks,

> Do we not see in our country some of that sex so excellently well trained and so rarely qualified in regard both to the tongues themselves and to the subject matter contained in them, that they may be placed along with, or even above, the most vaunted paragons of Greece or Rome?[37]

But it is only 'some of that sex'. How broadly spread female education in the upper and middling ranks was, is unquantifiable. Masses of boys went to grammar school, then university. Scholarships, bursaries and endowments enabled poor scholars to get an education otherwise beyond their reach. Such institutional learning was generally unavailable to girls, and such home tutoring as was provided has left few examples of its existence. Celia has obviously been taught Christian principles, but her speeches are devoid of classical allusions. In the attempted rape scene there is a clear contrast between the plain, ethical terms of Celia's defence and the rhetorical ornaments with which Volpone peppers his blandishments (Proteus, the horned flood, Valois, Antinous, the Catullus poem *Vivamus, mea Lesbia*, Egyptian queen, Lollia Paulina, Cretan wines, Ovid, Europa, Jove, Mars, Erycine, sprightly dame of France, Tuscan lady, Spanish beauty, Persian Sophy, Grand Signior, quick Negro, cold Russian, an image from Petronius, Nestor).

Unsurprisingly, Henry VIII's daughters, Mary and Elizabeth, were well taught. Elizabeth, who knew Latin, Greek, Hebrew, Italian and French, was one of the most learned rulers in Europe. Her speeches use rhetorical devices displaying her classical learning, but she insisted that a prince's education should be useful to ruling the nation. The princesses were tutored by leading scholars, including Juan Vives, the Spanish humanist. Vives, conservative, wary of providing a classical education because some political-historical

---

37 Mulcaster citations in Greenblatt, ed., *Norton Anthology*.

material was unsuitable and the poetry of Ovid and Catullus immoral, based their curriculum on his own *Instruction of a Christian Woman*, broadened to include Erasmus's *Paraphrases* and Sir Thomas More's *Utopia*. He believed 'most of the vices of women [...] are the products of ignorance, whence they never read nor heard those excellent sayings and monitions of the Holy Fathers about chastity, about obedience, about silence, women's adornments and treasures'. Women had to be obedient to their duties and needed their morals shaped and their virtues developed – as did men. Only 'a little learning is required of women' while 'men must do many things in the world and must be broadly educated'.[38] Women should confine their reading to works on chastity.

This outlook betrays orthodox Catholic anxiety about female sexuality. Men felt that independent female sexuality would lead to increased illegitimacy thus obscuring the fatherhood of any child and confusing matters of inheritance, the central concern of patriarchally controlled marriage. Erasmus, friend of More and a key figure in the development of Renaissance ideas, suggests (*The Institution of Marriage*, 1526) education is more effective than needlework in chasing away idleness, preserving virginity and enhancing matrimonial relationships.

It should not be assumed that humanist ideas greatly influenced the court or spread very far beyond it. Young women attending court would already be past the education stage. Their personalities and tastes already formed, they usually had more worldly matters on their minds. Away from court there was a huge variety of attitudes among the country aristocracy and gentry as regards rearing and educating daughters. Learned education (Greek and Latin) was briefly fashionable for aristocratic girls from 1520–60. Thereafter it waned. Other positive influences did emerge, though again it is impossible to chart their influence. One was Castiglione's *Il Cortegiano*. This important handbook suggested a little knowledge of 'letters' (classics, modern languages, history, literature) was acceptable for women, but that the social graces – playing music, singing, dancing, drawing/painting, doing needlework – were more civilized and made a woman more marriageable. Thomas Hoby claimed the book was 'to Ladies and Gentlewomen, a mirrour to decke and trimme themselves with vertuous conditions, comeley behaviours and honest entertainment toward all men'.[39] This new courtly ideal promoted the self-effacing but agreeable woman, witty, cultured, but chaste. Castiglione also acknowledged, in some detail, that cultured education should be more than a mere social ornament for women. He strongly endorses their virtue and their potential for positive influence in a court. This new courtly ideal

---

38 Vives citations in Greenblatt, ed., *Norton Anthology*.
39 Thomas Hoby, *The Courtyer of Baldessar Castilio*, from 'The epystle of the translatuor'.

promoted the self-effacing but agreeable woman, witty, cultured, but chaste. Renaissance courts could be centres of high culture but were also deathtraps of intrigue, of plotting, of power struggles, assassinations, political coups, rape and seduction. Court history exemplified that double-sidedness – culture and killing, music and murder, poetry and poisoning. Executions, torture, the rise and fall of favourites, hothouse animosities and sexual intrigue made English courts (from Henry VIII to James I) like the set of a bloody play. The splendour of the Venetian cultural cityscape, with its many church spires and domes, its luxuriously facaded *palazzi*, its rich music and paintings, contrasts with the decadent and corrupt behaviour of its citizens – a treasure box filled with dung with only two jewels buried in it (Bonario and Celia).

As evidence of some shift in attitudes to women, Thomas Campion (1567–1620) explores how women's restricted social opportunities encourage a vigorous inner life, while men are easily distracted by the world's superficialities:

> women are confined to silence,
> Loosing wisht occasion.
>
> Yet our tongues then theirs, men,
> Are apter to be moving,
>
> Women are more dumbe then they,
> But in their thoughts more roving.[40]

Female-authored literature was beginning to emerge. Lady Mary Wroth (1586?–1651?) from the high-status, literary Sidney family, wrote a sonnet sequence and the first known prose romance by an English woman, both contributing to the gender discourse. Elizabeth Cary (1585–1639), the first woman to write a history, also wrote the first female-authored tragedy. *The Tragedy of Mariam* (written 1602–4, published 1613), a 'closet drama' to be read in domestic surroundings, contributes to the gender debate, contrasting honest, principled Queen Mariam with devious, promiscuous Princess Salome and presenting the violent, absolutist patriarch King Herod. Another contributor to the man-woman question was Rachel Speght (1597?–?). A Calvinist minister's daughter, she entered the literary world with panache, stepping straight into gender-discourse controversy. Aged 19, with her name boldly attached, she published *A Mouzell for Melastomus* (A muzzle for Blackmouth, 1617), an articulate, spirited, clearly and logically argued attack on the bigoted misogyny of Joseph Swetnam's *Arraignment of Lewde, Idle, Froward, and Unconstant Women* (1615). Biblical and classical references reveal her religious background and education.

40 See Campion in Greenblatt, ed., *Norton Anthology.*

Living at the centre of London commerce and clerical debate, she understood the current polemical climate and had seen many examples of husband-wife cooperation among merchant families. She claims respect is due to women as God's children and sees the possibilities for companionate relationships between men and women. A lively style, often akin to the acerbic, insulting, combative language of male pamphlet polemics, makes her work readable, while her ideas make it convincingly sympathetic and reasonable. Marriage is a true union: 'as yoake-fellowes [married couples] are to sustayne part of each others cares, griefs, and calamities'. 'Marriage is a merri-age, and this worlds Paradise, where there is mutuall love [...] husbands should not account their wives as vassals, but as those that are heires together of the grace of life'. As 'Head' of his wife, the husband must protect her and lead her to Christ. To 'exclaime against Woman' is to show ingratitude to God.[41] Swetnam focuses female vanity and lechery, and Speght voices a new mood of companionship, shared piety and compromise between gender egotisms.

In religious thought the body (a temporary house for the soul) was considered corrupt and its sinful needs and dirty functions were to be minimized so the spirit could be kept pure and nourished. Subject to fleshly temptations and the vagaries of emotion, human beings were a comic treasure. The virtue/sin, duty/desire conflict produced a body of 'sex war' literature focusing the persistent hostility between men and women – men as bullying, lascivious brutes, women as devious, unreliable and bullying (shrewish) in their own way. Shakespeare addresses the virago-virgin polarity in *The Comedy of Errors*, *The Taming of the Shrew* and *Much Ado*. Lady Would-Be and Celia represent that polarity. The trickiness of women is often a source of comedy while their evil is fitting for tragedy. Contrast the polarities of the kite/tiger/wolf/monster sisters in *Lear* and the gentle sensitivity of Cordelia. Many negative implications resonate round the words and actions of Goneril and Regan. Both sisters are white devils – a common metaphor for hypocrites who disguised their evil. The sisters are a study in the evil that females can perform. Shakespeare had often presented the failings of women, but deep evil had only been explored through Queen Tamora's cruelty (*Titus Andronicus*, c. 1588–93), and in *Henry VI* with Queen Margaret, a 'she-wolf' with a 'tiger's heart wrapp'd in a woman's hide'. His other great study of female evil is Lady Macbeth. The middle period plays exhibit demure and humble women (Ophelia, Desdemona, Cordelia) and highly articulate, irrepressibly independent ones (Viola, Rosalind, Beatrice). The last plays project positive images of articulate but self-effacing women. The sinfulness of women is only hinted at in *Volpone*, though plays of the

---

41 Greenblatt, ed., *Norton Anthology*, 1036–9.

same period are full of misogynistic opinions and situations not projecting women's positive qualities. In *A Mad World My Masters* Follywit asserts,

Man's never at high height of madness full
Until he love and prove a woman's gull. (4.5.12–13)

The same play has Follywit's friend, Penitent Brothel, pronounce even more extreme views:

Nay, I that knew the price of life and sin

What crown is kept for continence, what for lust,

The end of man, and glory of that end

As endless as the giver,

To dote on weakness, slime, corruption, woman! (4.1.14–18)[42]

Men had ambivalent, contradictory views of women. As the source of human sin they needed controlling in order to repress their opportunities for tempting men. Men's inability to withstand the sexual allure of women is also held in a contradictory tension, for on the one hand men are persistently represented as stronger, more rational, yet at the same time their ubiquitous sexual weakness is portrayed. A multiplicity of pejorative terms – virago, termagent, shrew, Whore of Babylon, hussy, wagtail, punk and more – provides lexical markers of male suspicion. In opposition to the Eve/Delilah/Jezebel/whore image, twelfth-century courtly love projected an idealized woman of beauty, intelligence, elegance and chastity, while Mariolatry raised the Virgin Mary to an archetype of gentle, sympathetic womanhood and loving, nurturing motherhood, that partially redeemed women. Mary became a key human intercessor in approaching Jesus or God, and an icon of the respect men should have for women. In loving a woman you re-expressed your love and respect for your mother, showing the love you first learned from her. Martin Luther asserted Mary was 'the highest woman' and 'we can never honour her enough' and 'the veneration of Mary is inscribed in the very depths of the human heart'.[43] While lauding Mary's model status, Luther also made very derogatory remarks about ordinary women in general.[44] Despite some easing of

---

42 Thomas Middleton, *A Mad World My Masters* (c. 1605).

43 Sermon 1 September 1522.

44 'The word and works of God is quite clear, that women were made either to be wives or prostitutes' (*Works* vol. 12, p. 94). 'God created Adam master and lord of living creatures, but Eve spoilt all, when she persuaded him to set himself above God's will. 'Tis you women, with your tricks and artifices, that lead men into error' (*Table Talk*).

extreme patriarchy and improvements in the status of women, negative views persisted and progress was slow.

Medieval hagiographies (lives of saints) celebrated the virtues of women martyrs. This was problematic for Protestantism had banned statues, days, prayers, relics and oaths associated with saints. This hampered the assimilation into church dogma of any ideology applauding women, though veneration of Mary persisted in people's private faith. A small amount of literature iconized particularly virtuous women and applauded romantic, affectionate relationships as long as they remained rational. There are Geoffrey Chaucer's 'Legend of Good Women' and 'The Book of the Duchesse' and a scattering of references to courageous, faithful women in the Bible, but generally all churches were suspicious of sex and passion, encouraged men to control their own and female appetites and warned against women as the ready provokers of lust in men and vulnerable to fleshly temptations themselves. Polemic writing tended to highlight female failings. Literature uses the constant interplay of tension between the positive aspects (affection and love) of the appetites and the dangers of following them excessively. Men's susceptibility to female charms and love was seen as a madness, an illness caught from women. In *A Midsummer Night's Dream* Duke Theseus describes love's insanity:

> Lovers and madmen have such seething brains,
> Such shaping fantasies, that apprehend
> More than cool reason ever comprehends. (5.1.4–5)

The Church of England's second *Book of Homilies* (1571), which vicars used for sermons, includes 'On the State of Matrimony', defining the church's views on women and how fathers and husbands, being in authority over them and being more rational beings, should approach them:

> The woman is a weak creature not endued with like strength and con-stancy of mind; therefore, they be the sooner disquieted, and they be the more prone to all weak affections and dispositions of mind, more than men be; and lighter they be, and more vain in their fantasies and opinions. (503)

They were 'the weaker vessell, of a frail heart, inconstant, and with a word soon stirred to wrath'. A commentary in Matthew's Bible (1537) says that men, being intellectually stronger and in authority, had a duty to ensure their women conformed to the demand for chastity and modest behaviour. If she was 'not obedient and helpful to him, [he may] beat the fear of God into her head, and that thereby she may be compelled to learn her duty and do it'. Corporal punishment was common in the Renaissance. Whores and criminals were publicly whipped, children caned at home and school and servants beaten.[45] Legally a wife too could be beaten.

The Bible exhorts wives to be in subjection to their husband, counterbalancing this by requiring that the husband should honour the wife and that they should have 'compassion one of another' (I Peter 3:8). Bishop Aylmer gave a sermon before Queen Elizabeth, outlining the best and worst aspects of women, in polarities evident in Shakespeare and most other dramatists:

> Women are of two sorts: some of them are wiser, better learned, discreeter, and more constant than a number of men; but another and worse sort of them are fond [simple], foolish, wanton, flibbergibs [silly chatterer], tattlers, triflers, wavering, witless, without council, feeble, careless, rash, proud, dainty [fussy], tale-bearers, eavesdroppers, rumour-raisers, evil-tongued, worse-minded, and in every way doltified [made foolish] with the dregs of the devil's dunghill.[46]

Legally women had few rights. Neither did most ordinary men, but they had the key ones.

There were some shifts in behaviour, but how far they penetrated society as a whole is unclear. There had been a sixteenth-century increase in stern patriarchy as regards marital and parental relations. In the seventeenth there were countermovements against both.

Imperceptibly slowly the stern, patriarchal, authoritarian father became more affectionate and considerate. Stone's comment suggests the gradual emergence of the more companionate marriage and more affective family relations:

> For a considerable period, two conflicting trends were at work at the same time, and the growing authority of the husband can only be seen in a relatively pure form during the first half of the sixteenth century.[47]

Playwrights hint at the hope for harmonious, loving marriages at the end of comedies, but within the piece tend to use the dramatic possibilities of

---

45 Resentful, beaten servants could not legally run away and leave the parish. That was to become a masterless man/woman and carried a prison sentence. This implication that a servant was the property of the master was yet another of the ancient practices that restricted the liberties of English people.

46 Stone, *The Family, Sex and Marriage*, 137

47 Stone, 137.

conflict between the sexes. Offering more opportunities for humour, tension and the exploration of violent emotions, it is better theatre. Stone captures the essence of this in quoting a character in a play by George Wilkins:

> Women are the purgatory of men's purses, the paradise of their bodies, and the hell of their minds: marry none of them.[48]

In John Marston's *The Dutch Courtesan* (1604), Malheureux says, 'The most odious spectacle the earth can present is an immodest, vulgar woman' (1.1.154–5). Marston, a member of Jonson's Mermaid Tavern circle, worked in the same areas of problematic moral ambivalence central to *Measure for Measure* and *Lear*, in Jonson's comedies and in the work of Middleton. Freevill (his name conflating evil/freedom/free will), a libertine trying to terminate his relationship with the courtesan Franceschina so he can marry Beatrice, a respectable and wealthy heiress, offloads the whore to his friend Malheureux (the unhappy or misfortunate one), who tries to repress his powerful sexual feelings. Freevill and Malheureux represent two significant forces in contemporary society – traditional male unfettered sexuality and the newer moral code of Puritanism attempting to control the sex impulse.

Franceschina admits, 'Woman corrupted is the worst of devils' (2.2.201). Her remark has relevance wider than London's sex trade and applies to the conduct of some of the court ladies. Lady Would-be is corrupted (she attempts a sexual liaison with Volpone) yet in court accuses Celia of being a courtesan. She is vulgar, immodest, credulous and forward, constantly talking over people and has, like her husband, inaccurate views on everything. As a character she is only a partially realized caricature, for Jonson's main focus is on the corruption of the men.

Shakespeare presents the counterargument when the hitherto chaste Angelo, feeling the prickings of lust, asks, 'The tempter, or the tempted, who sins most, ha?' (*Measure for Measure*, 2.2.164). This acknowledges partial male responsibility for lust. Volpone expresses no moral concerns about his lust for Celia and his intention to have her. He assumes she will easily be persuaded by the lifestyle advantages he offers. King Lear makes sharp comments on lust and female lust in particular, his strictures as condemnatory as any Puritan preacher:

> Down from the waist they are Centaurs,
> Though women all above:
> But to the girdle do the Gods inherit,

48 Stone, 136.

Beneath is all the fiends: there's hell, there's darkness,
There is the sulphurous pit – burning, scalding,
Stench, consumption; fie, fie fie! pah, pah! (4.6.)

In different ways Marston, Jonson, Shakespeare and others explored the difficulties of keeping to virtue's path, mocking the pretensions and greed of contemporary London through theatrical satires, delving into human depravity, cruelty, self-delusion and folly. Jonson explores human evil but always closely allied to the times. While Elizabethan-Jacobean dramatists display considerable sympathy for women in a male-dominated world, they are also alert to women's fierce brutality and disturbed at how similar it is to men's.

Chapter 7

MAN IN HIS PLACE

First walk in thy vocation,
And do not seek thy lot to change.[1]

By God's will you were born into a particular rank (your lot in life). You were expected to know your place, keep it and work at whatever calling came within the scope of your family's position. Each family might rise, through hard work and God's grace. Small status rises were not too disturbing for one's neighbours, but great success provoked envy, jealousy and suspicion of overreaching ambition. Doubts about the honesty of the means by which you rose might arouse accusations of magic and devilish assistance. People would be all too ready to credit the Bible's view: 'he that maketh haste to be rich shall not be innocent' (Proverbs 28:20). The industrious, careful man, slowly improving his station, was safe from negative gossip, for 'wealth gotten by vanity shall be diminished: but he that gathereth by labour shall increase' (Proverbs 13:11). Rapidly increasing bourgeois wealth created an interplay between envy, condemnation of luxury, suspicion of avarice and dishonesty and fears of an upstart, ambitiously aspirational group rivalling the traditional ruling class.

Jacobeans were suspicious about social movement. If God made the world, putting each man in his place, was it not countering God's will to change your social status? A poor man becoming poorer was thought punished for some unnamed sin, but a man going up in the world was usually not thought of as being rewarded for virtue, but rather guilty of ambition, arrogance and using sinful means. Some argued that God gave men abilities or talents, expected them to be used and rewarded hard work. If that meant you could climb out of your birth rank, bettering yourself, then you could be said

1 Robert Crowley, *Voice of the Last Trumpet* (1550).

to be doing God's will and worshipping him by developing the talents he gave you. This was a popular view among Non-Conformists for whom the work ethic was central. They believed in industry, thrift and found the idea of making money acceptable. The age saw huge fortunes made. A rise in wealth, place and public status should not be accompanied by complacently making money at any cost. The means had to be ethical, the amounts within reason. Excessive gains should be redistributed through charities and the moneymaker and his family should avoid arrogance, ostentation and snobbery – in theory. In practice, silk-clad pride stalked the land and at each step the chink of coins could be heard. Hard-working shop assistants might marry the shopkeeper's daughter or his widow, might rise to be wealthy, become guild masters or town councillors, but were expected to give thanks by making charitable donations and remaining humble. Education could help a poor man's son to a government clerkship. Talented, active men could rise, particularly if they earned the patronage of someone of note and power. They could fall too if they followed a favourite who fell from favour. The court was a roller coaster of fortune where many people rose by intrigues, plots, lies, favouritism, ruthless opportunism (and sometimes by honest service) and could fall by the same means. It was a jungle where the bejewelled animals struggled for survival one against the other with little thought for the fact that death would level all and that you cannot transfer your bank balance to Heaven.

So many new men rising to prominence, caused conservative thinking unease about social mobility. Extreme reversals or improvements in rank portrayed on stage were seen as omens warning of impending disaster and social implosion that might engulf everyone. Subversion of any sort was disturbing and threatening to the orderliness of society. In *Eastward Ho!* the goldsmith's daughter, Gertrude, obsessed with becoming a knight's wife, contemplates the pleasure of having gained superiority over her father:

He must call me daughter no more now; but 'Madam', and, 'please you Madam', and, 'please your worship, Madam', indeed. (3.2.63–5)

Gertrude is suitably punished, marries Sir Petronel Flash for title and property, but finds he is like his name, all show, no substance, no castle, no money. He married her for her money. She married him for his status and the title it would give her. Each cheated the other and their pride is humbled. Additional to pride and ambition, Gertrude shows extreme disrespect to her father, thus striking at the very root of social order and breaking a commandment. *King Lear* demonstrates even worse subversion of family values. Many city comedies show disturbing threats to the fundamental basis of social life – the family. In *Volpone* family is distorted or unnatural.

Movement was not always upward. A third to a half of the sixteenth-century population existed at subsistence level and suffered acute unemployment. The majority of the lower sort suffered their hardship fairly stoically, but the urban underclass was always a worrying barrel of gunpowder. It took little to ignite it and regular outbreaks of riot occurred – in London particularly. At the other end of the scale increasing numbers of merchants, financiers, manufacturers and industrialists were making huge fortunes, becoming wealthier than established aristo-gentry families. They copied elite cultural habits, seeking titles, estates and political power. This latter aspiration frightened the ruling ranks. The bourgeois elite was well educated, with 2.5 per cent of males aged 14–20 receiving university training.

With male literacy improving (80 per cent in London), clearly life-enhancement possibilities were expanding. The middling sort was unstoppably on the move. Though the very poorest remained poor and their numbers increased due to enclosures, unemployment and inflation, those able to struggle upward to literacy, and thereby to effective commercial activity, were also increasing. This widened the divide between those succeeding and the failing underclass with no means of reversing their downward spiral. The growth of capitalism created many different levels of sophistication and increased the need for minutely observed differentiations to distinguish between people. When a merchant's wife could afford to dress as well and in the same fashions as a lady at court, it was the normal response of human nature to seek finer status identifiers to enable those with established rank to mark themselves apart from those newly arrived. Obsessive fashion-consciousness evolved to identify status.

In the 1600s voices were beginning to speak for the lower orders. The need to do so indicates growing tensions between the ranks. At the end of his progress south in 1603 James I, arriving at Theobalds, Robert Cecil's magnificent palace north of London, was handed the 'Poor Man's Petition'. Like such other appeals it demanded the new king promise religious uniformity and the purifying of public life, particularly attacking the legal profession: 'A pox take the proud covetous Attorney and merciless lawyer! [...] fye upon all close biting knaverie!'[2] The very existence of the petition indicates how social tensions had grown toward the end of Elizabeth's reign. Voltore is a prime example of the covetous attorney whose principles are in his fees. His twisting of the truth in presenting Volpone's case in court is just the sort of 'close biting knaverie' that made lawyers perennial hate figures.

2 Quoted in De Lisle, 195.

Social divisions showed in other more public ways. Luxury clattered by on the streets in fine coaches. Successful men, their wives and families displayed their new-found wealth in banquets, gold plate, marble mansions and portraits memorializing their elevated state. Ben Jonson showed his contempt for such spiritual poverty: 'O, but to strike blind the people with our wealth and pomp is the thing! What a wretchedness is this, to thrust all our riches outward, and be beggars within'.[3] The moral emptiness of the central characters is inescapable in *Volpone*. Conspicuous consumption and ostentatious showing off through carriages, horses, houses, furniture, clothes and expensive social events were all forms of vanity. The many mocking stage representations of the purse-proud nouveau riche and the wasteful excess of the aristocracy had little effect. Sumptuary laws controlling expenditure and regulating the types of clothing worn and the amounts/types of food consumed by the different ranks were ignored. Established in the Middle Ages, updated by Henry VIII and extended by Elizabeth, these laws officially claimed to restrain vain, wasteful habits and protect English trade, but were really the elite's attempt at maintaining the visual differences of rank. As everywhere else, there was hierarchy – in the fur trimming permitted for your level in society, the fabric you could wear, the headgear, the jewellery. To dress 'above your station' looked like pride. The laws were designed to discourage someone from one rank imitating the manners and appearance of another, but were frankly a form of social control and means of identifying a person's standing and reinforcing the distinctions between the nobility and the up-and-coming entrepreneurial groups. Attempts to regulate extravagant expenditure on clothes by aspiring, fashion- and status-conscious bourgeois women were put in moral terms stressing restraint and humility. Elizabeth's 1574 law declared the craze for fine show led to

> the wasting and undoing of a great number of young gentlemen, other-
> wise serviceable, and others seeking by show of apparel to be esteemed
> as gentlemen, who, allured by the vain show of those things, do not
> only consume themselves, their goods, and lands which their parents
> left unto them, but also run into such debts and shifts as they cannot
> live out of danger of laws without attempting unlawful acts.

The words 'show', 'vain', 'consume' and 'debts' suggest disapproval based on medieval ideas of moderation, evoking the deadly sins and stereotypes linking suitability of behaviour to rank. Rank, income and gender were the criteria

---

3 *Timber*, 45. He continues, 'to contemplate nothing but the little, vile, and sordid things of the world; not the great, noble, and precious!'

that decided what you could wear. Thus dress signifiers supposedly identified social rank and preserved 'degree'. Though there were harsh punishments for sumptuary infringements they were largely ignored and the laws were repealed in 1603–4 as simply unenforceable. To some this was opening the floodgates that would swamp distinction between the orders and herald social collapse. In 1583 Philip Stubbes remarked on

> such a confused mingle mangle of apparel [...] that is verie hard to know who is noble, who is worshipful, who is a gentleman, who is not; for you shall have those [...] go daylie in silkes, velvets, satens, damasks, taffeties and suchlike, notwithstanding that they be both base by byrthe, meane by estate & servile by calling. This is a great confusion & a general disorder, God be mercifull unto us.[4]

High-end fashion became more lavish and impractical; it was saying 'I don't need to work, so my clothes are for show only'. Snobbery drove people to seek minute markers to show their superiority. Drama from 1600 onwards is much concerned with how clothing disguises what people really are, how the discrepancy between appearance and reality relates to clothes and office and inner probity, and how fine robes suggest rank and rank implies virtue. Theatrical satire exposes how clothes hide sin, how gold covers it and how office (or authority) does not mean the man occupying it is there by merit. Volpone changes his nobleman's appearance by means of clothes suitable to a sick old man, a mountebank, a sergeant-at-arms. He rightly only briefly appears as his true self, the rich grandee, for he has debased that rank. Brachiano in *The White Devil* suggests that the Duke of Florence is all show:

> all his reverend wit
> Lies in his wardrobe; he's a discreet fellow
> When he's made up in his robes of state. (2.1.189–91)

This reminds us of Lear's remark on 'the great image of Authority': 'A dog's obey'd in office' (4.6.). People perceive and treat you according to your robes and accoutrements of office, regardless of the fool or knave you might actually be. 'Robes and furr'd gowns hide all' (*Lear*, 4.6.). Fine silks paraded in public simply emphasized the fact that some were rising fabulously while most were in the mire. Those, like Volpone, who already had wealth showed their moral emptiness by the lust for more. That is the link connecting the hustler and the hoodwinked. Admittedly Volpone does not seek to acquire wealth in order to

4 Philip Stubbes, *Abuses*, 33.

ostentatiously show it off. For him the process of acquiring riches by trickery is what drives him. This still damns him in Christian terms and debases him as a magnifico. His conduct in fooling the legacy hunters and in contemplating fornication is enough to demean his rank. He betrays his degree and shows that a privileged background does not always translate into characters being decent, reliable or admirable.

Each man was guardian of his own soul, his own virtues and is responsible for his own sins. But he had other associations to which he owed loyalty and responsibility – his family, his village, his trade or craft, his county, nation, his church, humanity, the whole of creation.

Family and community were the strongest bonds, though faith might take precedence and separate a man from these commitments. Each man occupied a station in the detailed stratification of society, from king to pauper. The theory of the natural order was based on harmony. Each rank, high or low, had its part to play if concord and perfect working were to be achieved.

> This is the true ordering of the state of a well-fashioned common-
> wealth, that every part do obey one head, or governor, one law, as all
> parts of the body obey the head, agree among themselves, and one not
> to eat up the other through greediness, but that we see order, modera-
> tion, and reason, bridle the affections.[5]

This theory of order and orderliness was conceived by those who governed and wished to preserve degree. Rulers were the brains and heart, and the nobles the important organs. The others – the limbs – had little else to do but obey. This often-voiced analogy is false. Society is not a body. If you cut off the head the body dies, but if you cut off the king's head or remove the aristocracy, society will continue with a new political settlement – as the Civil War would show. If the lavishly bedecked part of the audience thought the play would be a light-hearted romance with sophisticated witticisms and a little clowning to make them laugh outright, they were wrong. It is throughout an unremittingly dark and cruel play, relentlessly severe in its view of man and with little to suggest humanity has anything redeemable in it. It carried in its texture warnings to the frivolous and the self-satisfied, but mostly to the greedy. The deceptions of Mosca and Volpone have something great about them. They are not petty thieves – their sins are on a grand scale. But in the end their spirits are mean and degraded.

5 From 'King Edward's Remains. A Discourse about the Reformation of Many Abuses', *History of the Reformation*, Bishop Burnet.

Their bait (Volpone's will) provokes questions about loyalty and honesty. In 1631 Jonson wrote,

> All Repraesentations, […] eyther have bene, or ought to be the mirrors of man's life, whose ends, […] ought always to carry a mixture of profit, with them, no less then delight. (Preface to *Love's Triumph*)[6]

Jonson was not just referring to court masques. A classicist by education and inclination he is alluding to Horace's maxim 'He has gained every point who has mixed profit with pleasure, by delighting the reader at the same time as instructing him'.[7] How much profit and instruction would the audience take from this representation? Would any spectator leave the theatre determined to live a more elevated, upright life? Probably not. Laughter often diffuses and loses the underlying message and human beings have a great capacity for seeing how they should not behave but without necessarily amending their conduct. Plays tend to be a mirror not a medicine.

6 *Ben Jonson: Works*, 7, 735.
7 *Ars Poetica* (*The Art of Poetry*), 1. 351.

Chapter 8

IMAGES OF DISORDER: THE RELIGIOUS CONTEXT

The lay people know the Scriptures better than many of us.[1]

The seventeenth century was undeniably a religious age. Religion impacted all lives to varying degrees. The church, present in everyone's life, was an arm of the established power that ruled England. The parish church, often on the edge of the village green, was visible from the fields as you worked. Its bells punctuated your day. The city parish church was likewise nearby. The priest would be visible haggling in the market like anyone else, perhaps occupying a corner of the local tavern. He was part of the civic power structure as well as sitting in judgement over your spiritual life. He reported your civil and moral misdemeanours, convened and presided over the church court, arranged poor relief and preached. One form of sociomoral reinforcement was the homily he was obliged by his superiors to read out every Sunday. The *Book of Homilies* (the first 1547; the second in 1571) had 33 homilies, intended to bed in the ideas of the new reformed Church of England, to educate the masses and assist conformity. They covered doctrinal and liturgical subjects but included moral sermons: 'Against peril of Idolatry', 'Against gluttony and drunkenness', 'Against excess of apparel', 'Of alms [charity] deeds', 'Of the state of Matrimony', 'Against Idleness', 'Against disobedience and wilful rebellion'.

Religion was central to many of the age's controversies, but not all those who attended church did so in a spirit of devotion. Many went simply to avoid the punishments meted out for non-attendance, but 'there was no escaping the rhythms of the Prayer Book or the barrage of catechisms and sermons'.[2]

1 Bishop Edward Fox, 1537. Cited in Dickens, 108.
2 Cressy, 139.

Though a largely churchgoing society, there had always been those who claimed (and believed) they needed no church or priest to intercede between them and God. More and more people would assert they could worship in the field, the workshop, their home. Enforced church attendance was increasingly resisted. One sailor expressed the view in 1581 that 'it was never merry England since we were impressed to come to church'.[3] The pursuit and prosecution of non-attenders depended on the zeal of individual clergymen. Sunday worship was theoretically a time of communal affirmation of shared beliefs and values. That excludes those parishioners with rather different thoughts in their heads while the parson exhorted them to virtue. There would always be some who were doctrinally opposed to Anglicanism, but kept quiet. Though everyone was nominally Church of England, some in the congregation would be Catholics conforming to the law, others Puritans passively conforming while having more radical and aggressive beliefs about which they were mostly, but not always, quiet. Increasingly there were hostile interactions in the church that created simmering grievances in the outside community. For some congregations their priest was too zealously reformist, for others he was too lazily traditionalist. Some Dissenters separated from the official church and formed their own unofficial congregations. These were illegal and the congregants subject to dispersal or arrest. There were those who, indifferent to religion, called themselves Christian, but did not allow faith to interfere with life more than they could help. Atheists tended to keep their views to themselves (or share them only with like-minded others); denial of God was punishable by arrest, interrogation, torture, imprisonment. There were always those more concerned with the pint of ale in the inn after the boredom of the sermon was over. Some chatted, snoozed, made mocking comments on the priest and his sermon, laughed aloud or transacted business.[4] Others would be more preoccupied with the members of the opposite sex seated across the aisle. The parish church was a place where the community's social/religious differences were reinforced as much as the shared Christianity. Finally, there were those who had genuine faith in the Anglican Church and lived in as holy and virtuous a way as possible. It is impossible to say what proportion of the population at any one time fell into these categories; there was much genuine piety and much irreligion. The service was intended as a celebration of solidarity and a reminder of the demands and sacrifices faith and virtue required. The overarching zeitgeist was religious, though like a rainbow it was

3 Thomas, 179.
4 Falling asleep during the sermon (and they could be very long) and disrespecting the vicar were fining offences.

of many colours, and despite the various forms of internal, external, silent and vocal opposition to imposed worship, most English men and women were regular churchgoers and those who were not, those who moved away from their village community to the anonymity of the city, would nevertheless have the vestiges of religious upbringing and the remnants of biblical teachings still in their memories.

Another aspect of this structure, that all faiths agreed on, was that the orderliness of the cosmos and the natural world was fantastically varied and complex yet orderly, with each part of the system working and doing its allotted job, and that all this is God's doing: 'The heavens declare the Glory of God and the firmament showeth his handiwork' (Psalm 19).

8.1 Unsettling Questions

Astronomers contributed to the gradual dismantling of the Ptolemaic system, but plays too could unsettle. Audiences watching the Admiral's Men perform Christopher Marlowe's *Tamburlaine the Great* (1587) at the Rose would have heard Edward Alleyne declaim,

> Our souls, whose faculties can comprehend
> The wondrous architecture of the world
> And measure every wand'ring planet's course,
> Still climbing after knowledge infinite
> And always moving as the restless spheres,
> Wills us to wear ourselves and never rest
> Until we reach the ripest fruit of all,
> That perfect bliss and sole felicity,
> The sweet fruition of an earthly crown. (part I, 2.7.21–9)

This combines traditional views – man's distinguishing faculties of understanding that separate him from the animals and the glory of God's creation (the 'always moving [...] restless spheres') – with progressive, dangerously blasphemous views on man's restless seeking for knowledge that trespassed into the secrets of the divine. The final idea is unusual, for instead of 'perfect bliss and sole felicity' being spiritual, a heavenly crown, Tamburlaine's goal is the 'earthly crown' of supreme material power – a very Renaissance ambition. This work, by a restless, enquiring, turbulent young university man, was intended for an audience with some fairly sophisticated members in it. But 80 per cent plus of England's population was rural: landless farmworkers and small subsistence farmers with beliefs still primitive, basic, medieval. Many large-scale landholders, farmers and nobles, were similar. Centuries of Catholicism could not be erased overnight. Changes in thinking take several generations when few are literate, are without access to academic research and have closed minds.

Nationwide instant communication just did not happen and the church always stood in the way of the free sharing of intellectual ideas, especially if unorthodox. There was no organized dissemination of news, regular newspapers appearing first during the Civil War. There was also the normal monumental public resistance to change. The majority of the population was exceptionally conservative. Ignorance, fear and simple intellectual inertia played their parts as always. The Reformation changed the official outer world, but the private inner world of daily life and its cluster of beliefs lagged far behind. The Reformation had many fervent supporters, but was grafted onto a residue of long-ingrained beliefs and practices. Individuals, devoted to their faith, might conform to the new rites and liturgy of Anglicanism while still performing little acts of superstition such as crossing themselves or praying to a favourite saint. The lines between magic and acceptable doctrine remained as blurred as they ever had been, but, given the growing print culture and the spreading knowledge of what the Bible said, huge numbers of controversial debates sprang up as to what was orthodox, what heresy, iconoclasm, superstition, idolatry, papist mumbo jumbo or diabolic magic. Services in English made doctrine more accessible and as Anglicanism settled, versions of the translated Bible became more readily available and individuals could read for themselves the words that were the basis of a priest's hitherto unique and monopolist interaction with his congregation. This new-found capacity for personal interpretation allowed many doctrinally divergent views to spring up and this worried the Anglican hierarchy. In response bishops became more repressive, demanding greater conformity from priests and parishioners. This encouraged stronger opposition though Puritanism's rise was slow. The Puritan sectaries' drive to change religious thinking was regarded with irritation and new ideas in medicine, politics and science always provoked opposition. Puritans are almost always figures of fun and derided as hypocrites in plays, but there were growing numbers of genuinely devout men and women who had serious issues with the episcopacy. Growing numbers of them would flee persecution in England and seek freedom of religion in America. It is noticeable that neither Volpone nor Mosca display any faith or express any religious sentiments. Morality has no place in their world. Volpone, guilty of idolatry, has substituted gold for God, like the Israelites who made and worshiped a golden calf (Exodus 32:4).

The mass of people just wanted to continue living as they had always done. But, regardless of this conservatism, seismic shifts were rumbling in many aspects of life. John Donne's 'An Anatomy of the World' (1611) declares,

> new Philosophy calls all in doubt,
> The Element of fire is quite put out;
> The Sun is lost, and th'earth, and no man's wit
> Can well direct him where to look for it.
> And freely men confess that this world's spent,
> When in the Planets, and the Firmament
> They seek so many new; then see that this
> Is crumbled out again to his Atomies.
> 'Tis all in pieces, all coherence gone;
> All just supply, and all Relation:
> Prince, Subject, Father, Son, are things forgot.

In the light of this Volpone's misconduct is not just that of a man exhibiting the power of avarice, but becomes a symbol of the new iconoclasm, the 'new Philosophy' of individualism that was beginning to erode the old certainties. The Ptolemaic system represented God's order, a divine harmony, a coherence that reassured. To hear it questioned, to hear of old beliefs discarded by new science was destabilizing, forcing doubts into people's heads in an age already full of changes, with a new religion, new worlds being discovered, new economic practices, new towns growing (and creating new problems) and old feudal relationships breaking down. Family was the commonest, closest bond for everyone. Family history, family honour and family loyalty were central to the audience's thinking and feeling. It would be painful for people to see taken-for-granted relationships called into question, especially if the answers suggest family love is a thin veneer of pretence. City comedies show many examples of family bonds being broken. Volpone's lack of a true or real family is therefore significant. His lifestyle choices are all resonant – and disturbing. The probity expected of men of high status, the honesty expected of the professional man, the mutual affection and harmony expected in marriage, the fundamental family bond of father and child and the impartiality of the judiciary are all shown to be open to question in *Volpone*. Venice in crisis is a warning to the London audience.

Onstage familial and societal disassembly is averted by the restoration of order manipulated by the storyteller at the end of the play. This artifice is a pattern found in many plays. In *Volpone* restoration happens at the last minute and is in doubt until then. It is brought about by the court though it is clear that the members of the bench are not entirely men of honour.

They are fooled into believing by unsubstantiated accusations because they are made by a lawyer. They do nothing to establish the truth. The predatory greed of the *avocatore* who sees Mosca as a likely rich son-in-law does not inspire confidence. He is lured by Mosca's clothes as signifying he is a *clarissimo*. The justice finally done does not restore faith in a system where corruption goes to the top. It is only Volpone's decision to unmask himself that enables judgement to be made. The audience would recognize in all this the unreliability and bias of the English courts.

William Shakespeare's history plays and Ben Jonson's two Roman histories amply displayed the natural desire for order and peace. Political vacuums were dangerous and so was illegitimate rule. Both usually led to bloody struggles, generating uneasiness and repression, putting into perspective the desperate anxieties surrounding a queen's pregnancy and the nervous waiting for a hoped-for male heir. The audience had experienced the traumas of the Tudor continuities and discontinuities. Change was disturbing and dissension at the monarchical level was very frightening. Familial rupture in Corbaccio's household, marital rupture in Corvino's, professional dishonesty on Voltore's part and the enveloping situation of a magnifico involved in large-scale fraud provide an uneasy atmosphere running in the background of the play. From God to earth's dust, everything had its place. Man, man's communities and states were part of that orderliness. The fast-changing, apparently disintegrating, world disorientated the Jacobeans and the princely court dramas so frequently staged were commonly the source of order-threatening discontent. This play is not set in a formal regal court, but it does involve characters who have status and who are courting the favour of a man of rank.

Along with the household entertainers Volpone's house is his court and the legacy hunters are like the suitors who came to Whitehall seeking place, pension or family advancement from the king. It would be disturbing to see their corruption, but it probably only confirmed what most suspected already – that men of high status were as grasping and greedy, as devious and lying as the huckster pestering you in the street. High-ranking characters, the leaders of society, would increasingly be pilloried in the run-up to the Civil War. Mistrust of the apparent probity of its power brokers was a cause of social conflict that would eventually lead to actual hostilities.

The disorderliness of courtiers was regularly condemned. Concern about unprofessional conduct among judges and Justices of the Peace was similarly voiced. On 11 July 1604 Sir Philip Gawdy Member of Parliament describes the Commons Speaker addressing the problem of

> Justices of Peace of wch ther wer two kyndes he founde great fault withal, the one wer such as go downe into the country, and presently fall to

hawking, and other sportes, and yf any man comme about Justice, they
sende him to their next neybur Justice; the others be suche as put downe
one alehouse, and set vp two for it, set up one constable, and put down an
other, and yf any matter be stirring whatsoeuer he must haue an ore in it.[5]

The double standard of the apparently virtuous public man whose apparent
probity masked private corruption recurs in drama, in the court, in real life. But
suspicion was not confined only to those of the better sort. The city comedies
showed other categories of social exemplar behaving badly. Part of the play's
development is stripping back appearances and exposing the realities hidden
beneath. Middleton's 1605 city comedy, A Mad World, has the mother of the
courtesan Frank Gullman, declare in a neat epigram:

Who gets th'opinion for a virtuous name,
May sin at pleasure and ne'er think of shame. (1.1.164–5)

All not being what it seems is a recurrent image and theme in both
Shakespeare's tragedies and comedies and is central to the action of Jonson's
works. Volpone, by virtue of being a magnifico, is thought of as virtuous.
Yet his palazzo is a house of many sins. The trickery at the heart of Volpone
becomes an emblem of contemporary life.

5 Gawdy, 148.

PART II

THE JACOBEAN PRESENT

Chapter 9

BEN IN CONTEXT

All he writes, is railing.
>> (Prologue to *Volpone*, 10)

I'll strip the ragged follies of the time
Naked as at their birth.
>> (Jonson, *Everyman Out of His Humour*)

Ben Jonson is the most colourful and explosive character among the tribe of Elizabethan-Jacobean writers few of whom were self-effacing. Aggressively self-promoting, arrogantly confident in his view of the art of writing for the stage and his contribution to it, his personal life was as lively, sometimes as tempestuous as his public stage works and they (as opposed to his poems and masques) are full of snarling satire and mockery. A combative man, a combative writer, he crusaded to establish a morally earnest theatre and elevate it to artistic respectability. To the moralist and satirist railing is the natural mode. To rail is to criticize, protest or complain in a vehement manner. Such was very much the manner of Jonson. Though he became superficially more genial in his court masques, his works for Blackfriars or The Globe retained to the end his savage mocking tone.

A number of biographical factors may have produced the growling negativity in his works. Jonson claimed descent from a gentry family, the Johnstones, from Annandale in the Scottish Borders. The religious hatreds of the time touched the family and had lasting effects. His father, a Church of England minister, imprisoned during the brief reign of Catholic Mary Tudor, had forfeited the family estate. Jonson believed this caused the family's decline in fortunes. His father died a month or two before the playwright was born in 1572. How that loss, plus the depressed status of the family, might have affected him in later life is impossible to say, but these events may have been a source of aggression, a sense of being deprived, and explain why he strove so hard to get back at the world and punish it through extreme and bitter criticism. Jonson had a deep need to succeed, to triumph over what he saw as his disadvantages and outdo those who had had privilege on their side. Life for widows (unless already rich) was difficult in those times. His mother was living in the parish of Charing Cross (between the walled City of London and Westminster, which were separate locations in those days) at the west end of the Strand. They lived in Hartshorn Lane, one of the maze of alleys leading from the Strand to the Thames. It was a bustling area. The Strand connected Westminster to the City, its taverns, shops and houses servicing and accommodating the overflow of officials who worked in the political village of Westminster and the courtiers who hung around the palace of Whitehall.[1] The eastern end of the Strand led to the City walls and the intense commercial activity inside. Widow Jonson remarried two years after her bereavement. Ben's stepfather was in the building trade. Brickbuilders had a guild (a trade organization) but it was low in the hierarchy of trades, crafts and professions. Later in life Jonson was ashamed to be labelled the son of a bricklayer.[2] This derogatory description pointed to his background being less than gentlemanly, adding to his determination to show his talents were as good as those with a more privileged start in life. It is possible his stepfather was something more than a mere bricklayer, perhaps a master mason, owner of a small building business or an architect, for the family could afford to send young Ben to the nearby parish school established by the church of St Martin's-in-the-Fields. His abilities were sufficient for a family friend (possibly William Camden) to pay for him to attend Westminster School, which had a reputation for producing exceptional scholars. Housed in the precincts of the Westminster Abbey monastery since the eleventh century, it had had difficult times when the monasteries were dissolved, but had been successfully refounded by Elizabeth in 1560.

Under the tutelage of Camden, antiquarian, scholar and headmaster, Jonson developed his lifelong love of the classics, addressing one of his epigrams to the man who was not only his headmaster but also became his friend:

CAMDEN, most reverend head, to whom I owe
All that I am in arts, all that I know.[3]

---

1 The jumble of different buildings making up the palace had become the common residence for Elizabeth and then similarly for James I. Both spent time at other palaces, but Whitehall became the focus for their courts and for the apparatus of government and officialdom.

2 Henslowe reported Gabriel Spencer as 'slain in Hogsden Fields by [...] Benjamin Jonson, bricklayer' (*Henslowe's Diary*, 286).

3 Jonson, *Epigram 14*, Herford and Simpson, vol. 8.

Failing to gain one of the Cambridge scholarships annually awarded by the trustees seems to have triggered (or furthered) an inferiority complex and a sense of having been cheated that may underlie his anger against life. He also claimed he was taken from the school 'and put to another Craft'. This suggests that, failing to get to university, he was put to bricklaying. Even if his stepfather had been a self-employed owner of a business, Ben would have had to have started at the bottom if he were to learn the trade and climb. Apprenticeship began at 14 of age and lasted seven years, so he may have left school circa 1584. After working with or for his stepfather briefly, he enlisted in the army that Elizabeth had sent to help the Netherlands in their fight for independence from the occupying power of Catholic Spain. Joining the military might suggest a combative temperament and certainly in later life he did display a tempestuous tendency to fall out with people. It might also simply indicate desperation. Many young men, especially from gentry backgrounds, joined the army for adventure, for escape from dreary home life, debts, pregnant girls or simply to do something rather than drift through the impecunious life of young men about town. During his time in the Low Countries he fought a duel with an enemy soldier and killed his opponent 'in the face of both the Campes'. This sort of Hector-Achilles single combat was a common occurrence and the spectacle ended, according to Jonson, with him, like any classical hero, stripping his defeated opponent's armour. He returned to England between 1592 and 1595 and shortly after had somehow gained entrance to the theatrical world. His one-time opponent in the 'theatre war', Thomas Dekker, asserts (*Satiromastix*, 1601) that he acted with a troupe of touring players and then became a writer. Much the same history is attributed to William Shakespeare's early years in the theatre. Jonson's first play was written about 1596 and from then on a steady stream of plays, poems and masques poured from his quill. It is claimed he played Hieronimo, the vengeful father in the ever-popular *The Spanish Tragedy*. This was a meaty, ranting role. In the five years or so of his 'apprenticeship' as a writer, before his great achievements (*Volpone, Epicoene, The Alchemist, Bartholomew Fair*), he wrote what he called 'comicall satires'.

Because he personally prepared his texts for printing, with dedications, epistles, prologues and other explanatory/justificatory additions, we know more about the aims of Jonson the writer than we do about any other author of the period.[4] We can infer more about the man from such literary paraphernalia.

4 *Volpone* was first performed at The Globe in 1606, then at Oxford and Cambridge the same year (probably after plague had closed the playhouses). A quarto text was printed in 1607 with the dedication to the universities and some commendatory English and Latin verses by admirers. The dedication sets out Jonson's artistic principles and aims. The prologue would have been spoken before the performances. The acrostic argument

In the *Volpone* prologue, Jonson imagines a critic complaining that 'all he writes is railing'. This was a view that had already been voiced.

Jonson feared being linked with 'railing and tinkling rimers' and rejected the sort of 'vulgar' audience or readership that 'greedily' popularized 'the scurrility and petulancy of such wits' who, lacking moral aim, simply wished to make money out of people's love of slander, innuendo and bawdy. Jonson never sought cheap popularity or endorsed scurrility or knavish conduct. Though some may have found his scoundrels attractive they were presented for condemnation. The 'expectation of the vulgar', he remarked, 'is more drawn and held with newness than goodness'.[5] Novelty and fashion were becoming driving forces in society and therefore targets for satire. His work is strident in its protests about the life he saw and depicted. He is a mirror of his times and what is reflected is not pretty. His vision is distorted by anger, seeing people mostly as morally ugly, vicious, greedy, corrupt. While acknowledging there is good in the world, he uses his plays as vehicles for exposing evils of different sorts and degrees, while good limps along behind. He was not alone. Other contemporaries present equally deceitful, avaricious and self-interested characters. (See Chapter 10, Literary Context: 3. The Literature of the Time.) Good's low profile also serves to draw the audience's attention to how easily cheats get away with their scams, how naive virtuous people are and how slow to combat evil. Niccolò Machiavelli had voiced the cynical but realistic view that the 'princes who have achieved great things have been those who have given their word lightly, who have known how to trick men with their cunning and who, in the end, have overcome those abiding by honest principles'.[6] This seems to be reflected in Volpone's world, as does the idea that men 'are ungrateful, fickle, liars, and deceivers, they shun danger and are greedy for profit, while you treat them well, they are yours. They would shed their blood for you, risk their property, their lives, their children, so long […] as danger is remote'.[7] The moral thinking of the time believed God saw all, so audiences expected and demanded the bad be punished and the good triumph, but they also knew that the artificial endings of plays did not always match real life and that the world was awash with unchastized dishonesty. The Devil stalked every fetid city alley and strutted the corridors of palaces – in London and Whitehall as well as Venice.

imitates the Latin acrostics printed at the beginning of contemporary editions of Plautus's plays. All of this was part of Jonson's intention to provide authoritative editions of his works and give them classically backed intellectual authority. In 1616 he was the first playwright to bring out an authorized edition of his own works.

5 *Timber*, 15.
6 *The Prince*, chap. 18, 99.
7 *The Prince*, chap. 17, 96.

It is hazardous to assume incidents in a text stem from events in the writer's life, as if imagination played no part and he could only draw on personal experience to provide material for his narrative. It is tenuous to make such links without evidence. More dangerous still is theorizing about how writing expresses the psychological make-up of the writer.

Nevertheless, there was an aggressiveness in Jonson's life and a persistently adversarial, acerbic tone in his work. A belligerent character, often in trouble with the Establishment and often embroiled in rows with colleagues and associates, his writing for the stage was from the beginning savagely critical, as if he had contempt for most of humanity and an inner resentment against the world. Robert N. Watson sees his personal pugnaciousness as sublimated and 'evolving into its adult guise of scholarly arrogance'.[8] This bitterness is sometimes so venomously critical and angry it becomes almost deranged. A man who has a character declare his aim is to 'strip the ragged follies of the time' and sees 'the earth crack'd with the weight of sin' has either an overly cynical world view or anger management problems – or both.[9]

Much of the relatively little known of Jonson's life (though more extensive than other writers of the time) derives from Jonson himself. Biographical details were recorded by a friend, Drummond of Hawthornden, to whom he spoke in 1618. His views on life and art appeared in *Timber*.[10] In this latter he links language, tone and style to the character of a person:

> Language most shows a man: Speak, that I may see thee. It springs out of the most retired and inmost parts of us, and is the image of the parent of it, the mind. No glass renders a man's form or likeness so true as his speech. Nay, it is likened to a man; and as we consider feature and composition in a man, so words in language; in the greatness, aptness, sound structure, and harmony of it.[11]

If the language of his plays may be taken as a marker of his psychological profile, we see a very angry man with an acutely observant eye for the deformities of mankind and a readiness, even a relish, for snarling them out at people with the fire of a Puritan reformer. Yet his masques are altogether more moderate, counselling the court yet flattering it. Both Jonsons were promoting their art, gaining fame and making money.

8 *Volpone* (ed. Robert N. Watson), viii.
9 Asper, who speaks these words (*Every Man Out of His Humour*), is named from the Latin for bitter and abrasive.
10 See *Timber, or Discoveries* (published posthumously, 1640). Drummond of Hawthornden collected Jonson's anecdotes in *Conversations*.
11 *Timber*, 64.

Drummond's *Conversations* is autobiography reported. This opens doubts as to its accuracy as a guide to Jonson's character. Autobiography is notoriously untrustworthy. When it is a life reported by the subject to a third party it is even more unreliable. Jonson may have elaborated, misremembered, sanitized, invented. He was a combative, aggressive character in his personal life and some of that emerges in the content and mood of his writing. Whether he is transferring, displacing or sublimating (as Watson suggests) is impossible to tell. What is undeniable is that *Volpone* is a cruel exposure of humanity at its worst and that Jonson expresses a low opinion of his own kind. The bitterness of the writing is appropriately focused on the corrupt characters he presents. A writer with a more positive belief in man might have made the good characters more proactive, more dominant. That Celia and Bonario are so marginalized is perhaps reflective of Jonson feeling that goodness is a rare quality, often overwhelmed by bad and that the world is largely evil. His contempt for the world he saw – its deceitfulness, its cheating, its greed – was echoed in the work of Thomas Middleton and John Marston, both of whom were members of the group that met Jonson regularly at the Mermaid Tavern. His comic vision reflects a vicious world that they all agreed needed castigating roundly, soundly, bitingly.

More than any dramatist of the time, Jonson's work reflects his learning. Many other playwrights had attended university – the so-called 'University Wits'. Jonson's immense knowledge of the classics is so evident it looks like showing off, trying to prove himself. Being so intrusive it often deadens and diverts the liveliness of his writing, but at other times it can be beautiful and thought provoking. It may be an expression of a need to compensate for the fact that he had no degree. The level of classical knowledge, triggered by Camden during Jonson's schooldays, was maintained and extended during adulthood. Camden's influence persisted, for they kept in touch and his old headmaster is probably the source of the evidence of contact with many books. The old scholar wrote, published and collected books and it seems probable Jonson had access to his extensive library. Knowledge of Michel de Montaigne, Machiavelli, Erasmus and John Florio, evident in *Volpone*, reflects Jonson's awareness of current writing and the intellectual interchange within a small social network of scholars and artists living in London.[12]

Jonson's reputation was slowly building. He must have written tragedies (now lost), for in 1598 Francis Meres listed him with Shakespeare and

---

12 Florio's Italian dictionary, *A World of Words* (1598), and his translation of Montaigne's *Essais* (1603) appear to have been useful to Jonson. Florio was once tutor to the Earl of Southampton, Shakespeare's one-time patron, and was a member of a group of London-based writer-scholar-intellectuals who knew each other, socialized and shared ideas.

Christopher Marlowe as one of the best for that genre.[13] In August 1597 he ran foul of the authorities for co-authoring, with Thomas Nashe, a play called *The Isle of Dogs*. The piece was charged with being lewd, seditious and slanderous. Jonson, with two actors, Gabriel Spencer and Robert Shaa, was sent to the Marshalsea Prison. The text is lost so there is no definitive evidence of how it was seditious, but any perceived criticism of Elizabeth could be nominated treasonable by an oversensitive (even paranoid) Establishment. All written works had to be licensed by the Stationer's Office before they could be printed or performed. Sir Robert Cecil (and before him Sir Francis Walsingham) had spies everywhere listening for seditious talk, intercepting letters and watching ports for Catholic priests trying to enter the country. The security alert level was very high.

There had already been plots against Elizabeth and they did not stop after James I's succession. Jonson was freed by October 1597 and no further action taken. The authorities were exceptionally nervous at this time, constantly suspecting plots against the realm, always overreacting to writers and actors who seemed to be an anarchic, irreverent lot little better than thieves and vagabonds. On 22 September 1598 Jonson was once more in trouble for killing the actor Gabriel Spencer in a duel. Jonson much later claimed Spencer initiated the duel and wounded him first. Like Jonson, Spencer had a reputation for disputatiousness and violence.

Jonson was arrested, but escaped hanging by reciting the 'neck verse', an exemption called 'benefit of clergy', enabling priests to prove their education and clerical status by reading a verse from the Latin Bible. Thus avoiding the death penalty in a secular court they could be tried in a clerical court, which would usually be more lenient. This saved their neck, hence the nickname 'neck verse'. By the 1600s it had become a large legal loophole which enabled literate non-clerics to evade capital punishment. Jonson, branded on the thumb, thereafter carried the visible mark of his enduring shame. Such events indicate his violent nature, a sign of a constant need to prove himself, an indication of his aggressive opposition to the world.

Elizabethan-Jacobean England was a brutal place where life was cheap, men carried weapons as a matter of course and quarrelled easily over very little. Awkwardly for Jonson, he converted to Catholicism whilst in prison, an unwise move adding further suspicion to a man already on the government radar.

The fatal duel took place two days after the opening of the play that established Jonson as a writer to be reckoned with. *Every Man in His Humour* (possibly with Shakespeare in the cast) was immediately popular and printed soon after. It has many of the features that were to become characteristic of

13 In *Palladis Tamia*. Jonson's first extant tragedy was *Sejanus* (1603).

his comedies – stock types based on classical models (various shysters; Musco, a devious servant; a short-tempered father suspicious of his ne'er-do-well son; a country gull come up to town), each dominated by a specific personality trait or humour. The setting is Florence.[14] With his next play, *Every Man Out of His Humour* (1599), Jonson began to show the bitter sardonic tone that typifies his mature work and his eye for the follies social pretension could bring out in people. This play demonstrates more thoroughly his interest in characterizing through the presentation of a person's dominant humour and his natural tendency to 'comicall satire'. Both the comedy of humours and 'comicall satire' were to be features of his subsequent theatrical productions and are very evident in *Volpone*. Building a character on one personality trait (miserliness, snobbery, greed, deceitfulness), however dominant, while being amusing and sometimes hilarious, diminishes the psychological subtlety and nuanced nature of how real people are. People are often inconsistent and it is this ambiguity of personality that makes Shakespeare's characters more interesting. As a comic writer, however, Jonson was perhaps more interested in exposing social and moral failings through stock stereotypes than in creating complex psychologically credible figures. Satirical comedy deals in broadly drawn caricatures for mockery, rather than subtle ambiguities of personality. The justificatory source of his anger had literary origins in the classics, particularly the satirists. The poetry of the Roman Juvenal was much studied in schools and university and provided many of the subjects on which Jonson would write. Juvenal's Satire I suggests the tone that Jonson would adopt, with comments like, 'Need I tell you how anger burns in my heart?' and 'Don't you want to cram whole notebooks with scribbled invective?' and 'Indignation will drive me to verse'.[15] The same piece provided topics Jonson later targeted: cheating lawyers, informers, corrupt courts, husbands pimping their wives and an obsession with legacies. Juvenal's tone and subjects influenced the mindset of the young writer.

Verbal or written violence was another outlet for a man desperate to succeed. He got involved in an acrid squabble with Marston and Dekker, one of those frequent artistic spats (like Robert Greene's attack on Shakespeare) that indicate the delicately balanced precariousness of fame and popularity and the jealousies constantly erupting between writers competing for readership or audience. Jonson knew how his favourite satirists of ancient Rome, Horace and Juvenal, had also been drawn into such acrimonious poets' wars, accusing rivals of being poetasters (bad poets, mere rhymesters). The

---

14 He later wrote an anglicized version set in London. This was first published in the 1616 Folio edition of his works.

15 *The Sixteen Satires* (trans. Peter Green).

Poetomachia (conflict of the poets or war of the theatres), as Dekker named it, waged from 1599 to 1601, then died down. Dekker later collaborated with Jonson on an early masque and Jonson and Marston co-authored *Eastward Ho!* (1605), a satirical piece that got both of them (and co-writer, George Chapman) into trouble and into prison. The new king was very touchy about his status. Once an equally sensitive Scots lord had drawn the king's attention to the play's mocking the Scots accent and criticizing the hordes of place-hungry, cash-hungry Scots invading London, that was sufficient to activate his short temper and determination to punish any act that threatened his absolute power and his untouchable divine aura. Jonson's tragedy *Sejanus* (performed 1603, printed 1605) got him hauled before the Privy Council for perceived treasonable anti-monarchical sentiments. It was a Roman history play, but the times were exceptionally edgy and the authorities were neurotically suspicious, seeing plots everywhere. The historical distancing did not fool them. Jonson complicated his situation by becoming implicated in the interrogations following the discovery of the Gunpowder Plot. He had attended a supper party hosted by Robert Catesby (a leading conspirator). Also present were fellow plotters Thomas Winter and Francis Tresham. Some aspects of *Volpone* echo the intense anxiety felt by the authorities: the play's title 'The Fox' (similar to Guy Fawkes), Sir Pol's ludicrous comments about codes and spies, the play's pervading atmosphere of secrecy and deceit. Sir Pol's excited credulity may be Jonson expressing amused contempt for the paranoia of the authorities. In the previous reign Lord Burghley summed up the Establishment's view: 'that state could never be in safety, where there was toleration of two religions'.[16] It was a view still held by many.

Inevitably, once the plot was exposed, Jonson was questioned again by the Privy Council and may have been recruited to turn a Catholic priest into a double agent. He failed and spent the next four years as a fine-paying recusant. (Recusants were Catholics refusing to attend Anglican services.) His contempt for the law is echoed in the failure of the Venetian court to recognize Volpone and Mosca's crimes at the first hearing and the wrongful arrest of the victims, Bonario and Celia. In 1609, Jonson equally suddenly (though perhaps understandably) returned to Protestantism. He was both mixing with known, high-profile Catholics and yet writing masques for the very king and court the Catholics had hoped to annihilate. In *Sejanus*, the emperor finally turns on his one-time fixer/favourite, the title character. In his next play, *Volpone*, it is the servant who betrays the master. Both the fictional and the real world were precarious places of constant struggle to survive. Betrayal could come from any quarter. No one could be trusted. If Jonson

16 Chute, 79.

was, through Sir Pol, mocking the more extreme fears of Catholic plots and scaremongering about outrages, as some critics have suggested, it is as well to remember that the Gunpowder Plot and previous failed attempts, were real enough. The audience might have laughed at Sir Pol's fear of a tinderbox setting fire to the *Arsenale*, but the laughter might have been in grim recognition of how close the Gunpowder Plot had come to succeeding. The play is as full of misunderstandings, misperceptions and incomprehensions as pervaded the murky spy-filled atmosphere in 1605–6 London. Plots within plots accumulate as Mosca plays different roles to different victims and Volpone plays different degrees of incapacity to each predator he plans to fool, leaving his bed to masquerade as Scoto, leaping from it to prove his virility to Celia or dressing as a law officer to mock the disappointed *captators*. As the plots twist, turn and proliferate, the audience cannot be sure the hustlers will ever be caught – until Mosca decides to turn on his master. When the thieves fall out the whole edifice comes toppling down. The wily fox is at last imprisoned and the carrion-kissing buzzing fly chained to an oar in a Venetian galley. It looks as if Volpone will get away with it all, then as if Mosca will outwit his master and inherit his wealth, as if plots within plots, like Chinese boxes, will enable the deceivers to disappear in a mass of contradictions. Ironically, the plots the central characters fabricate come true. Volpone, feigning imminent death, lying immobile in bed, will end in prison, immobilized by chains. With unwitting prolepsis, when eagerly awaiting Celia's arrival and assailed by the unexpected visit of Lady Would-be, who drowns him in a torrent of words, he announces, 'Before I feigned diseases, now I have one' (3.4.62). The disease of sin was in him all along. Ironically he is treated to a host of medical advice by Lady Pol just like the jargon he spewed as Scoto. Mosca, acting as slave to everyone while secretly enslaving them to his will, ends as a galley slave. Corvino, who claimed his wife was cheating him, flirting with the crowd, ends up as a figure of public mockery, exposed to the crowd himself. Each becomes what he pretended to be. Jonson, as an actor, knew that if you imitate someone enough, you lose the sense of your own identity.[17] In a world where hierarchy ruled, rich men had a power aura which made everyone think they were always upright, virtuous and innocent, and which made judges assume they were and be ready to acquit them. At first it looks as if the court will go that way. Voltore's lies are believed because he is part of the top of the hierarchy, part of the Establishment, a member of a supposedly honourable profession tacked onto the upper echelons. The audience knew that lawyers, from time immemorial, lied, twisted facts and demonized witnesses to win

---

17 'We so insist on imitating others, as we cannot (when it is necessary) return to ourselves' (*Timber*, 36).

their case and earn their fee. As Bonario acutely says, Voltore's 'soul moves in his fee' (4.5.96). Jonson had personal experience of the prejudice of the 'better sort' toward players and of the power of the authorities over Catholics. Moving among the rich and powerful of both religions, and (like Mosca) using them where he could (doing well out of them, gaining many commissions for court and high-status masques), he nevertheless did not trust their probity. His predators are all (apart from Mosca) men of high standing and low morals, just like the courtiers Jonson worked so hard to entertain. Despising many of them probably, he mocked their type, made money out of them, but was part of the cannibalism of commerce he deplored.

From schoolboy scholar to bricklayer, soldier, actor, dramatist, from Protestant to Catholic to Protestant, Jonson had shown an ability (and necessity) to recreate himself and did so again when he began writing masques for court entertainment. (Compulsive role playing is Volpone's obsessive disorder.) He wrote plays almost until the end of his life but became increasingly embroiled in composing masques. Even then he fell out with his technical collaborator, Inigo Jones, who designed the costumes and stage machinery for these lavish events. He expressed great respect for Shakespeare ('I loved the man, and do honour his memory on this side idolatry'.) yet felt his style was sometimes too low, too casual and the facility with which he wrote did not become the creative anxieties and scholarly care Jonson felt were a necessary part of composition.[18] His own work is sometimes laboured and overburdened with unnecessary classical allusions. Marchette Chute is more supportive of his heavy pedantry: 'He became the one Elizabethan dramatist who was concerned with the spirit of the classics rather than the outward trappings and who was drawn to the world of which Erasmus had once dreamed – a serene, steady, ethical world made luminous by the principles of reason and order'.[19] This unrealistic utopia of high calling contrasts with the combativeness of his life and the bitterness of his stage works. The masques express a large degree of pastoral peacefulness. The earnest didacticism is still there, but it is transformed into a gentler tone. The allegorical titles, *Love Freed from Ignorance and Folly* (1611) and *Pleasure Reconciled to Virtue* (1618), and *Hymenaei* (1606) – a celebration of marriage – and *The Golden Age Restored* (1616) hint at the calmer but still morally engaged approach.

Contempt for money worshippers, greed, dishonesty and hypocrisy is still there, but disguised in the sorts of allegorical figures the Renaissance loved and a more persuasive instructional tone. Even Jonson knew he had to tread carefully when criticizing and preaching to a king and his nobility.

18 *Timber*, 23.
19 Chute, 31.

His greatest achievements, the comic classics *Volpone* and *The Alchemist*, spitting satires against his times, particularly focus greed. It is the authorial anger that gives them their bite, their interest, their vitality. His work is tougher to read than Shakespeare's. The syntax is often distorted from usual word order, the allusions sometimes obscure and pedantic, less homely than his friend and colleague's. Usually labouring long over his writing, seemingly envious of Shakespeare's fluent facility, he boasts in his prologue that *Volpone* took only five weeks to write. That inspiration fired him and anger drove his pen, shows in the pace and spiritedness of the action as the humans turned scavengers crowd to flatter Volpone and eagerly anticipate his imminent death. It shows too in the bustling glee of the two hustlers planning, plotting and grabbing the presents brought. They enjoy cheating the carrion scavengers, outmanoeuvring the greed of vulture, raven and crow and their excitement, for the most part, lends the dialogue a humming vitality.

Chapter 10

LITERARY CONTEXT

10.1 Genre – the Context of Comedy

Life does not cease to be funny when people die
any more than it ceases to be serious when people laugh.
(George Bernard Shaw, *Doctor's Dilemma*, act 5)

Tragedy is as old as human misery and comedy is its not-quite-identical twin, for laughter is as old as tears. One mask may smile, the other cry, but the faces are similar and in many respects so are the two genres, though their outcomes are different. Man's folly, his potential for evil, his potential for good and his ability to misunderstand the true values of life are common to both forms. One achieves correction of mistakes through disaster, pain and misery, and the other through tears turning to laughter as folly is mocked and humiliated and order is restored.

Ben Jonson acknowledged, what many in his time did not:

> The parts of a comedy are the same with a tragedy, and the end is partly the same, for they both delight and teach [...] Nor is the moving of laughter always the end of comedy.[1]

Tragedy has a set of terms used to define key aspects of how its story is structured dramatically. These were derived from Aristotle's series of lectures on Greek tragedy, *The Poetics*. The tragic hero/heroine has a tragic flaw of personality (*hamartia*) that makes them blind to how their confidence in their control of their life and fortune is ill-founded. This overconfidence is called *hubris*. At some point in the narrative the hero/heroine experiences a reversal of fortune (*peripeteia*) and recognition of their mistake (*anagnorisis*).

---

1 *Timber*, 81–2.

It is not generally recognized by critics that these terms apply in many comedies also. Sixteenth-century commentaries on Aristotle, who laid down the criteria for assessing the structure, development and success of tragedy, have some digressions into consideration of comedy. A developing plot must reveal character, character must be believable (even if exaggerated) and the story must reflect realistically the manners of the time frame of the play's setting. The plot must not be episodic but rather pursue a single story. The characters should represent flaws and follies. Lodovico Castelvetro identified four areas of imitative representation relevant and essential to comedy and the triggering of laughter: (1) 'everything that becomes ours after we have desired it long or ardently'; (2) deceptions that make characters say or do what they would not otherwise do or say if they were not deceived; (3) the portrayal of physical or spiritual deformity (that is, conduct that is counter to reason or ethical custom) and (4) anything to do with sex and lewdness.[2] Area one is inherent in the exaggerated longings of the five central characters, how they are lured to covet mistaken objects of desire and eventually cured by deserved punishments. Area two concerns most of the first half of the piece where the self-deceived and Mosca-deceived *captators* think they are shortly to succeed. Area three relates to the spiritual deformity of the central five characters and the physical deformity of Volpine's three grotesques. Area four is marginal, but emerges in the comic behaviour of Volpone as he tries to seduce then rape Celia. It is grimly amusing to see an oldish man lusting after a young woman and being physically thwarted just as he thinks he is about to achieve his goal.

In *Volpone*, the negatives, the upsetting and disturbing actions of men, almost overwhelm the positive outcome hoped for. The world of the play could have become a disaster zone, so dominant are the vile and greedy actions of its hateful central characters. The Corvino-Celia and Corbaccio-Bonario situations, two of the fundamental relationships of society (husband/wife, father/son), contain the seeds of sorrow. This world of crippled minds, ugly thinking and brutal emotions has not the physical savagery of Jonson's tragedy *Sejanus* or William Shakespeare's *Henry VI* plays, but the animal behaviour of greedy men lying and cheating, trying to do each other down – and all for money – is not so different. J. B. Bamborough says the piece 'comes nearer to tragedy than any of Jonson's comedies and contains more bitter and unpleasant scenes'.[3] Some situations develop that might threaten life and

2 Lodovico Castelvetro, *Poetica d' Aristotele Vulgarizzata et Sposta* (1570), from *Castelvetro on the Art of Poetry* (trans. Andrew Bongiorno), cited in *The Cambridge Companion to Shakespearean Comedy* (2010) (ed. Alexander Leggatt), 13.
3 Bamborough, *Ben Jonson*, 85.

order and certainly disgust the audience, but this is not a tragedy and the threats dissipate with the laughter and with the artifice of the ending. It is a world where a moment's lustful attraction transmutes into a wicked plan to seduce and rejection almost turns to rape ... almost. The generic features of comedy are there: intention to amuse, partly by depicting characters to whom the audience can feel superior, exposure of the corruption of the time, shocks, reversals, mockery, humiliation, but *Volpone* is not a happy comedy. It is dark, grimly critical of human beings, satirical and cynical. It has stock characters displaying dominant humours. There is crude physical comedy in the verbal abuse of Volpone by Corvino and Corbaccio thinking the old man too deaf to hear and Mosca playing along with them. Though close to farce the comments are disgusting, shocking reminders of the physical inconveniences of old age and the cruel readiness of people to smile to the face while criticizing behind the back. There is the cruelly humiliating, physical comedy of Sir Pol squeezed into a turtle shell, and the clever patter of Volpone as Scoto, ostensibly fooling the crowd while really catching a glimpse of Celia. There is the disgusting picture of Volpone giving Celia another line of patter as he outlines the advantages of becoming his mistress and then the farce of his attempting to force her and being thwarted by Bonario. These moments are ridiculous, absurd, but how superior can the audience honestly feel laughing as it watches characters so like itself?

It is fitting that Greek tragedies were followed by satyr plays and Elizabethan dramas by a jig.[4] Laughter is an antidote to overwhelming sorrow or a counterbalance reminding the audience that tragedy is a temporary interruption to the need to laugh at and mock a world that was a joke – all our proud possessions, all our pomp, brought to nothing so easily, after such a short life. And what fools men could be: spending so much effort in accumulating power, money and things, and neglecting their spiritual life. Your fleshly existence was relatively short and you were a long time dead. All flesh was as insubstantial as grass, as a flower, cut down by death. Eternity in Hell was a disproportionate price to pay for the transient tinsel pleasures of the flesh. Viewed through the teachings of religion, most aspects of this life were not to be taken seriously. The next life was the important one. This just a preparation for Heaven or Hell. The church promulgated the view that people are endlessly foolish and folly leads to sin, and that the wages of sin were death

---

4 A jig does not just mean a lively folk dance, but a mixture of dancing, singing, music and a comic sketch or farcical routine. In Tudor times these end pieces developed away from short, knockabout sketches, often satirizing topical events, into longer comic dramas in their own right. They often kept songs and music in them, but the dialogue became the main vehicle for instruction.

and death was the portal to Hell if you died unrepentant. Tragedy portrayed how folly led to sin and disaster. Comedy too deals in the portrayal of folly, but presenting it in such a way as invites laughter, exposes and eradicates folly (temporarily), and leads to a happy outcome. It is generally folly of a type that shames and humiliates but does not kill. It may drive characters to the edge of madness, however. In *The Comedy of Errors*, *Twelfth Night* and *Volpone*, mistaken perceptions spiral out of control until characters are near to frenzy, madness and desperation born of disappointment. There are elements in the play that follow closely the developments of tragedy and it is open to question just how much laughter it evokes. All the classic characteristics of tragedy are there: *hamartia* (character flaw), *hubris* (overreaching confidence), *anagnorisis* (recognition of your fault), *peripeteia* (the reversal of fortunes) and above all there is the fall of a great man. Volpone is talented, skilled and with a high position in society. How much good he could achieve with his drive and resilience. Mosca, perhaps even more talented, has immense management skill, if only his lowly rank had not restricted his scope in life. But both men have tainted characters. They are dedicated to evil. They probably do not at any point evoke our sympathy. They are great sinners who delight in sinning. They are therefore riding for a fall. We hope.

As Mosca, Volpone and the rest are *not* people we feel concern for – they are all too greedy and deceitful – where does the humour come from in their story? What sort of laughter does this play evoke? More often the cruel rictus of a grimace comes to the lips more readily than a smile or a laugh. It is a cruel play, about cruel people, and it brings out the cruel pleasure we feel in seeing bad people undone. Satire is not a friendly or life-affirming form. It aims to expose folly and wrongdoing by mockery and humiliation. It tends to reveal topical contemporary shortcomings. Its aims are positive but its means are often not pleasant. There are not many occasions where our response is likely to be of the open, warm-hearted sort that laughs at Sir Toby's drunkenness (*Twelfth Night*) or Lysander waking to magic-induced instant love for Helena (*A Midsummer Night's Dream*). Those antic, mad-cap plays have moments of dark humour, but *Volpone* is black throughout. Samuel Taylor Coleridge asserts, 'How impossible it is to keep up any pleasurable interest in a tale, in which there is no goodness of heart in any of the prominent characters'.[5] He sees the last two acts as 'a painful weight on the feelings'. A Jacobean audience would expect and demand the justice of the bad being brought down, but the delay begins to test one's confidence, especially as Mosca and Volpone are acquitted after the first court session. Further complications make denouement seem unlikely. The plot spirals into what looks like

5 Coleridge, *The Literary Remains* (ed. H. N. Coleridge), 2. 276.

an entanglement that is impossible to unravel. Indeed the whole piece is a risk on Jonson's part. How much interest can he generate and sustain in such vile action? Can we enjoy a play when we dislike the characters? Jonson's prologue calls Volpone 'quick comedy, refined/As best critics have designed'. By 'refined' he perhaps means without the low comic devices (slapstick, bawdy, clowns) that some writers deployed to gain the approval of the groundlings. If laughter was not always the end of comedy it was not always the means either. His art is serious even when comic and satirical, and makes intellectual and moral demands on the viewers. The relentless escalation of evil disgusts the audience with the sins and stupidities of the characters but also with their greed and dishonesty. J. B. Bamborough claims that apart from Celia and Bonario 'no one [...] has any genuine claim on our sympathy and admiration'.[6] Even those two characters may be seen as illustrating virtue's weakness when it lacks vigorous engagement in the unending battle against evil. Celia makes her defence of chastity clearly and spiritedly to Volpone, but is cowed and ineffective in court. Right, just, virtuous words are no defence when surrounded by lies and are of little help without direct action.

The only two characters who have any goodness are marginal. What they represent morally is important, but their part in the action, even in the denouement, is minimal. The majority of the action and the mood are blackly vile. There is little to break that mood. Mosca, the type of the devious servant, would normally make the audience laugh, with his antics, common accent, quick repartee and endlessly inventive improvisation, but his conduct is as vile, deceptive, lying and covetous as that of the other main characters. He does make us smile – up to a point. If we smile it is at how the foolish are fooled, but that soon loses its amusement and we long for Mosca to be caught, exposed and punished. Little mirth is derived from a morality play and in some respects that is what Volpone is.

The business of comedy was more important and serious than simply raising a laugh. It has always served a much graver purpose than mere humorous entertainment, but has also been regarded by religious, moral and cultural guardians as a lesser form than tragedy. Even the arts had hierarchies. In painting, devotional studies (annunciations, nativities, crucifixions) were thought to be the highest endeavour, and historical subjects were thought superior to landscape and portraiture. Grotesque topics of common life (card playing, village dances, tavern scenes) were thought very low art. In literature the epic, tragic drama, religious poetry, even lyrics and love verses were thought of as higher forms than mere comedy.

6 Ben Jonson, 90.

Though the plays of Terence and Plautus were studied, translated and performed by schoolboys and undergraduates, and the satires of Juvenal and Horace were similarly on educational syllabuses, comedy was regarded with suspicion. It was thought to be a too vulgar form, too associated with the bourgeoisie and commoners, too concerned with trickery, knavery and sex. Comic sketches performed at fairs commonly dwelled on the cuckolding of husbands by promiscuous wives and lustful young men. That was a low form, but comedy, properly handled, could use laughter to draw attention to personal or societal failings that need correcting. Comedy could therefore be morally instructive. To the Elizabethans-Jacobeans the didactic aim justified literature, but because comedy encouraged disrespect for the governing elite, debunking and exposing their moral failings, church and state remained uneasy about the whole range of comic forms. Furthermore comedies generally portrayed morally unacceptable (that is, sexual) situations. They might expose corruption, but the fear was that the laughter blurred the moral lesson, that delight and pleasure distracted from driving home the ethical point. Stubbes expressed the ambiguous status of comic drama when he has one of his speakers, Philoponus, assert, 'Of comedies the matter and ground is love, bawdry, cozening, flattery, whoredom, adultery. The persons or agents whores, queens [vulgar, base young women], bawds [prostitutes or pimps], scullions [kitchen servant], knaves, courtesans, lecherous old men, amorous young men with suchlike of infinite variety.' The other aspect is expressed by the second interlocutor, Spudeus, who says, 'But notwithstanding, I have heard some hold opinion that they be as good as sermons, and that many a good example may be learned out of them.' Pholoponus becomes incandescent in his response, condemning 'filthy plays and bawdy interludes' for spreading 'bawdry, heathenry, paganry, scurrility, and devilry itself'.[7] He deprecates how play-going encourages idleness given the numbers thronging the theatres and how plays display too many forms of flirting and promiscuous conduct and how audiences too indulge in similarly unseemly behaviour.

Love and the foolish things it makes people do was a traditional subject for comedy. Robert Burton devotes his Third Partition of *The Anatomy of Melancholy* to 'Love-Melancholy'. He prefaces the discourse by asserting that some will 'discommend' his focusing love at all for it is

> too Comical a subject [...] too phantastical, and fit alone for a wan-
> ton Poet, a feeling young love-sick gallant, an effeminate Courtier, or
> some such idle person. And 'tis true, they say: for by the naughtiness

---

7 *The Anatomie of Abuses* (11583), cited in King, *Voices of the English Reformation*, 224–5.

of men it is so come to pass, [...] that the very name of Love is odious to chaster ears.[8]

He later anatomizes the psychological consequences of love – jealousy, obsession, melancholy, madness and suicide – but opens by acknowledging the positives: the attraction to what is beautiful, good and fair and how love can 'sweeten our life'.[9] What makes him anxious (he was a clergyman) is the tendency of the emotion to turn into excess of lust or when a love relationship fails to become distorted into various forms of negative psychological reaction. *Volpone's* focus is excessive greed, a psychological, manic possession, touching on the sin of wanting riches, on hoarding money or valuables for their own sake, on the addiction of wanting more and more. These darkly serious matters are not immediately obvious as sources of humour. During the Renaissance comedy was expected to instruct, to teach a lesson, fully as much as tragedy, but moralists were as uneasy with the genre as they had been in the Middle Ages. The growth of public theatres and the concomitant accessibility of many plays to many more people made the censoring authorities and the church (both Catholic and English) ludicrously sensitive to the downsides of comedy. They feared that laughter often obscured what was serious underneath the situation being laughed at and that the content and subject of comedy were often immoral and handled distastefully. They suspected that the display of immorality, the basic human fascination with the rude and the lewd, was the real intent of the writers and actors and the real interest of the audience.

This uneasy suspicion is reflected in Sir Philip Sidney's *Defence of Poetry* (probably written 1581, published 1595). He examines in detail and at length the potential of tragedy to delight and instruct and does not look at comedy at all as a separate genre. He does consider the inappropriate mingling of comic elements with serious tragic subjects in that 'mongrel tragicomedy'. He deplores how dramatists 'thrust in the clown by head and shoulders to play a part in majestical matters with neither decency nor discretion'.[10] His attitude is aristocratic, superior, elitist and purist. He speaks for high poetry and tragedy as a cultural preserve of the privileged and learned.

> Having indeed no right comedy, in that comical part of our trag-
> edy, we have nothing but scurrility, unworthy of any chaste ears, or
> some extreme show of doltishness, indeed fit to lift up a loud laughter,
> and nothing else: where the whole tract of a comedy should be full

---

8 Burton, part 3, sec. 1, 611.
9 Burton, part 3, sec. 1, 612.
10 *A Defence of Poetry*, 67.

of delight, as the tragedy should be still maintained in a well-raised admiration.[11]

Sidney defines comedy as 'an imitation of the common errors of our life'. He would disapprove of the types presented in *Volpone*, but by 1606 a new range of targets and situations had become common – the sordid denizens of the city – and had generated a new subgenre – the city comedy. 'Nothing but scurrility' is an apt description for Jonson's cast here and in his other plays. Even his chaste characters, lamentably weak, do not combat evil in any effective way. But Jonson presents a tale that holds our attention by its awfulness and its artfulness. Though the verse might not be, as Sidney demanded, 'set in delightful proportion', yet Jonson fulfils the requirement of a poet:

> With a tale forsooth, he cometh unto you, with a tale which holdeth children from play and old men from the chimney-corner, and, pretending no more, doth intend the winning of the mind from wickedness to virtue.[12]

Sidney's ideal comedy would be the witty, elegant complications of courtly characters, as in the plays of John Lyly. He regards delight as the outcome of genteel comedy and distinguishes between delight (quiet pleasure) and the belly laugh. Delight derives from that which is natural while

> laughter almost ever cometh of things most disproportionate to ourselves and nature. Delight hath a joy in it, either permanent or present. Laughter hath only a scornful tickling.
> [...] we laugh at deformed creatures, wherein certainly we cannot delight. We delight in good chances, we laugh at mischances [...] the representing of so strange a power in love procureth delight, and the scornfulness of the action stirreth laughter. [...] the great fault [...] is that they [comic writers] stir laughter in sinful things [...] or in miserable, which are rather to be pitied than scorned. For what is it to make folks gape at a wretched beggar and a beggarly clown?[13]

For Sidney comedy's proper targets are 'a busy loving courtier [like Sir Pol] [...] a heartless threatening Thraso [like Corvino]; a self-wise-seeming

11 A *Defence of Poetry*, 67.
12 A *Defence of Poetry*, 40.
13 A *Defence of Poetry*, 68–9.

schoolmaster; an awry-transformed traveller [Sir Pol again]'.[14] The problem is
that Sidney's targets are narrowly exclusive stock types. Jonson's comic types
represent a wider social range but lack probity; knavery reaches all stations.
This irreverent cynicism earned Jonson a reputation for being so bitterly
misanthropic some might assert that 'all he writes is railing' (prologue, 10). It is
the lot of satirists to be labelled as perpetually mocking and detracting. Jonson
unswervingly mocks the failings of types from all classes and sees how comedy
can happen in moments of tragedy and that life is a complex mingling of what
makes us cry and laugh. In discussing the tragic playwright Seneca, Francis
Meres linked the Roman with the rising stars of English theatre: 'As Plautus
and Seneca are accounted the best for Comedy and Tragedy among the Latins,
so Shakespeare among the English is the most excellent in both kinds for the
stage.'[15] Among 'our best for tragedy' he lists 'Lord Buckhurst, Doctor Legge of
Cambridge, Doctor Edes of Oxford, Master Edward Ferris, the author of the
Mirror for Magistrates, Marlowe, Peele, Watson, Kyd, Shakespeare, Drayton,
Chapman, Dekker, and Benjamin Johnson'. Jonson is not mentioned among
the best comic writers or satirists, because Palladis Tamia was first published
in 1598 and Every Man in His Humour (the only comedy of note Jonson had
written at that point) was performed the same year and appeared too late for
consideration.

His best, in any case, was yet to come.

The impulse to correct mistaken or morally reprehensible conduct through
mockery, parody and deflation is as natural as breathing. Young children are
quick to imitate what is funny and deserves drawing attention to. Deflating
the pompous or self-important is a natural, human reaction. We laugh at the
authority figure who, full of his own self-importance, trips over. We mock
those with geekish monomaniac obsession, those too romantic, those too
cynical, those exhibiting any form of excess. The comic spirit's domain is man's
endless folly. Disproportion, affectation, pomposity, overfussiness, hypocrisy,
self-delusion, being tricked, plain stupidity, obsession, vanity, false vanity,
simple-mindedness and naivety all evoke various forms of humorous response
from the wry smile to gales of laughter. Laughter becomes possible whenever
reason is offended, whenever someone says or does something that is silly,
outrageous or irrational. Comedy aims to cleanse irrationality by mocking the
perpetrator into humiliation. It is a revenge against those who offend common

---

14 Defence of Poetry, 69. Thraso is a boastful soldier in the Terentian comedy Eunuchus.
   Representing the traveller distorted by visiting foreign cultures is, partially at least,
   Jonson's aim in creating Sir Politic. This was addressed in Shakespeare's As You Like It
   (1599).
15 Palladis Tamia (1598).

sense and balance. Any excess was seen as contrary to reason, whether it was being overdressed, spending too much on ostentatious display, thinking too much of yourself, being obsessed with money, being overly infatuated with another person, displaying snobbery, being caught out in a deception you were trying to work on others or just being stupid. As tragedy can have its grimly humorous aspect so too comedy can be black. The most serious happenings (death, lost love) often trigger jokes as if laughter were a way of dealing with matters so grave and hurtful they cannot be addressed easily by serious discussion. Laughter acts as a safety valve to relieve the pressure of something that affects us deeply but cannot easily be expressed. A serious situation made fun of has a shock effect, making us laugh involuntarily in response to its inappropriateness. Volpone, changing from assumed geriatric leaping from his bed to take on the role of charmer and seducer and then morphing again into would-be rapist is surprising, horrible, shocking and, ultimately, absurd.[16] Surprise often triggers laughter. The repulsiveness of the intended rape is interrupted before it goes far, but the language of Bonario is ludicrous too:

> Forbear, foul ravisher, libidinous swine,
> Free the forced lady, or thou diest, imposter.
> But that I am loath to snatch thy punishment
> Out of the hand of justice, thou shouldst yet,
> Be made the timely sacrifice of vengeance,
> Before this altar, and this dross, thy idol. (3.8.267–72)

There is something too formal in the verse, too wooden and unnatural. He speaks like a clean-cut hero – one of Puritan values – and the speech comes pat. Such controlled clarity is unlikely at such a dramatic moment and the genuine revulsion is smoothed out by the formality. The ludicrousness lies in Bonario, at a moment of quick action, being so fluent and philosophical. Though contextualizing Volpone's action with the correct Christian values, the effect is laughable. Bonario's way of talking is unnatural and rather superior. Some of the effect is lost because the audience knows all along that Bonario is concealed and watching, but it still makes us laugh. A common feature of what provokes laughter, seen in the punchlines of jokes, is the unusual, the unexpected juxtaposing of items that are normally not brought together – like playing the 'Dead March' at a wedding instead of 'Here Comes the Bride', or a man with an ass's head (as in *A Midsummer Night's Dream*). The basic situation

---

16 Volpone is not necessarily as old as he pretends to the legacy hunters. He seems active enough and is clearly not bedridden. The *captators*, at the beginning of their scheme, presumably did not know him well enough to realize he was not old and sick.

of *Volpone*, the pretence that the magnifico is dying, the gruesomeness of the legacy hunters ghoulishly trying to insinuate themselves into his will while really hoping for his death to follow quickly, the descriptions of the features of old age, all have a darkness, a repulsiveness to them that is disturbing in itself, but made worse by the acknowledgement that such things do happen, that fiction and fact unsettlingly overlap. This is a black comedy with a bleak view of man's inhumanity to man. Black comedy treats sinister and disturbing events with a humour that shocks or offends. It is a way of making an audience focus on something it would rather not, like a trio of men waiting for another to die so they can grab his loot, like a man of superior rank involved in an underhand, demeaning scam.

The play offers a wide range of humour. The unusual subject (fortune hunting) is amusing. The extemporizing skill of Mosca in responding effectively to all the twists and turns of the plot and to the reservations and demands of the scavengers, and the sight of Volpone masquerading as a disgusting old man excite amused admiration at their acting and improvisational skills. However wrong what they are doing may be we still laugh at the consummate ability this double act displays. But they both become ripe for a fall and comedy often displays overmighty characters brought down. Disturbingly, the two defeat each other rather than goodness destroying them. It takes a thief to catch a thief. As Volpone says, with more ironic truth than he knows,

> What a rare punishment
> Is avarice, to itself! (1.4.142–3)

Stock types are satirized: lawyers, merchants, physicians, the *avocatori*, the overdominant husband, the blushingly demure chaste wife. There is excess, wrath, lust, vanity, greed – all sources of humour.[17] Gullibility is widespread and many of the deceivers are also self-deceived. Celia has been gulled by her husband, having previously perhaps thought him honourable. Bonario is fooled into thinking his father loves him. There is the posturing knowledgeability of Sir Politic, pretending to have all sorts of secrets projects afoot. He is a version of the 'self-wise-seeming schoolmaster' combined with the 'awry-transformed traveller' of Sidney's acceptable comic types. There is his naive breathless astonishment at the petty news of 'prodigies' from England (the nesting raven, the whelping lion, the 'porcpisces', the sturgeon, the whale waiting to subvert

---

17 Apart from the Greek and Roman comic playwrights, Theophrastus provided stereotypical portraits in *The Characters*. The types he identifies – the Flatterer, the Chatterer, the Boor, the Skinflint, the Avaricious Man, the Boaster – commonly appear in Renaissance drama.

the Hanseatic fleet). His foolish belief that spies and plotters were all around sending cyphered messages in various fruits and other foodstuffs mocks the paranoid suspicions of Francis Walsingham and his agents in the previous reign and William Cecil in the current one. The serious reverse to that is remembering that the Babington plotters actually hid coded letters in beer barrels delivered to Mary Queen of Scots in prison at Chartley Hall. So, behind the excessive credulousness of Sir Politic's comments lies a genuine concern, made more relevant by the exposing of the Gunpowder Plot in the months prior to the play being written. This gains further traction in view of Jonson himself being questioned about his contacts with the plotters. There are many other topical references that would raise smiles around The Globe, for like Autolycus (*The Winter's Tale*) Sir Politic is a 'snapper up of unconsidered trifles', his mind is a ragbag of useless information and his 'diary' reveals he is a fool to be mocked. In parallel with his pathetic desire to be thought in the know about international matters is his evident ignorance of many matters he claims inside knowledge of. He wants to live up to his name and he would like to be thought a man of the world, a seasoned traveller, a politic (sound, prudent) man with his finger on the pulse. He is clearly not in Venice for its cultural ambience. His wife, a stock Theophrastian 'chatterer', driving Volpone crazy with her endless talking, seems only to travel in order to glean 'intelligence/Of tires [head-dresses], and fashions, and behaviour/ Among the courtesans' (2.1.27–9) and snuff up bite-size snippets of cultural information, presumably to regurgitate to others back in England to impress them with her worldliness. This couple present a satirical view of the English abroad, ignorant and vain yet pretending to knowledge of many matters. The expressive shortened version of their name – Pol – likens them to parrots, imitating and chattering nonsense unstoppably without understanding what they are saying. Both suffer from a form of logorrhoea. This is a communication disorder expressing itself through a persistent involuntary urge to speak. The sufferer is incapable of keeping quiet for any length of time, may be semi-incoherent in expression, but certainly virtually unceasing in flow. Sir Pol is suitably duped by Peregrine into believing he is about to be arrested for plotting to betray the Venetian state to their enemies the Turks. His panic is amusing in itself but is driven further when he is persuaded to hide in a giant tortoise shell. This presumably is a turtle shell rather than a tortoise for it must be big enough for Sir Pol to hide in. Coryat, in discussing Venice, mentions how 'amongst many other strange fishes that I have observed in their market places, I have seen many Torteises.'[18] The word 'fishes' suggests the marine rather than the land reptile and he presumably means the fish

18 Quoted in the New Mermaid (1968) edition, 164.

market (*piscaria*) near the Rialto Bridge. There is suitable absurdity in this absurd know-all trying to disguise himself thus. It is comic justice. Comedy often expresses a cruel streak in people. *Volpone* is persistently cruel, but the moral corruption of its characters deserves severe retribution and therefore the discomforting of the main characters appeals to the nasty, punitive streak in us, but also to our sense of justice. Sir Pol's boisterous confidence cries out for deflation. He is a grotesque, larger than life and yet another fool blind to his own foolishness. His many projects are laughable and as outrageous as Scoto's fake claims for the effects of his cure-all ointment. For most of the play Peregrine endures Sir Pol putting him down and adopting a patronizing attitude, constantly preaching and putting him right. Like his wife, Sir Pol does not know when to stop talking and Peregrine is eventually driven to take revenge. His long-sustained polite deference reminds us how much of social life is based on the agreement to pretend we like people or keep silent about their negative aspects. Peregrine's revenge pleases for it is what we all wish to do to those who persistently aggravate us.

The central characters are all caricatures. Their grotesquerie has some element of the comedy of humours. This latter is founded on the theory of the four bodily humours and the idea that some people have a dominant humour that rules their life and behaviour – jealousy, greed, lust, anger are common personality traits mocked.

There is great pleasure in watching cleverness succeed, even if it is criminal in intent. But there is also pleasure in seeing overconfident cleverness brought down. Even today, however, we demand that the wrongdoers be caught in the end unless they see the error of their ways and reform. Jonson's view was harsh: 'Natures that are hardened to evil you shall sooner break than make straight.'[19] The hustler who seeks to right wrong we may applaud. The con man who is only out for his own gain may be applauded so far as he cheats those who deserve to be cheated, but will be expected to be punished after he has punished. There is amusement too in the biter being bit. No one likes a clever dick who always wins. Excess is always wrong but was forgivable if humbly repented. Neither protagonist shows remorse and both go too far.

10.1.1 The dénouement and the trials

The denouement of comedy traditionally brings a restoration of harmony after misrule. This mirrors our persistent hope for and belief in life having a happy ending and involves the humiliation, downfall and/or punishment of the villains. To the Jacobeans, the punishment of wrongdoers, in tragedy

19 *Timber*, 4.

or comedy, though clearly artificially effected, was an affirmation of their overarching belief that God saw all and would, one time or other, exercise his judgement. Public shaming of the wrongdoers is palpably the key achievement of the second trial. Authority is imposed and order apparently restored, but there is none of the love-and-marriage symbolism found in the resolution of Shakespeare's comedies. Coleridge suggested, 'If it were possible to lessen the paramountcy of Volpone himself, a most delightful comedy might be produced, by making Celia the ward or niece of Corvino, instead of his wife, and Bonario her lover.'[20] That would have provided love interest, but would be a sentimental sop. It is vital that Volpone feel he is paramount, above the weaknesses that make others fail, above the law – that is his *hubris* and *hamartia* (character flaw). *Volpone* is too tough, too harsh a play to conform to the romantic fantasy of fabricating the outcome Coleridge envisaged. An alliance between Celia and Bonario would be too incredible, requiring major realigning of the plot structure. It would also be out of place in an unblinking exposure of man's inhumanity. It demeans audiences to assume they naively expect and want a soppy ending and have not the moral and intellectual strength to watch cynical crimes committed and severely punished. Jacobean orthodoxy, however, believed God did punish sin, and the judgement of sinners at the end of a play was in keeping with that. Pleasure in the theatre does not only consist in easy-going entertainment that makes no intellectual demands. On the grounds of convincing verisimilitude the play gets away with the second trial and the exposure of the cheats because they give themselves away. Postponing Mosca and Volpone being caught creates suspense and makes the audience wait for (and begin to doubt) the orthodox retribution. The resolution is drawn out, covering three long scenes in act 4 and the whole of act 5 (12 scenes). Coleridge saw the difficulty of maintaining interest when the characters are nearly all evil. The clue to Coleridge's misunderstanding is in the words 'delightful' and pleasurable'. The play's delight and pleasure do not consist of gentle things like love interest and 'goodness of heart'. The *Volpone* world is cruel and selfish, and the delight consists of seeing perpetrators of sin caught, exposed and punished. Throughout, the comedy is cruel. Amusement resides in watching the *captators* deservedly tricked, then longing to see the tricksters finally brought to book. Interest in Volpone begins to ebb when he adds lust to his sins and emotionally hurts someone who does not deserve it. After the first trial there is the dark humour of Volpone and Mosca teasing the hapless scavengers as we wonder how (or if) these two will finally be brought down. These final stages lead both into overconfident *hubris*. They go too far, are too sure of escaping the law, too proud of their ability. They are due for

20 *Literary Remains*, 2. 276.

a fall and each proves to be the other's *nemesis*. One of the features of Greek tragedy was the working of Nemesis, the ancient Greek goddess of retribution, representing the belief that whatever wrong you do will be done back to you, through the gods or a human agent of punishment. Nemesis (from the Greek for paying what is due) was a remorseless goddess pursuing perpetrators, for years if necessary, until vengeance was taken. Just payment for wrong done is postponed, involves further deception as Mosca masquerades as Volpone's heir (a servant in his master's clothes) and Volpone disguises himself as a *commendatore*, an agent of the law who will eventually catch him. While we laugh at how they trick the legacy hunters we also see their overreaching accelerating and wait for their luck to run out.

Beginning within Volpone's palazzo, the play moves gradually from the private to the public, from the privacy of Volpone's bedroom to the bar of public condemnation. His and Mosca's major sins (multiple greed, multiple deception with fraud and the revelling in it, multiple false witness, lust) are committed in their private space, but they are finally caught and sentenced in public. The intervening section, when Volpone as Scoto goes into the streets, foreshadows his public humbling. This is a set-up, another fiction, another trick for him to see Celia, but he retreats to his private space to seduce her. The failure of this ploy lures him to attempt to assault her sexually and the subsequent court hearings bring the Fox out of cover and into the open. It is right that Mosca and the legacy hunters should be exposed to the vilification of the citizens and that their punishments should be public.

Volpone, as a gentleman, will be quietly removed from the court to the prison and languish there until he is disabled for real. It is a sort of justice that a man who has pretended immobility and illness will actually be rendered immobile and will become ill. His 'substance' 'gotten by imposture' is confiscated and he is 'to lie in prison, cramped with irons,/Till thou be'st sick, and lame indeed' (5.12.119–24). Reality will at last match Volpone's art. The *Scrutineo*, the Senate court, was held in the Doge's Palace in St Mark's Square. Attached to it was a prison accessed via the famous Bridge of Sighs. Though it was not known by this name until the nineteenth century, the link from palace to prison was built in 1602. It was enclosed and had barred windows. Prisoners were taken directly from the courtroom to their cell. This privacy is apparently accorded to Volpone on the grounds of his rank. The two court scenes enable Jonson indirectly to expose the corrupt and inept dealings of the contemporary English judiciary and the double standard whereby those of higher rank could be treated with more leniency than the ordinary mass of citizens.

The first hearing shows the magistrates' naivety and foregrounds the *captators*' capacity for bearing false witness. Joining together, the villains pervert the course of justice. Mosca asks the trio, 'Is the lie/Safely conveyed amongst us?' (4.4.3–4). Voltore, whose public stage this is, spins a web of deceits to match the private ones previously shown and leads the witnesses in the perjuries they commit. It is fine theatre very professionally conducted, but, fittingly for such a play, it is all untrue. Some in the audience would be mindful that God's court would not be misled. He could see into every heart and his judgement would be eternal.

The second session portrays the truth finally struggling out. The high reputation of Venice's legal system is vindicated, but not without revealing the difficulty of establishing the truth when dishonesty pours from the mouth of a lawyer. The effect of the two sessions is to provoke thoughts about the impartiality and forensic acuteness of the English system. Both trials are firmly based on words and the difficulty of telling just whether the claims made are genuine or not. Michel de Montaigne, in 'On the Vanity of Words', deplores the art of fine speaking as 'deceiving not our eyes but our judgement, bastardizing and corrupting things in their very essence' so that feelings are 'inflated with rich and magnificent words'.[21] *Volpone* rests on the misuse of words. Voltore's virtuoso performance begins with the lying use of words to claim how moved the magistrates will be when they see the state of Volpone. He builds a picture defaming the characters of Celia and Bonario. She is a 'lewd woman', 'a close adulteress', 'a strumpet' and a 'stale', and he a 'lascivious youth'. He claims they were 'taken, in the act'. He several times flatters the court, calling them 'your fatherhoods' as a term of respect and a reminder that they act as guardians of the state, words dressing lies as truth – another masquerade. Using the image of 'danger' and 'vice' beguiling 'under the shade of virtue' is cynical beyond belief, for what he accuses Celia and Bonario of is exactly what the villains have done – private vice pretending to public virtue – and is what he is in fact doing as he speaks. Bonario's reminder of the 'mercenary tongue' of a lawyer is taken as disrespect rather than a truth many would endorse. Under oath Corvino and Corbaccio both lie. Celia's fainting is dismissed by her own husband as 'prettily feigned'. The discrepancy between what the audience hears and what it knows ratchets up the tension and creates doubt whether the truth can emerge at all. The drama is increased when Lady Pol accuses Celia of being a 'harlot'. Misled by Mosca she believes Celia is the courtesan falsely claimed to have been observed with Sir Pol. Bonario's attack on courts 'where multitude, and clamour, overcomes' is rejected as 'insolent' and ignored as Volpone makes his triumphant entrance masquerading 'as impotent' (that is, acting the part of a man completely disabled, weak and clearly incapable of sexual assault). Voltore's concluding address is cleverly

21 Screech, 343.

ironic – he suggests torturing the truth out of the old man and rounds off the irony by suggesting that if Volpone can be accused none of the *avocatori* are safe from similar slurs against their character. The 'evidence' has relied solely on perjured depositions by Corbaccio and Corvino and the high rhetoric of Voltore's innuendos. Assuming that taking an oath means witnesses will tell the truth the court has Celia and Bonario taken into custody. This marks the lowest point; the bad seem to have won. It is a trick to trick the tricksters. Their apparent invulnerability leads them into incautious carelessness and to the second trial, and their eventual public exposure and conviction. Justice being finally done is one end to a comedy.

10.2 Sources

No one source provides the story of *Volpone*. It is a collage of many ideas, moods, hints and character types from other writers, many of them classical as is to be expected with Jonson. The money-greed, deception, legacy hunting and city corruption themes are drawn from the literature of Rome. The cunning fox story and the likening of humans to animals derive from medieval folklore and beast fables, though the Greek fabulist Aesop also contributes to this aspect. Some male audience members would recognize some of the echoes of the classics, many more, male and female, might spot the beast fable elements. (The fable aspect is dealt with in chapter 12.) The text alone would work as a comprehensible story, but the contexts give extra dimension. The religious ethics by which it would be mediated and the classical sources resonating in the language and the situations turn it from a flat narrative to a disturbingly three-dimensional representation of human evil.

10.2.1 The classics

The satires of Juvenal and Horace are recurrent correlatives to the dramatic worlds Jonson creates. They do not constitute sources so much as triggers for the preoccupations of his work that become major themes in *Volpone*. The cynicism of Juvenal (late first century AD–early second century AD) focuses behaviour in the seething city of Rome which, for Jonson, had clear parallels with London. In Satire I we find a view that precisely locks the two poets together:

who

Could endure this monstrous city, however callous at heart,
And swallow his wrath?[22]

22 *The Sixteen Satires* (trans. Peter Green), 66.

Among the types Juvenal identifies as representing the corrupt ambience of urban life are (as already mentioned) 'some chiselling advocate', 'an informer', and 'men who earn legacies in bed'. He calls his 'an age when each pimp of a husband/Takes gifts from his own wife's lover'.[23] Juvenal's targets and tone are echoed in Jonson. Both had a fiery indignation against the deceitful, greedy, corrupt nature of their society. Both stare unblinkingly into the heart of the darkness of the human heart. Satire I provides a possible source for Volpone's sacrilegious adulation of gold:

> Though as yet, pernicious Cash, you lack
> A temple of your own, though we have raised no altars
> To sovereign Gold (as already we worship Honour,
> Peace, Victory, Virtue, or Concord) –

Jonson found contemporary money madness reflected in Juvenal's comments: 'Honesty's praised, but honest men freeze. Wealth springs from crime',[24] and

> has there ever
> Been so rich a crop of vices? When has the purse
> Of greed yawned wider?[25]

The central idea of *Volpone* – legacy hunters handing over presents as inducements to being named as the sole legatee – recurs in Juvenal's reference to 'men who earn legacies in bed' and 'inheriting legacies'.[26] *Captatio* (legacy hunting) was a common activity in the ancient world. In Greece some men made it a profession. Greek new comedy, like that of Menander, has it as a common theme along with some of the stock characters who filter into the Roman comedies of Plautus, Italian Renaissance commedia dell'arte and the works of Jonson: low types like grooms, cooks, market traders, parasites using demotic speech and vulgar jokes.

Other stock characters – the *senex iratus* (angry old man), the overstrict parent obstructing his son or daughter's love affair, the *miles gloriosus* (boastful soldier), the golden-hearted whore – are all found in Greek and Roman comedies. The Roman Lucian satirizes the gruesome activity of *captatio* in *Dialogues of the Dead*, where, in Dialogue 15, the underworld god, Pluto,

---

23 *The Sixteen Satires*, 67.
24 *The Sixteen Satires*, 67.
25 *The Sixteen Satires*, 69, 68.
26 *The Sixteen Satires*, 66, 67.

orders Hermes (messenger of the gods) to bring to Hades (the realm of the dead) all the fortune seekers and flatterers buzzing round rich men. Pluto talks of 'Eucrates the rich – the man with no sons, but with fifty thousand men hunting his estates', surrounded by toadies who 'shower attention on him in public' but 'make their plans obvious to everyone when he's sick' and pray privately for his death. Eucrates knows what the *captators* are about, 'often leads them up the garden path with great skill' and is 'a lot healthier than the young men'. Pluto deplores their 'open-mouthed greed'[27] and plans, as a punishment, to gather them to him in death while their wealthy mark is allowed to outlive them.[28] In Dialogue 1 Diogenes expresses a standard view of wealth that was echoed in medieval and Renaissance thinking and is part of the message of *Volpone*. He asks Pollux to give a message to the living: 'Why do you guard your gold, you senseless fools? Why do you punish yourselves, counting interest, piling talents on talents, when you must come here shortly with no more than a penny?'[29] Given Jonson's extensive knowledge of classical literature and the number of key features in *Volpone* raised by Lucian, it seems highly likely that the *Dialogues* provided some background stimulus to the writing of the play.

Petronius too in *The Satyricon* touches briefly on the topic of legacy hunting among the many others that characterized decadent Imperial Rome. His protagonists arrive at the city of Croton, described as a place where the population comprises two sorts of people: 'Either they have fortunes [...] or they are fortune-hunters.' The town is 'like a plague-ridden countryside, where there is nothing but corpses being pecked and crows pecking them'. That image alone conjures up *Volpone*, but *Satyricon* also provides the cannibalism element when Eumolpus, an ageing, lecherous poet, poses as rich, unmarried and close to death and instructs the *capatators*: 'All those who have legacies in my will, except for my freedmen, will receive them only on this condition – that they cut up my corpse and eat it in front of the citizens.'[30] The theme re-emerges in the Renaissance with Erasmus's character Folly commenting on greed: 'Others fancy they've found an easy road to wealth by cultivating childless old men'.[31] John Aubrey, the famous seventeenth-century diarist, records his friend John Hoskyns saying, 'All those who came to London were

---

27 *Dialogues of the Dead*, 79, 81.
28 See also Lucian's *The Dream* as possible source for Mosca's interlude (1.2.).
29 *Dialogues of the Dead*, 7. The penny is the coin (an *obol*) put in the mouth of a corpse to pay Charon the Ferryman to row the dead across the River Styx to the Underworld.
30 *Satyricon* (trans. John Sullivan), 127, 162.
31 *Praise of Folly*, 142.

either carrion or crows' (that is, victims or predators).[32] This remark ties the city and one of its many sins to how Jonson presents his view of mankind. Juvenal's Satire 10 also provides some useful evaluations related to the mood and views in Jonson's play.

> Search every land, from Cadiz to the dawn-streaked shores
> Of Ganges, and you'll find few men who can distinguish
> A false from a worthwhile objective, or slash their way through
> The fogs of deception. Since when were our fears or desires
> Ever dictated by reason?[33]

Both Mosca and his master are foreshadowed in the lines

> The gift of the gab, a torrential facility,
> Has proved fatal to so many [...]
> [...] But more are strangulated
> By the capital they amass with such expense of spirit[34]

The Venetian value system echoes in a series of observations:

> The courts condemned him
> But the verdict was a farce. Who cares for reputation
> If he keeps his cash? ....
>
> The malice of heaven
> That granted ambition's prayers.
>
> The thirst for glory by far outstrips the
>
> Pursuit of virtue
> Good looks and decent behaviour too seldom are found
> In the same person.
>
> Cash always wins in the end.
> .... ask
> For a sound mind in a sound body, a valiant heart
> Without fear of death, that reckons longevity
> The least among Nature's gifts, that's strong to endure
> All kinds of toil, that's untainted by lust and anger,
> That prefers the sorrows and labours of Hercules to all
> Sardanapalus' downy cushions and women and junketings.[35]

32 Quoted in W. David Kay, *Ben Jonson: A Literary Life*, 88.
33 *Sixteen Satires*, 205.
34 Juvenal, *Satire 10*, lines 10–13.
35 These views are all expressed in *Satire 10*.

The moral of Satire 10 resonates in the closing thoughts, emphasizing that Fortune (not the Goddess of Destiny, but wealth) is not a deity; rather, it is only men who have raised riches to heavenly status:

> .... there's one
> Path, and one only, to a life of peace – through virtue.[36]

Dante (*L'Inferno*, canto 7) has Plutus (the god of riches in Roman times) as a demon guarding the fourth circle of Hell to which the misers and spendthrifts are condemned. This reinforces how seriously Catholic theology regarded the sins of Covetousness (or Envy) and Avarice.

Horace (65 BC–8 BC), persistently present in school and university curricula and in Jonson's writing, also attacks the same scavenging in his *Satires*. Book 2, Satire 5 focuses obsequious, self-interested hangers-on. In it Tiresias addresses Ulysses, who needs to recoup his fortunes after the depredations of the parasite suitors who, after his presumed death on his way back from Troy, camped in his palace seeking the hand of his wife, Penelope. The persona Tiresias advises, 'You must fish cunningly around/for old men's wills', follow law cases and support 'which party is rich and childless' even if he is a rogue.[37] Another source of cash may be 'a man who is rearing a delicate son/in an opulent style'. Ulysses must 'creep softly towards your goal, that is, to be named second heir'.

> If an accident sends the boy to his grave, *you* can move into
> the vacant place. That's a gamble which rarely fails.[38]

This implies a readiness to 'arrange' a 'casualty'. Murdering Volpone is suggested by Mosca to Corvino (1.5.67ff) and Corbaccio (3.9.14). Tiresias warns that a fortune seeker needs to check the will to ensure he is the sole heir or co-legatee, for 'frequently a raven with open beak/will be fooled by a civil servant.'[39] This may have suggested giving his greedy legacy hunters names relating to carrion birds waiting and watching a dying animal. Similar to Jonson's approach is

36 The Greeks raised Ploutos (Plutus) – riches – to god status. Aristophanes had him blinded by Zeus in order to suggest the random nature of good luck. This deity later becomes a blindfold female – Fortuna – whose impartial and arbitrary bringing of luck (good or bad) does not only refer to gaining or losing money but also to all other happenings in life.
37 *The Satires of Horace and Persius* (trans. Niall Rudd), 99
38 *The Satires of Horace and Persius*, 99.
39 *The Satires of Horace and Persius*, 100.

> if the old dotard happens to be under
the thumb of some scheming woman or freedman, make a deal:
you praise them, they praise you when you're not there.[40]

This idea is used by Jonson employing Mosca, the pretended carer for the fake 'old dotard', repeatedly claiming to each *captator* that he constantly pushes their case and praises their solicitude to his master. Even closer to Jonson is the advice to pimp his wife:

> If he's a lecher, don't wait to be asked – do the decent
thing and hand Penelope over.[41]

10.2.2 Contemporary carrion

Horace, Juvenal, Lucian and Petronius specifically focus the commonness of *captatio* in the social culture of the ancient world. J. B. Bamborough points out that the practice was 'never […] customary in England. It was not usual in Renaissance Italy either, but Jonson presumably felt Venice was far enough away to make it credible'.[42] This fails to acknowledge how in city comedy narratives avaricious and unprincipled men (and women) persistently target any victim with money, title, land and how often the legacy hunter is a member of the wealthy man's own family. The devious designs people have on an inheritance is a recurrent theme in Western literature. *Captatio* seems to have been an emerging feature in the early seventeenth century. In *Bartholomew Fair* (1614) Widow Purecraft (in a revealing aside) refers to the ranting Puritan, Zeal-of-the-land Busy, as 'the capital knave of the land' for

> making himself rich by being made feoffee in trust to
deceased brethren, and cozening their heirs by swearing the
absolute gift of their inheritance. (5.2.65–7)

A man, claiming to be religious, acting as guiding voice of God on earth to the elect, has been wheedling his way into being made, by their wills, the trustee with power over the land of brother Puritans and then retaining control of it and its value rather than handing it to the heirs. Greed and duplicity apparently know no bounds. The theme of pervasive parasitism (as shown in *Volpone*) is ironically extended, for the widow admits she has, in pure craft, conned 'feasts and gifts' out of the men seeking to marry her and

---

40 *The Satires of Horace and Persius*, 100.
41 *The Satires of Horace and Persius*, 100.
42 *Ben Jonson*, 83.

collects alms for her church but acts as 'devourer, instead of a distributor'. Finally, her greed is capped by her admission that she is 'a special maker of marriages for our decayed brethren with our rich widows' and takes a third of the value as her commission. This is supposed to be given to the 'poor elect'. She also makes matches for 'our poor handsome young virgins' with wealthy bachelors or widowers and blackmails them in return for her silence once they have 'got all put into their custodies'. As wealth spiralled up within a small sector of society in England from the seventeenth through to the nineteenth century (coinciding with and consequent on commercial and imperial expansion, each feeding the other), the theme of wills and the disruptions caused by discontented or disinherited relatives becomes a frequent theme in plays and novels. The more people amassed the more was at stake to protect from predators. The danger came as much from friends as family. As Thomas Middleton says, 'What worse knave to a man/Than he that eats his meat? (*No Wit, No Help Like a Woman's*, 1.3.78–9). If foolery was universal, so too was knavery, the one feeding the other and being fed off by the other. Wherever money and land were at stake the circle gathered round to hear the last will and testament read was often under extreme domestic tensions. The rich miser and those trying to wheedle their way into his will was an ancient literary combination, but had real-life contemporary descendants. The struggle between the daughters of Sir Brian Annesley was a recent example of such family jealousies. Sir Brian, a wealthy gentleman of Elizabeth's court, became senile. In 1603 the elder two of his three daughters tried to have him certified insane and incompetent to manage his finances or estate. It seems possible that Lady Grace Wildgoose, the eldest, had seen the will, disliked the terms and sought power of attorney in order to declare incompetence due to insanity. That would have put her father's property in her hands. The unmarried youngest daughter contested the move and wrote for support to an old acquaintance of her father, Sir Robert Cecil, secretary to the king. When Annesley died (July 1604), his will was successfully defended by his youngest daughter, Cordell, who inherited most of the family property. An executor of the upheld testament was Sir William Harvey, married to the Duchess of Southampton, mother of Shakespeare's one-time patron the Earl of Southampton.[43] The chain of connections suggests strongly the possibility that this story of family conflict over the division of property coalesced in Shakespeare's mind with the ancient Leir story (in Holinshed's *Chronicles*) and may have prompted his writing of *King Lear*. Shakespeare and Jonson worked together in the King's Men company and spent time together socially.

43 See Geoffrey Bullough, ed., *Narrative and Dramatic Sources of Shakespeare*, vol. 7, pp. 269–71, 276–84, 287–92.

It is possible the idea for *Volpone* came out of discussions between the two. Both were writing plays highly critical of society's decayed values. The practice of giving gifts to your patron was common in Jacobean court circles. It was not only a way of showing gratitude for the government place he had procured for you but it also acted as a sweetener to encourage him to add you to his legatees. Such was the story of Sir Thomas Sutton, an immensely rich entrepreneur, who became a miser and recluse in later life.[44] He is an example of the fortunate placeman who, working for the powerful Dudley family, had their influence to back him, married the rich widow of John Dudley and was given a pension by Ambrose Dudley, Earl of Warwick. From 1569–82, nominated by the Earl, he held the lucrative post of Master of the Ordinance in the North Parts, adding massively to his fortune by speculation in mining. From 1582–1611 he made a further fortune by moneylending in the south of England. 'His days as a money-lender coincided with a time of great inflation, when wealthy families were scrambling for the cash they needed for conspicuous consumption or merely to keep themselves afloat.'[45] His debtors – Lords Darcy and Mounteagle, the Earls of Essex, Sussex, Oxford and Suffolk – were some of the most powerful and influential men in the land. His wealth evoked envy and resentment. Known as 'Dives Sutton' he bought up the estates of defaulters, thus gaining even more from the income of those lands. He was, however, considerate to his servants and generous to the poor. Among his 'good works' he left an endowment to establish the Charterhouse, a residential 'hospital' providing accommodation, food and education to needy men and boys. He had a very able financial adviser/assistant, John Lawe, a lively gossipy man, who acted as liaison between the increasingly sociopathic Sutton and the public. There was much manoeuvring to inherit his money, but he tricked them all. He was still alive when *Volpone* was performed, but it is possible some in the audience would have seen parallels between him, his man of business and the stage scamster and his servant. The diarist, John Aubrey, in his *Brief Lives* identified Sutton as a possible model: "Twas from him that B. Johnson tooke his hint of the fox, and by Seigneur Volpone is meant Sutton', for he 'fed several with hopes of being his heir. The Earl of Dorset [...] mightily courted him and presented him, hoping to have been his heir, and so did several other great persons.'[46] This attribution is seconded by William Winstanley: 'I have conversed with some of the Wits, who credibly

---

44 Robert C. Evans, 'Thomas Sutton: Jonson's Volpone?' (in *Ben Jonson's Plays and Masques*, ed. Richard Harp), 411.

45 Evans, 413.

46 Quoted in Kay, 88.

informed me, that Ben Johnsons Play [...] had some allusion to Mr *Suttons* manner of treating his kindred.[47]

10.2.3 The Golden Age inverted

In addition to the story of Adam and Eve in the garden of Eden before the Fall, as icons of the original innocence of man and the locus for the perfect life, many in the audience would have in the back of their minds another legend idealizing the beginnings of the world. Hesiod (750–670 BC), the Greek poet, had written of a 'Golden Age' of pastoral plenty, of peaceful harmony between men. Plato (c. 420s BC–c. 340 BC), in his dialogue *Cratylus*, gave more formal definition to the idea of a time before laws (or the need for them), a time before seasons, a time when the earth provided all men needed and when men lived at peace with one another. Another Greek poet, Theocritus (c. 270 BC), similarly fantasized a world of bucolic peace and plenty. Virgil's *Georgics* explored the same area – the contentment of country life as opposed to the stress of city and court life. The Roman poet, Ovid (43 BC–17 AD), provides a countercontext to the world of Venice as presented by Jonson and one with which many audience members would be conversant. *Metamorphoses* was much read, translated, commented on and discussed in the classrooms and lecture halls of England. In book 1 he set out what was for the Elizabethans-Jacobeans the archetypal idyllic life triggering a spate of writings using a pastoral setting.

> In the beginning was the Golden Age, when men of their own accord, without threat of punishment, without laws, maintained good faith and di what was right. There were no penalties to be afraid of, no bronze tablets were erected, carrying threats of legal action, no crowd of wrong-doers, anxious for mercy, trembled before the face of their judge: indeed there were no judges, men lived securely without them. [...] The peoples of the world, untroubled by any fears, enjoyed a leisurely and peaceful existence, and had no use for soldiers. The earth itself, without compulsion, untouched by the hoe, unfurrowed by any share, produced things spontaneously, and men were content with foods that grew without cultivation. [...] there flowed rivers of milk and rivers of nectar, and golden honey dripped from the green holm-oak.[48]

The deposition of the god Saturn by his son Jove (also known as Jupiter) degraded the world into the age of silver, and constant summertime turned

47 *England's Worthies*, 1684.
48 Ovid, *Metamorphoses*, Book 1, 31–32.

into the varying seasons and changes of weather. Before, corn had grown naturally like all other vegetation. Now men began the hard and sweaty labour of farming, wounding the earth to grow sown corn. Further decline into the age of bronze brought man a fiercer character and a readiness for war. The final stage was the lapse into the age of iron when

> [a]ll manner of crime broke out; modesty, truth, and loyalty fled. Treachery and trickery took their place, deceit and violence and crim-inal greed. [...] The land which had previously been common to all, like the sunlight and the breezes, was now divided up far and wide by boundaries.[49]

Jonson's 'Age of Gold' is a materialistic, greedy perversion of the 'Golden Age', his characters debased men for whom gold in the shape of money and valuables has replaced the metaphorical gold of harmony and happiness. This is Jonson's take on his money-worshiping infant capitalist age where luxury and extravagant waste have turned some sectors of society into decadent, self-indulgent drones. The court masques Jonson was composing, though they contain instructive guidelines, were at the same time the indulgent, extravagant frippery of a court detached from real life. Jonson sees a society no longer happily free from labour, living off the bounty of Nature, but a fractured nation where some are exploited, toiling to survive while others dance, gamble and pursue a variety of unhealthy appetites. The play's characters form a grotesque, morally ugly Venetian Carnival of liars, cheats and fools. They are fools because they misperceive the true values in life and because they are convinced they are in control of their lives and are making material headway in accumulating riches. In reality they are puppets manipulated by Mosca and Volpone because they are ruled by their appetites and their folly. The hustlers too are puppets controlled by their appetites and, ultimately, by God. Jonson would know full well how much his Venetian world contrasted with the classical idyll. 'He wanted to link the English Court with Ancient Greece and Rome and to use the masque as a vehicle for the moral wisdom that the classical writers expressed allegorically in their mythology.'[50] For him the classic poets always represented an unwavering moral compass, a source of correct ethical behaviour. The day-to-day world he saw in the streets and taverns of London and in the court represented all that was low and vile. The perversion of life is emblematized graphically in the strange trio of pseudochildren forming Volpone's grotesque distortion of a family – the dwarf,

49 *Metamorphoses*, 31–2.
50 Chute, 132.

the hermaphrodite, the eunuch. Fatherhood and family are dysfunctional and disabled in the play. The word 'unnatural' recurs frequently.

Volpone is 'childless', Corvino perverts the marriage bond, Corbaccio subverts the father-son bond, Voltore misuses the legal process and Scoto turns science into gullible superstition and a mesmerizing mishmash of misleading words. Sir Pol trivializes knowledge into lunatic fantasies and even the magistrates fail to live up to their title of 'fatherhoods'. The central bond broken is that of master and servant. For all their closeness and apparent comradeship, working as partners, Volpone and Mosca's relationship is subversive. Volpone fails to behave as a proper master, careful for his servant's moral welfare, by encouraging his sinfulness.

Mosca infringes the proper, orderly, hierarchical role assigned him, is too informal, too much in charge and commits the worst sin a servant could – betraying his master. It may be argued that Mosca, as a parasite, is not technically a hired employee (though he calls Volpone 'master' and 'patron'). Parasites traditionally sought to become established members of a household, not exactly menial servants, though they did run errands, carry messages and generally fix things for the host body on whom they battened like a leech. An effective parasite could become like a right-hand man or personal assistant to someone who was greater in rank, power or wealth. Mosca is invaluable to Volpone. Betrayal of this bond deserved, in Dante's view, damnation to Nether Hell.

Much pleasure would be derived by those who could identify the classical allusions. They give the work a degree of intellectual and scholarly authority. But the real effect of any play is not in spotting sources or influences or in the extent to which it entertains. To some, entertainment is simply relaxing and laughing. There were writers whose aim was simply to please the vulgar crowd and there were comedies with songs and jigs and bawdy humour to satisfy the groundlings. The aim of Jonson was to entertain through instructing and provoking thoughtful reaction to the moral complexities the piece offered. Comedy could exercise the mind as much as the most moving tragedy. Whatever the motives of the drunken apprentices crowding into The Globe, or the reasons for attendance of any of the other many types of spectator, the entertainment, as far as the author was concerned, lay in what a play might suggest as moral guidance after displaying humankind's capacity for moral transgression and self-seeking.

10.2.4 *The Mouse Trap* and the fox trap

Mosca, having got himself named Volpone's heir, turns the tables on his erstwhile partner in crime. He exults, 'I have the keys, and am possessed' and determines to keep everything 'till he share at least', concluding, 'Let his sport pay for't, this is called the Fox-trap' (5.5.12, 15, 18). (The fly trap will be sprung later as the thieves fall out and defeat each other.) There may be an allusion here to Hamlet's famous command performance of the 'Mouse Trap' wherein he catches the conscience of the king by staging the enactment of a crime similar to the murder of Hamlet's father by his uncle. *Volpone* certainly should have acted as a prick to the consciences of those lawyers, gentlemen and merchants watching who had acted in any way like the central characters. An odd little side issue occurs in a book of a hundred epigrams 'by one H. P.' and called *The Mouse-Trap*. This book aimed 'but at the silly mouse and not any greater or more venomous vermin'. This was the standard disclaimer to protect a writer from the revenge of some powerful man who might think his shady actions were being exposed. The book contains an epigram 'On Ben Jonson's New Play':

> Magus would needs forsooth this other day,
> Upon an idle humour see a play.
> When asking him at door, that held the box,
> 'What might you call the play? Quoth he 'The Fox.'
> In goes my gen'man (who could judge of wit),
> And being asked how he liked it,
> Said all was ill, both Fox, and him that play'd it;
> But was not he, think you a Goose [fool] that said it?[51]

This implies not everyone understood the subtlety of the piece, but those who missed the point were fools. Shortly after its performance at The Globe the play was presented at Oxford and Cambridge with great success. The countless overt classical allusions and the many coded ones would have appealed to a scholarly audience. The chance to have his play performed in such venues and be applauded by such august spectators would have pleased Jonson and furbished his pride in himself.

10.3 *Volpone* in Jonson's Oeuvre and the Literature of the Time

Volpone is among the great achievements of Jonson's career. It addresses the same themes through characters similar to those found in his early work, but is a more intense, concentrated study of human evil. The plotline is intricate and tight. *The Alchemist* would be even more claustrophobic in setting and

---

51 Quoted in Harrison, 340–1. The book was entered in the Stationers' Register on 17 October 1606.

similarly focuses greed and gullibility. Jonson's world is peopled by knaves and fools locked in predatory struggle. Like many writers in the period, Jonson was much preoccupied by questions relating to how lives and states should be run. Volpone misrules his public life by non-engagement with the sociopolitical role his rank automatically entails. He misrules his personal life by living as a form of parasite, a leech leeching off the leeches who come to leech off him.

The black cynicism in plays from around 1600 onwards reflects a widely perceived sense of spiritual and moral decline. This was inherent in Christian thinking, but coincided with fin-de-siècle (end-of-the-century) anxieties. These were exacerbated by nervousness due to the imminent end of Elizabeth's reign and uncertainties about the future. At 67 her health was visibly and quickly deteriorating. Social and economic change contributed to the sense of an old world passing and indeed it was transforming. In play after play, comedy or tragedy, the world presented, whether England or abroad, is full of dishonesty and civic and personal corruption at all levels of society, but mostly at the level of the governing ranks. For an age believing everyone was a sinner to greater or lesser degrees, the corruption of man was a basic given. Pessimism about individual probity (personal goodness, honesty, openness) is seen to extend into the wider workings of society and government. Individuals from all ranks are regularly shown as morally corrupt in different ways, but the supposed leaders of society – the titled governing elite – the expected exemplars of good practice, are persistently shown as selfish, indifferent and morally bankrupt. Deadly sins parade through the contemporary drama, but in this play they hold centre stage.

The public theatre was dominated in 1606 by city comedies and revenge tragedies, while the court, though hosting selected plays already performed in the commercial theatre, was turning more increasingly to the performing of masques. Other forms were available. History plays retained their popularity (but were declining in numbers composed) and there were romantic comedies and tragicomedies like Shakespeare's late plays and Francis Beaumont and John Fletcher's *Philaster*. The two dominant forms expressed in profusion satirical-critical views of city life and decayed morality. The revenge tragedies centred on devious court politics, misdeeds and the process of retribution. They were ever more bloodily ingenious in portraying the violence of small continental courts, but always invited parallels being drawn with the nasty intricacies of the English royal court. Edward Reynolds, a reluctant placeman, admits his 'fear of the cunning and undermining tricks which are practised in this age'.[52] Intrigue, adultery, jealousy and murder were as much part of

---

52 Quoted in Peck, *Northampton: Patronage and Policy at the Court of James I*, 49.

Whitehall life as that of the Florentine, Roman and Neapolitan settings of tragic drama.

In a more direct, identifiably topical way the city comedies displayed the tensions, pretensions and predations characterizing London life. Penniless gentlemen seeking to fool others (especially rich relatives) into parting with their cash are a recurrent type in Middleton, John Marston and Thomas Dekker. Greedy merchants, cheating apprentices, lascivious wives, foolish daughters, tricky tradesmen, thieves, cony catchers and whores fill the comedies of city life. Although it has individual features unique to Venice in its overall structure, in its character stereotypes, in its portrayal of human greed and predation *Volpone* is easily recognizable as typical of London. An audience would have no difficulty in mentally transferring their judgements of the actions on stage to an English environment. Middleton, who had sided with Jonson in the Poets' War, has a very similar view of society and shared the same world view. One of his characters in *A Trick to Catch the Old One* (1605) declares simply, 'The World is so deceitful' (3.1.202). She is an example of a deceiver doubly deceiving. She is Witgood's mistress (her seldom-used name is Jane, but she is called simply 'courtesan' throughout). She masquerades as his wife in order to impress Witgood's rich uncle, Lucre.[53] They set up a secondary scam in which she pretends to be a respectable rich widow who allows herself to become engaged to a usurer, Hoard. The tricks-within-tricks proliferate wildly, as they do in *Volpone* — and they all revolve around money. There are scenes in which, as in *Volpone*, each character is lying to every other character. The city comedies deal in narratives detailing complex scams, all focused in one way or another on money, with lust as a subsidiary topic and set in the framework of a London full of people preying one on the other. The real world the real audience inhabited stalked the stage, art imitating life. Everyone would recognize types they knew. They probably would not identify themselves among the rogues and fools, but they would be there.

Many of these plays and the revenge tragedies have lust as an inciting theme or as a prominent concern. The church was particularly worried about the growing promiscuity of the time, especially in London. As its population rocketed and commerce thrived the opportunities for theft and fraud expanded as did the legitimate service industries and the illegitimate ones, especially prostitution. Various drives were launched to repress the trade, close brothels and prosecute offenders. *Measure for Measure*, *Hamlet*, *Othello* and *Troilus and Cressida* all express concern about female sexuality. Marston's *The Dutch Courtesan* (1604), Dekker's *Honest Whore* (1604), Middleton's *A Mad World*

---

53 His full name, Pecunius Lucre, is Latin for Money Dirty-Money. He too is a wealthy usurer.

My Masters (1605), Cyril Tourneur's *The Revenger's Tragedy* (1607) and John Ford's *'Tis Pity She's a Whore* (1629–33?) all focus closely on the workings and complexities of lust. It is his determination to subvert Corvino's marriage and lure Celia with his status and wealth that triggers Volpone's downfall. The attempted rape sets in motion a series of responses that lead to the *Scrutineo.* It is lust therefore that precipitates the exposure of the two central villains so that the appalling avarice compactly occupying the first part of the play is only revealed as a by-product.

10.4 Some Critical Reactions[54]

While Samuel Pepys, not admittedly an acute or reliable critic, enjoyed *Volpone* and felt it was an 'excellent play', contemporary literary-theatrical professionals had severe reservations about the structure and tone. They questioned whether Jonson had kept strictly to the classical unities of time, place, action (that is, 24 hours, one location, one plot). Margaret Cavendish, Duchess of Newcastle, questioned whether 'the whole Play of the *Fox* could be the action of one day?'[55] As a dedicated classicist such a concern did influence Jonson, as being in his view necessary for the order and composition, but it was a petty point. The action of the plot is fast. Whether it fits into a day is not something an audience is likely to worry about as they watch the convolutions of trickery develop. They are more likely to revel in the portrayal of corruption, the rich satirical resonances that chimed with their own times and the questions of if, when and how the villains will be exposed and punished.

John Dryden felt the play failed to present a single unified narrative:

'The unity of design seems not exactly observ'd [...] for there appear two actions [...] the first naturally ending with the fourth Act; the second forc'd from it in the fifth: which yet is the less to be condemn'd [...] because the disguise of Volpone, though it suited not with his character as a crafty and covetous person, agreed well enough with that of a voluptuary: and by it the Poet gain'd the end at which he aym'd, the punishment of Vice, and the reward of Virtue [...] it was an excellent fifth Act, but not so naturally proceeding from the former.'[56]

Nicolas Boileau, seventeenth-century French poet and critic, felt Jonson was too conscious of pleasing the ordinary playgoer and 'debased his plays' with

54 The seventeenth- and eighteenth-century criticisms are cited in *Jonson: Volpone,* Casebook Series (ed. Jonas A. Barish), London: Macmillan, 1972.
55 *Playes,* third preface, 'To the Reader', 1662 (Barish, 27).
56 *An Essay on Dramatic Poesy,* 1668 (Barish, 28).

'low farce' and 'dull buffoonery'. This was precisely what Jonson thought was Shakespeare's flaw. His 'wit refined' would otherwise have 'borne away the crowne.'[57] John Dennis and the playwright William Congreve deprecated the making of humour out of personal infirmities like Corbaccio's deafness. Dennis declared, 'Personal Defects cannot be amended; and the exposing such, can never Divert any but half-witted Men.' Poking fun at personal defects 'is contrary to the end of Comedy'. This ignores the cruel fact that we find physical deformity, mental failings and personal idiosyncracies amusing. Dennis also considered the Would-bes as 'Excrescences' and Volpone is inconsistent – 'manag'd so Craftily' in acts 1–4 but then 'behaves himself like a Giddy Coxcombe' in act 5.[58] This is, however, exactly how *hubris* works: a character becomes so confident in his own skill that he assumes he is untouchable and cannot fail so takes unnecessary risks and makes foolish judgements. Congreve agreed with Dennis that it was poor taste when physical defects are 'barbarously exposed on the Stage'.[59] Sidney had earlier remarked that in comedy 'we laugh at deformed creatures, wherein certainly we cannot delight'.[60]

A generation later, in the middle of the cruel eighteenth century, when for all the elegance of its appearance, its fine furnishings, its clothes, manners and genteel taking of tea, the age revelled in crudity and insensitive exposure to the point where with cartoonists (like William Hogarth in *A Harlot's Progress*, *A Rake's Progress*, *Beer Street*, *Gin Lane*) its humour had become scabrous and mocking in portraying the poxed ugliness of humanity. In 1753 Richard Hurd felt the play focused 'a subject so manifestly fitted for the entertainment of all times, that it stands in need of no vindication'. He deprecates the 'farcical invention' of the Scoto scene, the tortoise device, Corbaccio's deafness and at the same time accuses Jonson of being by nature 'severe and rigid', which 'gave, at times […] an intemperance to his satyr. His taste for ridicule was strong but indelicate […] his *style* in picturing characters, though masterly, was without that elegance of *hand*, […] his wit is too frequently caustic; his raillery coarse; and his humour excessive.' A writer who wanted to 'spout ink' in the faces of the vile would have heartily agreed and been pleased to do so.[61] Jonson was by temperament intemperate when engaged in a fight – artistic or physical. 'Caustic' and 'excessive' are precisely the qualities to be expected in someone of such strong opinions. The morality of the time was expressed in similarly powerful terms. Witness the writings of John Knox and Stubbes.

---

57 *The Art of Poesy* (1674), trans. Sir William Soames and John Dryden, 1683 (Barish, 28).
58 *Letters on Several Occasions*, 1696 (Barish, 29).
59 *Letter to Dennis on Humour in Comedy*, 1695 (Barish, 30).
60 *A Defence of Poetry*, 68.
61 *A Dissertation on the Provinces of the Drama*, 1753 (Barish, 34); italics in original.

The play then experienced a long period of neglect in consequence of the elevation of Shakespeare's reputation and the relegation of Jonson's. This continued until 1919 with T. S. Eliot's essay that began a resurrection of the writer.[62] While feeling Jonson was too earnest, too keen to instruct, that he sometimes burdened his writing (particularly the tragedies) with 'the weight of pedantic learning', Eliot acknowledges 'his genius was for comic satire'. This gave *Volpone* a drive 'a unity of inspiration that radiates into plot and personages alike'. Jonson 'created his own world' and that 'beneath the theory, beneath the observation, beneath the deliberate drawing and the theatrical and dramatic elaboration, there is discovered a kind of power, animating Volpone' (and other vibrant alive characters in other plays).[63] It is true that while the central characters are universal stereotypes and caricatures of humours and sins, they vibrate with life. The world of Venice, or rather that part of it orbiting round Volpone, may be an exaggerated, pantomime reality, where everything is heightened. Jonson's characters live too because they represent the timeless deviousness of man, the persistent vileness of humanity present from ancient Greece to the modern day. They are the cozeners, tricksters, cheats, scroungers, hustlers and wide boys who are always with us.

L. C. Knights declares, 'The most effective way of demonstrating the value of the inherited standards of the period is to examine those masterpieces of Jonson's in which they are present as a living force.' He cites *Volpone* as 'Jonson's greatest comedy' where the author focuses his 'criticism of accumulation', what Knights calls his 'anti-acquisitive attitude'.[64]

In an article entitled 'Tragical Mirth: *King Lear* and *Volpone*', Stephen Musgrove sees a similar mix of tragedy with humour in both plays. This was a mixing that Sidney had deplored, though it reflects the nature of life not fitting neatly into artificial constructs of genre or mood. Both plays were written at the same time, both writers were colleagues working for the King's Men and both moved in the same social circles and may have discussed their work in progress. Musgrove sees imaginative and thematic links. Both texts for example address the breakdown of old values in the collision with new impulses in society. The intense bitterness of Jonson's vision of the world is echoed in *Lear* and in *Timon* where Shakespeare's cynicism focuses on greed and the destructive nature of money. Jonson evidently knew *Lear* because his wedding masque *Hymenaei* (1606) and *The Masque of Blacknesse* (1605) both contain 'several important phrases' from Shakespeare's tragedy.

---

62 Collected with other studies into *Elizabethan Essays* (1934) and later retitled *Elizabethan Dramatists* (1963).
63 *Elizabethan Dramatists*, 69, 69, 76, 78.
64 *Drama and Society in the Age of Jonson*, 168.

Since *The Masque of Blacknesse* was performed before *Lear* this suggests that while Jonson may have seen the tragedy in manuscript and incorporated phrases from it into his own work, it is possible Shakespeare saw Jonson's masque first and it was he who did the borrowing.

Whatever the truth of it, both *Lear* and *Volpone* use laughter as a means to mock folly rather than simply to amuse and both present a world that is not pleasant. 'Both plays, in their different ways, postulate a vision of things in which nature is assaulted and corrupted by this monstrous power of greed.'[65] Both plays use the words unnatural and monstrous and display monstrously unnatural acts – both are concerned with inheritance and disinheritance, fathers disown children, a child is accused of contemplating parricide, lust makes a sister poison her sister, a greedy man pimps his wife for gain and greed overwhelms conscience. Both pieces also show the corruption of justice and how villains destroy themselves. They first damn their souls and later damn their bodies. Their bodies will be punished in this life first and their souls later in Hell.

---

65 *Auckland University College Bulletin*, no. 51 (1957): 21–32.

Chapter 11

THE POLITICAL CONTEXT

Be sure to keep some great man thy friend [...] Compliment him often. Present him with many, yet small gifts [...] Otherwise, in this ambitious age, thou shalt [...] live in obscurity.[1]

Volpone offers little direct reflection of the national political mood of the time, but the atmosphere of posturing, deception, male dominance and the compulsion to acquire material wealth trigger identification with the cultural mood in England. Sir Pol's and Peregrine's comments make topical references to matters at home, and the lies and deceptions of the play, enacted between the central characters, echo the personal politics of the most active and public sector of contemporary society and parallel the 'cunning and undermining tricks' Edward Reynolds remarked on in government and court circles. The play's texture is that of the rivalries, adulteries, flatteries, ambitiousness and money-focused intrigues of the makers and shakers. The court gave the age its flavour and provided much of the rumour and titillating scandal that charged tavern gossip.

What exactly was the court? It had three layers – the Household (the 'Board of Greencloth') under the Lord Steward, the Chamber (under the Chamberlain) and the Bechamber (under the groom of the stool, responsible for arranging the monarch's toilet procedures). The Household comprised all the indoor and outdoor servants keeping a palace running: cooks, footmen, chambermaids, cleaners, gardeners, soldiers, officers of the guard, a butler in charge of those who served food, clerks dealing with the paperwork (orders for food and materials). The Bedchamber was the cadre of personal body servants (mostly Scots) dressing the king and serving his washing/toilet needs. The Chamber was the real court – a mix of true courtiers and an amorphous, constantly changing mass of hangers-on. 'Court life was a constant

1 Lord Burghley to his son, Robert Cecil. Quoted in Chute, 69.

canvassing of advances and rebuffs not only for the throngs of suitors but also for the highest officials of the Crown'.[2] The inner circle of courtiers (many from old-established titled families) had specific roles as waiting gentlemen and gentlewomen of the king and queen (with petty responsibilities like placing the king's cutlery, carving his meat) or general roles escorting visiting ambassadors, running errands or chatting with the king. This was the polished, elegant, public face of the English court and included government officials and the elite group of privy councillors – a board of top advisors. The audience of *Volpone* might comprise some of these true courtiers and certainly some of hangers-on (often relatives of a placeman, hoping to catch the eye of someone of power to help them get on the payroll).

Hangers-on were invited to make up numbers at festive and official events. Many were chancers. In Ben Jonson's satire *Every Man Out of His Humour* the vitriolic Macilente (played by the abrasive Asper) criticizes 'mushroom gentlemen,/That shoot up in a night to place and worship' (1.1.). Such a one is the aspiring Sogliardo, a petty country gentlemen come to town to make his fortune. Newly raised to gentry status by payment to the College of Heralds and not one recently dubbed by the monarch, he announces, 'I can write myself gentleman now; here's my patent, it cost me thirty pounds' (3.1.) and 'I have land and money, my friends left me well, and I will be a gentleman whatsoever it cost me'. A wealthy farmer (*sogliardo* is Italian slang for manure), he is one of the upwardly mobile middle class buying their way into the gentry. His lifestyle mentor, a con man, Carlo Buffone, instructs him,

> to be an accomplished gentleman [...] you must give over housekeeping in the country, and live altogether in the city amongst gallants: where, at your first appearance, 'twere good you turn'd four or five hundred acres of your best land into two or three trunks of apparel [...] mix yourself still with such as flourish in the spring of fashion [...] study their carriage and behaviour in all; learn to play at primero (a card game), [...] and when you come to plays, be humorous [severe-looking], look with a good starch'd face [...] and sit on the stage and flout, provided you have a good suit. (1.1.)

The going rate was £30 for a gentleman's patent and coat of arms and £40 for a knighthood. In *Eastward Ho!* Sir Petronel Flash is 'one of these forty-pound Knights'.[3] James I having debased the knightly rank, later augmented

---

2 Peck, 37.
3 A reference to the decree of 1603 whereby the king required all landowners worth £40 a year to become knights or pay a fine.

the Crown's income by selling peerages. Money was the measure of all things, which is exactly why *Volpone* attacks its creeping influence. Jonson adopts a very medieval morality play stance.

The court tone was set by the masques performed there or rather masques were symptomatic of the Court. On 6 January 1605 the notorious *Masque of Blacknesse* (by Jonson) was much criticized because the court ladies blacked up as Moors and wore revealing diaphanous costumes. Those Christmas festivities also included William Shakespeare's company, newly rechristened the King's Men, performing standard plays: *Measure for Measure*, *The Comedy of Errors*, *Love's Labours Lost*, *Henry V* and Jonson's *Everyman Out of his Humour*. The Boys of the Chapel performed *All Fools*, and the Queen's Players *How to Learn of a Woman to Woo*. More masques were presented in January 1606. The masque would become the dominant performance art form at court and during James I's time, court dramatic performances of both plays and masques trebled.

Small wonder that Jonson's mind turned so often to Horace's and Juvenal's satires. Their comments on the decadence of Rome were just the ambience he felt reflected Jacobean high society. The king himself was a poor exemplar. His long-anticipated, unashamed predation of England reverberates in his assertion to Parliament that 'the ane country [England] has wealth and the other [Scotland] has multitudes of men, sae ye may pairt [part] the gifts and every one do as they may to help other'.[4] He certainly envisaged pillaging England of as much as he could and his hordes of followers simply helped themselves once they got their fingers in the public purse. His extravagance began as soon as he left Scotland to progress south to take up his throne for he immediately dunned Parliament for thousands of pounds to pay for his travel.

In the month progressing from Edinburgh to London and the month following arrival, James I knighted so many of the gentry (and non-gentry) swarming to see him and parade their loyalty (a meet-and-greet ploy that might reap profit later), that he created as many new baronets as Elizabeth had done in the last ten years of her reign.[5] Francis Bacon called knighthood 'this almost prostituted title'.[6] On 23 July 1603 the king dubbed 300 new knights in the palace gardens at Whitehall. Sir Philip Gawdy, revolted by this, described the recipients of the new honour as 'a scum' enough to 'make a man sick to think of them'.[7] Such recipients were called 'carpet knights' for they were not

---

4 Chute, 151.
5 Davies, 1.
6 Davies, 1.
7 Philip Gawdy, cited in de Lisle, 157. Among the new hatched knights were the sons of pedlars and of a run-down lawyer. They paid less than £8 for the honour.

knighted on the battlefield for valour, but dubbed on a carpet for often trivial assistance to the monarch.[8] Many new promotions were from the Scottish horde accompanying his removal to the wealthy milch cow of England. This tendency to favour his compatriots regardless of merit caused friction and disgruntlement among the English nobility, who began to describe the newcomers as devouring and devastating the land like wild boar.[9]

Coupled with the king's persistent attempts to effect union between the two realms, the Scottish dimension provoked resistance from the Commons, Lords and the powerful City merchant community. Other conflicts with Parliament began early too. Increasingly Puritan in its thinking, the Commons was alienated when James I ridiculed them as constantly discontented, factious and quarrelsome. Hoping for some relaxation of the stringent restrictions on their freedom to worship, they found James I all too ready to ban Presbyterianism and expel the more extreme Puritan reformers. Catholics too anticipated greater freedom for their practices and were disappointed. Disaffection followed discontent and discontent bred the Bye Plot and Gunpowder Plot, which led only to further repression. The appalling shock of the Gunpowder Plot is a major part of the political context (for author and audience), resonating in the background as a play full of plots and stratagems unfolded. The 'honeymoon' period quickly ended. James I's assumed liberal attitudes and behaviour soon altered. The speech from the throne in 1606 informed the Commons that kings were God's vice regents on earth, 'adorned and furnished with some sparkle of Divinitie'.[10] James I's 'sparkle' rapidly dimmed. His extravagance emerged immediately in his demand for £5000 for his progress south. James I regarded England 'like a man that hath been wandering in the wilderness for forty years and hath at last come within sight of the Land of Promise'.[11] Court expenses for personnel, promotions and festivities rose rapidly. Surrounding himself with handsome young men who willingly flattered him, he became infatuated with a succession of favourites who, puffed up with pride and the confidence that came from royal protection, were domineering and obnoxious. The homoerotic aspect of his attachments (sodomy was a capital offence) aroused violent reactions. The king himself, from apparent initial affable openness, became withdrawn, disliking crowds and looking with contempt on the thriving, rising middling sort. On ceremonial occasions he

8 Sir Toby Belch describes the cowardly Sir Andrew Aguecheek as 'a knight, dubbed with unhatched rapier, and on carpet consideration' (*Twelfth Night*, 3.4.245–6). James knighted a jeweller for boring a hole in diamond for him (see Haynes, 102).

9 Davies, 9.

10 Davies, 8.

11 Quoted in O. J. Scott, *James I*, 263. This comment by Roger Aston, a messenger in James's service, provoked laughter at the Privy Council. It soon proved hollow.

never acted with kinglike dignity. His leisure interests did not endear him to the pious, for he loved horse racing, bear-baiting, hunting and sanctioned dancing and the playing of games on Sundays. This latter angered the Puritans particularly, but Anglicans too disapproved of breaking the commandment to keep the Sabbath holy. It was only a matter of months before people began to talk nostalgically of the old queen, the relative decorousness of her court and the human touch displayed in her public appearances when her love of her subjects, her approachability, were manifestly sincere. Her failings were forgotten in a wave of longing for times past that says more about the current incumbent and the nation's capacity for sentimental fantasizing than about the true nature of the old queen and her neglect of many crucial problems. In December 1602 Sir John Harington had complained (*Tract on the Succession*) how Elizabeth had let slide many urgent matters. By 1606 he was bemoaning the excesses of the Jacobean court where 'the ladies roll about in intoxication' and the men behave in 'wild riot, excess, and devastation of time and temperance'.[12] Hunting, the traditional gentry and aristocratic pastime, was an obsession with James I. It was noted how the decorous progresses of Elizabeth were replaced by the king's spontaneous hunting parties accompanied by a huge field of young nobles. James I's neglect of political duties for impromptu hunting trips, absent for days at a time at Theobalds or Royston, soon had courtiers commenting.[13] The Venetian ambassador reported the escalating problems James I was creating:

> *many members openly declare* that as there is no war with Spain, no war with Holland, no army on the Scottish border [...] they cannot understand why the king, who has the revenues of Scotland should want money. They add that the people are far more heavily burdened [...] for the king stays so continually and so long in the country [...] and whenever he goes a-hunting the crops are ruined.[14]

The court was not known for being sedate or free of moral or material corruption. The opening act of *Volpone* shows appalling behaviour: greed, lying, dissimulation and generally conduct unbecoming figures drawn from the political part of the Venetian state. But such intrigues give the play a topical sociopolitical edge at a time when misconduct by those in the upper

---

12 Sir John Harington, *Nugae Antiquae*, vol. 1, 352. Drummond of Hawthornden notes in a letter of 3 August 1606, 'There is nothing to be heard at court, but sounding of trumpets, hautboys, musick, revellings and comedies' (see Furness edition of *Macbeth*, 1873).

13 In 1604 he bought Royston Abbey, Hertfordshire, furbishing it as a hunting lodge.

14 Quoted in Brian Gibbons, *Jacobean City Comedy* (London: Methuen, 1980), 40; italics in original.

echelons was a burning subject and the air was full of rumours of rampant avarice, extravagance, plots, deceptions and hypocrisy.

In considering the views and values comprising the contexts of *Volpone* and underpinning the theoretical views and values of the audience, it is well to remember what interesting possibilities for tension and drama come from the discrepancy between morality's expectation of people's conduct and their actual behaviour. This applies to the real grandees, lawyers, gentlemen and merchants in the audience and the ones on stage. Niccolò Machiavelli claimed,

> I have thought it proper to represent things as they are in real truth, rather than as they are imagined. [...] The gulf between how one should live and how one does live is so wide that a man who neglects what is actually done for what should be done learns the way to self-destruction rather than self-preservation.[15]

The gulf between expected and actual conduct is the arena in which *Volpone* is played out. Corvino may be seen as conforming to both the familial and national view of a husband's authority – except that not everyone in the 1600s agreed with such rampantly absolutist patriarchalism. Corbaccio's planned disinheritance of his son focuses sharply the discourse about child-parent relationships. Voltore is simply as grasping and dishonest as lawyers were traditionally expected to be.

The governing ranks, the political nation (that is, that tiny part of the population with access to political power), was beginning more and more to come under critical scrutiny. The customary idea was that by being anointed during the coronation ceremony monarchs magically took on godlike qualities as if transubstantiated like the wine and the bread in Communion. Many disputed the doctrine that wine and bread turned into the blood and flesh of Christ and many were beginning to dispute that 'divinity doth hedge a king' (*Hamlet*, 5.5.) and question whether the 'better sort' were significantly superior to the rest of the nation in any respect. Despite the adulation of Gloriana as saviour of the nation against the Armada, her limitations were becoming obvious by the end of her reign. Obstinate and wilful, sometimes irrational, her motto, *Semper eadem* (Always the same), is positive and negative. Immovability, firmness are marks of consistency and strength, but can be obstinacy that precludes adjusting to advice. Ironically James's motto was *Beati pacifici* (Blessed are the peacemakers). He kept peace with Spain yet his every action at home stirred trouble.

---

15 *The Prince*, 15, 90–1.

Vacillating, influenced by the latest whisper in his ear, he was notoriously obstinate once his mind was made up. Elizabeth was equally immovable. Her persistent refusal to face the succession problem, strengthened by legislation making discussion of the succession treasonable (the 1571 Treason Act and in 1581 another reinforcing it), began to look like a very human failure to acknowledge, address and resolve a serious matter for fear of contemplating her own mortality. The anxiety this generated merely added to accumulating unaddressed problems. Her refusal to allow much authority to the House of Commons delayed resolution of constitutional difficulties that would plague James I and Charles I and would lead to civil war. While Elizabeth's failings made a new man welcome, her strengths and the natural resistance of people to change, made the role of the new king particularly challenging. James I was not up to that challenge and disillusion very quickly followed the euphoria of his peaceful succession. A wise king has counsellors and considers a range of actions. Theoretically James I supported this view, but in practice disliked Parliament's interference. In talking of Parliament he once told an ambassador on Parliament, 'I am surprised that my ancestors should ever have permitted such an institution to come into existence'. In declaring 'I will never be ashamed to confess it as my principal honor, to be the great servant of the commonwealth', what he meant was that he would do things his own way and saw the state's good as identified with his will. He saw himself as 'the great schoolmaster of the nation', but a very wilful one that did not lightly brook opposition.[16]

Volpone is not a king, but his rank gives him the status of a leader of society and therefore an exemplar to others. He neglects both duties. To see such a one presented as a mean-spirited, covetous trickster is a political comment by the author and disturbing to the audience. His sole adviser, his partner in lies, is a devious servant, but whose ready acceptance of the title 'parasite' betrays his wrong thinking. Parasites live off their host body and leave once they have drained its nutrients. The vulture and the carrion birds are simply parasites higher up the food chain than a fly. Jonson is heavily implying that human society is distinguished by the ubiquitous predation of every member by every other.

The Jacobean world was still essentially Elizabethan but with discernible changes stemming from a darkening zeitgeist. The new reign opened with eclipses, storms, gruesome murders, plots, freakish births and an outbreak of plague killing 30,000 people in London. For an age that believed in omens and saw God's hand in everything, the signs were frightening. For an age believing in hierarchies and that order reflected God's harmonious design,

16 Chute, 130–1.

disorder, treason, the decay of old certainties, debasement of the nobility, greed of society, callousness of parents and irreverence of children, all promised a dismal future, even perhaps the approach of Apocalypse. God punished sinful nations and it looked as if he had withdrawn his favour from his chosen people. The Jacobean theatre reflected this dark mood. Tragedies became more bloodthirsty, their plots more devious and intricate, presenting ever more ingeniously nasty ways of killing people. They presented too a world where no one is what they appear to be and all are corrupt. Shakespeare's work alone – omitting *Much Ado, Twelfth Night, As You Like It*, heartening comedies as they are (though not without dark aspects) – has a string of plays from *Hamlet* to *Cymbeline* grimly depicting human duplicity and cruelty. Even comedies at this time are black, grimly indicting the age. The cynical tone of *Volpone*, the jaded view of society, the scenes of destruction and despair, with thieves, liars, lechers, hypocrites, knaves and fools, is of a piece not just with Jonson's view of the world but with other contemporary writers. In *King Lear*, performed at court Christmas 1606, Gloucester's litany of social disarray ('Love cools, friendship falls off, brothers divide: [...] mutinies [...] discord [...] treason [...] machinations, hollowness, [...] all ruinous disasters', 1.2.) echoes how people felt. The year 1606 was dubbed 'The Black Year' in Anthony Nixon's book of the same name. He comments on the extreme weather, then moves to social matters:

> The fruitfulness of the fields is not such as it hath been before time. Lords and great men bend their cogitations to the oppressing of their poor tenants, and by often fines and exactions, bring honest men to beggary, and by example of Pharaoh make slaves of their servants and subjects.[17]

There were many other sources of anxiety, but what made them worrisome to the general public and particularly to dramatists and moralists was that they betokened a threat to order, disturbing people's need to feel that all was well.

If the court had its amorphous mass of hangers-on flattering the king and pecking about for scraps and advantages, so too does Volpone's 'court' of obsequious legacy hunters. He also has his entourage of entertainers who portray a parallel distortion of humanity. In the plays of the 1600s, among all the pretentious social climbers, whores, rogues and crooked scamsters pilloried for the amusement and instruction of playgoers, courtiers are the commonest target for mockery. If sufficiently well dressed you could gain entry to the court and attach yourself to whoever looked to be on the rise. If you looked

---

17 G. B. Harrison, *A Jacobean Journal*, 305.

the part you were mostly taken for being it, appearance appearing real. At the end of the play Mosca is taken for a *clarissimo* (an aristocrat) simply because he wears the appropriate robes. Clothes were the key first step in the social charade. Many young men got themselves heavily in debt with tailors, ruff makers, shoemakers, hatters and jewellers, just to dress themselves correctly. These were often debts they did not pay, adding fraud to the vain masquerade of their clothes.

Whilst seeking a patron, they also looked for an heiress.[18] An opportune wealthy marriage would make them. City comedies present many such peacocks and mock their shady pretensions. When Jonson wrote *Volpone* he had already begun to write court masques for titled patrons and experienced the predatory pecking order of the 'better sort': the royal entourage of titled aristocrats, their ladies, mistresses, hangers-on, parasites, yes-men on the make and government placemen. The court was 'extravagant and disorderly, frivolous and indecorous, with hard drinking common and immorality winked at'.[19] There was, as is normal among all groups of human beings, constant falling out, making up, allegiances formed, loyalties betrayed, sexual rivalries, status rivalries, backbiting, bitching and duels. 'There is much plotting and malice among the ladies of the Court striving for the offices of honour about the Queen', complained the Earl of Worcester. So virulent was it, he added, 'I think envy hath tied an invisible snake around their necks, to sting each other to death'.[20] The standard court ambience was a hothouse of some celebrities and many nonentities, all thinking they were at the centre of the world, the focus of all attention, the source of all that was chic, all that counted. As king, James I was responsible for this toxic charade.

11.1 The Wise Man and the Fool

Between man's capacity for sensible decisions and actions and his infinite ability for foolishness, lies the potential for tragedy and comedy. *Volpone* is a parade of folly. The interface between reason, feeling and appetite was the spark between steel and flint.

Lucifer's rebellion proving his first creation imperfect, the Almighty made a second attempt, creating earth and man. Because man, though endowed with the ability to think calmly and decide rationally, was open to the weakening working of passions, this world would be corrupted by the Devil and by his spawn, sin and death. As Genesis tells, this human 'angel's' tragic

18 Mosca uses the word several times to describe his relationship to Volpone.
19 Davies, 263.
20 Harrison, 107, quoting Edmund Lodge (ed.), *Illustrations of British History*, 1838, 3. 86, 88.

flaw showed in disobedience to God's command (not to eat of the fruit of the forbidden Tree of Knowledge) and in weakness (listening to Eve and acting on her encouragement rather than abiding by the diktat of God). Adam faced the age-old conflict between the stringent demands of religion and the easier human way of doing what others want. This foundation story of Christianity, a prophetic allegory of the difficulties man makes for himself, encapsulates the idea that the Almighty's way is hard and involves restraining natural instincts that draw us toward self-indulgence, comfort and the easy life. This bodies the tension between good and evil that was seen as an ever-present essential of human life.

Man had two qualities that none of the rest of creation shared: sensibilities and reason. Altruistic feelings of kindness and caring led to charity and showed in family love and community care which rationally accepted that some loss of self-will was needed if the benefits of group cooperation were to be accrued. Despite the positive aspects of some feelings, many others lured men into folly – the first step toward sin. It was, however, his ability to reason that raised him far above the animal world and drew him closer to the angels – the capacity to postulate action, speculate on causes, effects, consequences and then decide what course to take. As already seen, Hamlet sums this up most aptly:

> What a piece of work is a man! How noble in reason! how infinite in faculty! in form, in moving, how express and admirable! in action how like an angel! in apprehension how like a god! the beauty of the world! the paragon of animals! (2.2.303–7)

This idealized Renaissance man was rare, a theoretical model. Strip away the fine clothes and airs of the man of rank, remove the protection money and power give and he is a 'bare, forked animal' (*King Lear* 3.4.110). *Volpone* displays this process of stripping away the fine-looking veneer of power and wealth. The title character perverts the perfect form Hamlet describes. He shows great powers of reason and faculty (understanding) but distorts them to petty, evil and sinful ends.

This prick to the consciences of the fur-robed, silk-attired members of the audience reproaches not just the lawyers and merchants but also all who used their rank to cheat and exploit and then hid behind their reputation. More broadly, it appealed to all men to treat each other with love, with honesty. The comfortably off are made to watch what they would prefer perhaps not to think about. They would readily recognize too the stripping away of those rules of behaviour that keep men civilized, to expose the selfish savagery that lurks not too far below the polished surface, a barbarity that can emerge within the supposedly better ranks and not just the brutish lower sort. They would be reminded of the fierce rivalries and jealousies that seethed under the surface of supposedly orderly and cultured court life. This natural state of struggling for survival in conflict with Christian values of love, cooperation and brotherhood was a view reinforced in Michel de Montaigne's essay 'Apology of Raymond Sebond'. History and countless plays showed time and again the fall of powerful men from unbelievable luxury to the bleeding, broken wreck kneeling, head bent for the axe. Lear warns that without wealth and position, you are no more than a weak and shivering creature:

Is man no more than this? Consider him well. Thou ow'st the worm no silk, the beast no hide, the sheep no wool, the cat no perfume. Ha! here's three on's are sophisticated; thou art the thing itself; unaccommodated man is no more but such a poor, bare, forked animal as thou art. (*King Lear*, 3.4.)

Montaigne goes further in his contempt for man's claim to superiority, while Shakespeare maintains a more general deployment of the idea of humanity's lack of humanity. *Volpone* is full of examples of 'manifold imperfections' masked by clothes. The link between Shakespeare, Montaigne and Jonson is John Florio, whose 1603 translation of the Frenchman's essays both writers knew and used. Florio, whose Italian dictionary seems to have been a source of information for Jonson, was a scholar who was part of the network of writers and intellectuals who all knew each other socially. Titled patrons, like the Earl of Southampton, the Earl of Pembroke, the Earl of Salisbury and Sir Christopher Hatton, were often the means by which such men met and the cross-fertilization of ideas took place. Jonson paid homage to Florio as 'his loving Father and worthy Friend Master John Florio' and called him 'Ayde of his Muses'.[21]

Jacobeans were graphically aware of how fortunes turn, how poverty, sickness, sudden disaster can turn the world upside down, however virtuous you were. Those body servants who dressed and undressed them knew how poxed, scabbed and stinking their master or mistress might be under their doublet, their farthingale, their wig. Under showy tinsel and gorgeous stuff the lord might be as much of a conniving knave as the pickpocket among the groundlings, and the bejewelled duchess might be as wanton as the twopenny whore outside The Globe, but both worse for pretending to be better and demanding respect for the positions they occupied. Mosca certainly knows his

---

21 Quoted in 'Jonson, Scholarship, and Science' by Mark Bland (www.cts.dmu.ac.uk/occasional papers/Bland.2013.pdf).

so-called betters are no better than he and are all rogues. The 'sophisticated' men of Venice are artificial, impure fabrications, relying on clothing and rank for the position and deference they have, yet knaves under their surface impostures. This was an embarrassing point to make to an audience some of whom would be dressed in the costliest fashions of the day and others who would probably already be suspicious and contemptuous of their fine show. It is a view endorsed by Lear:

> Thorough tatter'd clothes small vices do appear;
> Robes and furr'd gowns hide all. (4.6.)

Across the texture of the play, clothing imagery symbolizes the way dress disguises what people really are or intend. Volpone is a focus of these transformations of dress – from his grand clothes at the beginning, to his robes and furs when masquerading as an old man, to his change of costume to play Scoto, to his sergeant-at-arms uniform donned to permit him to tease the legacy hunters when they think him dead. His final change will be the ragged, filthy wretch fettered in a prison cell. Clothing changes and language/attitude changes suggest throughout that identity is fluid, can be metamorphosed in a moment to suit the character seeing the shape-changer, just as Mosca changes his ploys and demeanour to match whichever legacy hunter he is tricking. Clothes were a political statement in Jacobean times. Sumptuary laws defined the types of cloth appropriate to people's place in the hierarchy. A law of 1574 required all males over the age of six to wear a woollen cap on Sundays. The 'statute cap' was, however, only for the lower sort, a badge of rank. The gentry and nobility continued to wear silk or velvet caps. Snobbish aspirants constantly subverted these categories, aping those above in borrowed styles. The maid on holiday, decked in her mistress's cast-offs might masquerade as a fine lady. Merchants' wives were perpetually criticized for parading in the silks and satins designated for their superiors. The gentry aped the aristocracy and the aristocracy kept adopting more and more outrageous fashions to preserve the differences marking them as leaders of style. Trends in dress became more sexually explicit. Male hose became tighter, codpieces more eye catching and court ladies wore lower and lower necklines. *The Masque of Blacknesse* provoked the comment 'Their apparel was rich but, some said, too light and courtesan-like for such great ones'.[22] Lear makes the point to his daughter:

> Thou art a lady;
> If only to go warm were gorgeous,

---

22 G. B. Harrison, 181. The quote is taken from Winwood's *Memorials*, 2. 43.

Why, nature needs not what thou gorgeous wear'st,
Which scarcely keeps thee warm. (2.4.469–72)

In drama costume becomes a marker of moral state. Overdependence on
show and the trappings of power indicates moral aberration. In *Measure for
Measure*, Isabella reminds the self-righteous Angelo,

No ceremony that to great ones longs,
Not the king's crown, nor the deputed sword,
The marshal's truncheon, nor the judge's robe,
Become them with one half so good a grace
As mercy does. (2.2.59–63)

She further remarks on how 'man, proud man, Dress'd in a little brief
authority'

like an angry ape
Plays such fantastic tricks before high heaven
As makes the angels weep. (2.2.121–3)

The image of an ape in fancy dress reflecting a man of authority overproud
of himself is not dissimilar to that of Lear's mocking gloss on 'the great image
Authority': 'A dog's obey'd in office'. Some at court clearly would bow and
scrape to a dog if he wore a badge of authority. Mosca is treated deferentially
when clothed as a *clarissimo*. However inefficient, useless or tyrannical a judge,
state councillor, general or king, might be, some people would still hurry
to obey his orders. There would be a frisson of subversive pleasure among
many in The Globe laughing at how sycophantically Voltore, Corbaccio and
Corvino cringe and play up to Mosca thinking he is on their side. How many
in the posher part of the audience (in the second- and third-level galleries)
had smiled and bowed to try and insinuate themselves into some lord's good
books and payroll? Mosca describes them as

those
With their court-dog tricks, that can fawn and fleer,
Make their revenue out of legs and faces [bows and appropriate facial
expressions],
Echo my lord, and lick away a moth. (3.1. 19–22)

The year *Hamlet* described man's perfectibility, another picture of what man
could be (and generally was) is voiced by the jester Feste (*Twelfth Night*,

1601) telling Viola/Cesario (another character in clothing disguise but also in gender disguise), 'Foolery Sir, does walk about the Orb like the Sun, it shines everywhere' (3.1.39–40). In theory rational, in practice foolish is how the dramatists generally defined mankind – and often not only foolish but roguish too. Everyone acknowledged man at his best –planning ahead, being commonsensical and reasonable, adjusting to changed circumstances, doing what was just and kind, constructing social agencies to fit the needs of a community, sympathetically desiring to redress imbalances of food, wealth and power caused by individual greed, laziness and intemperance and formulating this into a judicial system, developing a power hierarchy that enabled society to work effectively. It was the other aspect, the failure to achieve perfect social harmony and perfect personal government, the natural tendency to lie, cheat, grab and scrounge, that most exercised the pens and tongues of satirists and moralists. Acts of folly, those first steps on sin's high road, provided an endless, rich ground for description of failing and prescriptions for improvement. Man's infinite capacity for spoiling things was a much more exciting, titillating, sensational and fruitful subject for dramatists and religious polemicists than theorizing about ideal sociopolitical-personal structures. Making silly judgements, making a fool of oneself, deceiving others, engaging in self-deception, using trickery for gain, displaying greed, treading the minefields of sex and love, power and money, engaging in outright wrongdoing provided a complex network of failed right conduct and a wonderful parade of fools. It is this picture of men as animals consuming one another that gives *Volpone* its vitality and its depressing undertone.

The attempt to keep men on the rational, virtuous straight and narrow was formulated into a very detailed series of 'Thou shalt nots'. Life in Jacobean England was highly regulated. There were all the formal, official checks on one's actions – parents, neighbours, employers, the guild, the parish priest, the parish council, the parish constable, the night watch, magistrates and courts. But there were inner controls, or those checks on wrongful impulses stemming from conscience – the sense of right and wrong, of honour and virtue, of what God demanded. Significantly, Volpone dismisses conscience as 'the beggar's virtue' (3.7.211) when Celia appeals to him to desist from trying to seduce her. This suggests the rich can buy their way out of any difficulty that might prick their moral conscience. Mosca too contributes to the counterview of rational, charitable man loving his neighbour:

> Almost
> All the wise world is little else, in nature,
> But parasites, or sub-parasites. (3.2.11–13)

In practice, human beings being what they are for the most part – weak, feckless, lazy, selfish – many were indifferent to how they behaved. London bred a huge underclass of 'street people' – prostitutes, beggars, petty criminals, unskilled labourers, the poor in general – lying, scrounging, thieving and cheating their way through existence. Then there were the high-status criminals committing big, profitable scams and with position, rank and money enough to buy off prosecution. Corruption among the governing ranks, widespread among the patronage and power networks of court, recurrently features in city comedies and revenge tragedies. It is integral to *Volpone*.

The individual soul was felt to be in terminal decay, but civic life was too. Considerable attention was paid in pamphlets, philosophical studies, poems and plays to the question of Good Government, a particular Renaissance interest. As regards the individual character in drama this relates to conduct toward others and control of oneself, displayed in the perpetual battle to control the passions. As regards community and national politics this relates to theories of good governorship and real-life examples of bad practice and concepts of civic duty. From Sir Thomas More's *Utopia* (1516) through Sir Thomas Elyot's *The Boke Named the Governour* (1531) and James I's *Basilikon Doron* (1599), to Thomas Hobbes's *Leviathan* (1651), writers were much exercised by the questions 'What makes a good state?' and 'What makes a good governor?' Jonson's two historical tragedies, like Shakespeare's, are much taken up with those complex questions. So too, in different ways, are his comedies. *Volpone* makes a key contribution with its cast of leader figures involved in serious misconduct and criminal proceedings. Apart from the sins of greed, lying, flattery and personal frauds on each other that do not come within the reach of the law (but are offences to decent conduct), all of them are complicit in perverting the course of justice by lying in court to save themselves. None of this actually harms the state at large, though it does lead to Bonario and Celia being wrongfully held for a brief period. The moral and judicial failure of the first court hearing to establish the truth stands as an emblem of the general corruption of public life. The behaviour of the central protagonists, driven by greed, emblematizes contemporary personal life partly triggered by unfettered materialism, a problem that was being more and more discerned in Jacobean London. In an age when personal desires were gaining priority over civic responsibility, flawed governorship would be a major theme and flawed governorship stemmed from individual, personal, spiritual rottenness. The implications for the real-life social and national political state, the failure of real practice to match idealized theory, the tendency of monarchic and aristocratic government to be run according to personal whim and autocratic, despotic diktat, are evidenced by the descent into civil war (1642–9). In its immediate literary context *Volpone* gains value as a blast of a moral trumpet when seen in conjunction with other plays delivering similar warnings.[23]

11.2 New Philosophy, New Men

A host of new social subtypes was helping destabilize the old orders of society. The new families of the Reformation were, by the time of James's accession, well assimilated into the aristocracy and embedded in the power structure. James's wholesale creation of hundreds of new knights and sale of peerages debased the value of such ranks in the public mind and antagonized the old nobility. This was exacerbated by the king's appointing many new men to government and court posts. The fact that many were Scots newcomers arriving with the king made for a fractious atmosphere around Whitehall. Contemporary plays comment regularly on the dangers to kings of flattery by courtiers and remark much on the importance of honest loyalty. Jonson called flattery 'a fine pick-lock of tender ears' He saw, first-hand, how those in positions of power and rank 'whom fortune hath borne high [...] submit their dignity and authority to it, by a soothing of themselves'.[24] The predators flatter Volpone and Mosca, and Mosca flatters them back. All are dealers in lies. *Lear* comments on the loyal service of old courtiers, along with questions of the limits of service, of what is right to do in the name of your master or mistress when their orders are morally suspect. It was an age that believed monarchs were to be obeyed without question. What if your king ordered you to do something counter to the teachings of the Bible, supposedly the word of God?

Baldassare Castiglione was clear you should 'obey your lord in everything that redounds to his profit and honour, but not as regards things that bring him loss and shame. Therefore, if he were to order you to commit some treacherous deed not only are you not obliged to do it but you are obliged not to do it'.[25] In practice, men in positions of power tended to be entangled in, sometimes creating, networks of moral and physical corruption. Elizabeth raised high men who served her well. William Cecil, Elizabeth's Secretary, was made Lord Burghley. Burghley's son, Robert, became secretary of state after Francis Walsingham died in 1590, succeeded his father as Elizabeth's principal minister, smoothed the takeover of James, became spymaster for the new king and was rewarded with a peerage as Baron Cecil (1603) and then promoted Viscount Cranborne (1604) and finally Earl of Salisbury (1605).

---

23 Middleton's *A Mad World My Masters* (1605) and *A Trick to Catch the Old One* (1605) are just two examples. The plots of both pivot on intricate deceptions related to money.
24 *Timber*, 36.
25 *The Book of the Courtier*, 131.

Robert Cecil, to take one example, shamelessly milked the financial benefits to be made from all of his positions.[26] The fact that Volpone is not involved in the shady doings of the 'scurvy politicians' Lear talks of (4.6.), is only a minor positive. His deceitfulness is a sin nevertheless, and though initially confined to the small circle of *captators*, moves into wider moral dimensions when he adds lust to his sins. Pretending to be Scoto he misleads the gathered crowd by masquerading as someone he is not, pretending to sell unguents and ointments falsely claimed to be efficacious, while actually being there to catch a glimpse of Celia; he commits the sins of false witness, dissimulation and lust. He also betrays his rank in every aspect of this and his other behaviours. The play world of secrets and lies mirrors the intrigues and deceptions poisoning the corridors of power and the royal apartments. The word 'politician' has a number of related etymological meanings. Often it meant a trickster using 'policy' to cheat. 'Policy' was the word for the intricate lies told to gain what you wanted. It was the means by which Machiavelli's Prince was advised to achieve his will. It relates to politicians as administrators running aspects of the state and consequently implies politicians are tricksters cheating for self-gain, lying to cover what they are really up to. There was much of that in seventeenth-century government.

Further resonance is given to Volpone's behaviour when he is brought to court. This is a man out of control and the justice system finds it difficult to pin him down. Venice's reputation as a state was high; as a republic it was admired throughout Europe. Its judicial system too was much lauded, but by 1606 it had declined from its golden days and would become synonymous with arbitrary imprisonment, government corruption, personal decadence and dynastic struggles among the leading families. It was an ideal correlative for an England ruled as a family concern by a king who saw the state as his own and his people as his chattels. The Venice of the play is likewise a place where the laws of the jungle apply, beast preying on beast, each out for himself.

Great families could fall. Great men could fall. Fortune was fickle and royal favour all too human and unreliable. James's capricious behaviour, violently passionate in its verbal expression, is not unusual. Elizabeth too could be hysterically angry and dismiss courtiers for misdemeanours, petty or serious, real or imagined. James I despatched a stream of men to the Tower for thwarting him. Arbitrary exercise of absolute power was nothing new.[27] With the irresistible rise of the middle class, successful men were constantly being

---

26 See Haynes, 79ff.
27 Progressing south James indicated readiness to use his sudden access to absolute power, having a pickpocket summarily executed at Newark without trial. He pardoned many prisoners yet left Catholic recusants incarcerated with murderers.

promoted into the ranks of the privileged and titled. They were not always well received by those who felt their status was being tainted. Promotions for services to the Crown (not always moral), often bought (a means of appeasing ambition and the monarch's need for cash), made the very idea of titles a target for satirical comment. The court crackled with tense suspicion.

Villains in plays present the emerging dangers of individualism that puts self above morality, private profit above decency and humanity. They are usually one malcontent individual, but in *Volpone* all the central characters are villains. These new men with their new egotistical philosophy are part of the context in which Jonson and contemporaries viewed those who sought to rise, to gain wealth or consequence through immoral, violent, inhuman means. This applied as much to the Jacobean tragic writers exposing and punishing the ruthless psychopaths who entertain and horrify us as they murder their way to power (in *The Duchess of Malfi*, *The White Devil*, *'Tis Pity*, *The Revenger's Tragedy* and countless others), as to the satirists who decried and mocked underhand, exploitative behaviour by the powerful merchant associations, powerful politicians and individuals whose greed became a psychological obsession.[28] Volpone is this dangerous type of new man, pro actively, ruthlessly grasping and unashamedly devious. He voices no moral concern.

Conscience, to him, is the 'beggar's virtue' (3.7.211), operative only in those who have no choice. The rich man can afford not to worry about morality, and the parasite who is so much a partner in crime with his master, as Mosca is, can also live without conscience. Both know that what they are doing is wrong, but are so blinded by greed and the pleasure of deceiving that they do not care. This is a reminder how vulnerable masters and mistresses were to ruthless, deceitful, self-serving servants and how important was the bond of loyalty and honesty between master and servant. Machiavelli once asserted that 'the deceiver will always find someone to be deceived'.[29] The hustlers have found their victims and additionally Mosca has found another victim in his partner. It is impossible to tell whether he planned all along to cheat Volpone when the time came, but the plan shows the depth to which his sin has led him – to the sort of betrayal Dante condemned to Nether Hell. It is only as they are sentenced and are faced by punishment that they minimally express

28 This type was shown in Philip Massinger's *A New Way to Pay Old Debts* (written 1625, performed 1626, printed 1633). Sir Giles Mompesson, MP, a corrupt officeholder, the original of the fictional villain aptly named Sir Giles Overreach, used his position to gain licenses for businesses, charged for doing so and kept the money. His name became synonymous with speculative, accumulative, corrupt aristocratic government. He was found guilty, a fine levied, but he fled to France.

29 *The Prince*, 100.

any conscience or remorse. Volpone is a new man in an old Machiavellian way, a villain on his way to power, the power his greed and deceit give him over the greed of his victims. Mosca is a Machiavellian-plus; he works with his master, deceiving and leading the way much of the time, until ready to execute the final deception in which he turns on Volpone himself. History is full of such men. His people-management skills, his ability to react instantly to any change of circumstances and his drive and lust for power would have made him a formidable leader had his personality been virtuous and his rank given him access to power. In traditional comedies, suffering and humiliation usually cleanse characters of sins and misperceptions, making them new, giving them a second chance. In this play repentance is absent, no one is made anew and behind the punishment of the human court stands the shadow of the definitive judgement of God.

In Jonson's time, as in all ages, circumstances and character led some to rise and others to fall. Industrious habits could (and increasingly did) mean that a hard worker, a thrifty man, a canny opportunist could rise to a station much higher than that he was born to. These first glimpses of capitalism caused moralists and sermon makers considerable anxiety. Opportunities for making huge fortunes were increasing as were worries about the insatiable greediness of those who, prioritizing their own private gain above the common good, began to precipitate disgust, envy and disgruntlement among the exploited and those with no chance to improve their own standards of living. The 1590s saw a number of attempts at legislation to regulate merchant enterprises. It was felt that the state had to control unfettered capitalism to ensure it was conducted in orderly and moral ways. In *One and Thirty Epigrams* (1550), Robert Crowley reminded,

> You are not born to yourself,
> Neither may you take
> That thing for your own
> Whereof God did you make
> But steward and bailiff. (5.12.149–51)

Men of ability and drive were encouraged to see their success as the gift of Providence more than the reward of their own efforts. As stewards of their own talents they owed God a portion of their profits, paid in doing good works for others. The merchant making huge sums importing spices or cloth from the East had a duty to ensure the captains and crews of his ships, the dockers unloading cargoes and the market traders or shopkeepers to whom he sold, were fairly and honestly treated and that the 'superflux' did not all go into his pocket or onto his wife's back, but into fair wages and charitable works.

It was a feature of capitalism that this was already happening less and less. Acceptable levels of personal gain had to be offset against duty to the whole, the community. It was a medieval idea struggling to survive in a changing and greedy world. Biblical and Christian thinking exhorted believers not to set too great a store by the riches of this world, but to concentrate on enriching the soul. Celia alone in *Volpone* expresses in any detail such spiritual concerns. Her name means 'the heavenly one' and is not merely a reference to her beauty. The *avocatore* who delivers judgement on Mosca and Volpone makes some brief reference to moral irresponsibility at the close of the piece, declaring that they should stand as a warning to be taken heed of:

> Let all, that see these vices thus rewarded,
> Take heart, and love to study 'em. Mischiefs feed
> Like beasts, till they be fat, and then they bleed. (5.12.149–51)

Increasingly, as capitalism began to take hold of European trading, families like the Medici, Bardi, Peruzzi and Strozzi in Florence became powerbrokers loaning to governments and then governors themselves. Similar men thrived in Venice and England. The growth of trade increased the numbers of the entrepreneurial middle class. With more money washing around London there was an increase in the activities mushrooming to service a thriving city. Foreign visitors were astonished at the amounts of lavish goods in London shops. Merchants' wives dressed like court ladies, and snobbery, luxury, extravagance and ostentation flourished.

With their improved standard of living the bourgeoisie dreamed of gentrification. That meant selling out of the trade that made their fortune, investing the proceeds of the sale, buying a country estate, making more money from the rents of tenants farming your land and hoping to gain the respect of your gentry neighbours. A title increased the chances of that and money could buy a title awarded by a king whose coffers were always empty. This is a society based on the old orders but beginning to change as circumstances altered. It was a difficult transition and made many anxious that with too much change basic values were being forgotten or simply discarded. Individualism, a keynote of the Renaissance idea of man, took on dangerous potential when unregulated by law or personal moral self-control.

The audience watching *Volpone* brought a memory bank of family- and community-oriented reactions, differing according to rank and experience. Whatever the spectator's individual story, whatever their assessment of it, they also brought a set of learned values shared by society. The social context varied from family to family depending on the personalities involved and their social position, but would share at points the common values of the culture at large. Social context reflected not only the morality of the past persisting into the present but also the contradictions and conflicts created by current priorities that temporarily interested the time or dominated and coloured their views of the world. Another context is the nature of political experiences and views. Politics is about who has power, how they use it, where and how they apply it and who does not have power but wants it and why. Politics in this sense is found as much within local social groups as within nations. *Volpone* is a play that works on both levels politically, for the interpersonal politics of the central characters act as admonitory exemplars for wider society and for the state.

Finally there are the historical and literary contexts that help in interpreting a piece of writing. Whatever their social or religious differences, recent history is something Jonson's audience shared – a host of active memories going back into the recently ended Elizabethan era with all its dramas (though their experience and evaluation of it would vary according to religion, rank and age). Similarly, the literary context a spectator brings would vary enormously depending on education, breadth of reading and how frequently they visited the theatre. Jonson brings a hugely capacious knowledge of history and literature in the allusions, echoes and lessons presented in his dramas. The range of classical references is particularly striking and often outside the scope of common knowledge. He also brings a mind vibrantly responsive to what was going on around him. Sources, low and popular, high and cultivated, are absorbed in the play and a huge array of nuanced meanings are cached within the language and situations of a story referencing the anxious contemporary scene. For all its being set in Venice, with local dialect and slang words, city-specific locations and offices peppered throughout the text, *Volpone* is resonant with imaginative connections to contemporary London. Though the playwright was vastly better read than almost everyone else in the audience, they all shared a common text. They may have had different degrees of knowledge of it and would certainly have interpreted parts of it in differing ways, but to a large extent, theoretically at least, the Bible was a shared source of values. In practice many people, perhaps most, failed to live up to its demands, but they all knew how they were expected to live. It is the deviations from the expected Christian life that provide the play's most dominant context.

Religion was penetrated through and through with politics and politics was mixed up with religion. Thoughts of God, sin, salvation, death, Satan and damnation were as natural to people of this age as breathing. Coming to contemporary political contexts we must remember that the enveloping locus of *Volpone* is Volpone's 'court', an aristocratic household, whose 'courtiers' are smiling rogues bowing, scraping and saying what is wanted, yet playing the villain underneath, harbouring disrespectful, irreverent, self-interested, vengeful and destructive thoughts, ready to abuse Volpone when they think he is deaf while smiling and nodding to him – and all to grab his fortune when he dies. It is a sick world.

Respect, deference, politeness and honesty were major features of the old hierarchy – in theory. All households, except the very poorest, had a maid or a boy. A good, long-term servant was like a member of the family. A bad one was a disruptive force. Theoretically, servants were part of an aristocrat's extended family. Volpone speaks of Mosca in loving and admiring terms: 'my beloved Mosca' (1.1.30), 'Loving Mosca' (1.2.123), 'Excellent Mosca! Come hither, let me kiss thee' (1.3.78–9), 'good rascal, let me kiss thee' (1.4.137), 'My divine Mosca!' (1.5.84), 'Thou art mine honour, Mosca, and my pride,/My joy, my tickling, my delight! (3.7.68–9), 'Exquisite Mosca!' (5.2.4), 'my precious Mosca!' (5.2.15).

The traditional coupling of master and servant in plays, usually a bond of loyalty and shared amatory intrigue, is here subverted for both are involved in unworthy actions. It is subverted again when the apparently loyal servant betrays his master. There is another sort of betrayal and subversion going on here for Mosca is part of the family along with the eunuch, the dwarf and the hermaphrodite. Mosca is the steward/mistress/housekeeper, running things, working closely in harmony with the master/patriarch. But, it is a perverted family, a family turned upside down, a reverse image of father, mother and children, an evil parody devoted not to rearing offspring but to criminal greed, grasping and gain. In a monarch's court the whole body of people in royal employ was part of the ruler's family. The constantly expanding royal household was problematic logistically and costly to house and feed. Volpone's is not. His meiny is small and he is already wealthy enough to run it. Volpone, like a king, had a duty of care, the servants a duty of service and loyalty. In practice many servants were simply parasites and sycophants, and masters slave-driving, arrogant snobs. In a cynical sense Volpone's household reflects a family devoted not to loving support and guidance to living the virtuous life but to acquisition, deception and self-interest aimed at hoarding as much loot and doing as much evil as they wish. They are dysfunctional in the sense they are not a proper family, but highly functional within the parameters they have set as a gang employed in the magnifico's house and focused on cheating. The importance of the bonds of reciprocal care (master-servant, parent-child) is a recurrent theme in 1600s drama. Good servants and bad are frequently shown in contrast to each other as are good masters and bad and the consequences of their cooperation. The master-servant, parent-child interface required that personal and professional transactions be based on the truth. Social cohesion depended on both sides doing their duty properly and honestly. Once these bonds were broken chaos was possible – and in a tragedy, inevitable. In traditional comedies, bad service leads to misunderstandings, emotional complications, mayhem and misrule. In *Volpone* we trace the progress of evil, laugh at the inconsistencies and hypocrisies exposed on the way, admire the skilled duplicity of Mosca (particularly) and Volpone (to a lesser extent), and do not endorse their actions but applaud their punishment. They break the Biblical guidelines about loving your neighbour, not coveting other people's property, being charitable. In traditional comedy the characters tend not to be evil. Foolish yes, but not bad. They may be presumptuous, pompous and misguided, but are essentially foolish rather than criminal. Not so in *Volpone*. Once God's order is transgressed and excess is displayed a Jacobean audience would expect retribution.

That it is only narrowly achieved is Jonson's comment on how the real world works as opposed to the theoretical, obligatory ending demanded by theological orthodoxy. Aspects of the courtier's life as a servant are revealed through Edgar's speeches as Poor Tom in *King Lear*. In this play, contemporary with *Volpone* and by a writer who was a co-worker and in the same friendship group as Jonson, Edgar, in disguise as a madman warns,

> Obey thy parents; keep thy word justly; swear not [that is, do not take the Lord's name in vain by blasphemy]; commit not with man's sworn spouse; set not thy sweet heart on proud array. (3.4.)

Three of these four commandments are broken in Jonson's play. They relate to the common sins of the court in particular and society in general and finish with an admonition against vanity that would be highly relevant to the silken, pampered narcissists watching this disturbing drama and to Volpone's longing to possess treasure. Another form of 'proud array' in an acquisitive society was accumulating valuable objects and being known as a man of substance. This too is Volpone's sin.

Edgar continues reciting a litany of sins typical of young men about town and court: pride, personal vanity, lust, the breaking of oaths (probably blasphemous), lust, drinking, gambling, insincerity, readiness to believe the worst, violence, sloth, deviousness, greed, irascibility, predatoriness. He ends with warnings against amatory and sexual involvement with women, against involvement with moneylenders and with an exhortation to defy Satan. The city dramas of the time are full of young men regularly visiting brothels, entangled in irregular sexual attachments, in debt to moneylenders and who are less than God fearing. *Measure for Measure*, imbued with the same imaginative resonance as *Lear*, presents types from this world. So do Thomas Middleton and Jonson. Dupes, fools, prodigals and knaves populate his work in a vivid but disturbing depiction of the immorality of seventeenth-century London and exposure of the deeply flawed nature of man and the vile hypocrisy of what is supposed to be a civilized world.

Within two months of James I's accession uncertainties began accumulating and hopes of a new Golden Age evaporated. In July 1603 he was crowned and in early August a Catholic plot to kidnap him was uncovered and the plague returned to London. Its regular outbreaks always unnerved people. Apart from the natural anxiety about a disease whose origins were unknown, they imagined it was the work of the Devil permitted by God to punish man's unidentified sins. The context of James I's new court was initially an unknown quantity.

Doubts and fears circulated, but a pattern was emerging. By the end of 1603 government finances had lapsed into chaos and the king was already bickering with Parliament over money. It would worsen. Puritans and Catholics were disappointed, restless and discontented that no relaxation of restrictions on them had emerged. In fact the opposite looked likely. The court quickly earned a reputation for corruption – physical and moral. Luxury and extravagance, promiscuity, drunkenness and other forms of degeneracy became increasingly evident. A large agglomeration of people in a court unavoidably generates rivalries, grievances, hatreds, secrets and changing alliances and relationships. This pot of poison bubbled over when the established order was penetrated by newcomers, foreigners accompanying a new king and taking posts already occupied.[30] Monarchs have always raised cash by selling titles, honours and posts. James I awarded mass knighthoods and well-paid promotions. The devaluation of distinction did not end there. James I created a new rank, the knight baronet, available for £1,905, and elevated important local gentry.[31] His creation of 56 baronets, 19 viscounts, 30 earls, a marquess and 3 new dukes, raised a calculated £120,000, though in 1612 James I was still in debt and Parliament refused a huge payment request. The Elizabethans and Jacobeans were keen to have clear differences between the ranks; background, land ownership, income, clothing and spheres of activity, were the criteria. Any loss of the sharpness of distinction was a step toward chaos. The tawdry selling of titles provided playwrights with wonderful opportunities for humour, but the money gained did not replenish the public purse and the new promotions depleted it further. All this added to the general sense of the age's decay. Part of the cultural context of the play is the display of an age far from golden – an age of leaden despair, of decadence, of moral decay. Volpone points up how

30 Davies, 9.
31 Peck, 53.

the age has made gold its centre, its standard and by implication its moral lodestone. His perverted *aubade* (dawn song) to his treasure declares:

> Well did wise Poets, by thy glorious name
> Title that age, which they would have the best. (1.1.14–15)

The subsequent play unrolls to show how far contemporary life distorted the fantasy model that Ovid and other classical writers had imagined of man's primal innocence.

Other mental baggage Jacobeans carried focused in the spate of pamphlets recounting bizarre occurrences. Ghostly appearances, outbreaks of witchcraft, brutal murders, malformed births and unusual weather events were a staple of gossip and fear, for such events were always seen as portents of disaster. Sir Pol's naive wonder at the porpoises and the whale in the Thames and the various other freaks and 'wonders' that interest him mocks the general superstitious credulousness of people and Londoners' love of oddities, prodigies and 'monsters'. They would, as is remarked in *The Tempest*, rather pay sixpence to see an Indian on public display as an oddity than give it to an English beggar in the streets. Thomas Dekker wrote of 'a hideous tempest' that seemed to herald Elizabeth's death. It 'shook cedars, terrified the tallest pines, and cleft asunder even the hardest hearts of oak'.[32] Such events were believed to be omens of imminent death or disaster and were sent by God as punishment or warning. All natural disasters were seen as God's anger at the nation's sins and a warning to repent and reform. Any unusual event, earth tremor, comet, flood or unseasonable hailstorm provoked a mass of hysterical, moralizing pamphlets and stern homilies from pulpits. Samuel Harsnett's *A Declaration of Egregious Popish Impostures* (1603) stoked the always smouldering fires of anguished expectation of Catholic outrages, recounting a series of papistical deceptions. The year 1604 was difficult, 1605 worse. In January Barnaby Rich's *Faults, Faults, Faults* deplored the breakdown of love and marriage, clerical squabbles and literary decline, but the general economic depression, agricultural difficulties, scandals and other unsettling alarms were overshadowed in November by the Gunpowder Plot. The evil of the plan to annihilate the social and political leaders traumatized people and created an edgy, suspicious mood worsened when a great eclipse followed.[33] Such astronomical events were understood by a few but for the majority of the population they were imbued with all sorts of ominous superstitions. The year 1606 was no better. In January the Gunpowder plotters were tried and

32 Dekker, *The Wonderful Year of 1603*, 24.
33 It must have reminded James of the explosion that killed his father.

executed horribly. Father Henry Garnett, part of the extended network of Jesuit priests secretly working in England, knew of the plot, but did not reveal it as he was told it under the protection of the confessional. He was tried and executed in May. In February 1606 the pamphlet *Strange News from Carlstadt* reports a bloodlike sun, a woman bearing three children – one a blackamoor, one like death, the third with four heads – each speaking bizarre prophecies. Anthony Nixon's *The Black Year* expresses a broader sense of decline with barren fields, oppression of tenants and arts and learning despised. *Volpone's* atmosphere of intrigue and cheating, secrets and lies, and acts of disloyalty and subversion were more than matched by the realities of recent events. The sustained darkness of the action is not accompanied by happy laughter but by sneering snorts of recognition of human frailty and grasping human duplicity. The whole play cuts deeply into the roots of our need for the comforting belief that humans are kind and loving and the audience knows throughout that these happenings are not confined to Venetian society. Volpone's world is Jonson's, where civilization is as veneer thin as it was in pagan times. All around were instances of man's inhumanity to man. The recent public executions of the Gunpowder plotters involved their being hung and while still alive having their hearts cut out. The reality/fiction similarity was obvious. In July 1606 some of the courtly personages in the audience had been present (like Jonson and the King's Men) at Theobalds, the Earl of Salisbury's mansion, where he hosted the visiting King Christian of Denmark, brother of James I's queen, Anne. The drunken excesses of the celebrations, the inebriated lady performers in the masque and the copious vomiting of the Danish king were transgressions of decorum confirming the sense of social disintegration and moral decline recurrent in contemporary literature.

In this play about disguised identity, most characters want to change their status or enhance it by becoming richer: Volpone voluntarily changes his costume and personae and is prepared to dress down from his status to masquerade as a mountebank; Lady Pol behaves like a courtesan of her own volition; and Celia has courtesanship forced on her by, of all people, her husband. All, except Celia, are brought down by their overreaching ambitions.

Humiliation and imprisonment for some would remind the audience of the medieval image of the Wheel of Fortune that raises and destroys popes, kings, politicking dukes, merchant bankers and court favourites – a warning echoed in many Bible stories.

The fall of a great man is the key pattern of classical tragedy, but in a Christian Renaissance context the downturn of Fortune's wheel was a reminder of the precariousness of life and, importantly, a warning that an evil ruler's fall was a sign of Providence's purpose.

Figure 11.1 Rota Fortunae

With domineering hand she moves the turning wheel,
Like currents in a treacherous bay swept to and fro:
Her ruthless will has just deposed once fearful kings
While trustless still, from low she lifts a conquered head;
No cries of misery she hears, no tears she heeds,
But steely hearted laughs at groans her deeds have wrung.
Such is the game she plays, and so she tests her strength;
Of mighty power she makes parade when one short hour
Sees happiness from utter desolation grow.
(Boethius, *The Consolation of Philosophy*, 2. 1)

Humiliation and fall was also a device found in comedy. Chastening
excessive, irrational behaviour was part of the process of reforming manners,
but behind it loomed the larger shadow of divine punishment of those who
overstep moderation and balance. This carried in it latently the ultimate
fall: the decay of human society and the end of the world. Jonson's age believed
in Armageddon; it expected collapse.

Fear was in the air the Jacobeans breathed. Fears about doctrinal differences ripping society apart and fears of excommunication and damnation resulting from England separating from Catholicism had seethed in the subconscious and conscious mind since Henry VIII's time. The second half of the sixteenth century was awash with anomalous vestiges of the old faith coexisting with the rigours of the new. The outer world might change at a monarch's command and the stroke of a pen, but the internal habits of thought and feeling of 4–5 million people took longer. Rituals detailed in the Book of Common Prayer controlled Sunday worship in thousands of parish churches, but there was a difference between the conformity of the tongue mouthing responses and the dissent of the heart. No king, bishop or priest could control individual consciences. Whatever Henry VIII's motives in destroying the centuries-old religious houses scattered all over the country, ordinary people would have had doubts, reservations and terrified premonitions of God's wrath punishing the land for such impiety. Everyday life was a confusing mixture of new enquiry, the discarding of some old doctrines and corrupt superstitions, and little moments of instinctive resort to ingrained superstitious habits. These did not disappear overnight. To live in constant fear of unpredictable disasters, lurches in the Wheel of Fortune, as signs of divine anger might have made men neurotic paranoiacs. John Calvin taught that Christians needed to submit to God and trust that nothing happened (good or bad) by the working of chance. All was as God intended. Misfortune might be a deserved punishment for sin, but could also be a chastening good. The story of Job was commonly referenced to enforce the idea that misfortunes could purify and strengthen the sufferer. All you had to do was submit to the will of the Lord. Fear of divine vengeance for misdemeanours receded considerably as the Christian world moved from the medieval into the Renaissance period, but it was still there and became vibrantly active when a sin committed was followed closely enough by some misfortune to make it seem like God's punishment. The connection was naturally made. In an age permeated at all levels by religion and constant doctrinal realignment, many people still visited the wise woman or the cunning man of the village. People lived in three worlds. One had ancient pagan, popular roots in the rural community and the natural superstitions that people of all ages cling to. There was also the new world of science that debunked superstition. Then there was the aggressive, new religion, banishing magic, rejecting science (or very suspicious of it) and armed with a formidable range of punishments for non-conformity. Christians still wished ill luck on enemies and sought help from a conjuror to bring about misfortune. Such behaviour, ostensibly reprehensible, officially magic, was in reality understandable though growing less and less acceptable. In 1584 it was claimed, 'Three parts at least of the people' remained 'wedded to their old superstition still'.[34] There are many scriptural and contemporary accounts of possession. For the Jacobeans such schizophrenic or multiple personality behaviour had diabolic overtones. Some verbal hints suggest that in a sense Volpone and Mosca are possessed. They have an uncontrollable urge to deceive. It is a compulsion. They are psychologically driven, incapable of not lying, of not wearing different metaphorical and linguistic masks for different circumstances and different listeners. Elizabethans and Jacobeans were fascinated by unusual states of mind. Many plays introduce insanity (real or pretended) and other obsessional states. Volpone's infatuation with gold; Hamlet's extreme grief over his father's death and his anger at the evil of his uncle; Iago's racist psychopathy; Othello's jealousy; Richard III's single-minded ruthless pursuit of power; Faustus's obsession with the occult; and the various fixations of various malcontents in the revenge tragedies indicate interest in highly charged emotional states. Apart from the obvious excitement such explorations provoked in the audiences, many serious non-fiction writers – moralists, sociologists, medical scientists – described, defined and debated the workings of the human mind, its fragilities and aberrations. Madness mixed with diabolism was a heady, disturbing and frightening combination in any situation. There are moments in the play when Volpone and Mosca exhibit highly wrought states of excitement. When he escapes from the first court Volpone declares,

> To make a snare, for mine own neck! and run
> My head into it, wilfully! With laughter!
> When I had newly scaped, was free, and clear!
> Out of mere wantonness! O, the dull devil
> Was in this brain of mine when I devised it. (5.11.1–4)

The 'dull devil' may literally mean 'stupidity', but it carries a hint of awareness that he was not thinking rationally, but was possessed of sin, greed, personified as a state of possession. Mosca too experiences a state of euphoric self-congratulation after persuading Corvino to let his wife loose to Volpone:

> I fear, I shall begin to grow in love
> With my dear self, and my most prosperous parts,
> They do spring, and burgeon; I can feel
> A whimsy i' my blood: I know not how,
> Success hath made me wanton. I could skip
> Out of my skin, now, like a subtle snake,

34 Thomas, 84.

I am so limber. O! your parasite
Is a most precious thing, dropped from above,
Not bred 'mongst clods, and clotpoles, here on earth. (3.1.1–9)

Mosca's shameless, unconcerned pride in his parasite status and his manipulative skills is counterbalanced by the audience's judgement of his sinfulness. Jonson elsewhere comments more directly:

> These are flatterers for their bread, that praise all my oraculous lord does or says, be it true or false; invent tales that shall please; make baits for his lordship's ears; and if they be not received [...] they shift a point of the compass [...] deny what they confessed, and confess what they denied; fit their discourse to the persons and occasions. [...] They are an odious and vile kind of creatures, that fly about the house all day, and picking up the filth of the house like pies or swallows, carry it to their nest, the lord's ears, and oftentimes report the lies they have feigned for what they have seen and heard.[35]

The characters have little sense of an ever-watchful, demanding and vengeful God in *Volpone*. Most of them live without a present and active awareness of the demands of virtue. These two examples of hubris signal to the contemporary audience that both men have moved into a final stage of sin. As the events progress from bad to worse, there is little to give an audience any sense of hopeful upturn. Other comedies present little acts of kindness, little moments of understanding and support, hinting at an underlying impulse in man that is not so savage, not so selfish. Self-knowledge achieved through adversity, cleansing and instruction learned through suffering lead at the end to a mood of reconciliation, forgiveness, charity, redemption and reconstruction. That is absent in *Volpone*. Even Bonario's rescue of Celia looks to be doomed by obfuscation, lies, judicial prejudice and inefficiency.

Tensions between the vestiges of Catholicism and the drive of the new religion to establish itself led to many inconsistencies. The man who might automatically call on a favourite saint to help him because he had done so since a child, might be very vocal in opposing in his parish church any form of religious rite that looked like magic. The desire to banish any supernatural intercession had a long tradition stemming from the underground heresies and Lollardy of the Middle Ages that opposed the increasing doctrinal corruption of a Catholic Church that relied heavily on belief in miracles

---

35 *Timber*, 51.

and saintly intervention. The new Anglican Church wanted individuals to attend devotedly to their own faith and their own soul. It wanted them to see the priest, speaking in English, praying in English, as their spokesman with God. On one level the Venetian setting might encourage the audience to see the play as representing a rotten papistical society, without a moral compass, greedy, lustful, superstitious and gullible, provoking most of the spectators to xenophobic laughter. Sir Pol and his wife help link the action and its moral failings to England and theatregoers were used to seeing Italian or Spanish locations and seeing through them to an English problem being addressed. Is jealousy any less dangerous because *Othello* is set in Venice and Cyprus? Is obsessive greed and labyrinthine deception only confined to Venice? Human sinfulness is universal and whatever the setting the evils on stage evoked haunting fears at the dark edges of the mind. Satan and his legions were very real to the Jacobeans, a constant threat, and they knew no frontiers.

Dismantling Catholicism's infrastructure began with Henry VIII's Act of Supremacy (1534) and continued in 1536 with the first phase of the Dissolution of the Monasteries. This was followed by the extensive anti-Catholic Protestant reforms initiated in Edward VI's brief reign (1547–53). But there were still enemies to fight. Radical Lutheran doctrines worried conservative worshippers. More concerning was the Calvinist idea that some were born predestined to go to Heaven however badly they behaved on earth and others were damned however virtuously they lived. This raised the question of how much moral behaviour was only motivated by fear of punishment (on earth or in the afterlife) rather than by a genuine desire to behave well. Then there were the growing numbers of Puritan sects, gaining power on councils (especially in the City of London), vehemently calling for further church reform to root out vestigial Catholic ritual. Mixed with politics and religion were fears of a return to the pre-Tudor baronial Wars of the Roses, expressed this time through religious conflict like in France. These related to concerns about who ruled the country and how, especially as the queen crept closer toward death. Tensions between Mary Queen of Scots and Elizabeth had threatened civil war. Various plots against Elizabeth created a constant atmosphere of uneasiness. These anxieties gave history plays and tragedies the extra edge of not just being displays of past events, with pomp and ceremony, trumpets and battles, but also unnerving suggestions of how the past can come back to haunt a nation, how unresolved grievances, memories of violence done, of injustices committed and not righted, memories hidden like the fissures of an apparently quiescent volcano which, invisibly building pressure, will at some time break into seismic catastrophes in the body politic. Would there be a ferocious papist uprising against James I? The general expectation was that there would be civil unrest. Dekker asks,

> Who did expect but ruin, blood, and death,
> To share our kingdom, and divide our breath?[36]

With concerns growing about the new king's fitness to rule (given his background as the son of the plotting Queen of Scots), the spectacle of a play suggesting society was rotten to the core made tense and not very amusing viewing.

Much Elizabethan-Jacobean drama has an underlying motif about fitness to rule. There are examples of good and bad kingship, and studies of how not to rule a city, a household, a family and, most essentially, yourself. There is a persistent concern with the dangers of not controlling your passions. Jonson asserted, 'Passions are spiritual rebels, and raise sedition against the understanding'.[37] Not knowing yourself, not knowing your strengths and weaknesses, not focusing the right priorities, not being honest with yourself and others, not making rational judgements, not choosing safe friends and honest servants and not running your household, your family and yourself properly and justly are persistently discussed during the period. Chronicle plays offered instructive exempla from past history, displaying success and failure among rulers. Elyot's *The Boke Named the Governour* offered a detailed treatise on the education essential for those born to greatness, achieving it or having it thrust on them. Great place demanded moral principles if duty was to be properly performed. Transient fads and fancies, passing whims, innate personality defects, favouritism and other faults could all affect just conduct and behaving like a common criminal when you were a man of rank, put you beyond the pale of acceptability.

New centuries always create fearful anticipations of disaster. Contemporary literature reflected these fears in poetic satires and satiric dramas expressing a sense of England having lost its way morally and that the world had become old and rundown. John Marston's satiric poem *The Scourge of Villainye*, his plays *The Malcontent*, *Antonio and Mellida* and *The Dutch Courtesan*, and Dekker's *The Honest Whore* reflect moral ambiguity and concerns about the state of society, castigate the intrigues, lies and machinations of courts and present a range of psychopathic villains more disturbed and more fascinating even than Volpone or Mosca.

Shakespeare's great tragedies and problem plays contribute to this gloomy psychic state. *Lear*, *Volpone* and John Day's *Isle of Gulls* all appeared about

36 Dekker, *The Wonderful Year 1603*, 26.
37 *Timber*, 4.

the same time and, though very different in style, present worlds in which flattery, greed, hypocrisy and pretension are dominant features of a parasitical humanity where people are likened to the animals their major humour (personality trait) most resembles. Gloucester's picture of his times sums up the sense of the world's decay:

> Love cools, friendship falls off, brothers divide: in cities, mutinies; in countries, discord; in palaces, treason; and the bond crack'd 'twixt son and father. This villain of mine (Edgar) comes under the prediction; there's son against father: the King falls from the bias of nature; there's father against child. We have seen the best of our time: machinations, hollowness, treachery, and all ruinous disorders follow us disquietly to our graves. (*King Lear*, 1.2.110–20)

His son Edmund mocks this pessimistic credulity, but uses the same picture of social disintegration to fool his brother into believing in predictions of disaster:

> unnaturalness between the child and the parent; death, dearth, disso-lutions of ancient amities; divisions in state; menaces and maledictions against King and nobles; needless diffidences, banishment of friends, dissipation of cohorts, nuptial breeches. (1.2.151–6)

Though there was a natural tendency to sensationalize and emphasize the negative aspects of human sinfulness and God's warnings through violent natural events and grotesque unnatural births (like a calf born with two heads), there was a reverse to all that. Continued survival (the storm that dispersed the Armada, the exposure of numerous plots against Elizabeth and then against James I) indicated to some that England was a chosen nation, elected by God for special protection, justifying the Fifth Monarchists' belief that the reign of King Jesus would begin in England. Special-nation status resonates through John of Gaunt's 'sceptered isle' speech in *Richard II* (1593–6) where the dying duke calls England 'this blessed plot':

> This other Eden, demi-paradise,
> This fortress built by Nature for herself
> Against infection and the hand of war. (2.1.42–4)

This myth enabled Shakespeare and other playwrights to see English history in terms of good management leading to happiness and God's support, while mismanagement led to the misery of war and withdrawal of God's guardianship. Jonson presents a world endangered but redeemed. Satisfying as that may be emotionally, intellectually many in the audience might have felt it was an artificially manufactured ending. The world they stepped out into after applauding the actors was not likely to be one where they would 'fare jovially'. The omens were not propitious.

James I was notoriously generous with public money. He gave away Crown land and having promised to stop doing that gave his courtiers money instead. He exchanged the palace of Hatfield for Cecil's palace of Theobalds and threw in numbers of Crown estates all over the country to clinch the deal. Although the new acquisition was one of the most opulent and magnificent building in the land, he spent a further £12,000 on new furnishings. He further demanded nearly £6,000 for entertaining the visiting King of Denmark. Expenses for the dramatic festivities put on at court rocketed under him. James I did not particularly like plays though many were performed at court, probably more to entertain others than the king. He lacked his wife's enthusiasm for masques, but did not stop them.[38] On 15 January 1604, less than a year after his accession, a courtier's letter reveals,

[W]e had every night a publicke play in the great hale, at which the king was ever present [...] but it seems he takes no extraordinary pleasure in them. The Queen and Prince were more the players frends, for on other nights they had them privately, and hath since taken them to theyr protection.[39]

The first Christmas of his reign we learn that 'the Queen intendeth to make a mask' and 'It is said that there shall be thirty plays'. On Twelfth Night 1604 there was another queen's masque, and before Christmas 1604 again 'the ladies in the Court prepare to solemnize the Christmas with a gallant Masque which doth cost the Exchequer £3,000'.[40] By 17 December the cost had reached £4,000 and the Council wanted to halt it. Ultimately it was performed because withdrawal would look to foreign ambassadors present at Court as if the royal family could not afford it. The king's debts seemed a perennial, irresolvable problem. Since his succession James I had racked up greater and greater expenses. His personal extravagance and that of his court were a persistent aggravation. In 1610 the Great Contract, put forward by the Lord Treasurer, Robert Cecil, required Parliament to vote a sum to clear the king's debts and agree to James I receiving an annual sum of £200,000. In return he would give

38 Davies, 263.
39 Footnote, E. K. Chambers, *The Elizabethan Stage*, vol. 1, p. 7.
40 Harrison, 90–1.

up his prerogative rights over Wardships and Purveyance and cease to impose new import taxes. Entangled arguments over this, with both sides altering their aims, led to the plan being dropped, but the whole matter indicates the differences inherent in opposed perceptions of monarchical role, rule and the relationship with the Commons. In discussions between James I and 30 members of the Commons Sir Henry Neville had declared that 'where your Majesty's expense growth by the Commonwealth, we are bound to maintain it; otherwise not'.[41] This means public and national needs should be met by subsidies voted by Parliament, but personal expenses should not. Sir Henry went on to say

> that the King had received four subsidies and seven-fifteenths which is more than ever was given by any Parliament at any time; [...] yet withal they had no relief of their grievances. It is commonly said that the Parliament could be content to replenish the royal cistern of the King's Treasury were they assured that the King's largess to the Scots' prodigality would not cause a continual and remediless leak therein. Also, that one in the Lower House lately promised to produce a bill of £100,000 of debts owing to the Crown by Scotsmen who bear their creditors in hand that they shall all be paid when the new taxes come into the Exchequer.[42]

Worse than the material waste at court was the moral corruption. On 6 January 1605 was performed the notorious *Masque of Blacknesse*, much criticized on account of the court ladies blacking up and wearing revealing costumes. It provoked comments on costume costs and how they made the ladies look like courtesans. Lady Rich appeared in the masque. She was known to be living in open adultery with Lord Mountjoy. Pickpockets were common in the public theatres, but even at this Court event it was afterwards found that jewels and purses were 'lost' in the crowd and one young woman was caught having sex.[43] More masques followed after New Year. During James I's reign Court performances increased threefold.

There were other more pertinent examples of court decadence. The Overbury poisoning case created the most sensational court scandal when the king's favourite, Sir Robert Carr, and his wife were implicated. The court was *terra infirma*. When Carr fell, Buckingham and his faction and family instantly moved into places of power and money. Courtiers were always

41 G. B. Harrison, 232.
42 Harrison, 232.
43 Chute, 164.

struggling to fill vacated places. The Overbury murder was an unusual event, but the general atmosphere was one of sexual promiscuity, rivalries, feuds, debts, extravagant waste and indecorous conduct. The king himself was no exemplar. A physician remarked, 'He is very wrathful but the fit soon passes off'.[44] There was an incident when the king kicked a groom for losing papers which the servant denied having even touched. There were many other incidents of violent language and swearing when James I was thwarted. He regularly exploded in angry outbursts. Orazio Busino records an incident when some dancers became tired during a performance of Jonson's masque *Pleasure Reconciled to Virtue* (performed 6 January 1618 in the Banqueting Hall, Whitehall):

> [T]he king, who is by nature choleric, grew impatient and shouted loudly, 'Why don't they dance? What did you make me come here for? Devil take all of you, dance!'[45]

These incidents transgress various qualities thought essential to regal and gentlemanly decorum. The Prince of Wales even set up 'swear boxes' round the palace. 'King James was notorious for his habit of laughing and talking at divine service, but prince Henry sat alert and attentive through the longest sermons'.[46] James I also hated smoking, cosmetics and 'the clutter of overdressed, extravagant women who overran Whitehall'.[47] He wrote *A Counterblast to Tobacco* (1604), but the other problems he did nothing to curb.

The chancellor, Sir Francis Bacon, signed arrest warrants that allowed Sir Giles Mompesson to threaten with imprisonment anyone who hindered his projects. Mompesson was free to extort money from those applying to get licences to sell liquor. The whole of government was similarly riddled with political jobbery and chicanery lining the pockets of ruthless opportunists. The Volpone system was alive and living in England. Bribery was so endemic in Whitehall that James I said he would 'soon not have a single subject left' if he punished bribery on the Venetian system.[48] Aristocrats happily took inducements to allow projectors to name them in the list of backers of any new scheme or merchant venture. In the face of the universal corruption it is laughable that James I had announced, 'I will leave nothing undone that

---

44 Chute, 154.
45 Quoted in Stephen Orgel and Roy Strong, *Inigo Jones: The Theatre of the Stuart Court*, vol. 1, p. 284.
46 Chute, 171.
47 Chute, 228.
48 Chute, 222.

becomes a just king'.[49] In 1612, though he was an employee of the king, both as an associate member of the King's Men and as principal composer of court masques, Jonson published a book of epigrams in which he openly attacked 'the effeminate young witlings he had encountered at Court' and the 'fledgling statesmen who had spent a few weeks at Whitehall and considered themselves experts on every problem that was facing Europe'.[50] Sir Politic had evidently returned from Venice and was spouting his nonsense around Whitehall and Westminster.

49 Chute, 263.
50 Chute, 236.

Chapter 12

THE BEAST FABLE

Along with the mood and the stock types of the commedia dell'arte, another literary form that Ben Jonson collages into his text is the long-established beast fable. A fable is a story (usually short) conveying a moral lesson. It uses the device of speaking animals with human characteristics. They may represent allegorically particular personal qualities – like vanity, cunning, greed, gullibility, courage, resourcefulness. Volpone himself sees the symbolism of the bird names when he tells Corvino he has 'such moral emblems on your name' (5.8.12). He recognizes too his own name's meaning ('The Fox shall, here, uncase', 5.12.84). This implies some degree of recognition of the fox's traditional reputation and how it fits his conduct, though he may only see it as a badge of pride that he has been the clever bringer of justice to cheats rather than seeing it as badge of shame that he has stooped to greed, lust and deceit. The fable, often ending with an epigrammatic statement of the moral, has its origins in ancient folklore and proverbs and is traceable, in written form, to the sixth-century Greek writer Aesop. The classically educated in the audience would know Aesop's *Fables*. Many others would know improving or warning tales told them as children in which animals behave as well, as stupidly or as badly as human beings. Among the substantial collection of stories, each involving talking animals and each ending with an improving moral lesson, Aesop recounts ten tales depicting the cunning of the fox, including the one where the fox – like Volpone pretending to be so ill he will soon die – plays dead in order to lure in and trap a gullible victim – a carrion crow. Another tells how a fox flatters a crow which has a piece of cheese in its beak. The fox compliments the bird on the reports of its beautiful song and asks it to sing for him. The crow caws, the cheese drops to the ground and the fox gobbles it up.

The moral is, do not trust flatterers and is referenced by Volpone when talking to Corvino, the crow (5.8.13–14).[1] Another fable tells of a fox which, having broken into an actor's house, is frightened by a face staring at him. After a while he realizes it is a mask like the sort actors wear. He comments, 'What a beautiful head! Yet it is of no value, as it entirely lacks brains'.[2] Moral: fine show on the outside is no guarantee of inner worth. One might add that the gullibility of the fox suggests another moral: a cheat used to using artifice can also be easily conned by artifice.

Aesop's *Fables* were traditionally read to children, because they drew on the common appeal of animals talking, which children respond to very readily. Such tales are a way of teaching them about the ways of the world. While Aesop suggests that animals have human traits, Jonson turns this around and attributes animal and bird names and characteristics to his human characters as a way of saying humans have become brutalized, that they are animals in human guise. Each of his creatures (fox, fly, vulture, crow, raven) is a predator. Likening humans to animals – usually negatively – was a traditional way of speaking in sermons or writing in moral pamphlets. It was not unusual in plays either. Very close in time to *Volpone*, Shakespeare's *King Lear* is crammed with animal imagery. It is the major image type. The king likens two of his daughters to tigers, kites and monsters. Animals provide the major image type in that play as they do in *Volpone*. Some mutual influence may have been active. The two men worked together, lived near each other and spent time together socially. Who influenced whom is impossible to tell and does not matter. It was a common enough way of thinking.

Later in the century, in his book of political philosophy, *Leviathan* (1651), Thomas Hobbes referred to man's life as 'solitary, poor, nasty, brutish, and short' if not protected by a society or political community based on cooperation.[3] Without community (family, village, tribe), men would prey on each other like animals in a savage, primitive, might-is-right world.

Hobbes asserted that nature can be counterbalanced by men working together to protect themselves from brute-force robbers. Michel de Montaigne

---

1 Geoffrey Chaucer's 'Nonnes Preestes Tale' makes the fox the gullible one. Having grabbed and ran off with the cockerel Chauntecleer he is fooled into replying to the bird. At the moment his muzzle opens to speak, the bird escapes. The foxes moralizes, 'God yeve hym meschaunce/That is so undiscreet of governaunce/That jangleth whan he sholde his pees!' (God give him bad luck who is so careless of self-control that he chatters when he should hold his peace), 667–9.

2 *Aesop's Fables*, 230.

3 *Leviathan*, part 1, chap. 13, 'Of the Natural Condition of Mankind As Concerning Their Felicity, and Misery', 186. His title refers to the people as a huge, monstrous state like the Old Testament creature mentioned in the books of Job and Isaiah.

had said, 'There seems to be nothing for which Nature has better prepared us than for fellowship'.[4] This mutual cooperation is a signifier of civilization and incorporates Christian beliefs that validate the exercise of sympathy, neighbourly and community help, decency and respect for the individual. Without this socialization, Hobbes says, there would be no industry and commerce, 'no arts; no letters; no society; and which is worst of all, continual fear, and danger of violent death'. This vision of life as a jungle is within the same cultural thought patterning as Jonson's naming his characters after scavengers and is in the same tradition as medieval illuminated manuscripts containing margins full of animals – some merely the livestock of farms or woodland, but others grotesque imagined monster hybrids and some dressed in human clothes, like the bishop-fox in the *Smithfield Decretals*. A book of hours from Utrecht (c. 1460) depicts a fox sitting reading a book. He wears a monk's hood. In Erasmus's *Praise of Folly* (written 1509, printed 1511) is a description of a Doctor of Divinity under whose hood is a pair of ass's ears. Jonson takes up this anticlerical image:

> ...Hood an ass with reverend purple,
> So you can hid his two ambitious ears,
> And he shall pass for a cathedral doctor. (1.2.112–4)

For him it represents the foolishness of ambition for power, masked by the trappings of fine costume and the deference paid to rank, while the wearer of the clothes of office is actually an ass. It references government corruption allowing fools into office because they have contacts, rank and money rather than merit.

There is a substantial medieval tradition of tales about Reynard the Fox. A seminal text is the Old French *Le Roman de Renart* (c. 1170), thought to be by Pierre de St. Cloud. This comprehensive collection of the adventures of a fox with speech, acuteness and cunning established the basis for many other anthropomorphic tales and translations into English, Dutch and German. H. A. Guerber claims the story of Reineke Fuchs (Reynard the Fox) originated among the Franks and 'was carried [...] across the Rhine into France' and was first written down in the Netherlands.[5] He sees the enduring interest in the fox tales as reflecting the connection between the human hunter searching for game (in competition with the fox) and the shepherd protecting his food from the commonest predator: 'The root of this saga lies in the harmless natural

---

4 'On Affectionate Relationships', Screech, 207. 'Fellowship' here means company, society.
5 H. A. Guerber, *Myths and Legends of the Middle Ages*, 35.

simplicity of a primeval people'.[6] There is more to it. Such a character was likely to be of interest, as a warning, to a culture that was largely rural and relied on protecting its food sources from such a prolific and indiscriminate predator. But it developed into a more sophisticated allegory about human corruption and the deviousness of some types of people. More specifically, it became a criticism of hypocrisy, particularly that of a monolithic church whose personnel penetrated every region of Christian Europe, but more generally an attack on those whose acute intellects made them capable of conning the majority of simple folk

Guerber's account begins with a range of animals bringing charges against Reynard at the Merovingian annual Whitsuntide assembly set up to plan the coming year but also to address problems that had accrued during the previous 12 months. The fox is accused of physical brutality, food theft and insult to a she-wolf. The assembly is presided over by the king, a lion called Noble (or Nobel). The accused is defended by a badger who presents an alternative version of each statement and declares that the fox has found piety, turned hermit and spends his days in fasting and prayer. Just as it looks as if the fox will be acquitted a cockerel brings evidence of a massacre perpetrated by the predator gaining entrance to the hen yard 'in the garb of a monk'.[7] Piously pretending that a peace amnesty had been announced by the king, Reynard persuaded the fowls he had changed his way of life and that they were safe. When they went foraging in the forest the fox attacked them. Messengers are sent to call Reynard to court, but each is outwitted or killed by the accused. Eventually brought to stand trial the fox is condemned to death. He escapes by fabricating a story of a conspiracy against Noble. This apparently loyal honesty gains him a pardon. Further violent depredations bring Reynard to court a second time (like Volpone). Once again he wriggles out of punishment, fights in single combat, wins by trickery and thereafter 'enjoyed great honour as long as he lived', while 'his adventures have long been the delight of people, whom his tricks have never failed to amuse'.[8] Inventive and resourceful criminals have always fascinated people – as long as they were not the victim of their stings.

Among all the different fables those of the rascally but resourceful fox became the most numerous and popular. A recurring feature is the episode of the fox feigning dead in order to lure carrion birds, just as Volpone attracts his victims by pretending to be sick and close to his end. Another narrative leads to the fox losing his skin in a desperate attempt to escape.

6 Guerber, *Myths and Legends of the Middle Ages*, 35.
7 Guerber, *Myths and Legends of the Middle Ages*, 39.
8 Guerber, *Myths and Legends of the Middle Ages*, 58.

This is echoed in the phrase 'mortifying of a fox' (5.12.125) uttered by Volpone shortly after he senses he is caught 'I'mine own noose' (5.10.14). St Cloud's French version is a compilation of earlier literary strands in the emergence of the Fox tradition. These earlier strands drew on popular culture. The fox appears in Geoffrey Chaucer's 'The Nun's Priest's Tale' and in 1481 William Caxton printed *The Historie of Reynart the Fox*, translated from Middle Dutch. In one story Reynart is charged with raping Hersent, a she-wolf, and wrongly put on trial. In another strand Reynart is again put on trial for pretending to be dead in order to lure and catch the crow's wife. In the play, this is metamorphosed into the attempted seduction of Celia, where the supposedly almost dead Volpone leaps from his couch protesting true love. Lady Pol is called a she-wolf by Volpone who, like Reynart, attempts a rape and faces a court appearance twice. In another fable, Reynart is thought to be dead and many mourners deliver insincere eulogies at the graveside. Such hypocrisy lies at the heart of the legacy hunters' ploys.

Reynart takes his revenge on them in a variety of suitable ways. This is echoed in the disingenuous flatteries of the *captators* in *Volpone* and the twists and turns Mosca and Volpone devise to lure them in deeper. Other guises adopted by the continually shape-changing Fox are those of the quack doctor and the false preacher. In both strands he mounts a pulpit or bench or stage as Volpone does as Scoto. As a pretend doctor Reynart has the opportunity of giving personal consultations to women and taking advantage of them sexually. There are medieval illuminations of a fox as a pretend priest preaching either to hens, geese and ducks or to women. This relates to Reynart's proverbial lustfulness and ties in with how priests often used their oratorical skills in sermons to mesmerize and frighten pious women and then seduce them after discovering their weaknesses through their confessions. He is occasionally depicted as a pretend minstrel (another common seducer type), perhaps playing the fiddle well but singing in an unattractive voice. It would work as a comic touch if Volpone singing the lyric 'Come, my Celia' created a humorous tension between the beauty of the words and the discord of his voice.

The fox emerges as both downright scoundrel (though admired for his ingeniousness) and as an anti-establishment, anticlerical hero to be admired. From folklore stories, ballads and folk song these tales were assimilated into more literary form, part of the print culture's transformation of oral tradition into written format. Many of them are satires against authority with the fox typically as a peasant hero outwitting the nobility and the church. Aesop, St Cloud, folklore and medieval bestiaries all make their contribution to how Jonson's imagination builds his story. The Renaissance, with its love of allegory, gave abstract qualities to many animals – peacocks for pride, lion for courage and so on. Here the anthropomorphic animal is given a typically Renaissance emblematic treatment, suited to that allegorizing tendency and seeing people in terms of the animal characteristics they might display. Tying the animals then to sins – avarice, envy, pandering, flattery, lying, vanity, pride, lust – completes the moral circle and gives the edge to the satire that is the driving force of the play. It was not unusual in the period for characters to bear names that indicated their humour or dominant character trait.[9] Here the animal names point toward their dominant humour (greed as expressed through scavenging for money and money as a thing of death, like carrion feeding off dead meat). This is a pattern continued from medieval morality plays and early Tudor interludes. Bonario is so called because he is good (*bonum* is Latin for good) and Celia is heavenly, pure (*coelum* meant the skies, the heavens). The fox stands for cunning; the fly for its love of rottenness, which is its sustaining diet; birds of prey for their gruesome greed for dead flesh; and parrots for meaningless chatter. Even the freaks are named for their specific distortion. They are an antifamily, reflecting Volpone's own unnatural state – childless, without love, without friends, unattached to humanity. Even their names are not personal or real but point to their status – Androgyno (hermaphrodite), Castrone (eunuch), Nano (dwarf), as if they are merely household objects like a jug, a chair or a goblet. It was a common fad for dramatists to give humour names or significant names to characters, sometimes related to their job. In George Peele's *The Old Wive's Tale* there are semi-clown characters called Frantic, Frolic and Fantastic. Jonson himself commonly gave his characters similarly evocative names. In *The Alchemist* we find Subtle, Face, Sir Epicure Mammon and Pertinax Surly. But the choice of animal names for the central figures in the hunt for Volpone's legacy hints to the audience that their personalities are likely to conform to the bestial behaviour associated with the particular creature after which they are named and points the audience's attention to how they suit their animal. They do not even have Christian names. This further bestializes or dehumanizes them. It is entirely fitting that the animals are all predators (apart from Sir Pol and Lady Pol, the parrots who are just noisy fools).

Renaissance paintings are full of symbolism and such iconographic emblems seeped into literature. The primacy of the scriptures created this sort of thought pattern. We tend today not to think that way but in those days there were emblem books that informed set designers, costume designers, painters, engravers and writers what symbols were what and what they meant. Thus, when representing Faith, Dignity, Justice, Courage,

---

9 Other Jonson plays provide Zeal-of-the-Land Busy, Morose, Truewit, Amorous la Foole, Madame Haughty, Fastidious Brisk, Sordido and Fungoso.

Fortitude or Cowardice, a painter or writer could ascribe to the allegorical concept a personification and description that conformed to the current understanding of it. Many symbols related to religion – to death or salvation. Such symbology or semiology (symbolism and signification) enabled writers, artists and orators to describe the virtues, the vices, the various passions and the various types of arts and sciences, and to subtly insert secret messages and arcane meanings into their work, whether visual or written. In these handbooks the emblems were alphabetized and each had an engraving or woodcut of the subject (for example Justizia – Justice), accompanied by a description (with references to the Bible or classics) of the characteristics (Justice as a woman, erect, blindfold, holding a sword in one hand and scales in the other). All the features it required (clothing, posture, relevant instruments) were listed too, with explanations why these were chosen. The most famous and influential of these handbooks was Cesare Ripa's *Iconologia*, published in 1593. A second edition came out in 1603, with 684 separate emblem/allegory items and 151 woodcuts. Jonson would almost certainly have looked at such books when collaborating with Inigo Jones. Whether he had such images in mind when writing *Volpone* is impossible to say. There were English handbooks fulfilling the same requirements, like Stephen Bateman's *The Christall Glasse of Christian Reformation* already referred to in chapter 3.

Common folklore also contributed to the attributes of foxes, flies, vultures, ravens and crows. One of Jonson's own epigrams refers to the hawk as a creature that 'pursues the truth, strikes at ignorance, and makes the fool its quarry'. The peregrine was the hawk hierarchically prescribed for the nobility. The character Peregrine is meant then to be thought of as striking at the foolishness of Sir Pol and at his lies and fantasy aggrandizements of himself. Suitably Politic is shortened to Pol, a parrot. Peregrine's punishment of the garrulous chatterbox is ruthless and perhaps disproportionate, but is the one example of virtue opposing folly with rigour.

In a world where no one is what they purport to be, the servant becomes the master – by means of donning his clothes – just as flies infest carrion. The magistrate's order 'Disrobe that parasite!' carries a number of resonances. In *The Taming of the Shrew* Tranio is made to exchange clothes with his master, Lucentio, in order to fool the father of the girl he wishes to secretly woo in the guise of a schoolmaster. It is a device common to comedy, usually related to the metaphor for dress as a disguiser of reality. In practical terms, in a world where costume indicated rank, exchange of clothes was a means by which assignations and courtship are furthered. In *Volpone* dress works initially to disguise what people truly are and then in the denouement stage it works as an unmasking of deceit as each cheat is exposed. It also acts as an indicator that normality is being restored in Venice as Mosca the master deceiver (and deceiver of his master) is brought to book and disrobed.

Jonson's vision of man preying on man is picked up in the next century in Jonathan Swift's 'Poetry: A Rhapsody':

> So, Nat'ralists observe, a Flea
> Hath smaller Fleas that on him prey,
> And these have smaller yet to bit 'em,
> And so proceed *ad infinitum*. (337–40)

This references the tendency of humans to prey on each other as a part of the natural chain of being. Court life and the commercial 'food chain' are founded on everyone trying to outdo everyone else, to con them, to get money or place and power out of them. Everyone out to get what they can from others, either in a friendly mutual interchange of services or in selfish criminal theft is what hire and labour are about, what shops, investment, foreign trade and politics are about. Pieter Bruegel drew a pen picture in 1556 called *The Big Fish Eats the Little Ones*. It shows a seaside scene with two men in the foreground in a boat. One has cut open a fish and is removing another fish from inside. His companion points to the middle ground where a huge fish lies on the shore. It is disgorging a mass of other fish it has swallowed. Meanwhile another man with a huge knife has cut open its belly and many more fish have cascaded out. This works at one level as a political comment on how the great men of power, rank and money swallow up the little people, subjugating them, keeping them in subordinate positions, restricting their lives. It further suggests that such men can become 'beached' and fall from power and be cannibalized themselves as their property is redistributed like a fish being butchered for sale. At a broader level it is an allegory of man's tendency to scavenge from his own kind, like for example a usurer who plays on people's vanity, greed or desperate need, loans them money they cannot afford to repay, then takes over their property when they default. When the usurer's business fails or he dies, all sorts of scavengers gather to dismember his empire. It is the never-ending cycle of survival. Mosca puts this grotesque reality in a different metaphor:

> Almost
> All the wise world is little else in nature,
> But parasites, or sub-parasites. (3.1.11–13)

Be they fish, parasites or fleas, the picture is of a world where men predate each other in an endless food chain of cannibalism.

Chapter 13

TRANSGRESSIONS AND SINS: THE BITERS BIT

Sharp mustard rhyme
To purge the snottery of our slimy time.

(John Marston, *The Scourge of Villainie*)

In his compendium of psycho-emotional states, *The Anatomy of Melancholy*, Robert Burton, academic and clergyman, studies the causes and effects of covetousness. He sometimes conflates avarice with envy (greed with covetousness) because they do overlap. Avarice is wanting more and more of something to the point where you have more than you need but still are greedy for more. It can be the unquenchable desire for chocolate or cake or gold.

Usually it is applied to the obsessive accumulation of material goods or wealth. The possessing becomes the object of the act of acquiring; just having the gold, not using it to buy things, that is the compulsion. Envy is coveting what another has. It is a commandment that 'Thou shall not covet ...' It is another form of greed. Citing Plutarch, Robert Burton asserts that 'all the causes of our miseries in this life [...] have had their beginning from stubborn anger [...] or some unjust or immoderate affection, as covetousness, &c'.[1] On his own account he adds that 'usury, fraud, Simony [selling church offices], oppression, lying, swearing, bearing false witness' issue from 'this fountain of covetousness, that greediness in getting, tenacity in keeping, sordidity in spending'. Apart from simony, all are found in *Volpone* and are integral to its

---

1 Robert Burton, *The Anatomy of Melancholy*, 244. Subsequent Burton quotes come from 244–7.

ethical framework. Orthodox morality is so inverted that Volpone can assert
of gold,

> .... Thou art virtue, fame [reputation],
> Honour and all things else! Who can get thee,
> He shall be noble, valiant, honest, wise. (1.1.25–7)

He means that money can buy the appearance of having these qualities in
the eyes of others for, of course, in reality they are only to be earned by one's
deeds, not by simply having a title, power, rank or wealth. But Volpone (and
Ben Jonson) lives in such a world that if you have riches you are thought to
be virtuous, have a good name, are honourable and honoured by others. If you
have a noble title (often bought in James I's time) you are thought to be noble
courageous, honest and wise in your behaviour just by virtue of having the
title. This was the failing of the hierarchical system. Those with titles, money
and access to power were thought to be good. The word 'aristocracy' comes
from the Greek for 'rule by the best' and centuries of pressure had brainwashed
the lower orders into thinking the aristo-gentry were 'the better sort'. Jonson's
audience knew full well that the so-called great and good were often no better
than knaves and whores, but they clung to the belief (or desperate hope) that
the 'better sort' might really be better. Some were, but many were not. The
court attracted many of the worst of them. Those who came to court virtuous
would soon be corrupted.

Burton quotes the well-known saying 'The desire of money is the root
of all evil, and they that lust after it, pierce themselves through with many
sorrows' (see 1 Timothy 6:10). He might also have alluded to the previous
verse: 'they that will be rich fall into temptation and a snare, and into many
foolish and hurtful lusts, which drown men in destruction and perdition'.
He is part way to defining the title character's moral failing. Rich already,
Volpone has an inordinate (that is, excessive) desire to get more. Burton cites
early Church Fathers (St Augustine, Pope Gregory the Great, Chrysostom
and Bishop Cyprian) who defined avarice as 'a madness of the soul', 'a torture',
'an insatiable drunkenness', a 'blindness, a gilded torture, a plague subverting
Kingdoms, families, an incurable disease'. Along with greed, lust was a major
sin. Cyril Tourneur or Thomas Middleton saw the two linked: 'Were't not for
gold and women, there'd be no damnation'.[2]

Gold and women are the mental and emotional fire that burns and drives
Volpone. What Burton misses, because he is not doing a psychological profile

---

2 *The Revenger's Tragedy* (1607), 2.1.254. The authorship is unclear though the sentiment
   is not.

of the character but generalizing about the mental state, is that for Volpone, it is not the having more for its own sake, it is the thrill of getting more, the process of hustling and conning others that excites him.

> .... I glory
> More in the cunning purchase of my wealth,
> Than in the glad possession; since I gain
> No common way. (1.1.30–3)

This is a whole new level of greed that enjoys fooling others to add to his wealth more than revelling in the actual goods acquired. Volpone is excited by the means not the ends, by the deviousness and deception needed to gain material wealth not the material items themselves. For him there is pleasure in exercising intellectual and strategic dominance over people.

Burton's book (published in 1621) analyzes the various mental states with contributions from the accumulated material provided by ancient writers, Christian theologians and contemporary scientists.

> What makes a Merchant that hath no need, that hath enough and to spare at home, to range all over the world, through all those intemperate Zones of heat & cold; voluntarily to venture his life, and be content with such miserable famine, nasty usage, in a stinking ship, if there were not a pleasure & hope to get money? What makes them go into the bowels of the earth an hundred fathom deep, endangering their dearest lives, [...] when they have enough already, if they could be content, and no such cause to labour, but an extraordinary delight they take in riches?[3]

This is an old-fashioned understanding of the merchant venturer and miner. In his times, merchants were already investing in ships and paying others to undergo the dangers of commercial exploration. Those who bought or opened mines no longer even contemplated digging ore themselves but exploited the labour and needs of others to do the dirty work. Sir Walter Raleigh's dreams of Guyanian gold were not to be realized by his picking it up off the ground but by slaves driven to do it for him. Jonson seemed to understand this when he has Volpone snobbishly reject trade as a means of making more money. He prides himself on the uncommonness of his exploitation. Burton discusses the mental disturbance that drives those who are 'rather possessed by their money than possessors'. They are 'slaves & drudges to their substance'. He references Horace proving that 'all men dote by fits [...] but that covetous

---

3 Burton, *The Anatomy of Melancholy*, part 1, section 2, memb. 3, sub. 12 (pages 245–46).

men are madder than the rest [...] they are all fools'. The covetous workaholic 'is a perpetual drudge, restless in his thoughts & never satisfied, a slave, a wretch, a dust-worm; still seeking what sacrifice he may offer to his golden god, by right or wrong, he cares not how'. In this assertion Burton approaches something of the deranged and obsessional nature of Volpone's gold worship. But Volpone is different. The acrostic argument before the prologue states immediately that he is 'rich'. He has no need to work, has no need for more wealth and is a decadent patrician drawn into crime, partly for the enjoyment of tricking greedy men, partly because he has no civic responsibility, partly because he is disturbed. This is the Devil making work for idle hands. He is a Venetian example of Viscount Conway's definition: 'We eat and drink and rise up to play and this is to live like a gentleman; for what is a gentleman but his pleasure?'[4] He is disengaged from civic duties and is bored. This is why he is drawn to other tricks in the pursuit of his pleasures. Like any idle voluptuary he has to keep finding new sources of pleasure for his jaded palate. Hence he is tickled by lust for Celia. Seducing a merchant's attractive wife was common sport for gentlemen throughout the period. They believed themselves far more attractive than a mere dusty, money-grubbing husband more interested in his business than in his wife, more exciting than a counter-hugging pen-pusher, more cultured, a better catch altogether. Such were the excuses for lust. For Volpone, the Scoto of Mantua mask is not only a means of drawing Celia's attention and of allowing him to see her but it is also an extension into new material of his love of part playing. He is an actor, an orator, an inventive and an imaginative trickster and Scoto is another juicy role.

13.1 Volpone

Both the play and the person are a pageant of sins from the first lines to the last. The normally brief scenario of a commedia dell'arte situation is built into an elaborate and extended series of tricks, essentially a criminal fraud founded on lies. The means by which Volpone and Mosca fool the legacy hunters is a compound sin – bearing false witness and fraud. The *commedia* sketch expands into a fully developed narrative exposing a whole society that is corrupt and predatory. For an audience brought up to beware the snares of the Devil and the temptations of the Seven Deadly Sins it is a feast of moral instruction, like a contemporary morality play. It begins with blasphemy and ends with punishment. There is theatrical shock value in Volpone's morally and theologically corrupt morning prayer to his treasure hoard.

4 Cited in Lawrence Stone, *The Crisis of the Aristocracy*, 27.

His celebration of gold is a profane corruption of the matins service and the traditional dawn song of the lover to his mistress. The 'Te Deum Laudamus' of the Morning Service in the Book of Common Prayer begins,

> We praise the, O God, we knowlage thee to be the Lorde, All the earth doeth worship thee, the father euerlastyng.[5]

Its continuation makes it clear that man should prioritize the adoration of God above all things. The same attitude is found in other morning service prayers and in the Bible (notably Psalm 148), highlighting how much Volpone's 'prayer' transgresses Christian morality.

Acknowledgement of the glory of God and giving thanks for His light and the delight of another day's life are substituted by Volpone by the glory of his shining gold. It is the first of many perversions and inversions that emphasize the moral distortion of Venice (and by implication London). The language of the acrostic argument introduces the element of deception and punishment ('feigns sick', 'deludes', 'tricks', 'all are sold'). The depth of Volpone's blasphemous loss of grace is vibrantly evident in his invocation, not to 'my God' but to 'my gold!' It is a shock opening, at the same time throwing the audience immediately into the central concern and offending their moral sensibilities. Or does it? Jonson immediately includes the audience in this sin when Volpone, gazing on his 'shrine' and addressing his 'saint', hails it as 'the world's soul, and mine!' The audience is a representative part of that world and each must assess his own attitude to money worship. Edward B. Partridge agrees 'this perversion of religious imagery must have been shocking'.[6] This profane prayer would doubly mark the speaker as a sinner in the eyes of even the minimally godly in the audience. Firstly, he addresses his hoard as a 'saint', which would have been regarded as superstitious and idolatrous. The Reformation had done away with such papistical customs. The saints were revered by Protestants as people of special faith and ability who had suffered for their beliefs and spread the word of the Lord, but they were no longer addressed as particular intercessors capable of answering prayers or working miracles. Kissing his treasure 'with adoration', calling each piece a 'relic/Of sacred treasure' is another parody of Catholic faith. The tons and tons of holy relics (thigh bones of this saint, fingernails of that saint, a forest of bits of the cross), probably all fake, had been swept away out of churches by Henry VIII's commissioners. The Catholic habit of kissing the feet of statues of saints was regarded with mockery and revulsion by Anglicans. Secondly, treating gold

---

5 *The Book of Common Prayer* (ed. Brian Cummings), 9.
6 Edward B. Partridge, *The Broken Compass*, 72.

as if it were a holy thing is redolent of the Israelites making and worshiping a golden calf (Exodus 32:2). This was a subversion of the First Commandment ('Thou shalt have no other gods before me'). This is subverted again by the line that calls 'riches, the dumb god'. He adds to the idolatry of this a comment which sharply defines the power of gold to loosen tongues, for riches 'giv'st all men tongues [...] mak'st men do all things' and is 'the price of souls' (1.1.22–4). Ironically he asserts that even Hell is acceptable with gold. His soul has been 'sold' in the name of acquiring gold and he will end in the Hell of a prison cell, without his gold and shackled. Partridge calls Volpone's obsession with material wealth a barren and 'monolithic fanaticism'.[7] The Protestants in the audience (and they would be the majority) would be suitably horrified by his superstition and his blasphemy, but laugh too at his popish simplicity. Behind this reaction would be the sense that this is a topical reference to the growing money worship of some ranks in England. Such irreligion crossed all faith boundaries. Puritans and Anglicans were as guilty of materialism as Catholics. Volpone further reveals himself as a believer in astrology in referring to 'the horns of the celestial Ram' and as knowing something of alchemy in calling gold 'thou sun of Sol'. Punning on the words 'sun' and 'son' he is alluding to alchemists' belief that the moon (female) received the seeds of the sun (male) and conceived gold. Such beliefs would be abhorrent to a Protestant audience. The blasphemer goes further, for in another sense Renaissance men had made gold into a 'saint'. They worshipped it, fought to get it, died for it, stole it, tortured and enslaved to mine it and ventured thousands of miles across uncharted seas in search of it. And then they fashioned trinkets of it to vainly display themselves. There would be some in the audience with gold thread woven into their doublets and dresses. Most would wear gold rings and gold earrings. Some sported gold brooches. A few ate off gold plate. The whole of Europe was struck by gold fever. This was not just an aesthetic obsession. It spoke of the greed of an expanding capitalism. It was not just a mania for gold. Silver and precious gems too were coveted. All were misperceived as expressions of your rank, your wealth, your personal worth, your virtue.

Volpone admits the happiness he experiences in gaining and owning valuable objects ('the glad possession') is less than the excitement of how he actually gets the treasure ('the cunning purchase'). This is a view expressed too by Cressida in *Troilus and Cressida*: 'Things won are done; joy's soul lies in the doing' (1.2.292).[8] It is the chase, the luring in of his mark, the sting that excites Volpone. The ploys by which he gains his wealth are not yet revealed,

---

7 Partridge, *The Broken Compass*, 74.
8 Performed late 1602 or early 1603, by the Chamberlain's Men shortly before they became the King's Men. Jonson was a colleague and friend of Shakespeare at this time.

but Jonson broadens his satirical targets by referencing the ways Volpone does not increase his riches, but which greedy capitalists do.

> Since I gain
> No common way: I use no trade, no venture;
> I wound no earth with ploughshares; fat no beasts
> To feed the shambles; have no mills for iron,
> Oil, corn, or men, to grind 'em into poulder;
> I blow no subtle glass; expose no ships
> To threat'nings of the furrow-faced sea;
> I turn no moneys, in the public bank;
> Nor usure private. (1.1.32–40)

Apart from the manufacture of glass, for which Venice had become famous through its factories on the outlying island of Murano, Jonson's list of the usual vulgar ways of making money were to be found as commonly in London as in the city where his 'hero' lives. His mention of trade, arable and meat farming references traditional ways of making a fortune. The 'mills' straddle the old activities of flour and olive oil production, but also include the new factories making iron and grinding down its exploited workers. Jacobean England was beginning to see the expansion of industrial manufacture that would ever more quickly develop into the next century's Industrial Revolution. It is at the end of this speech, with the references to maritime merchant ventures, currency exchange and money lending, that the new capitalist enterprises, the speculation and investment aspects of London's financial services industry are alluded to. Volpone abhors these ordinary money-grubbing tricks. He leads no 'soft prodigals' into debt by lending them money. This was a common and growing problem with so many young men loose in London, living Prodigal Son lifestyles. He eschews ruining families by demanding exorbitant rates of interest on loan repayments and takes pride in the singular manner of gaining his wealth. There is vanity in his sense of differentness. His designation as a magnifico suggests he would already be rich, so his greed lies in gathering more, accumulating more than he needs and he does it for the thrill of cheating dupes who think to gull him into making them his heir. His character is emerging as a bored, idle man from the top rank of Venetian society who lives well (he is not a miserly hoarder of riches, living frugally), but has no political role in the state. He has no personal domestic role either as husband and father for he is unmarried and childless. The acrostic argument calls him 'childless' though Mosca tells Corvino his master has 'some dozen, or more' bastards 'begot on beggars/Gipsies, and Jews, and black-moors, when he was drunk' (1.5.44–5). This is so glaringly contradictory of the argument that it must be a fabrication by Mosca intended to reinforce his description of the libertine life of Volpone. He will also refer to Volpone's 'incontinence' and claim that "tis the common fable' that 'the Dwarf, the Fool, the Eunuch are all his' (1.5.47). Volpone himself asserts, 'The Turk is not more sensual in his pleasures' than himself (1.5.87). While Volpone may indeed be childless, Mosca's claims help make a general satirical criticism that might be applied to many wealthy men of status. It was common enough for aristocrats to sire illegitimate children. Many were reared in their father's household, others kept at a distance, acknowledged, supported, but kept secret. Others again were simply cast adrift without acknowledgement or finance. It depended on the character of the erring father. Nano and his companions make a suitably disfigured family that reflect the sinful lifestyle of their master: a voluptuary, a devious hustler. It is a debasement of normal humanity that echoes the corruption of Volpone and the decadence of Venice. Father or not, Volpone is an idle libertine and the Devil has made work for his idle hands. In addition to his vanity (he regards it as genius, 1.1.71), he defrauds by means of lies. The extent is revealed when he speaks of 'new clients' who visit him daily 'bring me presents, send me plate, coin, jewels'

> [w]ith hope, that when I die (which they expect
> Each greedy minute) it shall then return,
> Tenfold, upon them. (1.1.76–81)

The rest of the speech exposes Volpone's plans. He reverses the normal *captatio* situation, for this legacy holder strikes back and is consciously, purposefully leading on the greedy legacy hunters in order to squeeze more out of them. The educated part of the audience would recognize this feature of ancient life, but would they see its link to the predatory nature of their own times?

Volpone, a perverted magnifico, with no sense of social responsibility, with no political duties, partially signifies his state by debasing himself by adopting unsuitable costume. In an age when dress marked your rank, to wear other than the clothing appropriate to your rank was to blur distinctions. This was thought subversive. Volpone first adopts robes and furs suitable to a much older man, masquerades as a quack doctor and disguises himself as a *commendatore*, an officer of the court. Mosca signifies his transgressive aspirations by dressing as a *clarissimo* (a grandee), far above his actual rank in the hierarchy and it is his master who gives him his own distinctive costume (5.4.105), thus demeaning himself and encouraging another to be falsely dressed. Volpone, detached from community or civic office, lives entirely for himself. He further demeans his rank by being involved in criminal activity (fraud and intended fornication). All transgressors are given a punishment suitable to their sin. Volpone is ultimately sentenced to lie in prison, manacled until he is sick and lame. The bed where for much of the play he lies to purvey his lies is exchanged for a pallet bed in prison. The cramps and other pretended concomitants of old age and near-death are substituted for real cramps suffered from having his movements restricted by fetters. The fortune this childless, selfish man has scrounged and hoarded is to be given to the hospital for *Incurabili* – those unfortunates he should, according to the expected duties of his rank, have helped. It is doubly just that a man who showed such predatory, adulterous lust should lose his fortune to a hospital (founded in 1522) devoted to the treatment and palliative care of venereal disease. The Jacobean audience would expect punishment for wrongdoing to be very evidently meted out at the end. They would expect legal justice to be done (for the attempted rape), but would also expect moral justice for all sinners. Both are incorporated into the process of comic justice. The disappointments and public humiliation of the legacy hunters and the ultimate downfall of the two tricksters who inaugurated it all, are all part of this process. Our laughter at their cleverness turns to laughter at their being caught. Mosca is to be whipped (probably in public) and then condemned for life as a galley slave. Corvino receives a very public set of punishments: rowed round the canals wearing a cap with ass's ears 'instead of horns'. Then with a paper 'pinned to thy breast' (describing his sin – 'wife panderer') he is to be put in the pillory and have 'stinking fish/Bruised fruit, and rotten eggs' thrown at him (5.13.134–45). A pander is a man who procures women for others, a pimp. He is to be 'embarked from thine own house' before his display to all the canal-side households of the city, suggesting he is rich enough to have bought a house on a canal and with a landing stage. The cap and the paper were common features of public punishment. Paper hats, often long conical-shaped ones, were worn as signs of certain types of crime and might carry some written signification on them of the nature of the misdemeanour. The ass's ears signify his folly both in his greedy ambition and in his risking his and his wife's honour. Voltore is struck off from the list of approved lawyers and banished from the city. Corbaccio is to lose his property ('all thy state') and be held in a monastery. The word 'state' means not just his estate, his money, house and goods, but also suggests the loss of his rank. This is appropriate as he has not behaved like a gentleman. It is appropriate too that because he 'knew'st not to live well here,/Thou shalt be learn'd to die well'. His disregard for spiritual values will now be reversed and incarceration in a religious house will enforce them. It is a condemnation to Purgatory, but one imposed on earth and before death. Perhaps he will soon make a virtuous death.

Noticeably, the three members of the 'better sort' are not subjected to the gaze and mockery of the rest of the citizens. Hierarchy was still active in the ranking of punishment.

While it is satisfying to see all who deserve it getting their comeuppance, it is also meant to act as a warning to the viewers to avoid such behaviour. To amuse and instruct is, after all, the basis of comedy. This relates to the basic belief in a retributive God who saw and knew all and would punish. Between the opening scene and the last we see large-scale greed and deceit. Wrath, lust, deceit, blasphemy, greed, deceit, lust, wrath, gluttony, deceit, deceit and deceit are joined by a number of lesser failings – social pretentiousness, vanity about cultural knowledge (in Lady Pol), bullying and hypocrisy (by Corvino). The whole framework is founded on different sorts of trickery facilitated by the playwright's own plots and tricks. The two central characters are actors playing actors, for Mosca and Volpone are both consummate manipulators of appearance and both are supremely aware of their own ability to play parts.

And it is Jonson's imagination that has dreamed up all their tricks. This is the trickery of the writer's art. Paradoxically for two con men, their language is poetical, full of metaphors and learned allusions. This is at odds with their low intentions, but artificially and temporarily elevates them to the status of the heroic. Their fantasies of wealth and deception fly high.

Their ambitions are far from petty. Both are aware of their corrupted state morally and do not care. They are moral iconoclasts. Volpone is an idle man of rank with decadent desires and adulterous fantasies, and is excessively covetous. The reverse of a dignified patrician, god-fearing, engaged with the state and its people, he is a solitary voluptuary, stealing, cheating and seducing all to excite a jaded palate that needs stimulation. Mosca, from the beginning revealed as a parasite, represents in his name and his place at the bottom of the food chain the fly that sucks the juices of rotting flesh (so a carrion feeder like Voltore and the others), though in his skill he is intellectually and imaginatively top of the pyramid of crooks. But their crookery is an art that they exercise to a high level of proficiency and skill.

Whether gulled or gulling, the characters offer a range of social ranks. Those of the upper degrees are Volpone as a patrician, Corbaccio (an old gentleman) and the Would-bes representing the English gentry. The *avocatori* are part of the governing class as magistrates. This may just about include Voltore as a professional man of law. Corvino the merchant is of the middling sort, though in Venice, as a paramount trading hub, they had particular status.

The household and the crowd in the piazza are the 'base sort'. Mosca too is base born, but is accumulating gifts and tips and making his pile. In a sense too he is, as a consummate actor, artist and crook, an aristocrat of crime or, at least, something special and different.

Time and again Mosca and Volpone step from their own selves talking as master and servant into their assumed roles as dying old man and his servant who poses as confidant and fixer for the legacy seekers, pretending to have the interests of each greedy carrion feeder at heart while drawing them deeper into his and Volpone's greedy clutches. Each gull is engaged at different times in a dance duet with Mosca as he leads them into a more and more intricate commitment of money or goods, convincing them of the imminence of Volpone's death. It is amusing to see how clever the two crooks are, but disturbing too that they are so superior in inventive opportunism and understanding of the way the world works. Their skill in conning people extends from the small circle who visit the magnifico's house to a public arena when Volpone masquerades as a mountebank. Their deviousness penetrates the assumed acuteness of the legal establishment when they initially fool the judiciary at the *Scrutineo* and have Celia and Bonario imprisoned. It looks then as if evil has triumphed. Unnervingly, good only prevails because evil defeats itself. The only two virtuous characters, Celia and Bonario, are strong enough in their own principles, but do not engage vigorously with the evil of which they are the victims. They lack the virtue of fortitude, that is, the strength to engage with evil and combat it. These scenes display the foolishness of the mass of the public and exposes how the law too can be tricked by the lies inherent in the fake respect shown to it and the assumed outrage demonstrated by the prosecutors. The judges are shown as being as vulnerable as the fools in the piazza. Ultimately, the two protagonists defeat themselves. The official law is ineffective and it is the justice of *hubris* that prevails. The overconfidence of Volpone and Mosca brings them down. We may marvel at the skilful deviousness of the pair, but we do not endorse their dishonesty and we applaud the fiction that defeats them while knowing that in real life liars and cheats often get away with their crimes. There will be fascination in the inventiveness of Mosca as he masterminds the plan and reacts resourcefully to each new twist. He is a master improviser. From a distance an audience will admire such cleverness – as long as it is not going to affect their lives. But do we have the moral honesty to condemn him? Like all comedies we are invited to watch human weakness and identify our own on stage, but do we truly condemn wrongdoing or do we rather envy their material gains? Theoretically we may sneer at the shallowness of the money-grubbing legacy hunters, but greedily hope for a legacy ourselves from some distant or close relative. Hypocrisy is never far away in comedy or real life.

The story is incited by the pairing of a devious master and a tricky servant that has origins in the Greek comedies of Aristophanes and that continued in the comic work of the Roman writer Plautus. The knave gulling credulous victims is here extended to a pair, a dynamic duo, but with the twist that the apparently loyal servant, so cleverly improvising and manipulating in the interests of his master, is slowly revealed as serving his own interests and secretly planning to con his master as a final coup. Mosca becomes in a sense the villain of the piece, proving that there is no honour among thieves. He combines the ingenious servant role of classical comedy with that of the Vice of medieval interludes. He takes on the characteristics of allegorical figures like Hypocrisy and Dissimulation, though initially emerging as a comic but criminal instrument of the punishment of greedy men. The Vice was thought of as a persona of the Devil and Mosca is the demon of the play. The principal character pretends to be old and dying, with his gummy eyes and failing voice, but is actually cheating the *captators* into giving him expensive presents in order to keep in his good books and (more importantly) keep in his will as chief or even sole legatee. The legacy hunters pretend concern for him while only being interested in getting hold of his money and property. Mosca is not only tricking each inheritance hunter into thinking he is dedicated to furthering their cause, while in reality aiding his master's plan, but he is also tricking his master. This cuts at one of the key roots of society – loyalty of a servant. It is a morally corrupt world. Volpone's household is distorted and depraved. He has no family, no wife, no maid servants. It is unnatural in that there is no female input into the running or the atmosphere of the palazzo, and that the male inhabitants are all deformed in some way. Mosca, apparently the devoted servant, will ultimately betray his master. The rest of the meiny are a hermaphrodite, a dwarf and a eunuch. Two are sexually different from normality and the dwarf physically so. But they are the sort of freaks, 'monsters', curiosities that noblemen kept to entertain them. They might perform domestic service, but would be called on when the master was bored or commanded to amuse guests between the courses of a meal. Castrone, the eunuch, might sing. The castrato voice was much prized and in fashion. Nano, the dwarf, is named as Volpone's zany or jester. The zany was an Italian *commedia* character, a buffoon in old comedies who attempts feebly to mimic the tricks of the clown. His person, costume and behaviour were outrageous and extravagant, like that of a slapstick clown, but he could also be astutely devious. If Nano is the foolish servant, Mosca is the clever one. This coupling of sharp- and slow-witted servants, cunning and silly, appears in the Zannis of commedia dell'arte They are a double act. *Lo stupido* (the daft one) is clumsy and provides low, physical humour. The clever tricky one, *il furbo* (the clever one), acts as a fixer and go-between and, like Mosca, is resourceful enough to have the wit to cheat and mislead anyone. The name Zanni is a Venetian variant of Gianni or Giovanni (John), a common name among the *contadini* or country folk of the Veneto, the mainland, from where Venetian aristocrats recruited their servants. The whole drama becomes a series of linked *commedia* scenarios.

The *commedia* element resurfaces verbally (2.3.) when Corvino accuses Celia of having flirted with Scoto. He angrily beats away the mountebank, calling him Signior Flaminio, asking if he thinks Celia is 'your Franciscina' and fearing he will be nicknamed Pantalone de Besogniosi. These references alludes to Flaminio Scala, a highly reputed writer of *commedia* sketches and a leading actor (under the stage name Flavio). His company was associated with Venice and he cemented his European fame when he published a collection of comic tales in 1611. These *favole* (yarns, tales) furnish us with the most comprehensive range of situations that the *commedia* actors used for their scenes and improvisations. Scala is generally reckoned to have influenced the work of William Shakespeare, Lope de Vega and Molière as well as Jonson. Franciscina is a stock character in *commedia* playing the part of the frisky, sexually forward maid, and Pantalone (a stock Venetian figure) is the old man who is often cuckolded.

The double irony is that Corvino accuses Celia of intending to betray him with Scoto (which she is not), yet will shortly encourage her to lie with Volpone. Several *commedia* scenarios have a suitor serenading a wife at her window and fleeing when the husband returns. Another farce (*Flavio's Fortunes*) has Flavio, a young lover, disguised as a mountebank, serenading his lady, and another (*Pantalone Spezier*) disguised as a quack doctor (precisely Scoto's 'profession'). Pantalone, the foolish old miser figure, did, in some *scenarii*, become diverted from avarice to lust and then be fooled by the lady he coveted. This conforms to Volpone's downfall being precipitated by his relinquishing of the greedy deception hustle, lured out of his fox's den into playing the part of the disguised lover. The attempted rape is what brings him into conflict with the law. A further well-known figure is the Bolognese doctor, Gratiano (or Graziano), dressed in black hat, black mask and black cloak or robes. His sales patter was in the form of rambling, dull, pedantic discourses detailing at length the medicinal properties of his wares. Scoto does this. The style of Gratiano is to cram his speech (as Scoto does) with Latin names for medicines and processes, Latin proverbs, details of illnesses, lots of doctor's jargon, lists of satisfied celebrity customers and remarkable cures effected. Gratiano also used helpers to advertise his wares and gather a crowd. These *zanies*, like Nano and Co., entertain the assembled dupes and assist their master in projecting his persona and his medicines. The Scoto role is a demanding piece of tour de force acting with long speeches full of technically difficult words and phrases. It is also a triumphant piece of writing in its intricate interweaving of so many topical elements and its mastery of the medical terms. The success of passing himself off so effectively as a

renowned quack so excites Volpone that he is lured into overreaching himself
and determines to possess the beautiful Celia. From delight at her appearance
he longs to own her, the eyes triggering his lust to acquire. Though Corvino
enacts the Pantalone role and will later be reviled and exposed for pimping his
own wife, Volpone too, unwittingly, plays the old dotard fooled – but fooled
by his assistant, Mosca.

The biter is bit. Volpone betrays himself, by adding sex-greed to money-
greed, thus compounding his already great sin. Volpone has some of the
characteristics of the Pantatone character. His *commedia* counterpart was
traditionally named as a magnifico, in a nobleman's red costume with black
cloak. His half mask had a long nose (like a fox's snout) and a moustache. If
masks were not worn the foxlike look could be echoed by make-up and beard
and moustache. Pantalone was often portrayed as an old miser who is lured
into lust, thus following the evolution of Volpone. Another way of presenting
him was to make him middle-aged, but sexually predatory and energetic.
Pantalone plays the lute badly and sings badly too. The ever shape-changing
Volpone incorporates both aspects. It is hardly fitting that he should sing the
'Come My Celia' song as a beautiful, lilting piece of Jacobean madrigal. The
spirit of comedy demands a tension between the words and the performance.
The lyric's carpe diem subject is wistfully beautiful. Surely his rendering of it
should be coarse and cracked? The acrostic argument does not describe him
as old. His masquerade as terminally ill is heightened if a relatively robust man
changes before our eyes into one at the limits of life. Even if the song is well
sung there is still a contrast between his lewd and sensual offers to Celia and
the horrified reaction she makes: 'Some *serene* [poisonous mist] blast me, or
dire lightning strike' (3.7.184–5).

The I Gelosi troupe, formed in Milan in 1569 by Flamineo Scala, toured
Europe and helped spread the *commedia* form to England. In 1611, 50 scenarios
and roles were published by him in Italian. This is too late for Jonson to have
pillaged for his play, which suggests strongly that a troupe visited England at
some time during the period, triggering the copying of subject and style by the
various types of playing companies.[9] There are records of sixteenth-century
tours, but no evidence for performances in the 1600s. However, so many
elements appear in English plays and then in court masques that some direct
viewing of an Italian company performing must have taken place or returning
tourists recounted pieces they had seen, particularly in Venice. When
Volpone was written Jonson had already started composing masques and they
developed with fantastical costumes and masks.[10] The *commedia* characters

9 The view of E. K. Chambers, *William Shakespeare*, 1.494.
10 See the illustrations in *A Book of Masques*.

wore the half masks that are specifically associated with the mayhem of the traditional Venice carnival. This pre-Lent period of misrule, with its many different types of masks, fits the mood of a play where so much of the truth is hidden, where so many characters hide their true self and play parts different from their genuine feelings. The pace and intricacy of the plotting create a feel of carnival mayhem and unreality. Some recent productions have used masks to reinforce visually the deceptions on which the play is based and the mask image symbolizes how the characters hide their true selves and intentions. It has been customary to design masks that represent the animal the character resembles. This seems rather simplistic, even childish. The form of the play is that of a moral fable with characters behaving like animals, but it is more subtle and complex than a fairy story for children. The masks may add to the exotic and grotesque nature of what the play is dealing with, the distortion of humans into animals as representing the workings of sin, but the words they speak are more important for they show how the central figures verbally mask themselves from others. So much of human intercourse relies on the belief that people tell the truth in the common language exchanges of every day. Once the lies begin the whole edifice of society is endangered. Volpone and the others lie so persistently and intricately that masks would be superfluous. The masking is in the words people misuse. Contemporary audiences were used to following intricate arguments in verse and would not need the masks to help. Indeed, though Corvino references some *commedia* figure there is no evidence that the actors wore masks at all. The animal resemblances are clearly pointed up in the dialogue. That said, the use of masks in court masques was becoming quite a fashion, so it is not impossible they were used.

In his criminal deception Volpone betrays his rank and therefore the state. He does this by becoming involved in a criminal scam, a fraud, which is visually enforced by his changes of appearance. He does it by play-acting, not being open, honest and frank as a man of high degree should be, but by pretence and fiction. He and Mosca are both excellent actors. Volpone tells Celia he had been an actor in a comedy 'for entertainment of the great Valois'. He played the part of Antinous and 'attracted/The eyes, and ears of all the ladies present' (3.8.160–3).[11] The contextual resonance here reflects the increasing tendency of English courtiers to take part in masques and plays at court. This was a status subversion in itself. James I's wife, Queen

---

11 Henry of Valois visited Venice in 1574. Antinous was the young boy lover of the Emperor Hadrian. To the Jacobeans this would be an illicit (because homosexual) relationship. This fits with the corruption and unnatural aspects of a decadent Venetian society. It implies fears that English society was similar.

Anne, many of her titled gentlewomen, some titled gentlemen and the Prince of Wales all participated. Some regarded it as demeaning of their rank and questionable on sexual grounds. The audience sees not only the actor dressed up as the magnifico (the magnificent one, the great one), playing his part, but also a further transformation takes place as he puts on an old man's bed cap and furs and Mosca applies ointment to his eyes to make them look rheumy. In adopting the appearance and sounds of decrepitude (he pretends to be very deaf, speaks low, coughs and wheezes consumptively, feigns palsy, apoplexy, catarrh), he emphasizes the trick being played. Doing so onstage adds another dimension to the illusion that is theatre. Backstage in the tiring room, the actor has already prepared himself as Volpone. Now, before our eyes, he adopts a new persona – Volpone geriatric and terminally ill. We witness the magic of him assuming a new part, becoming a new person. The whole play is based on a series of tricks and, of course, drama itself is a trick. But through the illusion of fiction come a host of unsettling truths about human nature. *Commedia* sketches were short pieces, but by using many of the elements of the form and patching in many of the stock character types and extending them over the length of a full five-act play, Jonson concentrates and extends the depth of misrule and misconduct to fill a whole world with sins.

Yet another metamorphosis of costume and character takes place when the lust-driven Volpone disguises himself as Scoto of Mantua. Jonson turns the renowned Italian juggler into another sort of manipulator as the actor playing Volpone presents a theatrical tour de force in a series of long, complex speeches as a mountebank. He interlards his speeches with Latin and Italian mixed with copious medical terms and scholarly language. This impresses the crowd and the gullible Sir Politic and yet is all froth. It displays Volpone's improvisatory imagination more fully than previously, when much of the extempore trickery was created by Mosca. And it is all irrelevant for it is only a front to give him a chance to glimpse Celia.

Once again the words are misleading and the accomplished rhetorical flourishes mean nothing. They are a means of achieving something completely other than the tenor of their meaning. Volpone is the hero in the sense that he is the central character and we get to know and infer more about him than any other person in the play. Though he has resilience and perseverance, he is not heroic. Some critics see him as a Marlovian character, defying the world's theoretical values on a grand scale and seeking to be something wonderful, but he lacks decency, sympathy, charity and there is something mean and demeaning in his goals. He is twinned with his parasite and though we may admire their devious skills we cannot ever applaud their conduct. His character is coarsened and degraded as the play progresses and this process is accompanied by a lessening of admiration for his sheer effrontery. Possessed by greed and the excitement of cheating others, he is also taken over by lust. The trajectory of his story portrays the power of sin to debase and diminish a person and he becomes an emblem of the discrepancy between what a human should be and what they are. Even then he is surrounded by others who are largely as bad as he is or even worse. Can we sympathize with Volpone? Do we have any positive feelings for him? Are we meant to? In this sort of black comedy condemnation is perhaps more likely. We can both laugh at his clever successes and cheer his fall.

13.2 Mosca

There are two categories of flatterer: the domesticated ones are those who gather round someone's bath and table; but the flatterers who stretches his interference, slander and malevolence, like so many tentacles, into someone's inner chambers and into the women's quarters is wild and savage and hard to tame.

(Plutarch, 'How to Distinguish a Flatterer from a Friend', 86)

Musca domestica is the common house fly buzzing round constantly seeking food. Mosca too, whose name puns on the Latin for fly, is as busy playing his main part in the licking up of tips from the *capatators* and reminding them how much he does on their behalf. Like all parasites his aim is to eat, suck and drain dry. The host is unimportant. Anyone will do as long as they render profit. His name was commonly used in Roman comedies for parasite figures. It also occurs in medieval writing in association with diabolic familiars. Mosca is both sorts of parasite defined by Plutarch. He lives in and off Volpone's household and uses the visiting 'birds of prey' to gains tips and wheedles his way into their trust in his working solely for them. The parasite is by nature and by method a flatterer. In being a flatterer he is bearing false witness and defrauding those he plays up to. At the very least he cheats them of their ill-founded faith in him, he makes some material gains too and hopes for more substantial rewards. While much of the overt plot involves Mosca flattering the legacy hunters, he is also misleading his master by praise and ready service that ultimately is revealed as part of a cunning plan to outflank and outmanoeuvre Volpone. Plutarch describes the flatterer as 'one who inveigles others and leads them into the trap, by playing a variety of parts: he dances and sings with one person, but wrestles and rolls in the dust with another'.[12] Mosca constantly changes how he plays his prey. In this he displays

12 *Essays*, 68.

what Plutarch calls 'the octopus-like transformations of the flatterer'.[13] Mosca is a consummate improviser and shape-changer, being whatever each victim requires to flatter his ambitions – and fool him further. Plutarch also likens the flatterer to a chameleon that 'can assimilate itself to every colour except white'.[14] White symbolizes virtue, with its associated connotations of honesty and openness. Virtue is not one of Mosca's qualities. Flattery was much discussed and condemned in medieval and Renaissance moralistic writing. Most states were single-rule entities with a court surrounding the governor, and rulers were persistently vulnerable to the blandishments of sycophants. The danger of it is encapsulated in Shakespeare's comment in his 1607–8 play *Pericles*: 'They do abuse the king that flatter him:/ For flattery is the bellows blows up sin' (1.2.38–9).

Jonson has an ingenious servant, Musco, in *Every Man in His Humour* (in its Italianate form), but he is a loyal and honest character. Without doubt Mosca, *il furbo*, is, with Volpone, a key figure in driving the plot. In many respects, as the go-between receiving the scavengers and ushering them into his master's presence, inciting action, setting up the tone and mood of the meetings, improvising new approaches by confiding in the predators, he is the leading character. For much of the first part of the play Volpone is relatively passive, playing the bed-ridden apparently dying object of the legacy hunters' flattery. He has little to do other than lie groaning wheezily and pretending he is close to death. It is Mosca who dissembles, cajoles and lies to draw the gulls further into the net of deception. All of his actions involve forms of false witness, greed and betrayal. He and his master would be condemned to Dante's Nether Hell as fraudsters and sowers of discord. Mosca in particular would be damned for betrayal of a master, for the bond between servant and master was an essential social agent, a cement that maintained society's coherence. The parasite or toady sycophant was a common figure in classical drama and satire. He was given new life in the Tudor and Jacobean drama, often associated with courtiers and hangers-on at the court, flattering and scrounging, feeding off the rich and powerful, foraging for paid places at court or government office, and literally looking for invitations to dine with the rich and powerful. A seat at the table not only filled hungry bellies but also could result in contacts that led to advancement and patronage. It was a world where contacts were vital. Patronage could pay rich dividends.[15] Here the parasite has found his host body and is feeding off him by feeding his esteem and furthering his game of attracting wealth. Mosca is a parasite with

13 *Essays*, 69.
14 *Essays*, 70.
15 See discussion of Sir Thomas Sutton (ch 10, section entitled 'Contemporary carrion').

a difference; he is a triple amalgam of stock types. He is the witty, scheming servant of Roman comedy and *il furbo* of *commedia*, often helping to further his master's amatory plans (even changing places with him), combined with the legacy hunter and con-man parasite of Roman satire and, because he also insidiously plots against his master, he echoes some features of the Vice figure in Tudor drama. This latter was clever and devious, but did not have not good intentions like the witty servant. Often the Vice was definitively associated with the Devil. Much as Mosca may amuse by his cleverness and be admired for never being caught out, always able to provide a convincing answer to all new developments, some in an audience of the time might reserve judgement on him, but many might condemn him from the outset as untrustworthy. He fails Baldassare Castiglione's requirement that courtiers (or servants) should act to the 'profit and honour' of their master but not 'bring him loss and shame'.[16] We may be astonished at his stage-managerial skills in organizing his master, but are rendered breathless at his nerve in playing the 'harpies' on his own account.[17] He reminds Voltore to remember his assistance when he inherits Volpone's wealth. He accuses Voltore to Corbaccio of visiting only because 'he smelt a carcass' (1.4.61), then lures the so-called gentleman into considering disinheriting his son, Bonario, and making Volpone his heir as a sign of his devotion to the magnifico.

This prompts the gruesomely unnatural admission from the old raven that 'this plot/Did I think on before' (1.4.109–10). Mosca rightly calls this 'diverted love'. He might have called it perverted. All sorts of bonds are distorted in the play. Dante condemned flatterers to the eighth circle of Hell and for all his busy, buzzing cleverness Mosca is ultimately to be damned. He is guilty of *hubris*, overreaching himself ('I feare, I shall begin to grow in love/With my deare self'), becomes overgreedy in his determination to force Volpone to 'share at least' or he will 'cozen him of all' (5.5.15–16). Not knowing when to stop, being overconfident in his own abilities, ruins Mosca, as it does Volpone. In his 1610–11 comedy, *Epicoene*, Jonson picks up a similar theme where the villainous protagonist is eventually caught in a trap of his own making. Truewit asserts that it 'falls out often […] that he that thinks himself the master-wit is the master fool' (3.6.46–7). There was a proverb in the sixteenth century: 'When thieves fall out, honest men come by their own'. Jonson proves the old proverb – set a thief to catch a thief. But he elaborates it by making a

---

16 *The Book of the Courtier*, 131.
17 Harpies were monster hybrids in Greek mythology, with heads and breasts like women, but wings and claws like birds. They contaminated everything they touched and wanted to steal everything. As slang for a sponger the word is appropriate for the legacy scavengers and there were three of them in the play.

thief instrumental in catching his partner and catching himself while he is at it. There is no honour among thieves.

Jonson presents a cast whose characters are all fools in some way or other. They think they are in command of events and are fashioning their own destiny, but ultimately they all are proved to have been blinded by pride or greed or lust. The view of man as capable of being easily gulled and often self-gulled is locked integrally into Christian thinking. The medieval trope of 'The Dance of Death' shows pleasure seekers dancing blindly toward their own end, heedless of all they have been told about how wealth, fashion, pleasure and power are all mirages, all trumpery stuff that will not stop you dying however rich and successful you might be. You cannot take your gold to Heaven for 'it is easier for a camel to go through the ye of needle, than for a rich man to enter the kingdom of God' (Matthew 19:24). Sebastian Brant's trope of Folly, an emblem of life, is of a ship full of fools oblivious that they are drifting helpless and without a captain. Sebastian Brant's *Narrenschiff* (Ship of fools), published 1494, was a criticism of the church, comprising a prologue, 118 satires (on different aspects of Folly and church corruption) and an epilogue. It became very popular, was much printed and formed a template for other satires. The central emblem is life as a voyage on a ship that is rudderless, captainless, directionless. It is full of fools. This is an emblem of a life lived without the structure that faith and morality give. Hieronymus Bosch's painting *The Ship of Fools* (c. 1490–1500) has a motley group, drinking copiously. A monk and nun with a lute sit mouths agape leaning forward to bite at a cake suspended on a string from the mast. Two men also seem about to take a bite. A man climbs the mast to cut down a chicken carcass tied above him. Two figures swim alongside and others are placed about the boat. The vessel seems to be drifting toward the open sea, but no one aboard is concerned. Like *Der Totentanz* (The Dance of Death), a popular subject for paintings and woodcuts in the fifteenth century, the allegory, though complex and impenetrable or ambiguous in detail, is in general a comment on how most lives are lived without sufficient moral direction. Pleasure and other worldly pursuits distract people from the path of virtue. The most relevant form of this common emblem to Jonson was Erasmus's *Praise of Folly* (1511), for it addresses the stupidity of those who become obsessed with greedy acquisition and forget the demands of faith, moderation and humility. That Jonson knew something of Erasmus is evidenced by how the dedicatory epistle to *Volpone* echoes substantial sections of the *Epistola Apologetica*, which Erasmus wrote to Sir Thomas More.[18] In *Praise of Folly*, Erasmus gives multiple examples of

---

18 Harry Levin, 'Jonson's Metempsychosis', *Philological Quarterly* 22 (1943): 231–9. Reproduced in Barish's *Casebook*.

man's foolishness, how he is so often and easily cheated and how deceivers are themselves deceived. At a basic theological level, the deceiver, thief, trickster is self-deceiving, stealing from himself, tricking himself in the sense his sins will lead to damnation and he will have cheated himself of Heaven. Erasmus makes Folly the daughter of Plutus, god of Riches. This immediately suggests a potent satirical/critical link being made between the pretentious and hubristic self-esteem of the rich man oblivious of how his soul is endangered. Folly's attendants are self-love, flattery, forgetfulness, idleness, pleasure, madness, sensuality, revelry and sound sleep. The oddity of the last attendant is dispelled if we imagine that sound sleep is the forgetfulness that follows idle pleasure, sensual sexual indulgence and drunken revelry, oblivious of the precariousness of one's soul. Here we see immediately the moral weaknesses of Volpone. He is full of self-love, is flattered by Mosca and the *captators*, forgets to follow virtue, is idle as regards social responsibility (though active enough about his criminal intents), madly seeks his own perverted pleasures and is sensual and decadent (as witness the lifestyle he offers Celia). Jonson presents us with a 'Palace of Fools'. The rich leaders of Venetian society lived in fine *palazzi* (palaces). The inciting action is mostly located in Volpone's home where each inhabitant and visitor obliviously prances and plots his way into sin and dances his way to death and damnation. This is a location adrift from moral restraints, a closed world, a dystopia that looks disturbingly more like the real world than the utopias of Christian theologians and dreamers. This is Niccolò Machiavelli's view of reality.

An Erasmian source for the false blandishments of the would-be legatees is the assertion 'in the halls of princes [...] my "Flattery" holds first place'.[19] The overall atmosphere of the play is summed up in Erasmus's claim 'nothing happens in this world which isn't full of folly, performed by fools amongst fools' and 'the whole of human life is nothing but a sport of folly'.[20] The resourceful lies Mosca tells the foolish carrion birds are subsumed in Erasmus's comment 'man's mind is so formed that it is far more susceptible to falsehood than to truth'.[21] Mosca himself proclaims his world view in the first line of his song: 'Fooles they are the only nation' (1.2.67). He foolishly forgets to include himself among the list of types of fools.

The final lesson of the play involves the pleasure we feel at seeing two cheats cheat each other and be caught and punished. It is a case of the biters bit. In the seventeenth century a biter was slang for a trickster. Just as Erasmus provides examples of deceivers eventually deceived so too does Jonson. His

19 *Praise of Folly*, 85.
20 *Praise of Folly*, 99, 102.
21 *Praise of Folly*, 135.

contact with the chaplain to the Venetian ambassador may (as Harry Levin suggests) have encouraged him to use Venice as the setting for a series of intricate plots and greedy deceptions focused on gain, but he did not have to look so far afield for parallels for similar seething and decadent conduct.

13.3 The Three Unwise Men

In a play full of deceptions and profane reversals, the three main scavengers are an irreverent parody of the Magi bearing gifts to the Christ child in a manger. They bring their gold plate, gold coins and a pearl as bribes to an old cheat in his bed.

Voltore

It is entirely fitting that the character called a vulture should be a lawyer. The profession was much hated and figured commonly in satires on greed and dishonesty and in petitions against corruption in public life. Like vultures they were thought of as waiting for people to die so that they could help pick over the property, aid greedy relatives and charge exorbitantly for their legal help. Jonson delivers three satirical speeches criticizing merchants (1.1.32–40, from Volpone), lawyers (1.3.52–60, from Mosca) and doctors (1.4.20–5, from Mosca).

The first two set up audience expectation of Corvino and Voltore. The third correlates to Corbaccio, who, though much older than Volpone, believes he will live much longer and knows a great deal about medicines and doctors. Another speech about the miseries of old age (1.4.144–59, from Volpone) helps complete the contextualizing of the three dupes and the depth and type of their gullibility. Voltore it is who leads the defence of Volpone in court, misusing language to mislead the judges, defaming the only decent characters in the whole corrupt piece. He is suitably punished by being banned from following his profession.

Corbaccio

Called 'an old Gentleman' in the cast list, he displays none of the virtuous qualities expected of his rank. He is inhumanly pleased to hear how ill Volpone is, and is more than ready to disinherit his son in favour of Volpone as a mark of his devotion (to money) and as an inducement to the magnifico to name him sole heir. This shows how low a man will stoop in greedy depravity. Corbaccio does emphasize that the disinheritance will only be for 'colour' (to create the semblance), but it still indicates his willingness to be deceptive. There is none of the open, frank honesty expected of a gentleman. Four figures of status – a magnifico, a gentleman, a lawyer, a merchant – are presented in the play, yet not one of them conducts himself well. They are a microcosm of the decayed state of society in which people thought they were living in the 1600s.

The raven brings 'this great *elixir*' – a bag full of Venetian gold coins. These 'chequeens' are the slightly debased form of the Venetian ducat that had been the standard gold coin of European trade since 1284. From 1567 they were called *ducati de zecca* (ducats from the mint). They were known familiarly as *zecchine* (Englished as chequeens and corrupted into sequins) and were still a highly valued and trusted gold coin. Here they focus the money obsession of the play and the gold fever that struck Europe. They had been devalued or destabilized as a European standard by the power struggle between England and Spain that had raised the value of gold. The conflict was initially religious – Spain being Catholic, England regarded as heretic Protestant – but had shifted into a trade war in the West Indies and Americas that had political undertones related to colonial rivalry. The regular attacking of the Spanish treasure fleet and the theft by English pirates of the gold, silver and gems mined in South America were both cause and effect of the gold madness that swept through Europe.

Gold became the absolute signifier of status. Voltore brings a massy gold plate, Corbaccio his bag of coins. Corvino, the merchant, perhaps less wealthy, brings a pearl. These too were highly valued, were part of the treasures of both the East and the West being looted by Spain, England, Portugal, Italy and Holland at this time. They add to the contemporaneity of the personal looting going on among the humans, preying on their own countrymen.

Corvino

The 'spruce merchant' is no better than the other two main legacy hunters. The word 'spruce' suggests he is smartly dressed and that hints at a vanity about his clothes and appearance.

One of the fables, 'The Bird in Borrowed Feathers', tells of a crow that adorned itself with peacock feathers to appear more flashy and attractive (the peacock was a common emblem for pride in fine display). If Corvino is a merchant and smartly dressed he must be sufficiently comfortably off already, so to seek a grandee's fortune is sheer greediness. Giving him a name that associates him to the *Corvid* family sets off resonances of the various crow fables. If 'spruce' suggests he seeks to decorate his simple, respectable black costume with vain finery, the tale of the crow in peacock feathers is immediately activated in a viewer's mind along with the various moral lessons drawn from it. There is the warning not to put on a false appearance but to present yourself honestly as yourself. There is the reference to hierarchy and not reaching higher than your natural station in life. Though the Sumptuary Laws had been recently abolished, many would still consider Corvino as an upstart merchant dressing above his rank.[22] Yet his pose of superiority is belied his demeaning greediness, his bullying of his wife and his readiness to debase her. He brings a pearl and 'a diamant', which he meanly offers to take home again when he learns Volpone is so close to death. He is lured into abusing Volpone, thinking him deaf, and thus exposes his true hypocritical self, pretending respect but ready to show disrespect when he finds it is possible. It is a test of sincerity and honesty and is pushed to the extreme when Mosca pretends to start smothering his master. Corvino first tries to dissuade him, but then asserts, 'Do as you will, but I'll be gone', adding, 'use no violence' (1.5.70). He is willing to consent to murder, but declines to be an accomplice by his presence, though agreeing to it by leaving Mosca to accomplish the deed. To contemplate and mentally agree to a sin was regarded as being as bad as actually committing it.

The further sinfulness of Corvino emerges later in his readiness to pimp his wife for the sake of clinching the inheritance. His hypocritical inconsistency consists in his initial extreme patriarchy, abusing and threatening his wife for showing herself at the window and then his pandering her. He represents a stereotype of the mercantile mentality whereby money overrules all other considerations and ethics are overshadowed by economics. That appetite for gain is displayed among the other characters too. Corvino's treatment of his wife is open to serious criticism. It is exceptionally bullying, physically threatening, but worse, is breaking the sacrament of marriage. There seems to be no affection between them. It appears to be a typically arranged marriage: he is the traditional domineering husband and she the submissive wife. It is just the sort of situation where an unhappy woman would be easy prey for a wealthy man to seduce and make her his mistress. There would be such men as Corvino in the audience and such wives too as were ready to seek pleasure other than in the marriage bed.

There might even be a few chaste creatures like Celia.

13.4 Sir Politic and Lady Would-Be

Critics have seen the Would-bes as detached from the plot, an unnecessary excrescence. In performance today they seem often to be an interruption to

---

22 Robert Greene had scorned Shakespeare as 'an upstart crow, beautified with our feathers' in an attempt to denigrate the non-university background of one who had penetrated the theatrical world (*A Groatsworth of Wit Bought with a Million of Repentance*, 1592).

the impulse of the main plot and their humour rather awkwardly dull and contrived. To an audience in Jonson's time, however, their affectations would have been more readily identifiable. They are travel snobs, all too ready to pass on in a superior manner the experience they have of anywhere they have been. In the early seventeenth century only a relatively small, select group had been to Italy. The numbers of travellers was growing, but most of the audience would know little of Venice other than by rumour. What they would nevertheless have spotted is the triviality of the Would-bes' reactions to foreign parts and in many case their inaccuracy. Such people are to be met with everywhere and anywhere; they affect all sorts of airs and graces and specialized knowledge in order to elevate the public perception of themselves and to suggest they have more social or political power than they in fact have. Sir Pol is like Gratiano in *The Merchant of Venice*. Even his friend Bassanio admits,

> Gratiano speaks an infinite deal of nothing (more than any man in all Venice), his reasons are as two grains of wheat hid in two bushels of chaff: you shall seek all day ere you find them, and when you have them, they are not worth the search. (1.1.114–18)

Onstage Sir Pol would have been amusing as a caricature of the man of rank who speaks as if he spouted wisdom like an oracle, but is simply a self-deceived, pompous fool. Any gentleman figure speaking nonsense would be roundly mocked by the groundlings. His plots and projects are so petty yet spoken of as if they were high matters of state or finance. He would also have amused the middling and better sort, many of whom would have met such men on 'Change, where speculators trying to launch joint stock companies for the Virginias or the Indies were voluble and equally inaccurate in hyping up their claims.[23]

On the page, the Would-bes can be seen to be more integrated with the broad satire of the piece. They act as a parallel to the main plot and are linked to it physically and thematically. Lady Pol (the second of only two main female characters) actually enters the Volpone plot strand. She arrives unexpectedly when Volpone is waiting for Celia and acts as a rather inept courtesan trying awkwardly to be seductive and tempting in contrast to the chaste wife of the impure Corvino. She also plays an important role in the trial, falsely denigrating the character of Celia. She and her husband link

---

23 The Royal Exchange was founded in 1571 by Sir Thomas Gresham. It was the location for legitimate money-changing activities as well as the meeting place for the growing number of projectors (speculator-entrepreneurs) both genuine and shady.

England to Venice, portraying typical tourists, full of airs, pretending to great cosmopolitan knowledge, but largely merely exposing their crass ignorance. In a play full of misperceptions and misunderstandings, they fail to judge anything correctly. They self-deceive as much as the main characters and are prime examples of human folly – chattering, chattering and saying nothing. They are full of informational titbits which they have pecked up here, there and everywhere and utter at the least opportunity. They are both incessant talkers. Their marriage seems based on domestic convenience rather than real affection and both display an almost unstoppable pathological tendency to talk, talk, talk.

Anne Barton sees the Would-bes as 'harmless seed-eaters, no match for the free-ranging, carnivorous Peregrine'.[24] In this respect they are part of the bird-beast fable structure (endless clucking and squawking, pecking up tiny scraps of information) and part of the satirical element (the foolish traveller posing as suave cosmopolitan). The hypocrisies and affectations of both are humiliated in the denouement. Thus the subplot is a mirror of aspects of the main plot. Jonas A. Barish sees Venice as 'a looking glass for England' and Peregrine's trick on Sir Pol and the rejection of Lady Pol by Volpone, Mosca and Peregrine as moral correctives in keeping with the outcome of the other plot strands.[25] They are humiliated, though less publicly. Sir Pol squeezing into the tortoise/turtle shell and crawling across the floor, is both ludicrously funny and cruel, but deserved. It is also emblematic for the tortoise/turtle (thought to be tongueless) symbolized the rational quality of silence, not speaking unless you had something sensible and useful to say. Carrying its 'house' on its back it came to represent the ideal woman, reticent and keeping to her house, so becomes an ironic comment on these chattering wanderers.[26] Sir Pol inside the turtle shell becomes one of the monstrous prodigies he twittered about so readily. If the exposure of Volpone is the mortification of a fox, this is the plucking of a parrot and the silencing of his squawk.

Lady Pol visiting Volpone exhibits petty vanity about her ruff and her curls before demeaning herself and her soul further by making a clumsy sexual play for the Fox. Vanity about her looks and clothes, a readiness for promiscuity, a link between her and accessing a man's cash are indictments of the female character that go back centuries. In a Christian context the Would-bes betoken a concern for the fleshly and a neglect of the spirit. The morally misshapen,

---

24 From Anne Barton's *Ben Jonson: Dramatist*, 183–93 (included in *Ben Jonson's Plays and Masques*, 421).

25 'The Double Plot in *Volpone*', *Modern Philology* 51 (1953): 401.

26 See Ian Donaldson, 'Jonson's Tortoise', *Review of English Studies*, New Series, 19 (1968): 162–66.

the emotionally unnatural, are so pervasive in the foreground narrative that they become the normal world of Venice. Bonario and Celia alone represent what humans should be. They alone do not play parts, do not affect to be what they are not, do not metamorphose. The rest of the cast is scarcely human. They are, as Jonas Barish asserts, 'monsters of folly and monsters of vice [...] misshapen marvels'.[27] In a lesser way the Would-bes parallel this.

27 *Ben Jonson's Plays and Masques*, 410.

Chapter 14

THE VENETIAN CONTEXT:
CONSUMERISM AND CANNIBALISM

For all the law is fulfilled in one word, even in this, Thou shalt love thy
neighbour as thyself.
But if ye bite and devour one another, take heed that ye be not consumed one of another.

(Galatians, 5:14–15)

14.1 The Setting

Commerce, trade, traffic and exchange were as old as society, as old as farmers
bartering foodstuffs, as old as Phoenician galleys carrying goods to Sicily, as
old as the great annual fairs of medieval Europe, as old as the weekly market
in the nearest town. But things had changed in degree. The trade routes had
extended to the outer edges of the Continent, then across into Africa, into
Asia and then made the great leap into the Americas. Commerce had a global
dimension, the sums of money involved had become inconceivably huge and
growth and profit had become the new golden idols. Huge ventured sums were
also lost, and the greater the volume of trade the more the opportunities for
theft and fraud expanded. While foreign populations were exploited as trade
spread hand in hand with imperialism, so home populations too were exploited
by men who became obsessed with the accumulation of wealth. Within the
Court such greed flourished as parasites scrambled for places, pensions and
monopolies. In the City something of what we now see in our own 'Grab,
grab, grab' acquisitive society was already developing. And victims were being
created – the poorly paid workers who produced the luxuries the privileged
and wealthy lusted after and the fools who got into debt by living on credit.
The 1574 *Sumptuary Law* talked of how young men, addicted to keeping in
fashion, 'consume themselves, their goods, and lands which their parents left

unto them, but also run into such debts and shifts as they cannot live out of danger of laws'. Like so many of the better sort they fell into the hands of moneylenders. Big money was being made by a few and the rest all wanted a bit of it. Everyone seemed to be preying on everyone else in a delirious cycle of metaphorical cannibalism. Ben Jonson was sensitive to this, and it informs the narratives and moods of *Volpone*, *The Alchemist* and *Bartholomew Fair*. The structure of each play is very different, but the themes are matching – the greed, deceit and vileness of man.

How suitable it is that Jonson set this play in Italy and in Venice in particular. Italy was a magical, fascinating, yet dangerous place in the minds of the English. It was a different culture. Still resonant with the associations of the grandeur and gruesomeness of ancient Rome, it also had the fascinating yet frightening taint of being the source of Catholic power and the home of the Antichrist. It was the source too of the most wonderful art. Its paintings and sculptures were much admired. Its writers, thinkers and musicians too stood high in the cultural ranking of Europe. But the English mind always came back to the haunting recollection that it was the headquarters of the most hated religion with its Inquisition, its burning of so-called heretics. The word that crops up most regularly in Englishmen's writings about Italians is 'deceitful'. They are seen as cunning, devious, bloodthirsty and altogether untrustworthy, as likely to laugh with you, put one arm round you on one side and stick a stiletto between your ribs on the other. Plots, intrigues, poisoning and other exotic and ingenious ways of murder were also what the English associated with Italians. It was a nation with a corrupt church, with a venial clergy and which was teeming with ruthless political power seekers. The history of the city states in the Renaissance bore this out manifestly.

Venice was a state with numerous resonances for the Jacobeans. As a republic, as a state much less prone to despotic one-man rule, its reputation was very high. The truth was somewhat more mixed, but largely, since the Doge (the ruler of the state) was elected and had several councils and regulatory groups to supervise and control him, the sort of capricious absolutism of the English monarchy was avoided. It was still, however, a society ruled by the privileged, for those involved in selection and election were only from the leading aristocratic families of the city. It was in essence an oligarchy of the rich and powerful, and those men who ran it were most of them also intimately concerned with trade and profit.

As a centre for the arts it was admired and as an astronomically successful trading port it was a model to be envied. Though by the time of *Volpone* it was past its prime as a tiger economy, it was still immensely rich and influential, it still commanded admiration for its constitution and its relative stability and was a force in European politics that other power blocs sought to be allied to. It had been the first post-Roman medieval commercial success in Europe, acting as an immense warehouse for eastern and Mediterranean goods. Silks, ivory, spices and gems poured in from Syria, Lebanon, Libya and Egypt, and, with the Silk Road opened to China by Marco Polo, his father and uncle, it was the starting point linking Europe with the fabled cities of Asia. Its huge trading fleet carried these goods to the ports of Marseilles, London, Amsterdam and Antwerp to feed the acquisitive lusts of medieval and then Renaissance aristocrats and plutocrats. That fleet too carried crusading armies to Constantinople and set up Adriatic trading colonies that became the beginnings of Venice's maritime empire. With justice did Thomas Coryat call St Mark's Square 'a market place of the world'.[1] It was a cosmopolitan place where traders and tourists from near and far gathered. But it was not only goods that were traded as we see in *Volpone*. Venice was a model too for England's infant aspirations to become an imperial power through military superiority and commerce. It was a sophisticated playground for the rich of Europe seeking a variety of decadent pleasures away from the prying eyes of their individual moral guardians. It was a capital of naughtiness, renowned for its gambling, its fashion, its sumptuous living and its teeming courtesans.

Significantly, it is a location sufficiently distant from London to appear exotic and yet allow easily recognizable similarities with contemporary life in the English capital without being slanderously linkable to anyone in particular. It had already figured in two of William Shakespeare's plays – *The Merchant of Venice* (1596–8) and *Othello* (1603–4). The first flirts with tragedy mingling love, love of money and mirth. The second mixes passion with politics and jealousy and plunges into tragedy. Mention of the Rialto Bridge, the Senate, the *Scrutineo* (court), *avocatori* (magistrates), *mercatori* (merchants), *servitore* (servants), Scoto of Mantua, turtles for sale in the fish market (the *Piscaria*), the *Arsenale* (the shipbuilding yard), the *Procuratia* (High Court), a *commendatore*, a scattering of Italian words and all the Italianate character names serves to give the play a foreign feel.[2] But for all this attempt to make the setting seem like Venice, there is no mistaking that the satire and the morality/allegory nature of the story are distinctly relevant to the state of English society: the greed, the obsession with money (and gold in particular), the lure of luxury, extravagance and decadent pleasures. The flexible morality of the *captators*, of the magistrates and the universal predatoriness of the characters are all

---

1 *Coryat's Crudities* (1611).
2 The nine procurators were appointees of the Great Council. By the time of the play they acted as High Court judges with responsibility for orphans, the insane and the execution of wills. Their court was in the Piazza San Marco.

topics focused in the city comedies of the 1600s.[3] The play is saying that this is Italian viciousness, unscrupulous greed, cunning and trickery, but that these are becoming features of English life – beware! The acquisitiveness of the Venetians portrayed was something the audience would have readily responded to – some with embarrassment perhaps, others with revulsion. This distancing was regularly used. Revenge tragedies tended to use foreign settings often, especially in Italy, as a way of masking their concern with the political struggles and ethical failings of the English court. Foreign names were also thought to lend a tone of elegance and sophistication to comedies as well as transparently attempt to distance the stage action from any connection to real-life England.

The crude commercial predations of the streets of London, designed to spirit your money out of your purse, are a little distanced, just as the bustling markets of Venice are only mentioned or implied. The vulgar banter and pitches of Cheapside hucksters and stall holders are turned into the intricate and learned pastiche of Scoto's address to the crowd in the street outside Celia's house. Though it is in prose, while all the rest of the play is in blank verse, it is a clever mix of the sort of pseudomedical jargon quack doctors have always used to tout their miracle cures. Even that is a trick for it is all made up and is only intended as a blind to get a glimpse of Corvino's wife. The real commerce is taking place quietly, privately inside Volpone's palazzo. The language is clever, intricate, full of learned allusions, but at the same time full of very physical objects and concerns with wealth, value, high and low quality, material possession and conspicuous consumption. Volpone is no different from an aristocratic libertine in his attempted seduction and no different from a grasping merchant negotiating a business venture in his close interest in what his victims are bringing him and how much each 'gift' is worth. The obvious and intended irony is that for all the obsession with material value these characters have lost all sense of moral value. Even the beautiful, high poetry of Volpone's offers of a different life to Celia if she becomes his, is debased by its grubby object – fornication and adultery. Once again words are misused. The sensuous verse of Volpone's blandishments and his parody serenade, an adaptation of Catullus's famous poem 'Vivamus, mea Lesbia', are, like so many of his words, a trick, lust finely dressed up in the sort of scenario titled men used to lure merchants' wives or court ladies, offering them greater luxury and a more exciting sex life. The 'Come My Celia' song has some significant additions. While Catullus declares the lovers will 'laugh at all the sour-faced strictures of the wise' and celebrate the numberless kisses they have

---

3 For an excellent analysis of the new commercialism of England, see L. C. Knights, *Drama and Society in the Age of Jonson*, ch. 2.

exchanged, Volpone not only dismisses 'the eyes/Of a few poor household spies' but also claims they will 'his easier ears beguile/Thus removed, by our wile'.[4] This scornful dismissal of Corvino would trigger some in the audience to contemplate that other who would not be fooled – God, who saw everything. Volpone, situated in a state of sin – contemplating fornication and an encouragement to adultery – goes further when he asserts it is no sin 'love's fruits to steal' but to 'reveal' them:

> To be taken, to be seen,
> These have crimes accounted been. (3.7.182–3)

This shows how detached from any sense of sin or guilt he is; their fornication is acceptable, but being found out is not. Jonson has consciously adapted a classic love poem and used it to extend the negative moral profile of his protagonist. This is, on Volpone's part, a defiance of God. The language of his attempted seduction evokes the decadence of ancient emperors resurfacing in the luxury of the Renaissance. His household is in its small way like the court of Caligula or Tiberius with its parasites, its freaks, its barbaric conduct and sexual laxity, but Renaissance princes and their courts had them too and for all their supposed Christianity could be as licentious as any Eastern potentate. The grotesques (Andrgoyno, Nano, Castrone) appeal to the seventeenth-century public's love of monstrosities and curiosities, but also symbolize the moral distortion of Venice and, by extension, London. What is extraordinary is that for all their verbal and mental agility the two tricksters are so cynical they cannot begin to conceive that Celia will resist an attempt on her virtue or that Bonario will not turn on his father. They are so steeped in evil they are incapable of believing in good.

Some in the audience might have actually been to Venice on their continental travels. The Grand Tour as such had not yet developed. That would be a feature to emerge later in the seventeenth century and flourish in the eighteenth. Already, however, in the mid-sixteenth century young gentlemen (usually in their early teens) were being guided round Europe by their tutor, taken to the art galleries, museums and classical sites of France, Germany and, above all, Italy. The Roman remains scattered throughout but especially in Rome itself were a great draw to rich upper-rank men educated in the literature and history of Rome, but increasingly the Renaissance art of Italy was of interest and triggered the beginnings of the collection craze that would furnish with statuary, paintings, etchings, drawings, tapestries and furniture aristocratic mansions all over England. It was a marker of your cosmopolitan,

---

4 *Poems of Catullus*, 55.

man-of-the-world credentials to display such high-end, luxury status symbols. The Earl of Surrey (1516/17–1547) had introduced the sonnet into England from his contact with and translation of Petrarch's work, and translations of key Italian writers appeared in greater numbers as the century progressed. The scholar Gabriel Hervey (1550–1631) was well versed in 'Sweet Petrarch, divine Aretine, worthy Ariosto, & excellent Tasso'. He had also read Giovanni Boccaccio, Baldassare Castiglione, Francesco Guicciardini and Niccolò Machiavelli.[5] The Italy of the Renaissance had penetrated English thinking among the cultured, literate ranks and many ran mad for anything Italian whether in art, fashion or politics. As early as 1570 Roger Ascham had coined a phrase to describe those Italophiles who had travelled in the country and become fascinated/obsessed with it: '*L'inglese Italianato è un diavolo incarnate* [the Englishman who becomes Italianized becomes a devil incarnate], that is to say, you remain men in shape and fashion, but become devils in life and condition'.[6] This touches on the other views of Italy. To many it was the source of culture, artistic excellence and sophistication. To others it was the source of a malicious religion, the home of the Antichrist, the origin of those dangers that threatened to destabilize and topple the English monarchy and the English Church and a hotbed of violence, plots, poisonings and political killings. There were those who warned against those who travelled and returned discontented with their own land and all too ready to denigrate English customs in contrast to foreign lifestyles. For all his love of Italian poetry Thomas Nashe feared that Italian culture was a malign influence, turning Englishmen into sodomizing whoremasters, fantastical dressers, epicures and poisoners. Certainly the many plays set in city states reflect the awareness that for all its failings the English political state was sounder, more solid and stable than the ever-changing, violent turbulence of Italian politics with its court intrigues, plots and murderous coups. The courts of Florence, Milan, Ferrara and Naples were synonymous with cunning, subtlety and Machiavellian deviousness. Italian costume and etiquette were thought to have an effeminizing effect on male manners turning courtiers into bowing, scraping, insidious, untrustworthy flattering popinjays, which they had always been, though in a bluffer, plainer English style. Yet of the 400 separate titles of Italian works translated between 1540 and 1640 the most influential were the conduct or courtesy books. Some aspects of etiquette, table manners and the use of forks did improve social behaviour. New dances and music extended the artistic boundaries of the Elizabethan-Jacobean courts. There was clearly

5 See Hale, *England and the Italian Renaissance*, 9.
6 *The Schoolmaster*, book 1.

a love/hate, fascination/revulsion with a land so different from England. There was already a sizeable expatriate community in London – doctors, musicians, painters, scholars. Many were exiles fleeing religious persecution or the repressive censorship of the Catholic Church. Shakespeare and Jonson had links with a few of them where their skills overlapped with the needs of the theatre. Shakespeare knew the Laniers (musicians) and John Florio (scholar). Jonson knew Alfonso Ferrabosco, the composer, and Florio, whose Italian dictionary and translation of Michel de Montaigne's essays established his credentials as a scholar and provided useful material for dramatists. Roger Ascham, who loved the language, warned persistently against the insidious influence of Italian religion and the country's potential for luring unwary and innocent young Englishmen into curious vices. Reading Italian history, philosophy and poetry was best done at home, and even then impressionable minds had to be alert to the blandishments of Catholicism and the looser attitude to sex of a country whose courtesans had a Europe-wide reputation.

14.2 Commerce

Of those audience members who had not been to Venice (*la Serenissima*) many would certainly have heard about it as a place of immense wealth, a republic ruled by an oligarchy of rich patricians, the European trade hub for goods coming in from the East and being distributed overland or by sea to western Europe. It was a vibrant trading post where many cultures met – from Greece and Crete, from the Levant (Turkey, Syria), from north Africa and Egypt. Venetian shipping, for a period, carried a large proportion of the goods traded on the Continent and had had a merchant marine fleet larger than even Genoa. The Arsenale was once 'probably the biggest industrial complex of medieval Europe' building the many ships that started trading in the Far East and out across the Atlantic.[7] Venetian dominion, both of land and trade, gave much valued protection to local producers be it sugar, pepper, currants, silks or wines. This increased and reached its apogee at the beginning of the sixteenth century. Then began a long, slow decline. By the time of the play, Venice's power and commercial pre-eminence were severely in decline. Finance (investment, loans, banking) and the carriage of traded goods had shifted to Antwerp and Amsterdam. Throughout the seventeenth century Dutch carriage of goods increased while the expansion of London as a venture finance centre was growing. English merchant shipping also grew to the point that the Dutch wars of the later Stuarts were expressions not of military or political opposition but of the rivalry of an established trading power with a

7 D. S. Chambers, *The Imperial Age of Venice, 1350–1580*, 36.

rising one. Venice is an ideal setting that parallels the political and economic developments that were just beginning in England and a way of focusing the accompanying moral decadence that inevitably comes with wealth. Venice had had to achieve state security by colonizing the eastern Adriatic. This also made trading safer, so that expanding imperial dominion was inextricably linked to its commercial interests.

England too would discover the need to establish foreign plantations and fortify them to protect its Virginian and New England colonies and provide the raw materials for its growing industries, its growing navy, its growing profile on the world stage and the growing sophistication and complexity of its own native population. This imperial phase was opening up considerably at the time of *Volpone*. The play is not about colonization, but is about the effects on morality of suddenly becoming a wealthy nation with an expanding potential for luxurious living for the governing elite and those who increasingly serviced its governors and the state itself. This was a new angle on an old problem. From the early days of Christianity through to the High Middle Ages preachers and other moralists had criticized and warned of the dangers of wealth, the sinfulness of wasteful luxury and ostentation. Conspicuous consumption had always been a temptation to the rich and powerful governing ranks – the aristocracy, the court. Now those allurements spread into the growing group of entrepreneurs, financiers and manufacturers of the upper middling sort.

But, at the same time, Venice's long-established reputation persisted to make it a place of resonance. Its art and music continued to be highly regarded and influential. Much of the imaginative power of Venice focused on its past reputation as a unique city, a magical place, a different cityscape compared with Paris or London, surrounded by water, penetrated by canals, a place of extravagant palaces and great power, but a place too of decadence and corruption. The city had a profile much like that of nineteenth-century Paris – a centre of pleasure, of art, amour and plain lust – a tourist magnet that offered detachment from the strict regulation of life that pervaded life in England. London, it is true, offered similar pleasures – sex, gambling, drinking, theatre – but was still within the reach of disapproving parents and puritanical authorities. A tour to Rome, Florence and Venice, visiting churches, art galleries, artists' studios and sites of historical interest was a convenient cover for the pursuit of less cultural activities. The Grand Tour was not yet fully established, but since the Earl of Surrey's adventures in the time of Henry VIII, Italy had become increasingly a must-visit tourist venue and Venice specifically a place not to miss. Sir Antony Shirley was one visitor who published his impressions. His 1601 book, *A True Report of Sir Antonie Shirlies Journey Overland to Venice*, may have influenced Jonson to use the city for his location, though his own colleague Shakespeare had already used it as the setting for two plays. In 1611 Coryat published his *Crudities, Hastily Gobled up in Five Moneth's Travels*, an informative and moralistic guide coming out of his 1608 trip to Venice and back, including visiting France and Germany.[8] Such a travelogue was immediately popular for such ventures on the Continent were still largely rare and there was a growing market for such proxy experiences. Next best to having visited Rome, Florence or Venice was to have read about them and be able to talk of them as if you had been there. To appear conversant with the arts and politics of these states was to add materially to your social cachet. It is the sort of petty vanity mocked consistently in the representation of English travellers associated with the characterization of Sir Politic and Lady Would-be. Sir Pol is a caricature of the know-all who pompously spouts about places he has visited, who, on the strength of one visit, speaks loftily of the place as if he was a regular visitor who knew all the complexities of the place. Coryat's descriptions of the magnificence of the architecture, of St Mark's Cathedral, of a performance of the music of Giovanni Gabrieli in the Scuola San Rocco, fed a growing hunger for travel and appealed to the increasingly wealthy sectors of the upper sort and the middling sort who were profiting from the infant industrial manufacturing import/export merchant adventures, the proliferation of investment and various forms of financial speculation and the forays into the East and the New World of the Americas. This was the nativity of capitalism. Some people had immense amounts of disposable cash. The building of huge mansions or the refurbishment of an old family seat was one way to project your improved status. Foreign travel was another and would be a signifier well into the nineteenth century. For many, to visit a place was to somehow acculturate yourself, giving you greater social cachet, as if merely having been there meant you had absorbed it and become superior. This was often no more than a veneer appearance of having assimilated the place. There were many such cultural snobs like Sir Politic and Lady Would-be.

Coryat's book, dedicated to the much-loved Henry, Prince of Wales, touches on a number of very relevant features already presented in Jonson's play. He refers to the overprotective heavy-handed patriarchalism of Venetian men who 'do even coope up their wives alwaies within the walles of their houses' just as Corvino does Celia.[9] He describes the mountebanks:

> Amongst many other thinges that doe much famouse this Citie, these
> two sorts of people, namely the Courtezans and the Mountebanks are

8 Crudities comes from the French crudités meaning sliced fresh vegetables (carrots, tomatoes, celery, fennel) to be dipped into mayonnaise. Therefore, it means the raw thoughts, the spontaneous, unsophisticated reactions of an unseasoned traveller.

9 Quoted in Appendix I, New Mermaid edition, 163.

not the least [...] a mere novelty never before heard of (I thinke) by thousands of our English Gallants. [...] many of them are very counterfeit and false. Truly I often wondered at many of these natural Orators [who offer] a world of new-fangled trumperies.[10]

Tutors and tutees, as well as independent gentlemen, would many of them have been drawn to Venice as much for the amatory possibilities as for the art:

As for the number of these Venetian Courtezans it is very great [...] A most ungodly thing without doubt that there should be a tolleration of such licentious wantons in so glorious, so potent, so renowned a city [...] so infinite are the allurements of these amorous Calypsoes, that the fame of them hath drawn many to Venice from some of the remotest parts of Christendome, to contemplate their beauties, and enjoy their pleasing dalliances.[11]

The very setting would have brought back burning memories for some in the audience, as would the lie about Sir Pol in a gondola with a courtesan. It is unclear how Jonson knew of all these matters.

14.3 Gold Fever

A play about a Venetian grandee behaving like a common confidence trickster is entirely appropriate. The reputation of the 'better sort' was already tarnished. By 1606 Venice was in its decline-and-fall stage, but more resonantly, the situation in England, though capitalism and commercial expansion were relatively undeveloped by Venetian standards, was already creating an uneasy sense of the greedy consumerism and acquisitiveness growing out of the fortunes being made from the predatory opportunities available in the New World and the entrepreneurial possibilities developing at home. Piracy was already well established as a means of stealing huge amounts of gold, silver and other valuable commodities. The living gold of slavery was beginning to be exploited as a means of making money too, but there was a fever for the metal. For Romeo gold is 'saint-seducing' (1.1.) and Lear's reference to its power to corrupt justice is particularly pointed considering persistent contemporary pleas for reforming and purifying public life and James I's ignoring of complaints about venial judges:

---

10 Coryat, 161–2.
11 Coryat, 162–3.

Plate sin with gold,
And the strong lance of justice hurtless breaks;
Arm it in rags, a pigmy's straw does pierce it. (4.6.)

In *The White Devil* this idolatrous blasphemy is sharply described by Flamineo:

O gold, what a god art thou! And O man, what a devil art
thou to be tempted by that cursed mineral [...] there's nothing
so holy but money will corrupt and putrify it. (3.3.21–8)

Gold became a Renaissance obsession. People longed to own it, got it, wanted more, ruined others to accumulate it, undertook dangerous voyages to find it and attacked the annual Spanish treasure fleet to steal it. Foolish speculators gave huge amounts of money to alchemists experimenting to turn base metals into gold. Some seriously believed this possible. Others saw its potential for lucrative scams. This avaricious dream became the subject of Jonson's other powerful satire on human greed, *The Alchemist* (1610). Exploration of North America was triggered by the belief that limitless gold could be found there. Christopher Columbus had set the context (and the blasphemy) of gold greed:

Gold is the most exquisite of all things [...] Whoever possesses gold
can acquire all that he desires in this world. Truly, for gold he can gain
entrance for his soul into paradise.[12]

Raleigh fantasized a South American kingdom – El Dorado – where gold could be collected lying on the ground. This comforting concept conveniently ignored the slavery, exploitation, hardship, sweat and danger required to mine and process the metal. Gold thread woven into cloth, gold jewellery, gold plates and drinking goblets all showed off your pride in your appearance and your sad need to display your wealth. What a perversion of the idea of the 'Golden Age' the gold fever of this age was. Pride was a deadly sin and display a vanity associated with pride. Gold lust turned men into brutes as the history of colonization in the Americas demonstrated, but for all its long history of condemnation in homilies and sermons it seemed not to worry many at court or in the City of London. Gold, hoarding, avarice, miserliness and show had consistently figured in literature's 'bad list' from Greek times through the Middle Ages and into Renaissance Europe. Greed seemed to be part of man's psychological make-up. The lure of inheriting (legitimately or otherwise) recurs as a theme in play after play in this period along with other forms of

12 Quoted in Warwick Bray, 11. Cf. 1.1.22–5.

luxury seeking and money grabbing. Volpone is like a purulent spider drawing victims into his web in order to suck them dry of their wealth. Yet he does nothing with it. He does not live extravagantly, does not use it to buy power, does not recycle it to the poor.

High-end fashion became more lavish and impractical as a way of saying 'I don't need to work, so my clothes are for show only'. Gold madness, luxury and display, consumerism, materialism and moral decay are the matrix in which *Volpone* is located.

BIBLIOGRAPHY

Aesop. *Aesop's Fables*. Translated by G. Townsend. London: Collins Classics, 2011.

Apian, Peter. *Cosmographicus liber*. Antwerp, 1524.

Aubrey, John. *Brief Lives*. London: Mandarin, 1991.

Augustine. *City of God*. Translated by Henry Bettenson. London: Penguin Classics, 2003.

———. *Confessions*. Translated by R. S. Pine-Coffin. London: Penguin Classics, 1964.

———. *On the Good of Marriage (De Bono Coniugiali)*. Edited and translated by P. G. Walsh. Oxford: Clarendon Press, 2001.

Bacon, Francis. *The Advancement of Learning*. Edited by A. Johnston. Oxford: Clarendon Press, 1980.

———. *The Essays*. Edited by John Pitcher. London: Penguin Classics, 1985.

Bamborough, J. B. *Ben Jonson*. London: Hutchinson University Library, 1970.

Barish, Jonas A. 'The Double Plot in *Volpone*'. *Modern Philology* 51 (1953).

Barton, Ann. *Ben Jonson: Dramatist*. Cambridge: Cambridge University Press, 1984.

Bateman, Stephen. *The Christall Glasse of Christian Reformation* (1584).

Beier, A. L. *Masterless Men: The Vagrancy Problem in England, 1560–1640*. London: Methuen, 1985.

Berry, Helen and Elizabeth Foyster. *The Family in Early Modern England*. Cambridge: Cambridge University Press, 2007.

Bicheno, Hugh. *Vendetta: High Art and Low Cunning at the Birth of the Renaissance*. London: Weidenfeld & Nicholson, 2008.

Bland, Mark. 'Jonson, Scholarship, and Science', www.cts.dmu.ac.uk/occasional papers/ Bland.2013.pdf.

Bloom, Harold *Ben Jonson's* Volpone, *or the Fox: Modern Critical Interpretations*. New York: Chelsea House, 1988.

Boethius. *The Consolation of Philosophy* (translated by V. E. Watts). London: Penguin Classics, 1969.

Book of Common Prayer. Edited by Brian Cummings. Oxford: World's Classics, 2013.

A Book of Masques. Edited by G. E. Bentley. Cambridge: Cambridge University Press, 1980.

Bourghner, Daniel C. 'Sejanus and Machiavelli'. *Studies in English Literature, 1500–1900* 1, no. 2 (1961).

Bray, Warwick. *El Dorado*. London: Sunday Times/Royal Academy, 1978.

Bullough, Geoffrey, ed. *Narrative and Dramatic Sources of Shakespeare*. New York: Columbia University Press, 1957–75.

Burnet, Gilbert. *History of the Reformation*. 1681. Oxford, 1865.

Burton, Robert. *The Anatomy of Melancholy*. Edited by F. Dell and P. Jordan-Smith. New York: Tudor, 1938.

The Cambridge Companion to Shakespearean Comedy (ed. Alexander Leggatt). Cambridge: Cambridge University Press, 2002.

Castelvetro, Lodovico. *Poetica d'Aristotele Vulgarizzata et Sposta* (1570), in *Castelvetro on the Art of Poetry* (translated by Andrew Bongiorno). Cited in *The Cambridge Companion to Shakespearean Comedy*.

Catullus. *Poems of Catullus*. Translated by Peter Whigham. London: Penguin Classics, 1974.

Chambers, D. S. *The Imperial Age of Venice, 1350–1580*. London: Thames and Hudson, 1970.

Chambers, E. K. *The Elizabethan Stage*. Oxford: Oxford University Press, 2009.

Chute, Marchette. *Ben Jonson of Westminster*. London: Souvenir Press, 1978.

Coleridge, Samuel T. *The Literary Remains of Samuel Taylor Coleridge*. Edited by H. N. Coleridge. London, 1837.

Cressy, David. *Agnes Bowker's Cat. Travesties and Transgressions in Tudor and Stuart England*. Oxford: Oxford University Press, 2001.

Crowley, Robert. *One and thyrtye epigrammes*. London: R. Grafton, 1550.

Dabhoiwala, Faramerz. *The Origins of Sex: A History of the First Sexual Revolution*. London: Penguin Books, 2012.

Dante. *The Divine Comedy*. Translated by C. H. Sisson. Oxford: Oxford World's Classics, 2008.

Daunton, M. J. *Progress and Poverty*. Oxford: Oxford University Press, 1995.

Davies, Godfrey. *The Early Stuarts, 1603–1660*. Oxford: at the Clarendon Press, 1976.

Dekker, Thomas. *The Wonderful Year of 1603*. Edited by A. L. Rowse. London: Folio Press, 1989.

Dickens, A. G. *The English Reformation*. London: Fontana/Collins, 1974.

Donaldson, Ian. 'Jonson's Tortoise'. *The Review of English Studies*, New Series, 19 (1968): 162–66.

Eliot, T. S. *Elizabethan Dramatists*. London: Faber, 1963.

Elyot, Thomas. *The Boke Named the Governour*. Leicester: Scolar Press, 1970.

Erasmus. *Praise of Folly* (translated by Betty Radice). London: Penguin Classics, 1971.

Evans, Robert C. 'Thomas Sutton: Jonson's Volpone?'. In *Ben Jonson's Plays and Masques*, edited by Richard Harp. New York: Norton & Company, 2001.

Gawdy, Philip. *The Letters of Sir Philip Gawdy*. Edited by Isaac H. Geaves. London: J. Nichols & Sons, 1906.

Genest, John. *Some Account of the English Stage from the Restoration in 1660 to 1830*. Bath, 10 vols., 1832.

Gibbons, Brian, *Jacobean City Comedy: A Study of Satiric Plays by Jonson, Marston and Middleton*. Cambridge, MA: Harvard University Press, 1980.

Goldberg, Jonathan. *James I and the Politics of Literature: Jonson, Shakespeare, Donne, and Their Contemporaries*. Baltimore: Johns Hopkins University Press, 1983.

Greenblatt, Stephen. 'The False Endings in *Volpone*', *Journal of English and Germanic Philology* 75 (1976).

———, ed. *Norton Anthology of English Literature*, vol. 1. London: W. W. Norton & Company, 1962.

Hakluyt, Richard. *Voyages*. Edited by Jack Beeching). London: Penguin Books, 1972.

Hale, John. *England and the Italian Renaissance*. London: Fontana Press, 1963.

Harrison, G. B. *A Jacobean Journal, 1603–6*. London: Routledge, 1946.

Haynes, Alan. *Robert Cecil, 1st Earl of Salisbury: Servant of Two Sovereigns*. London: Peter Owen, 1989.

Henslowe, Philip. *Henslowe's Diary.* Edited by R. A. Foakes and R. T. Rickerts. Cambridge: Cambridge University Press, 1961. 286.

Hobbes, Thomas. *Leviathan.* Edited by C. B Macpherson. London: Pelican Classics, 1968.

Horace. *Satires of Horace and Persius.* Translated by Niall Rudd. London: Penguin Classics, 1973.

———. *Ars Poetica* (The Art of Poetry).

James I. *Basilikon Doron.* EEBO Editions reprint of the 1682 edition.

———. *Demonologie.* San Diego, CA: The Book Tree, 2002 (reprint of G. B. Harrison's edition, 1924).

Jonson, Ben. *Ben Jonson: Works.* Edited by C. H. Herford, Percy Simpson and Evelyn Simpson. Oxford: Oxford University Press, 1925–52.

———. *Timber.* Edited by Felix E. Schelling. Boston: Ginn & Co., 1892.

———. *Volpone.* Edited Brian Parker and David Bevington. Revels Student Editions. Manchester: Manchester University Press, 1999.

———. *Volpone.* Edited by Philip Brockbank. New Mermaids. London: Ernest Benn, 1968.

———. *Volpone.* Edited by Robert N. Watson. New Mermaids. London: Methuen Drama, 2003.

———. *Volpone, or The Fox.* In *Ben Jonson: Five Plays,* edited by G. A. Wilkes. Oxford: World's Classics, 1981; 1990.

———. *Volpone, or The Fox.* In *Ben Jonson's Plays and Masques,* edited by Richard Harp. New York and London: W. W. Norton, 2001.

Juvenal. *The Sixteen Satires.* Translated by Peter Green. London: Penguin Classics, 1970.

Kay, W. David. *Ben Jonson: A Literary Life.* London: Macmillan, 1995.

King, John N. *Voices of the English Reformation.* Philadelphia: University of Pennsylvania Press, 2004.

Kishlansky, Mark. *A Monarchy Transformed: Britain 1603–1714.* London: Penguin Books, 1996.

Knights, L. C. *Drama and Society in the Age of Jonson.* London: Penguin Books, 1937.

Laoutaris, Chris. *Shakespeare and the Countess.* London: Fig Tree, 2014.

Leggatt, Alexander, *Citizen Comedy in the Age of Shakespeare.* Toronto: University of Toronto Press, 1973.

Leinwand, Theodore B. *The City Staged: Jacobean Comedy, 1603–1613.* Madison: University of Wisconsin Press, 1986.

Lovell, Mary. *Bess of Hardwick.* London: Abacus, 2014.

Lucian. *Dialogues of the Dead.* Translated by M. D. Macleod. *Lucian Vol. VII.* Loeb Classical Library. Cambridge, MA: Harvard University Press, 1961.

Machiavelli, Niccolo. *The Prince.* Translated by George Bull. Harmondsworth: Penguin Classics, 1961.

Marchitell, Howard. 'Desire and Domination in *Volpone*'. *Studies in English Literature, 1500–1900* 31, no. 2 (1991): 287–308.

McIlwain, C. H. (ed.). *The Political Works of James I.* Cambridge, MA: Harvard University Press, 1918.

Middleton, Thomas. *A Mad World, My Masters and Other Plays.* Edited by Michael Taylor. Oxford: Oxford World's Classics, 1995.

Montaigne, Michel. *The Complete Essays,* trans. M. A. Screech. London: Penguin Classics, 2003.

Nichols, John. *The Progresses, Processions, and Magnificent Festivities of James the First.* London, 1828.

Orgel, Stephen, and Roy Strong. *Inigo Jones: The Theatre of the Stuart Court*. Berkeley: University of California Press, 1973.

Ovid. *Metamorphoses*. Translated by Mary M. Innes. London: Penguin Classics, 1955.

Partridge, Edward B. *The Broken Compass*. Westport, CT: Greenwood Press, 1976.

Peck, Linda Levy. *Court Patronage and Corruption in Early Stuart England*. London: Routledge, 1993.

———. *Northampton: Patronage and Policy at the Court of James I*. London: Allen & Unwin, 1982.

Petronius. *Satyricon*. Translated by John Sullivan. London; Penguin Classics, 1965.

Plutarch. *Essays*. Translated by Robin Waterfield. London: Penguin Classics, 1992.

Scott, O. J. *James I*. New York: Mason Charter, 1976.

Sidney, Philip. *A Defence of Poetry*. Edited by J. A. Van Dorsten. Oxford: Oxford University Press, 1971.

Stubbes, Philip. *Anatomie of Abuses* (1583).

Thomas, Keith. *Religion and the Decline of Magic*. London: Penguin Books, 1991.

Tillyard, E. M. W. *The English Renaissance, Fact or Fiction?* Baltimore: Johns Hopkins University Press, 1952.

Weldon, Christopher. *The Court and Character of King James I* (1650).

Wells, Susan. 'Jacobean City Comedy and the Ideology of the City'. *English Literary Renaissance*, 48 (1981).

Winstanley, William. *England's Worthies* (1684).

INDEX

Lightning Source UK Ltd.
Milton Keynes UK
UKOW03f2134240117
292787UK00002B/230/P

9 781783 085583